EVANSTON PUBLIC LIBRARY

3 1192 01291 8924

943.086 Koch.W
Koch, W. John.
No escape

W9-AMQ-656

MAT 2 4 2005

DATE DUE

IJUN 0 8 2008	

DEMCO, INC. 38-2931

NO ESCAPE

This book is dedicated to
my wife Maria and my son George,
to my forebears and the men and women
whose presence in my life
made a difference.

NO ESCAPE

My Young Years under
Hitler's Shadow

W. John Koch

BOOKS by W. JOHN KOCH PUBLISHING

©W. John Koch

EVANSTON PUBLIC LIBRARY
1703 ORRINGTON AVENUE
EVANSTON, ILLINOIS 60201

National Library of Canada Cataloguing in Publication Data

Koch, W. John.
    No escape : my young years under Hitler's shadow / W. John Koch.

    Includes bibliographical references and index.
    ISBN 0-9731579-1-7 (bound).—ISBN 0-9731579-2-5 (pbk.)

    1. Koch, W. John—Childhood and youth.
    2. Germany—History—1933-1945—Biography.
    3. World War, 1939-1945—Personal narratives, German.
    4. Prisoners of war—Germany—Biography.
    I. Title.

DD247.K63A3 2004   943.086'092   C2004-901368-8

First printing in April 2004.

Copyright © 2004 W. John Koch

All rights reserved. No part of this book covered by the copyrights hereon may be reproduced or used in any form or by any means without the prior written consent of the publisher, except for brief passages quoted by reviewers. Reproducing passages from this book by any means, including mimeographic, photocopying, recording, or by any information storage and retrieval system, is an infringement of copyright law.

Published by:

Books
WJK

Books by W. John Koch Publishing
11666 - 72 Avenue
Edmonton, AB, Canada T6G 0C1

Telephone: (780) 436-0581
Fax: (780) 436-0581
E-mail: wjohnkoch@shaw.ca
URL: http://members.shaw.ca/wjohnkoch

Cover design by Art Design Printing Inc.
Printed and bound in Canada by Art Design Printing Inc.

Table of Contents

Part III
THE WAR YEARS

Part IV
THE AFTERMATH

APPENDIX

About the Author

John Koch was born in the German province of Silesia. Following World War II, John studied history at the University of Würzburg before emigrating to Canada in 1954. After graduating in 1960 from the University of British Columbia with a Master's degree in social work, he worked in the social welfare and health care field in British Columbia, Saskatchewan and, from 1964 to 1987, in Alberta. Since retiring, John has devoted his time to writing.

John has published articles in professional journals in Canada, the United States, and in Poland. He is the author of the illustrated volume *Schloss Fürstenstein* (since 1945 Zamek Książ). He also wrote the German version of the biography of Daisy Princess of Pless, *Daisy von Pless, Fürstliche Rebellin*. Both books were published in Germany in 1989 and 1990.

In 1995, John and his wife Maria completed *To the Town that Bears Your Name*, a previously unpublished story by the German-Canadian pioneer and financier Martin Nordegg, written for his daughter Marcelle in 1912. Translated from German by Maria with a brief biography written by John, this book was published by Brightest Pebble Publishing Co. in 1995. It was followed by the German edition, *Zur Stadt, die Deinen Namen trägt*, in 1996. In 1997, Brightest Pebble published John's biography of Martin Nordegg, *Martin Nordegg, the Uncommon Immigrant*.

In 2003, John opened his own publishing firm, BOOKS by W. JOHN KOCH PUBLISHING, located in Edmonton, Alberta, Canada. In the same year, he published *Daisy Princess of Pless - A Discovery*, the English version of John's earlier biography *Daisy von Pless, Fürstliche Rebellin*.

Published in March 2004, his most recent book *NO ESCAPE - My Young Years under Hitler's Shadow*, has been translated into German by his wife Maria and awaits its publication in Germany.

* * * * *

Author's Note

On November 25, 2003, I completed the final draft of this book. I did so with some hesitation. I had not wanted to write my autobiography - I did not consider myself unique or important enough for that.

I did want to write about the world I grew up in, the world I witnessed from early age on, the world that had gone through so much turmoil, the world of the past 70 years about which there is such a divergence of opinion. What some people remember in horror, other people insist never happened. What some people can never forget or forgive, other people rationalize away with excuses and seemingly logical explanations.

As I will explain later in this book, my personal life and many important historical events during my lifetime have remained almost crystal-clear in my memory. Should I not put my recollections to paper to help later generations understand what happened before, during, and after World War II in Europe? If I did so, I would give confirmation and comfort to those who courageously stood up to Hitler. However, would such a book present a challenge to those who continue to rationalize or deny what really happened in Europe between 1933 and 1945, the years of Hitler's Third Reich? Did I feel competent to write about Germany and her years before and during Hitler's reign of horror and terror?

After much contemplation I decided to write about what happened, albeit as seen from my perspective. Here, I have to give one of several explanations: Even though I studied modern European history and European history has remained my field of interest ever since, even though I published two historical biographies, I did not want to write another general history of a particular period of twentieth century Europe. The book I decided to write was to have the character of a personal recollection and, further, an expression of personal beliefs and convictions. It should give the reader a picture of the world as I had seen, experienced, and understood it. In other words, the book was bound to become a book of an autobiographical nature. I must re-iterate that I did try not to write an autobiography. If some readers consider this book an autobiography pure and simple, then I apologize. In the end, the specific character of this book may not matter, as long as I have succeeded in my aim to present a personal picture of Germany and Europe under the shadow of Hitler and his reign.

While writing this book, my thoughts returned to hundreds of experiences and events and their meaning for myself personally as well as for my contemporaries: my parents, my relatives, friends of my parents and my own friends, and our acquaintances. From the beginning, I was determined to give persons who appear in this book, anonymity. In a number of situations I have not refrained from being highly critical of the attitudes and actions of certain people who touched my life. None of them are still alive, and I do not deem it fair to reveal their identity now that they no longer can defend themselves or explain their actions and attitudes. This does not include, however, my parents and members of the families of my father and my mother. On the other hand, I strongly felt that those whom I admired and who influenced my life, deserve to be remembered by their name.

Before concluding this note, I wish to beg the reader's understanding and indulgence for the enormous amount of detail found in this book. While this may, at first sight, seem overly meticulous, I am asking the reader to recognize this as my conscious attempt to re-create an environment that is long past and, thus, beyond the grasp of most contemporaries. Re-creating these past times in minute detail will assist the reader to find access to the true nature of the period, the events, and the people I wrote about. This is also the reason for giving so much attention to my family - I offer the history of the Koch and Hackenberg families as representative for the time of my youth.

I decided to restrict the customary acknowledgements to persons who assisted me in the completion of this book. Otherwise, where would I start, where would I end? How many persons would I fail to mention, by choice or by oversight? I believe the reader will sense and decide who deserves special recognition in this book. I also did not add a bibliography, as I did not use published texts or textual references to any extent.

I wish to assure the reader that whatever he finds in this book is not of an embellished or fictitious nature, but a reflection of the truth, a recollection of what I observed during a particular station in my life.

Thus, in the process of being written, *NO ESCAPE* has become an autobiographical narrative reflecting historical events. If this gives my book the character of an autobiography, so be it!

W. John Koch
November 2003
Edmonton, Alberta, Canada

Additional Notes

Throughout the book, I followed the CANADIAN OXFORD DICTION-ARY, 2000 by OXFORD University Press, Don Mills, Ontario.
 I consciously chose the old systems of measurement, i.e., miles and pounds instead of kilometers and kilograms, and so on. For added emphasis, I also took, very sparingly, occasional liberties with punctuation and spelling.
 To assist the reader to gain easier access to the locations named in this book, the spelling of names of towns, cities, rivers, and mountains gives recognition to their changes due to politicial circumstances. In any specific passage, such names are given in the version that existed at the time the author is writing about. When it comes to Silesian and Eastern European names, there have been in many cases frequent changes, after World War I, during Hitler's reign, and especially after World War II. Whatever the history of a place name, at its first mention in the book, the current name is added in brackets, if relevant. As an additional help, a comparative list of place names in various languages is included in the Appendix.
 The book was on its way to the printer when Ernst Brinnitzer, my Jewish classmate from Breslau found me after a long search.
 Ernst and his parents managed to reach Bolivia in 1939. He now lives in Buenos Aires. This brings his tragic story to a happy end.

Acknowledgements

NO ESCAPE differs so much from the books I have written before - in its research, and in the process of its writing. For a book of this nature, there was none of the usual prolonged research activity involving archives and libraries. Memories, reminiscences, and experiences and acquired knowledge formed the intellectual foundation for this book. While there are no institutions I can thank for assisting me with research, I want to thank a large number of people whose presence in my life and guidance and example became essential for my growth and my survival. Many of them left this world a long time ago.

I want to remember and thank my grandparents Koch and Hackenberg, my parents Georg and Hedda Koch, and, representing all my uncles and aunts, my courageous uncle Hubert Koch and his wife Käthe. They created a world for me where I could develop into the person I became, with my sense and courage required to survive.

I also wish to acknowledge the important role some of my teachers named in this book, and other adults and friends played at various stations in my life.

I acknowledge the urging of my niece Ines and my nephew Hans. Next to my son George and me, they are the only remaining representatives of the once so large Koch family. Ines and Hans challenged my sense of responsibility to preserve the story and the heritage of their forebears. I trust they will find in this book what they have been searching for.

I am indebted to my uncle Alfred Koch, my father's brother and grandfather of Hans and Ines. He was over 90 when he began writing about the Koch family, starting with Joseph Cuisinier. I thank him for the few pages that told me much about my early forebears I had not known before. The first half of Chapter I incorporates the reminiscences of Alfred Koch.

More than in all my previous writing projects, it was my wife Maria who gave me constant encouragement, who day after day worked at my side, correcting, clarifying, and modifying what I was trying to convey about the world I grew up in. Maria spent many hours correcting and proofreading my work. While I wrote, she completed the huge task of translating my work from English into German. If my wish to make this book accessible to German readers will be fulfilled within a relatively short time, it is entirely due to Maria's effort and support.

I thank my son George, who as a journalist, has done well in his own right, and took the time of giving me valuable advice.

My editor Nancy Mackenzie deserves great praise for help that went beyond using her exceptional editing skills. Her advice in how best to convey the intended meaning of complex passages was invaluable.

I thank Andrew Carlson, my friend for 25 years, for listening for hours and hours, letting me reminisce - at times praising, at other times raving - allowing me to reflect on my life experiences and the feelings they raised that have remained with me. If I have succeeded in writing with the emotional clarity I was striving for, it is thanks to Andrew.

Frank Walentynowicz, the computer specialist, was at my side whenever I failed to cope with the intricacies of my computer. I thank him for rescuing me many times and for proofreading the galleys, especially with respect to the numerous Polish place names.

To Lorna Offet, I wish to express my appreciation for her drawing of Joseph Cuisinier, my great-great-grandfather.

There are many more persons too numerous to mention whose example and guidance I wish I could acknowledge individually. I believe the reader will find that recognition expressed at the relevant passages in my book.

For their meaningful comments, I thank Manfred Prokop and Ray Djuff from Alberta, Tim Coates and Paul Minet from the United Kingdom, also for accepting the onerous task of reading the galleys and giving me advice and reassurance.

I acknowledge the superb printing and art work provided by Herb Ratsch, president of Art Design, and his staff, and the special interest and imagination he brought to printing this book and creating its cover.

I am grateful to all of you and the many others not named.

Introduction

This is the morning of Saturday, January 1, 2000, the first day of the new year, of a new century, and of the new millennium. In front of me on my desk lies the old-fashioned, one-page calendar sent to me by the *Süddeutsche Zeitung* in Munich, with the digits *2 0 0 0* printed across its top. In my mind, the figures transform themselves into *1 9 2 9*, in an archaic script.

Do I really remember the first day of 1929, when I seemed to comprehend the purpose of a calendar and its meaning, as my grandfather explained it to me? Or is this one of those incidents of early childhood, which is forever retold so fondly by parents that it finally becomes part of the child's memories as though it was something he remembers as a personal experience?

Whatever, this is what I remember from this morning in the house of my Grandparents Franz and Therese Koch in Waldenburg in the then German province of Silesia:

I stand next to my grandfather, who sits at his desk. I look at the new calendar and slowly read out the figures 1 9 2 9, one by one. And my grandfather explains to me how they are read, what they indicate, that this is a calendar that shows every day of the month for the entire year, and that the names of the patron saints are provided for each day (my grandfather and my grandmother were Catholics). He also explains to me that many years from now, one day, there would be a calendar reading *2 0 0 0*. Perhaps, I would look at such a calendar and by then, I would be as old as my grandfather is right now.

Did I really comprehend what my grandfather patiently tried to explain to me? Has my imagination added to this reminiscence later on in my life? This event seems too far in the past to speculate as to what is fact and what is imagined. But I am certain that this incident did occur on this particular New Year's Day exactly as I remember it today because there is at least one other incident I clearly remember, that predates January 1, 1929:

My parents, my grandparents, and their servants crowd around the windows of the parlor and the study in my grandfather's house. There are four windows altogether, and I sit on the sill of one of them, with my mother's arms holding me tightly so that I will not fall. Below us, many people line the street and wave and shout, while a large, black automobile slowly passes my grandparents' house. "This is President Hindenburg," my mother says to me, pointing to the open automobile. In its rear corner, I see an old man in a dark suit, with close-cropped, snow-white hair and a huge moustache. He looks up to us, smiles, and slowly waves his hand.

Many years later, while doing research for another book of mine, the biography of Princess Daisy of Pless, I discovered some old clippings from the Waldenburg daily *Neues Tageblatt*. With the help of one of the clippings, I can precisely determine the date I first saw Paul von Hindenburg, the second president of the Weimar Republic. According to the newspaper report, Hindenburg visited my hometown of Waldenburg in Schlesien on September 19, 1928. This day and event, which I so clearly remember, predates by a little more than three months the day 71 years ago, when my grandfather explained the calendar to me. Whatever I understood then of the meaning of the year 2000, I have reached it today!

It is today that my mind drifts back across the years of my life and its experiences and events. People have asked me, "Do you have regrets, do you wish your life had been different, easier, with fewer tragedies and hardships, but with more fun?" I always have trouble finding an answer to this question, even for myself. I ask myself how much of my life and its course was shaped by my own conscious decisions. How much of it unfolded simply out of the customs, traditions, and expectations of my parents and grandparents? From what time on was my own identity strong enough to no longer automatically obey the expectations of my parents, if not yet in action, but at least in thought? What about the political upheavals in Germany during the years of Adolf Hitler's rule, which affected me directly or indirectly? If, to a degree, I was aware of them when they occurred, in their breadth and depth I understood them much, much later in life. What about World War II, which affected me even more, not only because I was shot, wounded, and nearly killed at least three times? What about the experience of starting one's life all over again, when I escaped from a prisoner of war camp, but was barred from returning to my family's home by post-war political changes? Did I develop a new identity at the age of 29, after leaving the country of my birth and settling in Canada? And where does my heart belong now, at the age of almost 75?

There are so many questions, and throughout them run the primary questions: Did I do things right? Was it all worth it? Did I succeed in steering my own life, or was I the helpless victim pushed into unexpected directions by fate, political circumstances, or other changes at various stages in my life?

Beginning in my early childhood, I witnessed dramatic events, cataclysmic changes that deeply affected me, although I often did not grasp their far-reaching effects. I have always been a voracious reader, especially of historical and political literature. I have learned much from books – good things, bad things – especially from texts that helped me form my own conclusions through understanding the background and meaning of the political events that affected my personal life at earlier times. I have also read hundreds of books that caused me great anger because of their political slant, their superficiality, and their glibness. I have felt like shouting, "I was there, I was a witness," when I read what the events described and analyzed in thousands of books and articles meant to the individual – whether he be the little guy, or the guy in command.

In hindsight, I look at a gallery of images of people, mostly ordinary men and women who I respect for their decency, sense of responsibility, and morality. Yet there is another gallery of individuals - some I knew personally, others were public figures - who exhibited the opposite of decency, responsibility, and morality. To this day, certain matters have not been resolved in my mind and in my heart, and I am still battling with the memories of conflicts I have witnessed and with the reactions and actions of other individuals involved.

I write to gain clarity for myself. I dare to think that I also write for others of my generation and the younger generations. Am I qualified to do this? Can I offer something which adds to the surfeit of books written about the times I personally experienced during my life? Perhaps I do have a reason to write - not just for myself - but also for others. While not blessed with even average ability in mathematics and the natural sciences, my memory for events, people, and environments is such that I do remember things from my early childhood on with extraordinary clarity. This includes faces, voices, what people said, where they lived, and what their homes, towns, and villages looked like. Even today, I can still draw every façade on the street where I was born, and I can draw plans of the apartments and houses where I lived and where my grandparents and uncles and aunts lived. If I want to write about what I witnessed in a life that stretches over periods of world history, and about events that have formed my experiences, I shall have to begin with the aftermath of World War I, which was still very much present in the lives of my family in my early childhood. From there, the context of my life in Waldenburg, Silesia included the world-wide depression beginning in 1929, the rise of Adolf Hitler, World War II, the re-arrangement of the political map of Europe in 1945, the fall and rise of Germany after 1945, and the Cold War which overshadowed my generation for more than 40 years.

Our present and our uncertain future - in which humanity faces technological changes and moral challenges beyond imagination - I view from a base of accumulated historical observation and experience, and from my personal situation in Canada, from where I continue to travel and gather research material about the past history that has shaped my life.

* * * * *

Illustrations

Photographs

Maps

Silesia before and after World War I

Until the end of World War I, Lower Silesia and Upper Silesia formed one province — Silesia.

Following the Upper Silesian Plebiscite of 1921, the shaded parts of Upper Silesia were ceded to Poland.

After World War II, all of Silesia (except the district of Görlitz west of the river Neisse) became part of Poland.

Part I
My Family

1 | *The French Connection*

For centuries, hostile foreign armies originating from inner Asia, from Sweden, France, the Balkans, and various German states flooded back and forth across Silesia. Some only plundered and ravaged the country while the presence of others brought about complete changes in Silesia's political configuration, control, and eventual allegiance. During the Christmas days of 1812, hundreds of thousands of soldiers, remnants of Emperor Napoleon's Grande Armée, after being defeated at Moscow, crossed Silesia on their flight from the horrors of the Russian winter to their homes in Western Europe. Many soldiers were wounded, ill, exhausted, or simply tired of wearing a uniform to which there was no longer any glory attached. One of them, a French soldier, decided to remain in Silesia. His name was Joseph Cuisinier.

* * *

Are stereotypes to be believed? Of course not, but. . . .

Thinking back, though, to the times when people and nations were still summarily characterized — the English were reserved, the Italians amorous, the French sanguine and so on — sanguine temperament and other attributes ascribed to the French did seem to be quite congruent with the character and temperament of my Grandfather Franz Koch and the five oldest of his seven sons (my father Georg and his younger brother Hubert were of a noticeably different temperament).

From my childhood memories, I can only describe my grandfather and my uncles as vivacious, full of vitality, boisterous, loud and, more often than not, talking dramatically with the help of their hands and with vivid facial expressions. If one did not know them well, one could have been easily offended by some of their words and expressions. They were always ready to argue with each other — and others outside the family —

but just as quick to forgive and forget. Joie de vivre was a noticeable part of their nature, but they also had a certain tendency towards risk-taking. They were clearly upper middle class in their education, living circumstances, and dress, but they loved to utilize the local variety of the Silesian dialect which, their home town being a coal mining town, was quite expressive and often drastic. They had picked up a little vocabulary of Yiddish from their playmates in the immediate neighbourhood, yet they just as much loved to put each other to the test of their French, which my grandfather still spoke fluently. The latter was part of the "French connection" of the Koch family. Seen by all its members as an ancestry to be proud of, our Frenchness seemed clearly established, but quickly, within less than 100 years it was clouded in obscurity. This French heritage began with the life of my grandfather's grandfather, my own great-great-grandfather, Joseph François Cuisinier.

The first evidence of Joseph Cuisinier's existence is a document certifying that the *Médaille de Sainte Hélène* was bestowed on him by Emperor Napoleon III on behalf of his uncle Emperor Napoleon. Even though this document only dates back to the 1850s, it does tell a lot about Joseph François Cuisinier. Indeed, it is the only evidence giving his descendants some idea of who he was and what he did during his lifetime.

It appears that following the French Revolution, Joseph Cuisinier entered the army of the young French Republic in 1792 and continued as a soldier in Napoleon's army of the French Empire. Whether he was demobilized during any period after 1792 is not known. In view of the never-ending succession of wars and campaigns during this period and, particularly in view of the decoration of the Medal of Saint Helena that Joseph received, it is not unlikely that he never left the army of the French Republic and the Empire of Napoleon.

He participated in Emperor Napoleon's disastrous Russian campaign of 1812, when the *Grande Armée* of Napoleon, of which one-third consisted of allied German soldiers, entered the huge Russian Empire to reach Moscow within weeks, in September. This was the end of Napoleon's seemingly endless series of victorious campaigns. When fires set by the local population destroyed the mainly wooden buildings of Moscow, supplies became scarce and the *Grande Armée* abandoned Moscow to retreat westwards. The unexpectedly early and unusually cold winter caused enormous losses among the retreating troops which were attacked and decimated by the Russian armies again and again.

Napoleon had taken an army of 450,000 men to Russia. In the end, only about 200,000 survived.

When the retreating soldiers reached Poland, the first large contingents began to desert. Some soldiers disappeared among the local population, which was very sympathetic to the French soldiers and to

Emperor Napoleon. It was Napoleon who had returned a modicum of independence and sovereignty to Poland when he created the Duchy of Warsaw at the end of the eighteenth century, before Poland disappeared from the map of Europe after its third partition between Russia, Austria, and Prussia.

Its once so glorious combatants wounded, sick, and starving, the *Grande Armée* lost more and more of its men. Joseph Cuisinier was one of them. When his unit had reached Prussian territory, he decided to stay in the province of Silesia, whether forever or only to regain his strength and health, is uncertain. At any rate, in spring of 1814, he found shelter and work at Castle Fürstenstein.

Castle Fürstenstein dates back to the years of the Polish Piast princes who reigned in Silesia during the early Middle Ages. Strongly fortified and part of a chain of castles designed to defend the country against neighbouring Bohemia, Fürstenstein was famous as *clavis ad Silesiam*, "the key to Silesia." As part of Silesia, Fürstenstein fell under the crown of the Bohemian kings in the fourteenth century and eventually Silesia became one of the richest provinces of the crown lands of the Habsburgs. In 1509, Konrad I von Hochberg purchased the castle from Emperor Maximilian I. The Hochbergs remained in the possession of Fürstenstein until the end of World War II. In 1763, at the conclusion of the Third Silesian War, when Prussian King Frederick II finally wrested Silesia from Empress Maria Theresia (who called the province her most favourite possession), the Hochbergs swore allegiance to the King of Prussia. By that time, the once heavily fortified medieval castle had become one of Silesia's most luxurious and beautiful palaces. When Joseph Cuisinier reached the gates of Fürstenstein, the glamour of the buildings and their terraces, and the natural beauty of the surrounding forests and hills impressed him sufficiently, and he decided to seek employment there. French was still the often-used language among the aristocracy of Prussia. That Joseph was fluent in French constituted an extra asset. He was hired as "Gräflicher Leibkutscher," as one of the personal coachmen of Count Hans Heinrich VI of Hochberg.

It must not have taken Joseph Cuisinier long to decide to remain in this country for the rest of his life. On February 21, 1817, his oldest son Karl Johann was born. In the church registry, the place of residence of Joseph and his wife Anna Rosina née Seideln was given as Ölse, a village not more than 10 miles from Fürstenstein (since 1945 Olszany). Nothing is mentioned about his occupation. It is obvious that his years in the service of the Count of Hochberg were only a few. Long before the Counts of Hochberg acquired the Principality of Pless in Upper Silesia and were elevated to the rank of Princes of Pless, Joseph Cuisinier's name had been changed to Koch, the German translation of

Cuisinier. The change is recorded in the registry of the Catholic Church in Ölse.

If dates remain spotty or totally void, even as to the date and place of his birth, this was another incident where war affected our family. In 1968, I visited Paris intending to find traces of my great-great-grandfather. I had high hopes, as the French capital had not been seriously damaged during the two world wars. I had to discover, however, that once more, war had interfered and my research was stymied. The cause was not a war between nations, but the revolt against the French government by the *Commune* that had seized power and ruled the French capital. While Paris was under siege during the Franco-Prussian War of 1870/1871, an old fortress within the city of Paris, the Chateau de Vincennes, had been bombarded by the troops of the *Commune* and set on fire. Only parts of some of its buildings, which housed all the archives of the French armies from 1789 on, had been burned out, and to those belonged the rooms that contained records starting with the letter C. I had to learn that the records of my great-great-grandfather Joseph François Cuisine had become the victim of the conflagration. What a tragedy! Some of the undamaged records shown to me by one of the soldier-archivists gave me an idea of the richness of the data preserved. Huge linen-bound volumes contained complete histories of each soldier's military life, beginning with his enlistment, and followed by the campaigns he participated in, his war injuries, promotions, and decorations received and finally, his demobilization. Still, this was not all. The histories, in many cases, continued to the end of the soldier's life and listed his marriage, occupation, children, and the date and place of his death. How much I could have learned, had war not interfered! All further efforts to unearth data about Joseph Cuisinier's life proved fruitless. All I can do is attempt to reconstitute the world he lived in after deciding to remain in Silesia and become a subject of the king of Prussia.

After becoming part of Prussia in 1763 as a consequence of the three Silesian Wars, the devastated and impoverished province of Silesia stretched in south-easterly direction like a hand between Bohemia and Moravia (today's Czech Republic) to the west and Poland to the east. Silesia needed decades to recover from the ravages of war and the political and economic consequences of its separation from the Austrian Empire of which it had been a part for centuries. A modest prosperity had reached at least some parts of Silesia when the Napoleonic Wars brought renewed troubles.

Waldenburg had been one of the centres of the Silesian linen industry. Indeed, Waldenburg was the first location on the European continent where mechanical looms were put into operation, the signal of the end of weaving as a cottage industry. This, of course, meant the first step into the era of industrialization that caused untold suffering for the Silesian weavers. As a consequence of the large-scale introduction of mechanical looms in ever larger mills, the weavers lost their livelihood in increasing numbers. After years of a precarious existence of lack of work and poor remuneration for their products, markets were poor and flooded by the first products made of cotton. Near starvation, the Silesian weavers became more and more restless. Even though the Prussian government introduced some public works programs, the population remained sullen and angry and could not be pacified.

A highway that was built with government funds not far from Waldenburg by the out-of-work weavers in the early 1840s was called the "Hunger Road." This name persisted among the local population for generations. Throughout the province, there was widespread poverty that reached such proportions that the king proclaimed *Königliche Betteltage*, "Royal Begging Days" where begging became legal and the better-off families were expected to freely share from their wealth with those less fortunate.

In 1844, the Weaver's Revolt erupted. Uprisings in many towns and villages could only be quelled by Prussian troops. These traumatic events at the beginning of the industrial era of Silesia were immortalized in Heinrich Heine's poem "The Silesian Weavers" and two generations later, by the play "The Weavers" by the famous playwright Gerhart Hauptmann who, incidentally, was born in Bad Salzbrunn (since 1945 Szczawno Zdrój), only a couple of miles from Fürstenstein and Waldenburg.

Four years after the uprising of the Silesian weavers, the coal miners in Waldenburg and the surrounding villages began to rebel. Coal had been mined in the Waldenburg area for several centuries, but only with the early industrialization of the nineteenth century did coal mining become a significant industry in Waldenburg. As a matter of fact, in the early years, the output of the Lower Silesian coal mines almost equalled that of the coal mining enterprises of Upper Silesia, which would soon outpace Lower Silesia by several hundred percent. Under the influence of the Revolution of 1848, which had erupted in most of the German kingdoms and principalities, the Waldenburg miners marched on Castle Fürstenstein, the seat of the major owner of the Lower Silesian coal mines. Hans Heinrich XI of Hochberg, just elevated to the rank of Prince of Pless after inheriting the Principality of Pless in Upper Silesia, was prepared for the arrival of the miners. He cordially received the miners at the gatehouse of Fürstenstein, treated them to food and wine and, after accepting a list of their demands, suggested they return home before it would get too dark. This the miners did willingly, and for years this incident became a popular anecdote in Silesia rather than being seen as the precursor of serious social unrest. Nothing was done to ease the primitive, dangerous working conditions in the mines. The poor wages and the general poverty and want among the 7,000 miners and their families continued. In 1853, 5,000 miners went on a well-organized strike that could not be broken until after the occupation of Waldenburg and the surrounding villages by Prussian troops. After several angry confrontations, the miners went back to work. Nothing had changed except that the bitterness and the hatred towards the upper classes increased.

Superficially, there seemed to be progress. More mines opened and a range of other industries that were dependent on ready access to high quality coal settled in Waldenburg. These new enterprises attracted workers from other parts of Silesia, and after its existence as a small, unimportant town of not much more than a couple of thousand inhabitants, Waldenburg became the centre of the Lower Silesian Industrial Basin and started a sustained period of growth.

Among those who were attracted by the opportunities in and around Waldenburg was Joseph Cuisinier's son Karl Johann. In 1862, he moved from the village of Dätzdorf (since 1945 Dzierzków) in the Silesian plains near Jauer (since 1945 Jawor) to Waldenburg. At the edge of town, he bought some property, which became the new home for his family, consisting of his wife Maria née Stache, his three sons Karl, August, and Franz (the latter my grandfather) and his three daughters, Marie, Therese, and Anna.

Great-grandfather Karl Johann Koch had been a manager of several estates before he decided to go into business for himself. Putting his knowledge and experience to good use, he started his own business selling various agricultural implements and supplies, which he promptly moved to the expanding town of Waldenburg, once he was certain that he would succeed in his new enterprise. And succeed he did. Next to the house he had bought, he erected storage buildings, barns for his horses and wagons, and a building housing his office. How well he did in becoming a prosperous man is demonstrated by how he tried to provide for his children.

He also looked after his father, old Joseph Cuisinier-Koch, who had lived with his son's family since becoming a widower in 1848. There was one photograph of him in our family that, fortunately, I remember very well, as it got lost during the last days of World War II, when the entire family had to leave Silesia forever. It was a sepia photograph, probably taken during Joseph's last years, as he looked very old, though very dignified. I remember his heavy-boned, lined face and his snow-white thick, long hair which was cut in the fashion of earlier times, when men wore their hair quite long and coiffed. He wore a dark suit with a thick cravat and a silver or gold chain around his neck on which hung a heavy crucifix. As a child I was enormously impressed by this photo the size of a postcard. This was my great-great-grandfather Cuisinier, and he did look different, not really exotic, but obviously from another age. If I had only talked more with my grandfather about his own grandfather, the Frenchman! I spent so much time in my grandfather's company when I was a child, and he told me so much about everything, and he taught me my first words of French. But somehow, we never talked about Joseph Cuisinier. I was told so often that our family had roots in France and that there was that mythical forefather who had fought in Napoleon's army in Russia. I was shown the document that had accompanied the *Médaille de Sainte Hélène*, which, incidentally I had never seen. Somehow, a small photograph of the document, taken by my Uncle Hubert, who had created marvels with his Leica camera, ended in my wallet when I was taken prisoner towards the end of World War II, and this small photograph, which so clearly showed every word of the certificate proving that I had a French forebear, almost made me into a Frenchman myself, had I wanted to become one![1]

The only other frequent, although unspecific mention of Joseph Cuisinier concerned the old Catholic cemetery in Waldenburg where my great-great-grandfather was buried after his death on December 14, 1868. This cemetery, which dated back to the later Middle Ages, was located at the edge of town across from the tiny legendary St. Mary's Church, which is standing in its old location to this day. The church was built above a spring reputed to have saved a medieval knight who bathed his wounds in it. He was promptly healed and, in gratitude, built a small church above the miraculous spring, which became a place of pilgrimage until the spring dried up in the eighteenth century. As children, we were fascinated when taken behind the altar of St. Mary's Church and shown the stone basin, dry for many years.

It was not the old church to which the final story about Joseph Cuisinier related, but the old cemetery across the street. In order to accommodate the needs of the growing town, Waldenburg received several new schools, among them a very large, beautiful Catholic elementary school for girls. The school became an adornment of the Church Square, but unfortunately, it took the place of the old cemetery, which

---

1   While a prisoner of war of the French Army in 1946, I showed this photograph to a soldier who was guarding our work detail. The next day, a French officer appeared and advised me that in view of my French ancestry, I should consider applying for French citizenship to which I was entitled. This, of course, would also mean the immediate discharge from camp. I declined, thinking of my mother and my other relatives, none of whom were included in this offer.

was levelled rudely and without reverence. When earth was moved for the foundations of the new school building, human remains — skulls, leg, and arm bones — were unearthed in great numbers. My father and my uncles told me more than once how the boys would play soccer with the skulls, while the girls grabbed thigh and arm bones and playfully chased after the boys and tried to hit them. This custom continued until the 1930s, as an old friend from Waldenburg told me. She remembers how during recess there were always girls digging for human remains in the corners of the schoolyard.

I never knew whether to laugh about this rather gruesome story. Today I deeply regret that my great-great grandfather's last resting place and gravestone disappeared in such an irreverent way. This way of doing things was not untypical for a rapidly growing industrial town, where needs for housing, roads, and schools obscured the demands of piety and the sense of history. At this time, the old Gothic St. Michael's Church, which had been erected in the fifteenth century was also razed to make way for the huge, quite beautiful Guardian Angels Church. Whatever was razed was comparatively small and not always beautiful. The beauty that existed was one of age, patina, and history and these qualities did not enjoy much priority at a time of rapid progress where everything new was perceived as better, bigger, and more beautiful.

My Grandfather Franz Koch was 12 years old when his grandfather, the Frenchman Joseph François Cuisinier, my great-great-grandfather was buried in the old cemetery. This meant the end of the French connection in our family, of a story of many unknowns and gaps, which is so fascinating, perhaps just because there were so many unknowns. My great-great-grandfather, at least for me, exists on the level of a mythical forefather.

* * * * *

2 | *The Family I Knew*

I must explain that I was an only child growing up in the centre of the town where there were no other children except the daughter of my grandfather's chauffeur. If my mother wanted me to enjoy the company of other children, she had to take me to their homes or have them brought to our house. I was the typical only child, but I never felt like a lonely child. I was always with adults, my parents first of all, my uncles and aunts, and then my grandparents, who were retired and lived in the house where I spent the first eight years of my life.

* * *

I have now reached the times and events that I remember myself, and the people I am going to write about include those who were part of my growing up and of my later life. Some of these people were very important to my identity, others less so.

So far, I have said very little about the Hackenbergs, the other branch of my family, that of my mother Hedwig or, as she called herself since her teens, Hedda. Everyone liked that name except her mother, who to the end persisted in calling my mother by her birth name, Hedwig.

I must confess that as long as I can remember, I have felt as a "Koch" and not even remotely as a Hackenberg. I say that without malice, because there are rational explanations for it, above all the fact that the first eight years of my life took place in the house of my Grandfather Koch. His house was the centre of the Koch family, and a powerful and large one it was. Even after we moved out of this house, for me, it always remained my home. Then, there were the six surviving Koch sons (the seventh had died in World War I), and this was a powerful clan. I was a boy, and as much as I loved my mother and my aunts and, above all my Grandmother Koch, I also felt very close to all my uncles in the Koch family.

My Grandfather Franz Hackenberg was born on February 3, 1878 in the village of Naasdorf (since 1945 Nadziejów) near Neisse (since 1945 Nysa) in Upper Silesia (Górny Śląsk). Son of a farmer, he was one of three brothers, none of whom continued the family tradition of working the land. August, the oldest son, became a businessman in Liegnitz (since 1945 Legnica); Johann was a police officer, who was as part of his career moved throughout Prussia many times; and the youngest in the family, my Grandfather Franz, who worked in the Prussian justice system.

My maternal Grandmother Martha née Herde was born in the village of Köppernig (since 1945 Koperniki),[1] located two miles from the birthplace of her future husband. She was the daughter of a well-to-do farmer and, all her life was filled with an incredible sense of pride in her family background and in herself. A photograph from early adulthood shows a very beautiful woman with harmonious, evenly-formed features, and a face that spells out strong will and pride. She was loving, but in a possessive kind of way which, as long as she lived, I tried to escape from, always trying not to hurt her feelings. In contrast, my grandfather was a gentle giant, tall, erect to the end of his life, bald with not a single hair left on his large head, with a large face dominated by a big black moustache that, nevertheless, could not hide his friendly, good-natured, and gentle disposition. He adored his wife and gladly fulfilled every one of her many wishes and desires, and he was a loving father to his three daughters and his one son.

My mother was the oldest child in the family, born on July 22, 1901 in Neisse (since 1945 Nysa). During the Middle Ages and the Habsburg times, Neisse belonged to the archbishops of Breslau (since 1945 Wrocław) who were powerful and influential. Then, in 1763, the principality of Neisse became Prussian. At that time, Neisse was made part of Upper Silesia, which in contrast to Lower Silesia, had a predominantly Polish population. It was always said that Neisse was expected to have a Germanizing influence on the rest of Upper Silesia, a hope that was never fulfilled.

---

1   It has always been maintained by credible historians that the famous astronomer Nikolaus Kopernikus was born in the village of Köppernig. There is no absolute proof, but a memorial stone erected after 1945 near the church celebrates the village of Koperniki as the birthplace of Kopernikus.

As with many young civil servants at that time, my grandfather was, in the course of less than 10 years, moved from Neisse to three different towns. In each town, one of his four children was born: my mother Hedwig (Hedda) in Neisse; her brother Georg (called Peter) in Steinau (since 1945 Ścinawa); her sister Elisabeth (Lisa) in Trachenberg (since 1945 Żmigród), and her youngest sister Martha (Martel) in Waldenburg, where my grandfather's family remained until the end of Word War II.

What made the Hackenbergs, a family that seemed so loving and much more gentle, so different from the Kochs? I must confess that I know less about my Hackenberg forebears than about the Kochs, even though in contrast to the Koch forefathers, the Hackenbergs had resided in Silesia for centuries. I never seemed to be that interested in the history of the Hackenberg family, and I do not know any names or stories about the Hackenbergs or Herdes that predate my Grandfather Franz Hackenberg and his wife Martha née Herde.

Nevertheless, I was blessed with having both sets of grandparents close by. I also had four married uncles and two unmarried aunts (my mother's sisters) living in my hometown. In contrast, I had only one male cousin, Manfred, in Waldenburg until another cousin, Brigitte, was born in 1930. It is interesting and, perhaps, significant for the times, that the six surviving sons of my Grandfather Koch produced only four children among them, two boys and two girls, while among the four Hackenberg children, there were only two boys in the following generation. Altogether, the children of my father's and mother's generation produced only five children, and each one of them was an only child![2]

Although I always wished for a brother, I did not suffer. Rather, I was loved and spoiled and seemed to have the best of all worlds. If I often lacked for playmates, I also became quite self-reliant, and I received an extraordinary amount of attention from adults. I did not seem to be harmed by that but, instead, seemed to benefit by learning from them a lot more than I could have from children my age. Perhaps I lacked a bit in social skills when being with kids my age, perhaps I was a bit fearful, and not sufficiently aggressive and assertive as kids are who come from large families. For years, I suffered from shyness and timidity. No matter where we lived later on, I did not outgrow my insecurity and awkwardness in the presence of others until I was an adult.

This trait in my personality was reinforced by the environment in which I spent my early childhood, which was Grandfather Koch's house, situated 200 yards from the town square, called *Ring* (Rynek in Polish)

---

2   There was one more offspring among the six Koch sons, the oldest of my generation by the name of Günter who tragically died at the age of three.

as in most of the other Silesian towns. This part of Waldenburg was home to very few children; it lacked even a single playground, and the few little parks seemed to be put there for the convenience of war veterans, retired miners, invalids, and old people. The park benches were occupied by these folks all day. Our house stood in a narrow street with high buildings that was dominated by the huge red brick Catholic church. Directly across from my grandfather's house, the church had a set of five bells — one of which started ringing early in the morning at six o'clock every day, while on Sundays, all five bells were in operation almost incessantly. Their loud clanging reverberated all the more because of the narrowness of the street and the height of its buildings.

The house as it still stands today dates back to the middle 1880s when my great-grandfather bought property that stretched to the next street behind, and then gave it to his favourite son Franz, who had returned to Waldenburg after an apprenticeship in retail business in the Silesian town of Landeshut (since 1945 Kamienna Góra) and a year of travel through Germany to learn about retailing in foods.

There was a much older house at the front of the property that had two deep basement levels, one more than 12 feet below ground, the other only rising above ground by a few feet. This remarkable property was used as foundation for the entirely new five-story building my grandfather completed in 1888, as a plaque in its façade proudly proclaimed. The main level contained two large stores. The second floor housed the seven-room apartment of my grandparents, and there were large apartments on the next two floors. On the top floor, there were rooms for personnel and storage for the businesses (this pattern of usage changed, of course, with later times).

Throughout my childhood I was in absolute awe of this huge house and the other buildings that my grandfather had erected along the side of a spacious courtyard that, at its far end, reached to the next street. Rather quickly, thanks to the prosperous times when the German economy expanded rapidly, but also thanks to his hard work, his talent, and the support my grandmother gave him, my grandfather could fulfill his dream of creating the foremost, largest, most elegant, and sophisticated food shop in Waldenburg.

I am using very fancy words to describe my grandfather's business, but it was the type of food store that one would only find in large cities like Berlin or Munich. The foods were mainly specialty items of a fancy sort, much of it imported and designed to attract a clientele consisting of the local aristocracy, and of the business and professional class, although it did not refuse to serve the average citizen. To realize this dream did not only call for a spacious, fancy store, but also for all sorts of storage areas and dedicated buildings. In the end, my grandfather's business was quite unique and blossomed beyond expectations, until the outbreak of World War I in August 1914 brought everything to a standstill.

After the war, my grandfather decided to retire and devote himself to the management of his properties and financial interests. In spite of a lost war, a depression, and a devastating inflation following it, my grandfather managed to keep his businesses going. Despite substantial losses, he remained a prosperous man who found it possible to set up four of his sons in their own businesses (the oldest, Bernhard, was given the main store) and still retain the moniker *Millionenkoch* (the million-dollar Koch).

Naturally, in the 1920s, the style of business changed and its volume shrank considerably. Several of the buildings that were used to the fullest when my grandfather operated the business at its best times prior to 1914, stood now empty. They were still there when I was a small child. I could roam around them under the tutelage of the personnel of my Uncle Bernhard, or the exclusively female staff of the fine china store "Gebrüder Koch" (Koch Brothers) which my uncles Waldemar and Hubert had opened in the early 1920s with the support of my grandfather. The ownership of the Koch Brothers quickly changed, however, when Uncle Hubert bought out his brother and became the sole owner. Uncle Waldemar showed his nature, which was that of a lovable, talented guy who, however, would not work very hard unless he had a strict boss. Uncle Hubert would open the store at eight in the morning, he would buy and sell, hire and fire the staff, and altogether was the soul of the business, while Uncle Waldemar would usually show up after 10 in the morning, dressed elegantly, with a cigar between his fingers, and affably welcome the customers. While Uncle Hubert took his business very seriously, Waldemar would not work, demonstrating a pattern that he would maintain throughout his life. He had several business failures but in spite of them, always seemed to land on his feet again. Still, among all the Kochs he seemed to be the happiest and most carefree.

The main store, now owned by Uncle Bernhard, retained the appearance of an elegant shop from the pre-1914 era. The office behind it still had space for four clerks, but only two, now both female, worked there when I was a child. The office tract was a link between the store and a five-story building consisting of two floors of storage space and three floors of housing. In the old times, the rooms were used to accommodate the unmarried clerks and the young apprentices, who in their life outside work hours were the responsibility of my grandmother. At the time of my childhood, the rooms were made into small apartments and rented out.

Next to this building was another large building with a hayloft, where horses and wagons used to be kept. When I was a child, this building stood emp, y except for the parked car. The horses from past times were replaced by a dozen chickens and pigeons, which my grandfather kept for breeding purposes, as a hobby. On the other side of the courtyard, there was the *Fischhalle*, the fish building, where a huge white-tiled basin was used to keep fish alive and well until they were sold. This basin was also no longer in use and I always wished that it were filled for my convenience as a swimming pool, but this, of course, never happened.

During the winter, something truly special was created for me. Uncle Bernhard's apprentices would shovel the accumulated snow onto a hill at the end of the courtyard. I would be able to start my sled on top of this hill and slide through the long yard right up to the main building. Next to the *Fischhalle* were large freezer rooms, unique in Silesia at that time because of their size, and then came the building where coffee was roasted daily on a large, slowly turning grill measuring 12 feet across. My grandfather's coffee and its various mixes and mélanges were famous and in demand throughout Lower Silesia. Above and below, there were yet more storage areas, all of them now unused.

If I early on developed a sense that times can change the world a great deal, sometimes beyond recognition, the experience of my grandfather's once-thriving business was my first lesson. So often I was told in glowing words how my grandfather's business used to employ more than 100 people and how busy things were before 1914. How true that must have been I could see in the variety of the surviving buildings and their size. I could see the outside lifts that used to transport goods to the top floor of the big house up front and the other smaller lifts above the Fischhalle and the freezer rooms and also above the coffee-roasting rooms. In the store up front, there were still the colourful framed posters advertising *Liqueurs Cuisinier* which my grandfather had manufactured.

What was left and still used at my time was my grandfather's garden, a tiny, sheltered oasis behind a high fence presenting a surprising variety of flora. It had a couple of rows of rare rose bushes, a few trellises with special varieties of fancy pears and apples, and an arbour of wild roses with garden chairs and a table. Towering in one corner of the garden was a pear tree so huge it looked like an oak or maple tree. As I remember it, it was at least 50 feet tall. At harvest time, several apprentices from my grandfather's, or later my Uncle Bernhard's store would climb on long ladders to the highest branches to pick the old tree bare of its fruit. The harvest always seemed plentiful.

Was my young life interesting despite much of it taking place within the confines of the Koch property? It always was!

Part of this world was my Grandmother Therese Koch née Schneider who was born on January 8, 1858 in the village of Volpersdorf (since 1945 Wolibórz) near Neurode (since 1945 Nowa Ruda) in Silesia. She was the daughter of a prosperous family who owned a large farm and a brewery with a busy restaurant and, in summer, a beer garden. She was 28 years of age when she married my grandfather, who at that time was building his big house and store in Waldenburg. My grandmother, I can say unequivocally, was the ideal wife for my grandfather. Actually, they were both ideally suited for each other. They were both very religious, family-minded and, while generous to others and filled with a wide range of interests, they were, for all their lives, modest and unpretentious people, even though they always commanded the attention of others by their appearance and demeanour. Her years of working in her father's businesses gave her much experience, especially in dealing with people. It enabled her to make one of her greatest contributions to the success of her husband's business. Under her care, tutelage, and supervision, more than 200 apprentices were educated in the Koch business. At that time, it was the invariable custom that apprentices would live with their masters, no matter how close their homes were. This assigned an essential role to the master's wife whose interest, dedication, teaching, and example would be essential for the future careers of these apprentices. One must realize that most of them came from very modest backgrounds; quite a few of them were the sons of poor miners. So the training received from my grandmother was in the end almost as important as what they learned in my grandfather's business.

How successful my grandmother was I realized when apprentices from pre-World War I days came to visit during my childhood. In awe, I heard some of them talk about the businesses they now owned in faraway cities like Berlin, Cologne, Bremen, and others. They were important men now, but in talking with my grandmother, they would often fall back into the dialect of their youth and thank her for teaching them all the good manners and habits without which they probably would not have made their way into the world so successfully. One must also realize that my grandmother was given precious little time to broaden the education of the apprentices. As one former apprentice from 1910-1914 wrote, businesses at that time opened at 6:15 a.m. and did not close until 8 p.m. and on Saturdays stayed open till 9 p.m. In addition, stores were also open between 9 a.m. and 2 p.m. on Sundays, and after closing time, the apprentices needed permission to visit their own families at home.

When one reads about such hours, it becomes clear that my grandmother was not only a teacher to the young apprentices, but she also must have assumed the role of a caring, part-time mother, to balance the strictness and discipline with which my grandfather ran his business. One former apprentice mentioned to me some years ago that my grandfather's methods would always show that Franz Koch had completed his military service in the Royal Garde du Corps in Potsdam. He was not militaristic, but his life was governed by discipline. The bearing of this over six foot-tall man remained proud and erect to his last days.

It is all the more astounding that my grandmother, with all her duties connected with her husband's business and that of running a huge household, albeit with the help of a cook and several maids, bore nine children, the fifth and ninth being girls who died a the age of four and in infancy respectively. The seven sons were notorious throughout town because they were quite wild. Together with the three sons of the Jewish menswear store owner Korn next door, they represented a formidable force, which was an essential component in the legendary battles between the youths of Waldenburg and those of the neighbouring miners' village of Dittersbach (since 1945 Podgórze), that periodically took place in the plain between the two settlements. According to my father, amongst the youth from Waldenburg, there were other offspring of the better class families, while Dittersbach was represented exclusively by miners' and labourers' kids, which gave these juvenile battles a distinct social class flavour.

By the time the war came, my grandfather's sons knew what they wanted to do in life, although not all their choices found the approval of my grandfather. Bernhard and Franz, the two oldest ones, chose the career of their father, which meant that as the oldest one, Bernhard would take over the father's main store, while for Franz there would be a brand-new store of great elegance on the main floor of the apartment building that my grandfather had completed in 1913 at the corner of the busiest square in Waldenburg where all streetcar lines crossed. I do not know what Alfons had elected for himself, as he did not return from World War I. Waldemar and Hubert also were ready to enter the business world, but their businesses were not set up until after their return from the war. Alfred and my father Georg did not show any interest in retail business.

While Alfred wanted to enter a banking career, my father, who had no doubt inherited his artistic and musical talents from his mother, wanted to study music. He was extremely gifted, early in his life became an accomplished pianist, and also played all string instruments. To the great unhappiness of my father, which he never overcame throughout his life, my grandfather would not hear of a career in music because he considered it too risky. Finally, he would reluctantly consent to my father becoming a teacher, possibly even eventually a music teacher. But he steadfastly refused to accompany my father for the interview at the teachers' seminar. Although my father was almost 18 years old, it was mandatory that the candidates were accompanied by at least one parent. It fell to my grandmother to accompany my father. He was the only candidate whose father was not present and was told that his mother's presence was not sufficient and the scheduled interview was simply cancelled. My father was heartbroken, but before he could decide on another career, the war broke out, and he was drafted.

My father returned from the war a sick man. He had never been physically very strong and would never regain his full health. He brought from his army years a sick stomach and was continually plagued with ulcers and chronic gastritis (today one knows that bacteria are responsible for this condition that eventually caused my father's early death). He was sent to rest homes, got better, got worse, and then better again, but he never became really well. One wonders how happy he was in the banking career he had chosen for himself, perhaps to please his father, perhaps to at least find some emotional acceptance and recognition from him. He did spend all his free time with his music, gave recitals and concerts much to the pride of my grandfather, but to make a living, he had to stay with banking.

It was music that brought my parents together. They were both singing in the same choir, but due to the interference of my Grandmother Hackenberg, their long courtship never seemed to end. There was no doubt that with his family background, my father was considered an excellent marriage partner, but my grandmother had great difficulty to let go of her oldest daughter. It had been my mother who had almost single-handedly raised her siblings when my grandmother took to bed during most of the war in protest against the long absences of her husband at the Front. Eventually, my mother received permission from her mother to marry my father (my grandfather had long ago agreed with my mother's choice of a husband). In 1924, the wedding took place. There would be problems in my parents' marriage, but they had nothing to do with my parents' relationship, which was one of love, happiness, and harmony from the first to the last day.

There would be one more wedding in my mother's family, that of her brother Georg (Peter) six years later, who was never quite forgiven for marrying into the Lutheran faith. My mother's sisters, both lovely women who had a good number of suitors, never managed to escape the interference of their mother and, consequently, never experienced marriage or raised a family. They both would have made good wives and wonderful mothers.

Around the Kochs and the Hackenbergs who sheltered me in a warm, secure family life, there were influences from the more distant relatives, friends, or even just acquaintances of my parents in Waldenburg or from elsewhere in Silesia or, a few even from further away, as far as the United States and Brazil. For a young child, some of these men and women were most intriguing or awe-inspiring, be it because of the remote countries they came from, or because of their eccentric personalities. They were not part of my life all the time, but entered it at regular intervals over the years. Some were simply interesting, memorable characters. Others, for better or worse, left their indelible influence on my life or determined its course in some unique way.

* * * * *

3

1925 – 1930
A Few Good Years

S omewhere between the end of World War I, the revolution that deposed the emperor, the post-war hunger years, the inflation that turned so many self-respecting Germans into paupers overnight, and the crash of 1929, there were the legendary "Golden Twenties." They were by no means "golden" for everybody, but in retrospect, they provided a breather for many Germans, especially those from the middle class. These were the years that brought about a surge in the arts, literature, theatre, and architecture, and a better standard of living for many. They were also the years when popular culture reigned; they were Germany's jazz age. People danced and amused themselves like never before. There were the fabulous nightclubs of Berlin and the other large cities, but even smaller cities prided themselves for having nightclubs of sorts; big or small, nearly all of them closed quickly when the Golden Twenties came to an end with the crash of 1929.

* * *

Were the 1920s good years, the "Golden Twenties?" It depended on where you happened to live. The 1920s were an unsettled decade that struggled to come to terms with the devastating years of World War I and its aftermath. Three empires had been toppled by the end of the war. New countries emerged after 1918, borders of other countries changed, and revolutions and unrest kept Europe in uproar and suspense for the first five years of what was supposed to be peace.

Some people were full of hope, even in Russia where the millions of poor people and the formerly suppressed intellectuals saw a new millennium on the horizon. What was to be a new era of prosperity and happiness, but especially of a never before known intellectual and ideological paradise, began with untold suffering and the deaths of millions. Still, this was seen by many as a necessary prelude to a better world, which, of course, never came, although for a few years until Lenin's death on January 21, 1924, a sense of intellectual and artistic freedom seemed to have entered the new Soviet Union, only to be crushed by Lenin's successor, the ruthless Joseph Stalin and his version of Bolshevism.

The fear of Bolshevism spread across Europe with good reason considering the many revolts, uprisings, and coups that occurred, particularly in Germany. It was a state of "permanent revolution" following the toppling of the three great monarchies of Germany, Russia, and Austria-Hungary – it also gripped France, Italy, Spain, and the new countries of the European East that bordered on the Soviet Union. Except for France, none of these countries had an established democratic tradition that would protect the democratic freedoms, especially of the middle class. Under these circumstances, it was understandable that the German middle class was frightened of Communists, Spartakists, anarchists, even of Social Democrats, although the latter had helped to create the new German Republic with its remarkable constitution and had also provided the first president of a democratic Germany, Friedrich Ebert, who proved to be a staunch democrat.

Not only were there uprisings in all parts of Germany by both left and right forces, there also were the consequences of a lost war – the unpopular Treaty of Versailles, the occupation of the Rhineland by Allied troops, and the uprising in Upper Silesia prior to the plebiscite that would result in the loss of valuable industrial real estate to Poland. There was, finally, the great inflation that devastated the German economy and impoverished the middle class.

For all the problems of these first years of the 1920s, the new republic and its supporting parties were blamed by all those who belonged to the more conservative factions, the ones who were still faithful to the idea of the monarchy, those who had served the emperor as officers, judges, and civil servants and, finally, those who would aim at the destruction of past and present structures, the Communists. There were too many factions and parties that did not support the new Weimar Republic;[1] they at best despised it and, at worst tried to destroy it.

Looking back, people perceived the 1920s as a decade of horror, death, and deprivation which, after the end of a lost war, continued in different ways unabated until the middle of the decade. What followed then was finally some kind of stability, hope, and economic progress,

---

1   So called, because the seat of its constituent assembly was the city of Weimar.

which in retrospect perhaps was over-glorified. Things were not that good for a lot of people, especially the working class. What was real was the sense of finally being freed of fear of chaos, the sense that stability had finally been regained and that things could only go forward. The government was stable and in control of the country, the inflation had ended, and there was new money; it paid again to work, to save, and to enjoy oneself. For the middle and upper classes a period of relative prosperity definitely began.

It was at this stage that I entered the world on August 7, 1925. But my arrival still seemed to be affected by the past unsettled years.

My parents had married in July 1924 after looking in vain for decent housing, which was still at a premium after the lack of construction during the war and the unsettled post-war years. A solution was finally found when my Grandparents Koch divided their large apartment into two with the slightly smaller one given to my parents. There were still shortages and only after the end of the inflation was everything available again. This was the other reason for my parents to delay their wedding, even after my Grandmother Hackenberg had finally blessed their union.

In the end, everything went well, up to a wonderful wedding and a happy start in a new home. Both my father and mother were looking forward to their first child expected in late summer 1925. My mother felt very well and had an easy pregnancy. No particular precautions were indicated, and although there was a renowned private clinic only five minutes away, its chief physician, who looked after my mother, thought it entirely appropriate for her to have a home-birth with the attendance of a midwife. Unfortunately, things turned out very differently. As my father explained to me much later, I "refused to come out," my mother was haemorrhaging heavily, and in this emergency the obstetrician from the private clinic was called. My birth became by necessity a forceps delivery. As I was told, my little head was terribly bruised and I always wondered whether I had suffered slight neurological damage because of what became obvious during my school years – a pervasive restlessness, being easily distracted, constant facial twitching, a poorly controlled left foot, and other mild but noticeable symptoms, most of which gradually receded or disappeared.

Despite this dire emergency, my father was happy and proud and carried me across the hallway to the apartment of my grandparents, quietly opened the door with his key, entered their living room, and with the words *"Wolfram von Eschenbach, beginne!"*[2] he tweaked me so that I

---

2   "Begin, Wolfram von Eschenbach!" From a scene in Richard Wagner's *Tannhäuser*. A historical figure, Wolfram von Eschenbach was a famous medieval minstrel.

burst into a loud scream. My father's great love was Richard Wagner. So from his opera "Tannhäuser" my parents had chosen names for their expected offspring, Elisabeth for a girl, or Wolfram for a boy. This is how I became stuck with a first name, which at that time, especially in an industrial city, if not unknown, was never used. Only in the last grades of high school did I find another boy who carried my first name. In the meantime, I was not only teased by other boys, too many of them did not even know how to spell my name and mispronounced it in all sorts of ways, the easiest or most acceptable one being "Wolfgang."

During the Hitler years, "Wolf," commonly thought of as the short form of Wolfram, came into widespread use. I did not mind being called Wolf. However, of the irony of this first name, so very popular in Hitler's Third Reich, I did not become aware until years later. It was only in the 1960s that I discovered "Wolf " as quite a common and respected first name among the Jewish population in Eastern Europe! For the adherents of Hitler and his Germanic ideology, the name "Wolf" could not sound more patriotic and Germanic, but the Nazis were wrong without realizing it. If I never really became reconciled to the first name chosen by my father, neither was my Grandmother Koch. She immediately protested that Wolfram was not a good Christian name. She could not even find its name day in the Catholic calendar (she actually did so, but not until 1936 — my name day was March 20), and it wouldn't be possible to fashion a loving pet name out of Wolfram. I do not think she ever used my first name very much, calling me instead "Bübele" ("little boy"), which caused immediate problems for me as soon as I entered school where I was endlessly teased by the other kids. Interestingly enough, my Grandparents Hackenberg and their daughters, my aunts, quickly adopted "Bübele," which I could not get my aunts out of the habit of using until I was in my thirties! They did, of course, consciously try to avoid this pet name in public, but too often forgot to do so.

My mother had some other thoughts that, while well-meant expressions of fondness, were directly responsible for setting me apart from nearly all other kids except those who belonged to the same group my parents belonged to. As I had thick blond hair, my parents decided to let my hair grow long. At cooler temperatures, a red beret was placed on my head. Most kids seemed magically attracted by my appearance, simply for the purpose of destroying it or teasing me about it. I can recall several occasions with my mother at my side, when somewhat older boys would race up to us, yank the red beret off my head, and throw it on the street, hoping it would be run over by a bus or by the streetcar.

I am not relating these episodes to elicit sympathy, but to demonstrate that in this almost exclusively working class town, even the better off had to find ways to help their children in their daily lives outside home. I was certainly protected within the Koch property, while we were visiting friends, or in the kindergarten that I attended for a year and to which I was taken by the staff in the morning and returned at noon. But even before I became of school age, my mother realized that she would truly help me by adapting my appearance — within reason — to that of the other kids.

I had long hair — their heads were cropped bald. I would wear handcrafted suspenders — they would wear suspenders discarded by older brothers or their fathers. I would wear boys' oxfords — they would wear high winter boots, and so on. What a blessing that my mother eventually began to see the light! She dressed me inconspicuously, asked the barber to cut my hair very short, and in summer I was allowed to go barefoot to school. All this helped immensely, especially since I could not defend myself very well. I was born very weak, had a slightly malformed spine and a beginning little humpback.

I received various treatments, such as ultraviolet lights, which I liked, but I was also taken to a very famous orthopaedic specialist from Breslau, who had a part-time practice on the outskirts of Waldenburg, in Bad Salzbrunn. In his office which, for me, was approaching the aura of a torture chamber, I was put, actually shackled, into a contraption mounted on the wall that would quite forcefully straighten my curved spine and my entire back. Each treatment ended up becoming quite painful and, without myself realizing it, very humiliating and demeaning, especially since the doctor was a very harsh man, looking like someone from the past century. He always wore a black suit, a pince-nez, and he had a little grey goatee. He never wore a white physician's coat. He had a high-pitched, squeaky, always excited voice, and he never smiled at me. He just did not look like a doctor, certainly not like the few doctors I knew.

What else happened in my earliest childhood, events that I did not remember but was told about them? After my dramatic entry into the world, there was another calamity a few months later, which scared my mother very much. We had a little dachshund, called Rex, which one day, while my mother left the room for a moment, managed to get into the basket I was sleeping in and settle on top of my face. When my mother returned, I was blue in the face and apparently close to death. Needless to say, the dog was sent away, but only across the hallway to the apartment of the grandparents, where he lived for another 12 years. As I spent hours in my grandparents' quarters every day, Rex more or less remained "my dog," but my mother never again tolerated Rex in our apartment.

If I gradually became aware of my immediate surroundings and the world of my hometown and, later of Silesia, I can say that this world uniformly looked happy, secure, and always invited me to find out more about it; in other words, it was stimulating my curiosity from early on. Later, I asked myself whether as a young child of preschool age, I had simply been too innocent and ignorant. However, when I look at family pictures from these early years and compare them with photographs from the early and later thirties, I know that my perception of the world and of people as I developed it before I turned five or six, was correct — these were gentle, prosperous years. They were also very important for my parents, whose lives changed dramatically and abruptly when these so-called golden years ended overnight in 1929.

My father worked at the Deutsche Bank located on the Ring, after having survived the absorption of the Disconto Gesellschaft, his former employer, without losing his job. He had a well-paid position, and whenever my mother and I visited him, he used to sit in his office with a smile on his face, and everybody treated him with respect. I loved to go downtown with my mother. There were stores where one would get treats, a wiener sausage at the butcher's, a little piece of pastry at the baker's, always sweets at my uncles' stores of course, and little toys or similar attractions at other stores. These were good times. After the onset of the world economic crisis, all these treats seemed to be discontinued, except at the butcher's, the baker's, and at my uncles' — these businesses were essential for survival, people still had to eat; these merchants might have lost some business, but none of them went bankrupt, as did a number of other stores, like those selling clothing or furniture.

I loved to walk with my mother through the streets of Waldenburg, and as young as I was, I realized that very few women were dressed as elegantly as she was. I did not, of course, comprehend the reasons for this difference. I was merely proud of my beautiful mother. I particularly remember her grey fall coat with the fur collar and her little cloche hat so typical for this era. Being with my mother brought other surprises like streetcar rides, which always fascinated me (I have remained a streetcar buff to this day). I was delighted by the snow-covered motormen in the harsh winters of Silesia, who stood on the open platform of the old streetcars that had survived from before the war. One day in the summer of 1929 (as old clippings confirm), my mother and I were on our way home from a visit to the Hackenberg grandparents when there was a sudden commotion on the *Ring* that we happened to cross. A strong humming sound was getting louder and louder, until the *Graf Zeppelin*, Germany's first large intercontinental airship, appeared in the sky above us. Yes, they were happy days. There were always hundreds of people on the Ring and in the adjoining shopping streets because so many workers worked shifts, and those with their time off during the day spent it in the streets of the city. They all cheered when the huge low-flying airship drew a big loop over the centre of the city. The crowd was genuinely enthused and, I think, proud of what they were witnessing. I could see tiny little figures behind the windows of the cabin on the underside of the Zeppelin's silver skin that glistened in the noon-day sun. People were still cheering when a large number of papers were released from the Zeppelin and everyone wondered what these papers might say and could hardly wait until the answer floated to the ground. One of the papers literally landed in the outstretched hand of my mother: it was a voucher for a pair of genuine ELBEO silk stockings, which was quite a generous gift at a time when a lot of people could not afford silk stockings. I thought this world was wonderful and full of magic.

On another occasion, we went to the air show in Bad Salzbrunn to watch the filling and ascent of a huge passenger balloon and the landing of a small *Junkers* passenger plane. This was the first time I got close to a plane. It was one of the planes that my mother pointed out to me when they flew above town on their way from Breslau to Hirschberg (since 1945 Jelenia Góra), probably full of tourists destined for the resorts in the *Riesengebirge* (the Giant Mountains, in Polish Karkonosze), or the planes that crossed Silesia on their way from Prague (since 1918 Praha) to Warsaw (Warszawa in Polish) without landing on German territory.

There was little or nothing that could dispel this Pollyannish view of mine. Nobody was ill or died during these years except Uncle Karl, my grandfather's older brother, who was born in 1846. Just old enough to serve in the army, he took part in three wars within a period of only eight years: the war between allied Prussia and Austria against small Denmark in 1864, the war between Prussia and Austria in 1866, and the Franco-Prussian War of 1870/1871. Uncle Karl was fortunate never to be wounded, but in the war of 1870/1871, he was taken prisoner during the battle of Mars La Tour. As Uncle Hubert told me later, Uncle Karl spent his life as a prisoner of war of the French as a guest on a large farm south of Paris. His hosts were delighted with his near perfect French that he had learned from his grandfather Joseph Cuisinier. He was not treated like a prisoner, but more like a member of the family. This story came to my mind more than once when I spent 14 months in a prisoner of war camp in 1945/1946 under rather different conditions. How times had changed, but how fitting for Uncle Karl to spend his time as a prisoner of war like this! Unlike his brother Franz, Uncle Karl had never been ambitious, but he was notorious for his curiosity, which perhaps I inherited from him. Uncle Karl never managed to learn a trade, but he apparently was a very good and intelligent worker, liked by his employers. Invariably, he only worked until he had enough money to live footloose and fancy-free, as long as his money lasted. With this attitude, he apparently saw a good part of Europe. He even reached the Holy Land, and one of the few things my mother managed to rescue from home at the end of the war was a little hand-carved incense container he had bought in Jerusalem as a gift for my parents. He would be gone for months or a year or longer without writing more than the occasional postcard. Eventually, my grandfather stopped worrying about his brother, but he never stopped feeling responsible for him until Uncle Karl's death. I remember him as always smiling at me and always fishing a little candy out of his vest pocket. He had a round face with a reddish complexion, a little moustache, and a wicked, tight curl of silvery hair on his otherwise short-cropped head (apparently, he had been quite a ladies' man when he was younger). He always had a radiant expression on his face, as if he would never get over how wonderful and intriguing this world was. And I believe that is how he saw the world and all human beings. When I became aware of him, he was already an old man, but still good on his feet. He would march through town every day, spend hours on the market looking at produce and was always listening to people's conversations. At lunchtime — he ate at the table of my grand-parents where I often sat, listening in awe with my mouth open — he would relate all the news from town, some funny, some tragic, sometimes just plain but always interesting gossip.

Uncle Karl's death was the first time I saw someone expire. He had been sick for a few days and remained in bed in his little apartment on the top floor of my grandfather's house. One evening, on September 11, 1929, we were called upstairs to Uncle Karl's bedroom. The room was packed full with people, not only with members of our family, but also with the young women who worked in my grandparents' and my uncles' households, and lastly about a dozen old people, men and women who had worked for my grandfather in their younger years and had since lived in the small rooms on the upper floor like pensioners. My grandfather had never charged them any rent and they in turn helped around the house and the yard with whatever tasks they could still handle. There was Uncle Karl sitting up in his bed, leaning against the thick propped-up pillows and smiling as happily and brightly as ever. His head turned from one side of the room to the other. He seemed to be looking at everybody, also at me, as I remember distinctly — I also remember the twinkle in his eye as he looked at me. People were talking with subdued voices, but nobody was crying. Then, his head fell on his chest. I was not sure what was happening and thought Uncle Karl would again play a trick on me and on the others in the room. But my mother said gently, "Uncle Karl has fallen asleep; he will now go to heaven," and took me away. It seems that such a gentle introduction to the phenomenon of death can only have been offered by a gentle person of perfect goodness like old Uncle Karl. He was 83 years when he died and that was quite a rare age at that time. During the last years of his life he really had not done much but be there and spread a good mood among people. Not just in my childish perception, but truly so, this crucial experience during my early life fits into the few brief years when life was carefree and happy.

Nothing makes me fonder of these years than the memories of social occasions and festivities in the houses of my grandparents, my uncles, and my parents. There were special days like the birthdays of the grandparents, which were elaborately celebrated, beginning with a large dinner at noon, some rest for the older generation afterwards, while the younger generation went for a stroll. Then family and guests assembled for a large coffee party which was followed by an evening with fancy cold plates and other delicacies. In between, there was music provided by my father and his brother Hubert who played the cello, and sometimes skits, again put on by these two, often myself included as a little messenger boy or something like that. Frequently, events of the day were reflected in these skits. I remember my father appearing as Mahatma Ghandi after the Indian statesman's visit to Berlin. My father, just clad in a loincloth (actually a towel) was suitably slim and bony for this part. About the same time, there was also the state visit to Germany by Aman Ullah Khan, King of Afghanistan, a name that we young ones loved to mispronounce and mangle between our teeth. For the enactment of this visit, Uncle Hubert had procured a white silk turban and other rich clothes, while my father played the attendant and I followed up the procession waiving a whisk to provide a fresh breeze for the king. The applause was always enthusiastic, of course. We three grandchildren — my cousins Christel, Manfred, and myself as the much younger one by almost five years — loved to be by ourselves after the adults had moved from the dining room to the parlour. We would do wild chases around the dining room table each sitting on a little footstool and propelling it as fast as possible. We would also sit quietly listening to the great variety of laughs of the adults in the next room guessing whose it was we had just heard.

Birthdays were celebrated in a large way by all the uncles and aunts, and if one adds those up, one understands that the Koch clan enjoyed festivities as often as possible. Aside from these special days, there was a family tradition that lasted to the end of the war, although the group maintaining it became smaller over the years. Sunday afternoons, beginning right after lunch, were usually reserved for longer walks or a drive into the mountains. Sometimes, the entire weekend was used for a trip to Breslau, the Silesian capital or to the *Riesengebirge* or the *Grafschaft Glatz* (the Glatz Duchy, Ziemia Kłodzka in Polish), a particularly charming part of Silesia, very Catholic and quite Austrian in its character. I cannot explain how the family managed to do this, but with very few exceptions the entire Koch clan would end the Sunday outing with a visit to my grandparents. There were always some special foods waiting, and the mood was always harmonious, which, in hindsight, truly astonishes me and calls for my admiration, because there were not infrequent spats between the brothers or their spouses. Not once would these be noticeable during those Sunday afternoons in my grandparents' house. Towards the end, these Sunday afternoon get-togethers were, as my uncle Hubert told me, very subdued. There was only my grandmother and two or three of their sons left. My father had died, Uncle Alfred was in the war, my cousin Manfred was missing in action in Russia, my cousin Christel was with the Red Cross, and I was in the war. By January 1945, this long-lived tradition came to its end. If I think of all the festivities, these Sunday afternoons provide the most precious memories to me including a sense of belonging to a solid family.

If I recall those years, I also recognize the uniqueness of these "good years." Not only was the mood carefree, everybody laughed and talked, but we also felt unrestrained to offer our talents, be it singing, play-acting, playing an instrument, or doing magic tricks. The women, as photographs from those years still show, were at their best. They were dressed elegantly, their hair coiffed in various styles and their faces looked beautiful. All my aunts were still quite young and life had never been so enjoyable for them.

There are two more pictures that tell much about the happy years my parents, their siblings, and their friends experienced. One was taken after my parents' return from a holiday at the Baltic Sea in Binz on the Island of Rügen in the summer of 1928. The other captures a small party on New Year's Eve, 1929. I never fail to look at this lovely scene with other than very mixed emotions. Everybody appears so happy, no doubt optimistically looking forward to the coming year without a worry in the world. It is not that my parents were still quite young at that time and naturally looked well; it is that I would never see them looking that well, carefree, and happy again. Five months later, banks in Austria and in Germany crashed, a collapse that was repeated in other countries across the continent. Together with millions of other people from all walks of life my father lost his job. Life for us changed overnight, and would never be the same again!

* * * * *

4

1931–1932
A World is Lost Forever

On October 24, 1929, the papers had reported about the Black Friday, the day of the crash of the New York stock market. Hundreds of thousands of people had suffered severe financial losses overnight. When stocks lost their value, banks experienced difficulties, and the level of productivity in the economic powerhouse of the United States dropped dramatically. Factories drastically curtailed production or closed down altogether. There was mass unemployment, and many people went without food.

* * *

There had been periodic recessions and depressions before, but none had arrived overnight like the current one. Things seemed stable in Germany for a short while. Still, the national debt rose to astronomic figures, the lifetimes of governments became shorter and shorter, and for the first time, Hitler raised fears in the country. His National Socialists and the Communists had both made dramatic gains in the *Reichstag* (the German Parliament). It seemed as if the country was preparing itself for an internal war. The divisions became clearer and clearer. On the one side were the organizations of the Left: the Communists and their troops, the *Rotfrontkämpferbund* and — not at all in unison with them — the Social Democrats who created the *Eiserne Front* (the Iron Front), which encompassed the mass organizations of the *Reichsbanner Schwarz-Rot-Gold* (black, red, and gold, the colors of the Weimar Republic), the unions, and the workers' sports clubs.

Against these powers of the Left, Hitler's shock troops of the *SA* (*Sturmabteilung*) and the *SS* (*Schutzstaffel*) battled in the streets of the big cities, often with the open or tacit support of other right-wing organizations and the more conservative parties. On October 11, 1931 — the day of the rally of the National Socialists, the German National Party, and the veterans organization of the *Stahlhelm* — Hitler and the centre-right media czar Hugenberg created the *Harzburger Front*. Now the battle lines between Left and Right were drawn. Their troops increasingly controlled the streets, while the governing parties, which tried to keep the flame of democracy alive, lost more and more power and respect.

My political education was beginning! Most of what I picked up listening in on the conversations of the adults was vague and confusing. Almost daily I heard terms such as *Die Roten*, or *Die Nazis*. *Die Roten*, or The Reds included those on the Left, ranging from the Communists to the Social Democrats and their organizations. The major force on the Right were the *Nazis* and their organizations such as the *SA*, the *SS* and numerous other groups under the umbrella of the *Nationalsozialistische Deutsche Arbeiterpartei* (NSDAP), but also other conservative groups like the paramilitary *Stahlhelm*. All of a sudden, politics or the little I dimly comprehended of it, entered my life, and it was a new experience because whenever talk about parties came up, I felt a sense of threat and danger.

I soon learned to recognize the men of the social democratic *Reichsbanner* in their green uniforms, and their marching bands, that had fewer brass instruments than the Nazi marching bands, or the *Stahlhelm* members in their old army uniforms and their traditional military bands. There seemed to be more and more demonstrations and rallies, especially on Saturdays and Sundays. The demonstrations also seemed to get bigger and bigger and louder and louder, because they would often march through the narrow streets of the centre of our city and shout rhythmic, repetitive slogans. I found all this quite scary and would hang on to the hand of my mother.

I first saw Hitler when he stopped in Waldenburg in 1932 for an afternoon to speak to a huge crowd of *SA*, *SS*, and other Nazi supporters. His rasping, excited voice and the hysterical screams and applause of the masses could be heard from the Hackenberg grandparents' apartment. With its large corner windows the apartment opened to the civic stadium, which had been dedicated to health and well-being, especially of the workers, when it was opened in 1925. But now, it seemed to serve primarily political rallies, which brought the national party leaders to town. From one of the windows, I saw Hitler leave the crowded stadium at the end of the rally and step into a black Mercedes. Enthusiastic people pushed in on his car shouting and waving.

When we went to visit the Hackenbergs after this first view of Hitler, a girl I used to play with in the street whenever we visited there proudly showed me a picture of herself offering a bouquet of flowers to Hitler who held her one hand while bending down to her. What the girl showed me was a clipping from the local NSDAP daily that showcased the photograph with the poem she had recited for Hitler. It was a type of poetry that did not tell me very much. Much later on I learned from my Grandmother Hackenberg that the girl's father, a motorman with the local streetcar system, was given a very rough time after this event by his neighbours. Most of the houses on the street were rented to miners and other workers, and few of them were as yet devoted to the Nazi cause; neither had the girl who was really a very sweet child an easy time with the other kids on the block. All that changed dramatically after Hitler came to power. She was then wearing her little uniform quite frequently, and her father was quickly promoted to an office job.

What a different world that was, and it became louder, angrier and, it seemed, more threatening and dangerous by the day. Other things were changing too, all the things which had made our life enjoyable and memorable. If the rallies and marches were daily events, I could only remember one where I took part with my parents, and this was not a party rally but a religious procession which, however, had a presence in our city on this day like any of the largest political marches later on.

This was the procession on *Corpus Christi* in 1932. This particular year the procession was very special, as the archbishop of the Archdiocese of Breslau, Fürstbischof Kardinal Bertram, was present to lead the procession, a rare occasion. Thousands of people moved through the centre of the city to reach the square in front of City Hall where a huge altar had been erected for an open air mass. All along, the people were praying and singing. There was much incense wafting over the procession, the little bells carried by the altar boys were ringing, and all the time, the powerful sound of the five bells of the Catholic Guardian Angels Church were reverberating through the narrow streets. Also participating in the procession were all the dignitaries of the city and the provincial government, regardless of their creed or party affiliation. I saw my grandfather (who had done a lot for the Catholic church), in his black suit. Just ahead of him, I saw the archbishop walking under the richly adorned canopy. He was a small man of delicate build who was carrying the heavy golden monstrance. For me this was a rather overwhelming experience the significance of which I only understood later. I do remember that I experienced a sense of peace and elation. The huge groups that I would see a year or two later were so different in their loudness and hostility.

This was also a memorable day in another aspect. It was the last time the archbishop would enter my grandfather's house after his arrival in town. This was a tradition that went back to the archbishop's predecessor on the day of the consecration of the new church across from my grandfather's house in 1904. Always on this occasion, a special small settee and two delicate little upholstered armchairs, all covered in red velvet, were brought down from the attic into the parlour in my grandparents' apartment to seat the archbishop and some of his party. Small refreshments were offered, and after a short while, the archbishop would move on to the church across the street. This early tradition in which initially all the Koch sons were involved in some task or duty, continued whenever the archbishop would come to Waldenburg. His presence on *Corpus Christi* in 1932 was the last of these visits. I remember that I was absolutely frightened when I was presented to the archbishop, not so much because he was a strange man to me, but because of the prior coaching I had received as to my conduct. I was instructed — and I had to practice — to genuflect (on one knee) in front of the archbishop and then take the hand he extended to me and kiss the *Petrusring*, the St. Peter's ring. It was not the last time I would see the archbishop, but it was his last visit to Waldenburg. When after Hitler's accession to power, it was obvious that the archbishop would probably never return to Waldenburg and to my grandfather's house, the delicate red velvet covered furniture was taken to an upholsterer to be modernized in shape and covering. From thereon, it became part of our living room.

There were, in looking back, other "for the last time" events or activities such as our visits to Uncle Alfred and Aunt Käthe in Breslau. While these were always exciting, quite glamorous days, I found out later that my uncle and my aunt were living far beyond their quite substantial means at that time. They lived in one of those somewhat pretentious apartment houses in an upper class district with an elevator, servants' entrance and maids' quarters. There were parties in the house, and my cousin Christel and I listened to their noise while we were already in bed. I found it most intriguing to watch the grown-ups getting ready to go out. There were my uncle and aunt, my parents, and often, their friends. The men would all invariably wear a tuxedo. I was overwhelmed by what looked to me like the supreme elegance of the women's dresses. There was happy excitement, laughter, and jokes. It seems to me that I had as much fun in partying without attending parties or balls, simply by just being there and watching the adults get ready. After the bank my uncle worked with collapsed, he and his family left Breslau. Their life of partying resumed a couple of years later, and so did our visits, but my parents were neither in the mood nor had the means to rejoin the party crowds of Alfred and Käthe.

From sometime during 1931 on, I am still aware of the pall of worry, anger, and depression that was present in our little family despite all the love and harmony that existed between my parents. I do not remember the day when my father was fired from his good job at the bank. I believe my parents hid this fact from me until I eventually realized that something had changed drastically because my father seemed to be at home more hours of the day and his absences were irregular, obviously no longer determined by working hours. I, of course, could not comprehend what this all truly meant for my parents. I was, however, in a state of fear and uncertainty. I became a very quiet child, seemed to walk on tiptoes in the house, and almost completely stopped asking for things or treats.

My mother and I still went shopping, but mainly for food. There was certainly no longer window shopping or browsing through the stores. Often, my mother would abruptly cross to the other side of the street, and I learned very quickly that she was avoiding friends or acquaintances she used to love to chat with when we met by chance. In the beginning, I pointed such a person out to my mother with a loud voice, as I liked most of these ladies very much myself. But from my mother's reaction — she would speak in a tense voice to me like never before, and she would grab my hand and drag me along like never before — I soon learned how to conduct myself in such situations. I am sure that most of these people were kind and understanding, but some were obviously nasty and enjoyed their triumph of still being well off. I remember how the wife of my father's successor at the bank replied to my mother's polite "How are you?" with the incredible sentence: "Very well, of course, after all, my husband is playing the first flute at the bank now." My mother beat a hasty retreat, we rushed home, where my mother broke into tears. As always when she cried these days — and I could never remember my mother crying in my presence before — I did my pitiful best to console her and all I could do was stroke her cheek and say "Mummy, do not cry, please do not cry."

I was upset myself, but not as fearful as I was another time, when my mother returned in tears to our apartment after being away for a short while. She directly walked to the kitchen cupboard, took out a large bread knife, lifted it to her neck and screamed "I am going to stab myself to death, I am going to stab myself to death." In utter panic I screamed, "No, Mummy" and grabbed her arm and hung on to it. This scene is still so horribly present in my mind and feelings, but I never raised that incident with my mother again, and therefore did not know what its cause was. I know there were conflicts with one of her sisters-in-law, and I know that my mother often did not have a penny in her purse, but was too proud to ask her parents or her husband's parents for help. Why no help was forthcoming from these parties I can only speculate about, and I will do this at a later chapter, as it was much later before I would gain a reasonable understanding of what went on at that time. I know that shame, anger, and depression so filled my mother's heart that it made her life almost unbearable, because by nature she was always positive, cheerful, and took the good with the hard parts of life in stride.

My father handled this situation quite differently, mainly through keeping things to himself and being outwardly as cheerful as he used to be. This must have been often rather sad, as even I at my young age sensed that his humour, for which he was famous, was no longer the same and my laughter in response to his jokes was often subdued, or forced, as if I laughed only to fulfil my duty. I never noticed him being different to my mother. He was always gentle or cheerful with her. I recall often being confused and frightened when I heard him argue and fight with his brother Hubert. Being the two youngest in the family and of very like character, disposition, and talent, the two brothers always had been inseparable and were very close emotionally. It seemed incredible to me and very alarming to hear those two attacking each other in loud and angry words.

The event that nearly shattered me at my young age of not quite six years was a scene involving my father with myself the helpless and frightened bystander. I had started elementary school at Easter 1931 and was enjoying a beautiful sunny day during my first summer holidays. I am sure my father's mood was not like the weather this morning when he got ready to leave the house. I begged to go with him, as by that time I had realized that he no longer had to leave home to go to work. But he seemed reluctant to have me with him and got quite angry when I persisted in begging him, but eventually he agreed that I could accompany him. As he said that he was on his way to the *Neustadt*, the new part of town, I immediately assumed that we would visit the Grandparents Hackenberg. We crossed through the park that separated the old from the new part of town, and as we climbed the hilly path, my father became more and more silent. I finally realized that it was the *Arbeitsamt*, the Employment Office my father was turning towards for reporting on his job search and to pick up his meagre unemployment pay. One must understand that by that time Germany had more than four million unemployed workers; industrial cities such as Waldenburg were particularly hard hit. As a consequence, the *Arbeitsamt*, a recently completed building of very attractive architecture had become far too small to accommodate the daily numbers of the unemployed. As a result, there were several queues stretching out from the front doors and reaching backwards perhaps a hundred yards across the vast square. My father and I ended up in the middle queue.

There were men standing close on either side of us. We were literally trapped between people — there were no women, just men, and some were quite rough-looking. Many certainly spoke in rough voices and someone guffawed with sneering words: "Sattock dan reecha Koch, dan Millionärssohn, nu ies a ahner vo insel!"[1] There was loud hollering and nasty laughter. I am sure there were only a couple of men who knew my father's face. Hearing his name was enough for the rest to join in, making my father the representative for an entire class and the mark of their hostility against that class. My father, no doubt, did not know how to defend himself, and there would have been no way for him to defend himself (any altercation would have likely ended with my father being badly beaten up). The ridiculing of my father went on for a long while, but my father had no way to escape from the crowd, and he also could not afford to walk away, as he would have lost his unemployment money.

I do not know how to describe my feelings. All I knew was that I must not cry. I said nothing. My eyes were cast to the ground where I saw dozens of worn boots, dusty shoes, blue work pants, scuffed corduroy pants, and I heard the persistent rough voices. I was sweating profusely, and it was not the warm sun that caused it, as I hung on to my father's hand, to seek safety and to comfort him. Somehow we managed to get through this shattering experience. We walked home silently and by the time we were with my mother, my father had become his usual self and was seemingly cheerful and happy. He told my mother about our beautiful walk through the park but did not mention the incident with a single word; neither did I ever do so. This must have been one of the hardest, most devastating days in my father's life. Similar things must have happened to him more than once, when he was on the street, at gatherings, or even in the midst of his family.

Only if one knew the extreme poverty and want, even among part of the employed in this mining area can one at least partly understand the hostility that had descended on my poor father on that day outside the *Arbeitsamt*. It should be helpful to give a brief view of the uniqueness of the Lower Silesian Industrial Basin among the other coal mining areas in Germany. Although of great importance in the early half of the nineteenth century, the Waldenburg Basin was soon surpassed by the mines of Upper Silesia and the Ruhr Basin. In addition, the mining conditions in Waldenburg were geologically among the most difficult in Germany. There was also no access to a river or a canal for the economical transport of coal. However, the Waldenburg coal was of high quality,

---

1   "Now look at him, the rich Koch's son, the millionaire's son; now, he is one of us!"

especially for steel making — some of it was even shipped to Upper Silesia. Otherwise, the entire mining industry might have died an early death, as at all times the Waldenburg mines found it hard to compete.

As a result, the working conditions in the coal mines in the Waldenburg Basin were most difficult and dangerous; the hours were longer and the wages lower than anywhere else in Germany. There were years when the mines were not working at their capacity, but there were also times when the coal sold well, especially after more and more industrial enterprises settled in Waldenburg with its ready access to coal. The working conditions and wages, however, remained poor and so did the housing conditions.

During the years of economic expansion of the German Empire before World War I, a large number of labourers moved to Waldenburg from other areas of Silesia. For them, contractors erected housing of the poorest quality around the centre of town and in the formerly rural villages, which now became industrial settlements with ugly housing filling the narrow valleys. None of them had clean water or proper sewage, and until World War I, typhoid and cholera outbreaks were common occurrences.

The miners' housing consisted of four- or five-story buildings placed haphazardly through the villages or the suburbs of Waldenburg (only the centre of town had a development plan). For most families, their home consisted of one large room or at best a kitchen and a room. If they were fortunate, there was a common water tap and one common toilet at the end of a long corridor. In many cases, however, there was a pump in the courtyard and a row of outhouses. No wonder there were outbreaks of various epidemics and the poor health of school children was loudly deplored by the public health officials.

After World War I, the social democratic city government performed near miracles in building decent workers' housing and especially beautiful schools. But even at my time as elementary school student, I visited chums from my class at home and most of them were still living in the terribly overcrowded and ugly, unhealthy buildings, often in one-room flats.

The purpose of President Hindenburg's visit to Waldenburg on September 19, 1928, which I remember so well, was to inspect these notorious housing conditions in Waldenburg. Deeply disturbed by what he had seen in just a few hours, Hindenburg addressed the city councillors: "Most deeply I was touched by the horrendous situation of the overcrowded housing. I truly wish that it should be possible for employers and employees to alleviate this situation. Whatever I am capable of doing to help within the constraints of my position, I promise to do." And later, after the end of his speech, "Once more after the official part of my address, I must reiterate my profound distress about what I have seen and heard today. Help must come forth, things cannot be allowed to go on like this!"

Within a year, a film crew appeared in Waldenburg to document the living conditions of the miners and their families. The film "Hunger in Waldenburg" became a milestone in the history of social comment by the picture industry. What the film showed to the public in the rest of Germany was so horrendous that its press was not very positive; rather, its author and director Leo Lania was accused of blatant propaganda.

There were more attributes typical for a mining town like Waldenburg, which other towns and cities in Lower Silesia did not possess. One was the phenomenon of the *Schlafburschen*, young bachelors, who did not have a place of their own or would not even live in board and room with another miner's family (which would have been rare in any case, as miners' apartments were too small). Instead, in order to make a few extra pennies, the father's or the parents' bed would be rented out for about six hours to one of these bachelors while the father was away at work on a shift different from that of the *Schlafbursche*. My mother, who once wondered how the woman of the family would manage this man while she would wash herself or dress herself, asked our household help, a wonderfully brave miner's wife about it. The answer my mother received in pure Waldenburg dialect was that *"Olles was iech sog ies Morsch, imdrahn!"*[2] This woman was a true representative of thousands of miners' wives who maintained the family after their husbands went on an early disability pension. The wife going to work was essential for the economic survival of the family. Our cleaning lady came to us a couple of times a week with a boy of my age whom I thought to be her son although I always wondered, why Achim's mother was so much older than my own mother. Only later did I learn that Achim was her grandson, and his mother was the daughter of my mother's helper.

How the hard-working miners got enough rest was a miracle, as the overcrowded houses were always noisy. It became the custom for the fathers in the family to come home from night shift and in summer leave for the forest which was always near, the way the town was built, and get their needed sleep there. When we would go for walks into the forest, we would see quite a few men lying in the shade of trees. I was always afraid, but my father or my mother would tell me to look at their faces and if their eyelids were black, they were trustworthy working men; because all miners one could recognize by their pale skin and the coal

---

2   "All I say to him is "Turn to the wall!'"

dust that had imbedded itself permanently between their eyelashes and which gave their faces a very unique expression. Still, there were also other fellows hanging around the forest and sleeping there, and those were the drifters or *Bummler* (bums). They were often not trusted, although many of them were, I am sure, harmless and just unfortunate to have neither job nor home. They came to the houses to ask for food and when mass unemployment had descended on our town, each household in the wealthier parts of town had their daily guest for dinner at noon.

I got to know some of them, especially those my mother asked to come in and sit on a chair in the hall while eating their meal. But there were others she would not trust and they would have to eat on the stairs outside our apartment. Complications arose one time when my Grandmother Hackenberg was looking after me while my parents were away for a couple of days. My mother had left instructions to look after the daily dinner guests, but had failed to let my grandmother know who could eat in the hall, and who should be kept out on the stairs. At noon the doorbell rang and one of our regulars appeared, a surly looking war veteran with a wooden leg, a man of huge proportions with rarely a smile on his face who would also hardly ever thank my mother. Not surprisingly, my grandmother felt uncomfortable with this man and reached his plate to him and quickly shut the door. Within a second or so, the plate crashed through one of the large panes of glass of the door. Through the broken glass, I saw a terribly angry face and heard equally terrible swear words. Then the veteran took off his wooden leg. How he managed to remain upright while he swung his wooden leg from left to right and smashed the entire glass wall to the right and left of the already broken glass door, I still cannot imagine. Before my grandmother could get to the phone to call for help, he hobbled down the stairs using his wooden leg like a cane. He never came back. First, I felt frightened, then I felt sad, because I always had admired this big strong man who seemed to have a powerful presence. I have never forgotten his face with its huge grey beard.

The large number of single men who really did not have a home and the number of family men who lived in the noisy overcrowded tenements had an enormous effect on the appearance of the town's main streets. To escape the crowding, the men would spend most of their off-work waking hours on the streets and in the parks. Since the mines were operating continuously on three shifts a day, there were always large numbers of men off work and on the streets, and mingling with them were those who were on their way to work or going home after shift. While some were moving along fast, those on their free hours would literally shuffle along the sidewalks, stop, look at shops, talk, and amble on again. Why there were so many workmen on the streets is also explained by the fact that a lot of them were no longer capable of working. The harsh conditions underground resulted in various lung diseases. Beginning in their forties, miners would be medically declared unable to work and become *Berginvaliden*, living on a meagre pension with not much to do other than perhaps, as quite a few of them did, tend their garden plot, feed a few rabbits, chop wood or sweep courtyards, all for a few pennies. Their wives would continue making their contribution to the household by working as cleaning women, washerwomen, or working full-time in factories, the latter being rare, though, as factories preferred younger women.

In between these crowds in the streets, there was the endless stream of horse-drawn wagons that brought the coal from the mines into town. Their owners were essentially self-employed men who had a couple of horses and a little barn or shed somewhere at the edge of town. Their income was meagre, but they were busy all day into the night. Their wagons, with their ironclad wheels, made very loud rumbling noises rolling over the cobblestone pavement while the steel handle used to tighten the brakes would loudly and incessantly clank. Altogether, this noise was so typical and to me becomes part of the street scene of Waldenburg whenever I remember it. This was all very different in winter when the town often drowned in snow. Then the noisy streets became almost silent except for the human voices, but even they were muffled. The coal wagons now on steel sleds had also become quiet, and so were the normally noisy streetcars that were now gliding through the streets without making a sound save the occasional clanging of their bells. Life for the poor people must have been so much harder during these long and cold winters, but for a child, the town with its hills around it looked just magical. As soon as one left the narrow streets of the centre, one became conscious of another noise, which literally had not ever stopped for over a hundred years, and this was the conglomerate of sounds that emanated from the half dozen big mines that surrounded the town. It was a mix of steam hissing, coal cars squealing on the tracks or bumping into each other, of entire coal cars being unloaded in one swoop and above all, a deep rumbling sound that seemed to be of a subterranean origin.

Rarely can a town or city dominate one's awareness as much as a coal mining town or a town full of steel mills. Only such establishments can permeate the entire organism of a town and determine the nature of its population. Most of the phenomena I have described were somehow connected with various noises and sounds, but there was also a strong visual impact beginning with the truly imposing panorama of the city dominated by the huge mines elevated above town like modern industrial or technical castles, their power symbolized by the huge plumes of steam emanating from the numerous cooling towers and the equally powerful, although muted noises they produced. They also spewed out an incredible amount of dirt, coal dust, and noxious gases, which necessitated very frequent wash days for the housewives, and the cleaning of windows sills, door handles, and other parts exposed to the air. A silently creeping consequence was the poor health not only of the miners, but of a much larger than normal part of the population, foremost among the children.

Finally, a daily scene, which one would not find anywhere else except in a coal mining town, was the habit of drinking among the miners. In the streets while off shift, they would frequent the large number of pubs throughout town, drink beer or a cheap kind of brandy. The pubs opened early in the morning and were always busy into the late night. After shift change in the afternoon, and especially on paydays, the pubs were so overcrowded that their patrons, glass in hand, spilled onto the sidewalk making lots of noise and being quite intoxicated. Payday was the worst, and not a few wives waited at the mine gate trying to catch their husbands and wrest the little paper envelop with the weekly pay from them. Thus, drunkenness became a major problem. There were so many drunk men on the streets that we kids, rather than ridiculing them, became disgusted with them.

This is the setting where I got to know the world beyond the confines of our home. It was a fascinating world and, emotionally, I have been deeply attached to it ever since. But for the adult, whether poor or better off, this was not a pretty environment, but one where social and personal problems stared one in the eye every day. What must it have meant to my father, when he was claimed by the unemployed workers as one of them!

I never heard my father grumble about hard times, the stupid government or society's injustices, although he had plenty of reasons to complain about what had happened to him in this society and also within the sphere of his family. He must have been very unhappy, angry, and troubled inside. And I wonder whether the incident at the *Arbeitsamt* pushed him just too far. Whether this was accidental or a result of it, later in that year, sometime before the end of 1931, he joined Hitler's party. He became a member, but of all the many things I remember from that time, I cannot recall him going out to a meeting, joining a march or in any way promoting the NSDAP. Rather, it seemed to be a silent protest, a self-isolation from the class he was born into and belonged to, or even from his own family, especially his own father who did nothing to help him in this terrible time when he had no work and no money and struggled with shame and a deeply hurt pride. My Father was the only one in the large Koch family or among our friends at that time who had taken out a membership with the NSDAP. This was often enough discussed in the family when my parents were not there but while I happened to be around playing and my presence was usually forgotten by the adults, I would always listen very intently. This is how I found out about my father's membership, and when I asked my mother, she said not to think about it, which was an unusual way for her to answer a question of mine. I sensed that this was a very troublesome matter for her and never raised this question with my father.

On the surface, things improved in 1932 when my father went back to work, although he still must have remained bitter about his fate. This was a job as an accountant in a newly established firm which was a joint German–Russian (i.e., Soviet) venture of importing oil from the Soviet Union to Germany. The plant was a small terminal in a suburb of Waldenburg that my father could reach by streetcar, although he would walk home to save streetcar fare on the rare days when he did not have to work overtime. Overtime, of course, was not paid, not even when it occurred on a Sunday. I do remember how on most Sundays my father would get ready in the early morning, unsmilingly, while my mother hovered over him, being secretly as unhappy as he was. I only once met his boss and I can say that he was probably the person who frightened me most in my earlier life. He was very tall but also very heavy. His face was reddish and his head was completely shaved. He also wore a monocle – until the end of World War I the trademark of the Prussian officer – which gave him a fierce, wicked appearance (I only knew monocles as objects of fun when my father and his brother Hubert used to wear one during some of the skits they put on). His voice, however, was strangely high-pitched, but ice-cold and cutting. When my mother and I entered the office, he clicked his heels when greeting my mother, but except for asking me for my name and giving me an ice-cold stare for just a moment, he ignored me for the rest of our time in the office.

My father seemed strangely subdued in his presence. At home in the evening, he told me that his boss had been a very high officer in the Imperial Army and had just returned from the Soviet Union where he had spent a couple of years. Now, I assume that he was one of the small groups of German military personnel that were sent to Russia under a secret German–Soviet agreement designed to benefit both countries. This secret project had been spearheaded by the German Generaloberst von Seeckt who saw this arrangement as an opportunity to try out new advanced weapons and have German soldiers being trained on weapons that Germany was not allowed to produce or use under the terms of the Treaty of Versailles. This also included military planes, which were totally outlawed for post-war Germany. For the Soviet Union, there were tremendous advantages in having their relatively young Red Army trained by experienced German officers. There was self-interest on both sides, but also an important commonality which was the hatred and mistrust of the western democracies, a feeling both Germany and the Soviet Union shared. While on the surface, the relationships between the Weimar Republic and the western democracies had become much more normal, this change towards the positive did not include the German military, which remained conservative to the extreme and essentially monarchist in the tradition of the old Prussia.

Having seen my father's boss, I can only feel for my father to this day, thinking of this terrifying man and of the endless hours of work he pressed out of my father. And, to add to this terrible position, my father's pay was incredibly low and must have felt like an insult. However, I think my father would have worked for less, only to feel respectable again and to bring some money home for his family's survival. By 1932, while my father was still working for this German-Russian company, I was quite capable of reading words and figures. One day, I sneaked over to my father's desk where some papers were spread out and read on one of them "Monatsgehalt 122 Mark" (monthly salary 122 Marks). Even at that time, this was a pittance.

It was a miracle and speaks for my mother's strength and for what my father possessed in inner resources that in spite of all this anguish and the shortage of money, there was much that made life entertaining and enriching for us as a family. First of all, there was always music in the house. Whenever my father was at home and not engaged in other work, he would sit at his beloved Steinway grand piano for hours, no doubt grateful that he had purchased this precious instrument at a time when he could still afford it, at a price for which he could have bought a well-appointed automobile as several of his brothers had. Just by being around, I amassed an enormous amount of knowledge (by ear) of classical music and if later I had no trouble to quickly identify the composer of a piece unknown to me it was because my father rarely would tell me the title of the music but always the composer's name.

One of the things for which I am grateful is that with all his love for the great composers and their music, from Handel to Wagner and Richard Strauss, my father was not a snob when it came to popular music. He played all the great waltzes of the years before and after World War I, such as the "Destiny Waltz" by Sidney Barnes, the dark, mysterious French waltz "Quand l'amour meurt," and many others. When sound was introduced to movies, he played all the show tunes of the German UFA films and some of the American movies. He had a small sheet music collection of jazz for the piano, and I remember one piece for its absolute brilliance but also for its extreme complexity — the "Eccentric Fox" by

Fred Caplush. And there were the grand operettas of these years by Lehár, Kalman, and others, with their melodious tunes that my mother would sing along with.

I am immensely grateful to my father for opening a world of music to me that included popular music. It was originality, artistry, and competence of creation and play which my father honoured at a time when it was almost *de rigueur* to dislike popular music if one professed a liking or understanding of classical music.

He was also deeply involved in playing music with others. He played the large organ in our church, which at High Mass on Sunday would often include not only the choir but also an orchestra. He would sing solo parts with his trained tenor voice, temporarily giving the organ over to someone else for the length of the solo he sang. He also appeared as soloist in concerts of the local orchestra, as a vocalist or as a pianist. The next day, he and my mother would excitedly read the reviews that were always positive and sometimes very laudatory.

Once a week he met with others to form a trio or a quartet consisting of some of his musician friends and his brother Hubert at the cello. On such evenings I would lie in bed and not fall asleep for a long time because of the wonderful music next door. His love for music would even lead us to the Café Enderlein, a rather unlikely place to find good music, and that was the single large concert café in our town, a very elegant setting, where my mother used to go and meet her friends for an afternoon of coffee, conversation, and listening to music. She would usually take me along and I would meet the children of some of her friends. But these afternoon outings ceased altogether after my father lost his job with the bank. When he was back at work, however, we would sometimes go to the Café Enderlein on Sunday afternoons because of the exceptionally good musicians my father loved to hear. This was a temporary phenomenon, when a number of professional musicians playing in the great orchestras of the country lost their jobs and to support themselves, appeared in restaurants or coffee houses.

My father was still unemployed and had much free time, when a friend of his, who was a school teacher in a suburb as well as a very gifted painter, asked him to sit for a portrait. My father's friend Karl Boehm — endearingly called *Boehm Karle* — wanted to expand his oeuvre from landscapes and still lifes to portraits. So during the winter 1930/1931, we went to Karl Boehm's studio where I sat and watched my father's likeness slowly gaining shape. It turned out to become a beautiful portrait. Its survival at the end of the war was a feat my mother accomplished and I cannot thank her enough for that. It seemed hard to believe that this portrait was the first *Boehm Karle* painted. He chose the appearance and the surroundings of his subject very carefully. As the

British-American portrait painter John Singer Sargent used his subject's background, dress, and posture most carefully in order to convey the person's character, so did my father's portraitist. In front of a primarily red background with a white female torso placed on a bookshelf (a figure which I interpreted to be that of a little dog sitting upright) my father stood dressed in his black suit, white shirt, and a special bow-tie, of which he had a quantity specially made in his good years, and he holds an unlit cigarette in his hand — in real life, my father more often than not, would be seen with a gold-tipped cigarette between his fingers. He looks the viewer straight in the eyes through unusual black-rimmed glasses that convey his artist personality, as does the bow-tie, which his friends used to call *die Künstlerschleife,* his "artist's tie." As with any good portrait, it says more than first meets the eye. It is beautiful, but very serious, quite different from the portrait the same artist painted of my mother.

For a variety of reasons, my mother was not able to rescue her portrait at the end of the war and I can only describe it from memory, although were I a gifted artist, I could recreate it, because I remember it so well. In a sparsely furnished, but brightly sunlit room, my mother sits in an armchair and wears a short blue silk dress that with its narrow shoulder-straps is quite free around the shoulders. Like my father, she holds a cigarette in her hand and the smoke seems to curl slowly straight up into the air. It is a scene of calmness and serenity. My mother's hair is quite short and she does not look the viewer into the eye. The viewer can easily see her facial features, which seem to convey happiness, contentment, and beauty. This is so different from the nature of my father's portrait and I still wonder how the painter succeeded to give my mother's portrait and my mother herself, such a carefree, happy appearance. One has to remember that due to my father still being unemployed at that time, my parents were now in the midst of the most difficult period in their married life.

During the winter, my mother would once in a while take me to the movies, which were still silent. I remember my first one being the famous film about the *Nibelungen.* This was when I first heard about Siegfried and Brunhild (the one I thought was bad) and Krimhild (the blond, good one, I thought). I was captivated, spending most of the time on my feet standing next to my mother in the first row of the balcony. I was excited for days after that, but not fearful as I later felt after seeing the silent film "Snow White," which probably was produced quite a few years earlier, as the actors, especially the evil stepmother, made fearsome faces and used exaggerated gestures to show their feelings.

On summer Sundays we would often go on outings, especially hikes in the hills around Waldenburg, always taking a knapsack full of food for a wonderful picnic. To get to the hills we would usually take the streetcar to the end of town. My uncles, who all had cars, often invited us to go along with them, but my parents were reluctant to accept. We would, however, readily go on automobile trips or outings with the Körners, Georg and Emma who, for me, were the best aunt and uncle I could ask for. They were not blood relatives, but the Koch and Körner families could not have been closer. Already my father's grandfather and Uncle Körner's grandfather were close friends, and that includes their families as well. As the generations evolved, the friendship between the two families remained loyal and solid. Some of the Koch sons and the two Körner sons maintained separate friendships as well.

The Körners were an excellent example of the progress of Silesia's industry during the nineteenth and twentieth centuries. My own Great-Great-Grandfather Joseph Cuisinier was still a loyal soldier of Napoleon and had not even arrived in Silesia yet when Anton Körner already operated a factory around 1800 in the little town of Liebau (since 1945 Lubawka) close to the Bohemian border. In 1822, Körner relocated to Waldenburg to benefit from the first industrial boom there. He succeeded to expand his modest enterprise of producing various wire mesh articles into a busy factory that specialized in all sorts of materials made from wire that were in demand by the local mines and industries.

When my father was a child, both my Grandfather Franz Koch and Paul Körner were close friends. I have an old photograph from 1904 where the men proudly sit with their wives in front of the garden pavilion of the Körners surrounded by their children (10 in all). When I got to know the Körner property in the late 1920s and very early 30s, their situation was at its best. The factory was booming, employing more than 300 workers. A large, very attractive house had been built accommodating the offices on the main floor and a huge apartment on each floor above for the two young families of the Körners. I still marvel at the elegance of Uncle Georg and Aunt Emma's apartment. It had a large central hall with a huge fireplace, the walls were paneled in precious wood, and there was an enormous dining room, a library, and a number of other rooms. They often entertained quite lavishly, but I most remember the great time we had with them singing around the piano, especially the operettas by Franz Lehár, which were so popular after World War I.

On the floor below, Uncle Georg's married sister and her family lived, and her three children were ideal playmates for me. There was much to explore outdoors, as between the house and the highway, there was a large piece of property (the factory was situated on the other side of the house). Next to the house were the garages and the flats of the gardener and the chauffeur (the Körners had four different cars just for their personal use). There was a vegetable and flower garden and a large greenhouse and next to it the park with a long driveway and various smaller paths. In its centre was the garden pavilion with swings and sandboxes. Nearby was a large pond with a fountain. Secluded among trees and bushes, there was a swimming pool. I have nothing but wonderful memories of the Körners and of the children. All this ended most abruptly.

It must have been in 1931 or 1932, when Aunt Emma arrived at our house in tears with the words "we have lost everything, we are poor, we don't have our house and our cars anymore." This must not have come as a complete surprise for my parents, but for me it was. It was as if access to paradise was suddenly denied. We never went back to visit there again. When we passed the property in the streetcar, I longingly looked towards the little garden pavilion half hidden by trees. For me, it was like a miracle, when during my first visit to Poland in 1968, I found that in its substance, the old private park of the Körners had survived World War II and the post-war years. Its fence was taken down, the pool and ornamental pond were dried up and overgrown, but during my most recent visit in July 2003, the magnificent trees were still there and, in their midst, the garden pavilion now about 120 years old. I also found the former Körner plant with its adjoining buildings in Piaskowa Góra (formerly the Waldenburg suburb of Sandberg) in full operation

This was the closest I came to one of the countless tragedies experienced by German entrepreneurs who had worked hard and had done extremely well. After the short boom in the later 1920s, many of them simply folded when the entire economy slowed down to a crawl.

The next time we visited Uncle Georg and Aunt Emma, they lived in a single room in one of the poorest workers' houses in the Waldenburg suburb of Altwasser (since 1945 Stary Zdrój). It was a noisy and smelly house with not very nice people living in the building. There was a cold-water tap on the ground floor and the toilets consisted of wooden outhouses, shared with unknown others in the yard. I was truly shattered and cried. I remember that my aunt wanly smiled at me and caressed my cheek. The next time I saw her was in a large room in an abandoned factory. She was standing at an old wire weaving machine, which my uncle had been allowed to take from his former factory, as it had been discarded. At this machine, my aunt stood, I am sure for more than the normal eight-hour-day and operated the weaving process. A loyal foreman from the factory had joined my uncle and aunt to do all the heavy work of lugging around the big rolls of wire, packing the orders, and so on. During the same time, my uncle was on the move from morning to night trying to get some orders for his tiny business. Instead of going by car as in the past, he walked with his briefcase from one potential customer to the next, even trying to save the cheap streetcar fare.

About two or three years later, the Körners had overcome the loss of the big factory and its surrounding property. Uncle Georg used a second-hand car, Aunt Emma ran the little office, and there were a few employees now. They were also fortunate in their housing arrangements, as the awful house they had been forced to live in had been sold for restoration as a historic building (it had served as the old post office in the early 1800s when this dirty industrial suburb had been a charming, much-frequented spa, until its famous springs disappeared as a result of the increasing coal mining activities). The old post office building became a very pleasant place to live. My uncle and aunt now occupied the entire second floor. They enjoyed indoor plumbing, hot water, and central heating again as in better times. The once-dirty yard was adorned with lawns and flower beds and a little ornamental pool. I felt very happy for the Körners, especially when for the first time I accompanied my uncle on a short business trip in his new car. I always think that their story is representative of the fate of a lot of people and their stamina at that time.

The world around me remained confusing in certain ways. When I saw poverty and hunger in the streets, when we suffered ourselves because of my father's unemployment, when the well-off and seemingly secure Körners went from riches to rags overnight, we had two visitors from overseas: my father's cousin Grete Pohl, who had emigrated to Brazil after the war to become a school teacher in one of the German settlements there, and my mother's cousin Hildegard Hackenberg, who had gone to New York after her father died leaving his wife with four children and no pension. Both women looked prosperous, although in hindsight I doubt that they really were very rich. "Pohl Gretel" had brought a lot of exotic things like snake skins and Indian artifacts from Brazil, which to me looked utterly precious. Aunt Hildegard was a tall woman of striking beauty with jet-black hair and vivid brown eyes. She had a tiny little grey cap on her head with some iridescent feathers on it and wore a grey suit. I know I kept staring at her because I thought of her as being my rich aunt from America.

There was also some confusion I faced when I started school. I learned easily and was apparently very well behaved. But the world of the children in my class was one I had never been close to, and each teacher seemed to differ from the other. There were some teachers the children were truly afraid of, not because they were necessarily cruel, although they freely used the cane and their hand, but mainly because they were such remote figures of authority. It did not help that they all wore invariably dark, probably black suits, and if they had grey hair and a grey beard, which several of them had, they looked even more formidable to a little boy of six years.

When I started school at Easter 1931, I was the only kid in the classroom coming from a family known to be wealthy. When my father had lost his job, I felt as poor as the others (although that certainly was not so, considering the abject poverty most of them experienced at home). There were 60 boys in the classroom. All were poorly dressed, almost all had their head shaved (by their father to save money), and many looked ill or had some deformity. This was a constant with us, and in each school year one or two boys would unexpectedly die. I still remember the first one — I had hardly started elementary school — who complained about a headache and was dead the following day. There were several boys with dislocated hips; some had a short leg or arm; one had only an arm of a few inches with a tiny hand at its end; one had only one eye, and so on.

Interestingly enough, these kids were not persecuted by the healthy boys, but rather seemed to be objects of constant curiosity. They were not always called with the nicest of names by the other boys, but in the relationships in the classroom there seemed to be a good measure of good will and tolerance. We all kept playing with the one boy's tiny hand on the short little arm, and we would greet him with fancy words. The boy with one eye, we called *Einäuglein* (Little One-Eye) after a character in a Grimm's fairy tale the teacher had read to us. I also was an object of curiosity, as I was often dressed in a sailor suit, typical for a middle-class boy at that time. I kept explaining that this was a suit already well used, which I had inherited from my older cousin. Eventually, the fact that I wore used clothes from older boys, like most of the other kids, seemed to make me one of them. My mother also sewed *Manchester* pants and jackets made from corduroy for me, which were worn by a lot of working-class boys. She did not want me to have a hard time coming from a background different from all the other boys. I also did not take a mid-morning snack to school after the teacher suggested that I should be like the other boys and have only the Quaker breakfast.

After the film "Hunger in Waldenburg" was shown in movie houses, the Quakers, who had several branches in Germany, decided to provide all elementary school kids in Waldenburg and its suburbs with a daily breakfast. A huge bun and a cup of milk were placed on top of a little *Traktat,* a religious tale in form of a comic book strip. This we received during the 10 o'clock recess every morning and we all loved it. A few days after Hitler acceded to power, the Quaker breakfasts were ordered to be discontinued for political reasons.

I was incredibly fortunate to have, after a bad start with one of the tough teachers, a teacher who was not only a wonderful, understanding, and loving human being, but a person who employed methods of teaching and working with the children that were decades ahead of their time.

This was Lehrer Geisler, the *Geisler Alfons*, as he was called everywhere in town, because he was so well known for his many community activities.

I will only recall here a very few of his unique educational practices. He discarded the timetable, but requested that we bring all our books to school every day of the week. Each of us had to report something from the daily newspaper. Several times each summer, he would send us home, although we had just arrived at school, with the directive to get a snack and quickly return. In the meantime, he would order a special streetcar that would take us to the edge of town from which we proceeded into the hills. Naturally, this made the school day longer than usual (it normally ended at 1 p.m.), but we did not mind at all. Such a day was taken up with learning in the broadest sense and experiencing nature in a way young children would rarely do.

Our teacher Alfons Geisler also turned out to be a speech therapist of a kind. One day, a rather timid little boy joined our class and remained totally silent until the teacher asked him a question. It then turned out that the boy was afflicted with a terrible stutter. Before we could all focus on this poor boy's stutter in a teasing way, Alfons Geisler immediately proclaimed a class project designed to help this boy, Paul, to learn how to speak without a stutter. We were to start immediately. Paul was asked to write on the blackboard a sentence or two he would like to say, but was to remain silent for the time being. He was then asked to sit on the teacher's knee. We boys were told to form a queue and the first in line was instructed to stand very close to Paul, place one hand firmly on his back and stick the other hand as deeply into Paul's mouth as Paul would permit without gagging. Then the boy had to slowly say the first of the words Paul had written on the blackboard and while doing so, close the fingers of his hand in Paul's mouth slowly and gently and "pull the word out of Paul's mouth." This was repeated perhaps 10 times, and then again on the following day by the next 10 kids and so on. We were all quite excited, each one of us having a personal stake in relieving Paul's speech problem. Never mind that our hands were not very clean, often really grubby, never mind that Paul was sitting on the teacher's knee — this would present a real problem today — Paul's stutter slowly diminished and by the end of the school year it had totally disappeared. For us, Paul was like somebody we owned, a responsibility no other class in the school had. I would meet Paul occasionally on the street long after I had left this school. His speech remained clear and free of any stutter, as long as I knew him.

One day, when he was not yet 14, Paul told me that during physical education, Alfons Geisler had started dancing lessons for the boys. First, they all wanted to lead and nobody wanted to take the part of the female partner. But when the teacher, taking the part of the female, began to start dancing with one of the bigger boys, the boys lost their inhibition. I was the only one in this class who transferred to high school at the age of 10, while the rest of the boys finished their elementary school at age 14 and went into an apprenticeship or started work as unskilled labourers. In other words, they were all too poor to continue their formal schooling. Socially, however, their teacher Alfons Geisler helped them in teaching them how to dance and in talking about issues of the world. None of them would have been sent to dancing lessons by his parents. This was the type of "Head Start" as it is now called, that they received, thanks to Alfons Geisler's intuitive teaching ability.[3]

Being employed in a Catholic school, Alfons Geisler was also a pious man without being a hypocrite. He taught us a bit of Latin so that we could understand the Latin mass, and he formed a choir out of our class, which would sing in various churches. Over the years, we not only became a very tight-knit class that never experienced any disciplinary problems, we also were exceedingly proud of our class and, as individuals, a little proud as well and also more self-assured, as the years went on.

The problems that affected us were of external origin. Occasionally, we had a special assembly in the assembly hall or in the school yard, where the colors of the Republic were displayed. There were, ironically, several colors present: first of all the black and white of Prussia; then the black, white, and red colors of the old Empire, which had ceased to exist more than 15 years ago; the white and yellow flag of the Catholic Church; and finally, the official color of the Republic, black, red, and gold, which dated back to the very short-lived first German Republic of 1848. These colors were never recognized by the conservative establishment of the Weimar Republic and not even by a large segment of those employed by the Republic, although they had given their oath of allegiance as civil servants to the Weimar Republic. Many teachers, while at least in the beginning no supporters of Hitler, were nevertheless arch-conservative and monarchist and totally rejected the current Republic, which employed them and gave them their livelihood. I remember how at one assembly in the schoolyard, when the colors of black, red, and gold went up the mast, an older teacher standing near me said sneeringly with a loud voice: *"Da*

---

3   Alfons Geisler was able to achieve the optimum as an elementary school teacher thanks to a practice, common in Germany for decades, which permitted teachers to stay with the same class of students for several years.

hängt sie, die Fahne Schwarz, Rot, Kinderkacke.[4] Some time later, he was one of those who used every opportunity to come to work in the Nazi uniform.

We never saw our own teacher Alfons Geisler in uniform. The only uniform he eventually was forced to wear was that of the army into which he was drafted towards the end of the war from which he did not return. I wonder how hard a time he had, once the Nazi regime was getting established. Things began to get worse soon enough after I started school. The marches and rallies of the Right and the Left increased in frequency, size, loudness, and violence. There were street battles now, which the police found difficult to control. I heard more and more talk about a coup, perhaps another revolution, and a huge upheaval that would be near.

I did not assign any particular significance to this special day, when in the later evening the maid of my grandparents came to our door to tell us in her broad Waldenburg dialect, "There is a lot of smoke on the Ring and a huge crowd; they are marching around singing." It was the 30th of January, 1933, and I heard my father say, "The Nazis have won."

* * * * *

---

4   "There it hangs, the flag of black, red, and babyshit!"

Part II
A Different Germany

5

1933 –1935
Hitler's Capture of Germany

A new power took possession of Germany in the person of Hitler. It seemed to happen overnight. From the day Hitler assumed power, events never stopped moving at a pace, that kept all people breathless, many confused, and a minority of them in a constant state of fear. Not a few men and women had reason to fear for their lives and, in the end, many of them lost their lives to a government the likes of which Germany had never experienced.

Germany lost its democracy before democracy ever got truly established. The turmoil of the post-war years did not give democracy a chance to prove its superior worth as the best form of government. On the contrary, rejected or openly attacked by many, misunderstood by others, the Weimar Republic ended in dismal failure. Many blamed its demise on Germany's economic situation. Germans were so intent on their own salvation that they failed to notice that other countries had as severe or even more severe economic problems without losing their democratic form of government and the support of their people.

Neither had the German people ever faced a dictator such as Hitler. Authoritarian governments and emperors yes, but never "a man of the people" like Hitler who seemingly without effort, but in reality ruthlessly and bloodily, dismantled all the freedom enshrined in the idealistic constitution of the Weimar Republic.

Never before had the German people been confronted by a demagogue like Hitler, who with his promises and his condemnations and his monsterizing of the enemies of National Socialism confused the majority of Germans, creating an enormous mass of followers and a comparatively small number of sceptics and anti-Hitler citizens.

Hitler disregarded, abolished, broke, and destroyed every rule in the book of humankind. He misused Christianity and the name of God as a means to legitimize himself in the eyes of the common man, creating an enormous reservoir of faith and trust to such an extent that all up-to-now valid and observed ethical, moral, and religious standards were no longer applied by the ordinary citizen in judging Hitler's intent and actions. Such was his power and magnetism that the majority of Germans enthusiastically, faithfully, and willingly followed him, and while captured by his successes, they ignored or denied his increasingly horrible deeds.

* * *

1933 was to be an exceptional year in several ways. Important changes occurred in our family. We moved to a new apartment in another part of town, a move my parents welcomed. The other important event was the change in my father's work situation. Both changes were entirely positive for him and, at least for a while, for my mother as well. But around us there were dramatic, threatening changes. And even at my young age of seven and a half years, I sensed that the world I knew was being disturbed — the ground on which it rested, seemed to move as if a slow earthquake was occurring.

If before January 30, I had heard the words *Hitler* and *Nazis* with increasing frequency, after that fateful day more than just words like these began to fill our daily lives. Now, it was more than talk about Nazi demonstrations or about a speech by Hitler. Everyday life seemed to be affected, infringed upon, and swayed in almost all decisions, topics, opinions, and by the overwhelming presence of the *SA*, the *SS*, and other groups and their thousands of flags, posters, and slogans.

Even I felt that the world had changed, that at least in our family, everyone seemed to be constantly in a state of surprise, anger, and foreboding. Laws, unwritten but always adhered to, customs, morals, and attitudes had governed and guided the German people for generations. All of a sudden, everything was done differently, and too often no longer by unspoken agreement or established customs and norms, but by new ways that were dictated from above and did not leave room for choice. Whoever did not follow these expectations began to feel that he was being steered into an ever-narrowing tunnel from which there was no escape. If he managed to get by from day-to-day, he probably felt lucky, although his conscience or adherence to former traditions and morals might lie heavily on his mind and soul. He was unlucky, if he expressed his diverse opinion too openly or if he was known to be an adherent or member of a group, party, or race which was known to be anti-Hitler and anti-Nazi. From the first day of Hitler's rise to power over Germany, people who thought or felt differently were intimidated, censured, imprisoned, or murdered. Those who began to fear or experience persecution after January 30, 1933, realized that an overwhelming number of their compatriots were captivated in a trance-like adoration of Hitler and his movement. This adoration bordered on a state of excitement and enthusiasm in permanence, that was intoxicating in an unstoppable way. It was accompanied by branding those who did not fit the image of the new Germany.

Too many were overwhelmed by the sudden enthusiasm, the overpowering, shrill propaganda, to realize that, overnight, something had changed irreversibly. Some thought that things were so outrageous, so against common sense, so against all human decency and the true German traditions, that the entire outbreak of Nazism, from the jubilant masses to the threatening presence of the *SA* and the *SS* and the brutally different government, would not last more than a few weeks. There is no doubt that people living in small towns and remote villages had no sense of what was actually befalling Germany. Most people did not have a radio at that time, which would bring the happenings from the bigger cities, the screaming masses at party rallies, and the hysterical voice of Hitler into their peaceful living-rooms. Radio could bring an immediacy which no newspaper or word of mouth could.

Our hometown Waldenburg was a big enough city with an explosive socio-economic mix of parties and classes, of workers who were far to the Left, of civil servants who had faithfully served their government, of Catholics and Protestants. The new regime could not establish itself without turmoil, threats, violence, and even immediate death. This is what we felt in our family within 24 hours of Hitler's ascension to power.

Before the daily paper, which was not published before two o'clock in the afternoon, was delivered to our house, rumours had circulated in the city that "someone high up" had been murdered during the previous night. When my mother glanced through the paper during our usual cozy afternoon break with a buttered bun with jelly for me and a cup of strong coffee for her, she suddenly let out a scream. She discovered a rather brief but frightening notice on the front page. The *Polizeipräsident*, our city's chief of police, had been found in the ditch of a highway leading out of town. He was obviously murdered by a gunshot. No mention was made of any suspects.

The victim was a member of my father's string quartet that had met once a week for about eight years. Not all of them were the original members of the group. The police chief had only joined my father's quartet a couple of years ago. Aside from the fact that a police officer would invariably impress me because of his position and rank, I was also rather in awe of my father's musician friend. He must have been indeed a very special person, as I later realized that he and my father had fast become close friends.

The morning after the last time the quartet had played in our house, my father had shown me a small Russian icon made of bronze, which his police officer friend had given him the night before. My father told me that he had been reluctant to accept this precious gift, especially when he heard that his friend had received it during World War I from a Russian officer who had been wounded before being taken prisoner. My father's friend had taken him to a field hospital and seen to it that the Russian had been looked after properly. My father spoke often about this precious gift and the circumstances and especially the timing under which he had received it, which was a week prior to the day his musician friend had been murdered. When I left our house for the last time towards the end of World War II to return to my unit, I took this icon with me. It stayed with me and was not taken away during the many searches I experienced as a prisoner of war. The Russian icon still hangs in our living room and reminds me of my father's friend, who from all I know was a good person and a good German who had the misfortune to also be a stalwart social democrat in a high position for which he was no longer deemed tolerable by the Nazis.

The day after the discovery of the murder, there was a short obituary notice in the local paper that merely referred to an "unexpected and untimely death." In my mind, I still see the obituary notice in front of my eyes, especially his very distinct name which included a *von*, as he was a member of the nobility. Not one further word was said in the newspapers about this incident. People who knew and trusted each other would cautiously whisper to each other that he had been taken by several *SS* men from his office, shot somewhere, and then dumped into a ditch along the roadside. For my father, it was most painful to walk on his daily route to and from work past the Police Headquarters, a huge recently completed building with a wing containing apartments for the most senior officers of the force. This is where his deceased friend and family had lived and where my father had shared his beloved music with him. It was made worse for my father to hear how his friend's widow had been ejected from her apartment and hurriedly had left town with her two children for an unknown location.

So soon after January 30, official censorship had not yet been fully introduced by the government. My father was deeply disturbed that our paper, which was conservative and definitely not sympathetic to the Nazi movement, had not dared to report such an evil deed, the first political murder in our area. This, however, was only the beginning of rapid and continuous changes, restrictions, illegal acts, and laws contravening the after-all still existing constitution and the morals of the country. I do not

The Kochs

1. Joseph Cuisinier-Koch, my great-great-grandfather, who was born around 1770 in France. Died December 14, 1868 in Waldenburg, Silesia.

2. Certificate 138 of the Médaille de Sainte Hélène issued to Joseph Kochinier (Cuisinier)[1] in 1857.

[1] When the medal was issued to him, my great-great-grandfather, once a citizen of France, was a subject of the King of Prussia and had changed his name from Cuisinier to Koch. The Chancellery of the Légion d'Honneur confused the two names and entered the name Kochinier into the certificate.

3. The Médaille de Sainte Hélène. Fulfilling the wish of his uncle Emperor Napoleon I, Emperor Napoleon III created the Medal of St.Helena in 1857. The medal was awarded to the 405,000 soldiers, who had fought under Napoleon I during the 1792 to 1815 wars and were still living in 1857.

4.
The Médaille de Sainte Hélène — front and back.

The Kochs

5. Karl Johann Koch,
   my great-grandfather.
   He was born 1817 in Oelse,
   Silesia, and died 1893 in
   Waldenburg.

6. Waldenburg (1860).
   Drawing by F.A. Tittel.

The Kochs

7. Stationary of
   my grandfather
   Franz Koch's
   business (1905).

8. Franz Joseph Koch.
   My grandfather, 1856 - 1936.

10. Catholic Church in Waldenburg.
    Erected after 1900 across from my
    grandfather's house.

9. Therese Helena Koch
   née Schneider.
   My grandmother,
   1859 - 1951.

The Kochs

1. Friedländerstrasse, the location of my grandfather's house and business in Waldenburg.

12. My grandfather's house on Friedländerstrasse 8 (later 16).

3. Vierhäuserplatz.
The location of my grandfather's second house and business.

The Kochs

14. Families Koch and Hötzel were good friends (1908).

15. So were the Koch and Körner Families.

16. The Körner factory in Sandberg (now part of Waldenburg).

The Kochs

Brau- u. Brennerei-Ausschank
des Paul Kretschmer Etablissements

7. Volpersdorf. My grandmother Koch's birthplace.

18. My grandparents Koch.

The Kochs

19. The seven Koch sons, (left to right)
Alfons, Bernhard, Franz, Alfred, Waldemar, Georg, and Hubert.

20. Bernhard and Hubert. The oldest
and the youngest of the seven sons.

21. Franz.

The Kochs

22. Alfons died as soldier in 1915 in Russia.

23. Waldemar's and Aunt Mieze's wedding.

24. Alfred and his wife Käthe. at the Tauentzienplatz in Breslau.

25. Georg. My father.

26. My father as a three year-old. His hands are already shaped like a future pianist's.

The Hackenbergs

27. The family in my grandmother's garden (1930). Back row: my grandparents, Lisa. Front row: myself, Martel, my mother, Georg/Peter.

28. Martha Hackenberg née Herde. My grandmother, 1878 - 1965.

29. Franz Hackenberg. My grandfather, 1872 - 1937.

30. My grandfather's 50th birthday. February 3, 1922.

The four Hackenberg children

31.
Hedda (Hedwig).
My mother,
1901 - 1976.

32.
Lisa,
1907 - 1968.

33.
Peter (Georg,
1905) and
Martel (1910).

34.
Peter and his
wife Hannchen
née Tietze.

35. Martel and Lisa.

The Golden 1920s

Only a few years were "golden" and even these were not golden for everyone.

The Poverty

36. Banknote 1924.
    My parents married at the height of the German inflation. They paid for their wedding and their home, billions and billions of marks.

37. Heinrich Zille.
    Berlin working class district.

38. Käthe Kollwitz.
    Demonstration.

39. Marlene Dietrich.

40. Hans Albers.

41. Hilde Hildebrand.

Our Family

42. My father in 1919.

43. My mother in 1920.

44. The Wedding in 1924.

45. My father's portrait.
1931 by Karl Boehm.

Our Family

46. My father at his Steinway (1928).

47. Sunday outing (1929).

48. In our living room (1931).

Our Family

49. My mother's 27th birthday

50. In the Silesian hill country.

52. Outdoors with my father.

51. New Year's Eve 1931.

53. Uncle Hubert.

54. Aunt Käthe,
wife of Uncle Hubert.

55. Hubert and Käthe.

56. Uncle Alfred and
the other Tante
Käthe and my
cousin Christel
in Trebnitz.

The Koch grandchildren

57. The three oldest grandchildren, Manfred, Christel, and myself.

58. Myself (1932).

59. The fourth grandchild Brigitte (Gittel), born 1930.

60. Myself (1928).

61. Silver anniversary of Uncle Alfred and Aunt Käthe 1944 in Trebnitz.
Aunt Käthe with her daughter Christel, granddaughter Ines, and mother.
Uncle Alfred, away in the war, was present by his portrait only.

62/63. My grandparents Franz and Therese Koch in their later years.

My Waldenburg

65. The Altstadt, centre of the city.

66. The Ring, the town square.

67. End of Sunday
Mass. View
from our
window.

58. Marienkirche (St. Mary's Church), Waldenburg's oldest building.

59. Catholic Church.

70. Lutheran Church.

My Waldenburg

71. The City Hall Square with the Rathaus.

72. Auenstrasse with the other Koch house and store (at right).

73. The house on the Vierhäuserplatz my grandfather built in 1912 as it appears on today's Plac Grunwaldzki in Wałbrzych. Uncle Franz's fancy foodstore continues its tradition as a Polish store; it has never closed since 1912. Crest of Uncle Franz's store from the 1930s.

Religious and political events

74. Mass celebrated on the City Hall Square by Archbishop Cardinal Bertram on Corpus Christi Day 1932.

75. Procession on Corpus Christi Day 1929. In the first row l. to r. Uncle Hubert and Grandfather Koch; in the next row Bernhard Koch.

76. Archbishop Cardinal Bertram with Arch-Presbyter Peikert[1] in 1932.

Arch-Presbyter Peikert lived in Breslau during the Red Army's siege of the city from January to May 1945. After the war, he published a moving account which reflects the actual events and the life of soldiers and of civilians more accurately than most other publications. Peikert, Paul: 'Festung Breslau' in den Berichten eines Pfarrers 22. Januar bis 6. Mai 1945. Hrsg. von K. Jonca und A. Koniecny. Union Verlag 1971.)

77. Corpus Christi Day 1933.

Other events I remember or was told about

78. President Paul von Hindenburg in Waldenburg to inspect the desperate housing and food situation in the city (October 1928 leaving the city hall after addressing the city councillours).

79. Hindenburg arriving at his hotel.

80. Adolf Hitler in the Waldenburg Stadion during his 1932 election campaign.

remember all events, many of which I did not even comprehend, but I distinctly remember the apprehension and nervousness which pervaded our family, and the anxiety with which the adults discussed the steadily worsening news every single day.

By the end of its first week, the new government introduced censorship of the press. The police force changed dramatically, also being complemented by the so-called *auxiliary police*, which consisted mainly of SA men whose job was to promote and enforce the new ideology among the members of the established police.

On February 28, the front pages of the newspapers showed pictures of flames shooting out of the glass cupola of the *Reichstag* in Berlin. This was the signal for large-scale apprehensions of known Communists, as the Communist party was blamed for the burning of the *Reichstag*. Within days, Germans of other political persuasions were imprisoned as well.

On March 5, there were elections, which, despite enormous propaganda, did not bring Hitler the expected absolute majority. This was the opportunity for Hitler to do away with what was left of the constitution of the Weimar Republic, its symbols, and finally all its parties except Hitler's NSDAP.

Within a week of the elections, the German president Paul von Hindenburg proclaimed the colors black, white, and red as the colors of the new Germany, this flag to be flown side-by-side with the Nazi Swastika. The flag of the Weimar Republic with its traditional republican colors going back to the short-lived German parliament of 1848, was outlawed.

On March 21, Hitler and Hindenburg met at the Prussian shrine of the Garrison Church in Potsdam in the presence of the generals of the German Army to cement, in front of the German people, a partnership which was to symbolically meld the old Prussia and its traditions with the National Socialist Movement. Within 24 hours, posters appeared everywhere showing Hitler, not yet in uniform but wearing a cutaway, giving his reverence to the old field marshal.

The day of Potsdam had taken place on Sunday. Three days later, a law was presented to the *Reichstag*, which empowered the government to pass laws and decrees outside the established constitutional framework, including laws that would violate the still existing constitution. This law, to be effective for a period of four years, was passed by all parties of the *Reichstag*, but against the votes of the Social Democrats (the Communists had already been removed from the *Reichstag* and all democratic institutions). With this law, the door was open for Hitler to drastically change the character of the nation in a seemingly legal way. It especially allowed Hitler to do away with all laws, institutions, parties, and groups that would not be loyal to the new regime but would try to uphold what was left of constitutional law and order.

At the same time, a propaganda machine of never-known dimensions descended upon the German people for their indoctrination, after Dr. Joseph Goebbels was appointed as Minister of People's Enlightenment and Propaganda. To celebrate the achievements of the new government and its leader Hitler, Goebbels immediately concentrated on "the enemies of the people," the Communists, the Social Democrats and, above all, the Jews. On April 1, the first boycott of Jewish businesses was proclaimed and led by the *SA*. Citizens were prevented, with ridicule and shaming but also at times by physical force, from entering shops and stores owned by Jewish citizens or corporations.

This was also the beginning of the complete removal of Jews from public life in Germany, whether they were civil servants, professionals, or artists. The latter, especially, were so persecuted in the press that many of them decided to leave Germany immediately. This only helped Hitler and Goebbels to present them as degenerates or enemies of the pure Aryan, that was, German soul.

To symbolize this process of cleansing, on May 10, books of Jewish or left-wing authors were burned in a large bonfire in front of the university in Berlin, an act which was repeated in many other German cities during the next few days.

If a part of the German people were horrified by what was happening, whether it was the violations of established law or the discrimination and persecution of the Jews, fewer and fewer means remained to express this disgust on the one hand or demonstrate moral support to those persecuted on the other hand. The strongest, best organized opposition Hitler had faced — the Communist party and its organizations — had already been declared illegal. For all intents and purposes, it no longer existed. The democratic parties, increasingly intimidated, tried to rescue what seemed possible, but perhaps clung too much to a conciliatory approach.

The once powerful and influential trade unions were abolished on May 2 and all their property and resources were consolidated in the *Deutsche Arbeitsfront,* the German Labour Front, which started immediately as a rigidly controlled unified organization that kept the German workers in line.

In less than two months, the German parties were put under great pressure to disband. This they more or less reluctantly did, except for the Social Democratic Party, which was banned outright and declared illegal. By the end of July, Germany had become a one-party state.

On October 14, Germany left the League of Nations after the population had been indoctrinated to perceive the League as a body whose goal was the continued enslavement of the German people.

There was another election on November 12, still called a *Reichstagswahl*, a parliamentary election. But there was only one party to vote for. This was the absolute end of the German constitution. Barely 10 months after he had seized control, Hitler was the sole source of authority in Germany. What he had accomplished was a true seizure of power, a *Machtergreifung*, as Goebbels' propaganda machine would proudly glorify it.

That this barrage of frightening events impinged on our family life to a considerable degree, is understandable. We always had a radio and I grew up with listening to the news, first the news from the Breslau broadcasting station and then, usually while we had our supper, the German news from Prague, which gave not only news that had been censored out of the German press and radio, but also viewpoints and political commentaries from the "other side," that is Czechoslovakia, Poland, France, England, and the United States.

For having this window to the rest of the world, the daily *Prager Aktuelle Zehn Minuten* (the Prague Up to Date Ten Minutes of News) were vitally important for us. I will never forget the voice of the Prague announcer who spoke perfect German, but with a slight Bohemian accent. His voice would have sounded more charming, had the news he read to us been more pleasant and uplifting. After listening to his voice for years, I could, with a perfect Czech accent, repeat the announcement of the Czechoslovakian broadcasting system, *Praha, Brno, Bratislava, Moravska Ostrava*.

Thanks to the Prague radio, we knew what the consequences were of the new laws and announcements by the German government. We knew of large-scale imprisonments, and listened to the interviews of those German politicians and artists who had managed to escape Hitler's wrath before being imprisoned.

What the Czech radio told us was reinforced by what we saw in the streets of our city. It is true that life continued its daily pattern and pace, but the SA and SS seemed to be everywhere. While in town with my mother, I saw men being manhandled and beaten up by the SA and I sensed fear and apprehension among the bystanders. Although the SA was supposedly controlling the enemies of the state, the crowds rarely applauded them, and instead looked away in disgust and fear. To this day, I remember that the sullen crowds in the streets did not give an iota of support or sympathy to the SA and SS, while the much bigger crowds that would attend the frequent party rallies seemed to be shouting and screaming in support of the new era, of Hitler, and of his movement. Perhaps some were forced to attend or thought they better do so in order to protect their jobs and their families — but why did they all express their approval with such unnatural loudness?

All political events had their immediate fall-out in our city. After Hindenburg abolished the republican flag of Germany on March 12, on the following day my mother and I happened to witness the sad parade of the Mayor of Waldenburg, Herr Schubert, the deputy mayor, and the social democratic members of the city council, who formed an overwhelming majority in the council. The mayor, his deputy, and his councillors were carrying the republican flags that up to now had graced the roof of the city hall and other civic buildings. They were led by shouting *SA* men from the city hall to the Ring, the town square, around which they were marched several times and then back to city hall. What happened at the *Rathausplatz*, the City Hall Square, my mother and I did not witness, but we were later told that a bonfire had been prepared, which the mayor was ordered to light. He and the other legally elected representatives of the city were ordered to throw the flags of the Weimar Republic into the flames. They were then forced by the *SA* with threats and physical abuse to raise their right arms in the Nazi salute, while the flags slowly disintegrated in the flames. What kind of an audience the *SA* had, I do not know.

Via the Prague radio, we also heard about Dachau for the first time. If it had not been for Hitler's first concentration camp, opened at Dachau on March 20, 1933, I wonder how much time would have gone by, before the name of this small obscure Bavarian town would have become part of my factual knowledge.

On April 1, a Saturday, the busiest day of the week for Germany's retail trade, the *SA* started its first boycott of Jewish stores in a long-prepared and well-coordinated action throughout Germany. None of the unpleasant or worrisome events of the past eight weeks came as close to us! Our street was home to the largest number of Jewish businesses in Waldenburg. On a stretch of not more than 250 yards, there were eight Jewish businesses! Alarmed by the noise in the street, we saw from our window the SA milling around in front of three adjoining Jewish stores, Grünberg, Rahmer, and Thomas. And right below our windows, slightly to the left was the large elegant menswear store of David Korn, where the same commotion occurred. I noticed that slogans and Stars of David had been smeared on the shop windows. There also was some jostling between *SA* men and customers insisting to enter the stores. Only in the evening news did we hear that throughout Germany the same scenes had occurred, in some cities far less gently than in Waldenburg. In our town, all Jewish shops were affected except one, whose owner was a decorated officer from World War I. If he escaped persecution on this day, this bit of good luck turned into tragedy later. He would not believe that sooner or later his exempt status as a Jew would be terminated, and so, tragically, would be his life.

Only at one store did the *SA* action come to naught before it began. This was the large Schocken department store that had been opened about two years before. Not welcomed by the local merchants and considered an unfair competitor, Schocken became immediately popular among the miners and the rest of the working class because of its favourable pricing policies, which put a number of articles within reach of low wage earners. Its spacious restaurant and café was also well frequented, because it offered a huge selection of ready-made foods at very reasonable prices, which low wage earners could otherwise only dream of. Thus, Schocken had immediately become a local institution of the shopping scene in Waldenburg. It also was the first store in town with an elevator. If I think of Schocken during that time, I see its main entrance consisting of six doors always black with people getting in and coming out. By their attire, the customers were readily recognized as working class people. Inside, kids would swarm all over the store, but they were never told to leave when not accompanied by a parent. It was an altogether friendly environment, crowded, hot, a bit smelly, but happily exciting.

It was therefore not surprising that the *SA*, when beginning its action against Schocken, the biggest store in town, found itself quickly outnumbered by the mass of arriving shoppers. As we heard the next day, there was loud noise and anger expressed without restraint, mainly in the colourful language of the Waldenburg working class. After a comparatively short time, the *SA* retreated and Schocken remained untouched on this fearful day, enjoying business as usual.

If it seemed that except for the "Brown Shirts" (the *SA*), nobody supported this action, things began to look doubtful soon afterwards. As we lived in the centre of town, my mother and I would walk past all the downtown stores every day, among them a fair number under Jewish ownership. The damage of some broken glass, defaced store windows, and so on had been quickly removed. What was entirely new were the signs at non-Jewish stores, restaurants, or cafés announcing *Juden unerwünscht*, Jews not wanted.

Three months before, hardly anybody would have imagined what was happening now in Germany and in our city. Still, only a few were ready to believe that these were not isolated incidents but portents of worse things to come. Among them was a man who was well known to my parents, as they were his customers. A prosperous and well-liked businessman, Mr. Pollack owned a large drugstore. When my father met him on the street a few days after the boycott of the Jewish stores, Mr. Pollack confided to him that he was packing his bags to leave for Palestine. He did not announce his decision to leave Germany publicly, but he shared his plans with many of his customers. So within a few days, the entire town knew that the first Jewish merchant was leaving town. During the next 12 years, millions of people throughout Europe, German Jews and non-Jews, Poles, Czechs, Austrians, Russians, and many others, and millions of Germans again in early 1945 when the Eastern front rolled into German territory, would be facing this question, whether it was better to abandon one's home and security for the sake of freedom and one's life, or whether things would not get that much worse. In other words, should one be steadfast, brave, and not panic too early and hold out, or should one exercise prudence?

As it turned out in millions of cases, few people had as much initiative and foresight as our druggist Mr. Pollack had in the spring of 1933. He safely reached Palestine, but never regained his past prosperity. He sent colourful postcards of Haifa and its busy main street to my father and others in town. He did not hide that his family's home was only a tiny apartment and that he was a mere taxi driver. He never complained. But people in Waldenburg would say again and again: "How foolish that Pollack was; the wonderful store he owned, the beautiful house he lived in here in our town. And now, he has nothing!" After a while, Mr. Pollack seemed forgotten, and when the situation for Waldenburg's Jews became ever more dangerous, people fearfully watched what happened to the remaining Jews. People never talked about Mr. Pollack to say that he had done the right thing after all.

Of the rest of the year I only remember two events of a political nature. One was the book burning on the *Rathausplatz*, which I did not see but remember my parents talking about as a rather pathetic affair. In a working class town where most people were still pre-occupied with maintaining a half decent life for their families, an action against intellectuals and artists had no appeal. What the impact of the much larger book burnings in the big cities throughout Germany was, we heard in the Prague news on the evening of that day.

There was one more event, that I witnessed by chance. As it was Sunday, we happened to visit my grandparents after attending church across the street. This Sunday was also another election day, which had been preceded by enormous propaganda. Already while walking around the church and crossing the street, we noticed elderly people being helped along by *SA* men or carried on stretchers, or *SA* men pushing invalids in wheelchairs towards the polling station (which was located in the Catholic *Vereinshaus*, a restaurant, ironically owned by a group of Catholic clubs).

When we arrived at my grandparent's apartment, my grandfather in a state of excitement related that two *SA* men had come to the door wondering when Mr. and Mrs. Koch would come to give their vote to the Führer. The maid had opened the door and my grandfather instructed her to say that Mr. Koch's heart was bad and Mrs. Koch's leg was giving her trouble. Both conditions were actually plaguing my grandparents, but did not incapacitate them. It was common knowledge that the two attended mass every morning throughout the year. We had hardly arrived in my grandparent's home when the doorbell rang again. The maid and I answered the door to come face-to-face with two *SA* men who presented themselves with a stretcher to take my grandmother to the polling station. Before I could get my grandfather, he came to the door, moved the maid and me aside and in a loud, excited voice told the *SA* men to instantly leave his house. As there was no longer a *Zentrums Partei*[1] for which he and his wife had voted all their adult life, there was no party they could vote for; there was nothing for them to do at the polling station. I only remember that my grandfather shut the door with a loud bang. The *SA* men must have left with their stretcher and my grandparents were never bothered again when Hitler's elections took place.

This event took place about five months after we moved out of my grandfather's house. My father's youngest brother Hubert had finally decided to marry, hoping that he could exchange his bachelor quarters above us for our apartment. Having his business on the same property, it made sense for him to remain in the same building. My parents were quite willing to accommodate my uncle. My father had been born in this house, but ever since he had lost his job with the bank, neither my mother nor my father had been very happy in this house.

On June 1, 1933, we moved to the *Neustadt,* the first large, expertly planned addition to the city of Waldenburg. Located on an expansive plateau above the *Altstadt,* this new district was primarily designed for the working class. It did not have a single building of the type that shaped the depressing character of the older working class districts, which consisted primarily of drab, flat-roofed four- to five-story houses accommodating a large number of small flats without any comforts or conveniences.

In contrast, the *Neustadt,* seen from the surrounding hills, was a sea of red tile roofs. All buildings were at least outwardly attractive, although the worker's blocks still contained one- or two- room flats only, and many were without water and toilets, with both facilities located at the end of the hall on each floor. Still, this presented a great deal of progress and the *Neustadt* became the preferred residential area for the miners and other working-class families. In between these workers' houses, there were apartment buildings with comfortable, large flats for the middle

---

1   The party united most of Germany's Catholics. Since Bismarck's time, it also represented a large section of the exclusively Catholic Polish minority in the Reichstag.

class. Over the years, I can say from my own experience that this conscious attempt to mix social classes, rather than separate them in their own districts, turned out to be very successful. In addition, no matter what the shortcomings were that still existed in the workers' flats, all residents of this district lived in an attractive part of town with squares that had little parks in their centre, tree-lined streets, other amenities such as streetcar connections to the rest of the city, a theatre, kindergartens, large areas with garden plots, and a main street filled with attractive stores, restaurants, and a couple of cafés.

This is where I spent the next three years of my life. I left the house of my grandfather with great regret, but I was happy that we lived only a 20-minute walk away. This was also an attractive arrangement for my parents, and my mother quite happily vacated her first apartment as a married woman, saying to my uncle Hubert's young wife Käthe,[2] only half in jest, "In this house , you will never be truly happy!" Uncle Hubert promptly called this the *Heddafluch* (Hedda's curse).

My mother in particular, looked forward to the exceptional comfort and beauty of our new home, which had been erected only a year ago. Although the city administration had built this attractive block of three houses of three stories each for their own officials, most of the officials lacked an adequate salary to pay the rent. The flats were then placed on the open market and taken by families who could afford such accommodation. We lived on the second floor, enjoyed amenities that were still rare at this time, such as central heating, hot and cold running water, and a beautiful backyard with lawns and a play area with a sandbox for the children. In addition, truly exceptional for its time were the fully automatic laundry and drying facilities in the basement. Gone were the days, when once a month our washerwoman would come for two days, to do all work by hand and then carry heavy baskets of wet laundry five flights up to the attic to be hung for drying there.

Above all, the building was of exceptional quality when it came to the building materials used including small artistic touches in the design of doors and windows, the tiles in the kitchen and the bathroom, and so on. My mother went all-out to buy beautiful drapery for the windows, though no shears for the living-room. They were not needed, as this room looked down on an old, unused park, and hills and mountains beyond.

---

2   She was, by the way, the second woman by this name who entered the Koch family through marriage. The other Käthe, wife of my father's brother Alfred, perished tragically at the end of World War II when the truck she travelled in was blown apart by a landmine. After the youngest Koch, Hubert, took his life after the end of the war, the two widowed family members Alfred and Käthe married in 1946.

My father finally had his own music room, which was decorated by another artist friend of ours, Martin Sternagel, who painted the ceiling in art deco. He divided the ceiling into four squares of different pale pinks and used silver for the art deco designs on it. In contrast, the floor was painted blue (in the dining room it was light grey). My father's Steinway, in its massive shiny black, had found ideal surroundings. We were also given the upholstered furniture (redecorated for our music room), that for years had been reserved for the archbishop's visits at my grandfather's house. This was truly an exceptional room, although not all our visitors liked its unusual colours.

The windows of the front rooms, however, looked onto an ordinary workers' street. Indeed, during the warm season, the open windows in the houses across were always occupied by men off-shift with nothing to do. There was steady conversation between them and people on the street, where miners off-shift also spent long hours just standing around or sitting on the front steps and talking to neighbours and friends. In between, there were the swarms of kids playing on the street. I am happy to remember that there were no class distinctions or hard feelings. Neither did religion play a part. Waldenburg consisted of roughly equal groups of Catholics and Protestants and there were also several hundred Jews living in our city.

There was one Jewish boy in our street. He and his older sister were not looked upon as being different, and his lovely mother, a quiet beauty, was especially liked by all of us, while the father was much respected, even feared a little by the kids, because in his bearing and with his moustache, he looked like a true Prussian officer. Another boy on our street, Peter, was mentally somewhat slow and awkward. We did take advantage of him and his gullibility, but not in a nasty way, and in whatever we did, he was included in one way or another. We shared toys freely and also took each other to our homes, no matter how small or how fancy they were.

This was the time when I realized how fortunate I was, especially when visiting other kids in cramped homes with often one room serving as combined kitchen/living/bedroom. And I remember one little incident which demonstrated to me what a different and much harder life the miners' kids coped with at already a very young age. On the day when I got a brand new scooter for my birthday and proudly cruised with it on the smooth pavement of our street, at that time the only black-topped street in the city, a girl of my age asked me whether I would let her ride my scooter for a while, if she would give me 10 pennies. First, though, she would have to earn these 10 pennies by cleaning the stairwells of one of the houses. This was a job that took at least two hours. And she would also have to ask her mother, whether for once, she could keep the 10 pennies rather than turn them over to her mother for the general household budget. I was truly shocked and certainly did not take any money. I could not forget how this skinny, poorly nourished girl who was not even 12 years old yet, had to do such hard work carrying pail after pail of water up and down the flights of stairs, and clean every step with a rag in her small hands, doing that work several afternoons each week.

I remember the years in the pleasant *Neustadt* as entirely happy. I had much freedom, as there was little traffic compared to the bustle in the centre of the city. A wonderful, huge swimming pool was just around the corner, which I used, alone, with friends, or on weekends with my parents. My parents were also happy during these years, especially my father, who finally managed to escape the terrible boss he had, when the firm was taken over by a large local business and his boss was fired. My father had now a very pleasant walk to work through the city park, he had very nice colleagues, his office was located in a spanking new building, and his pay was considerably better, although it was obvious that we still had to be a bit careful. When I entered junior high school in 1935, in view of his income, my father qualified for an exemption of paying the monthly school fees of 20 Marks, which must have put us in the upper range of workers and lower civil servants. This puzzled me, as we lived so differently from most of the kids I played or went to school with.

During these years, I was also on very happy terms with my father, without being conscious of it, of course – only a few years later, when things were very different, did I remember longingly the years in the *Neustadt*. We went for walks and hikes, took trips to the high mountains, and visited relatives in other parts of Silesia. My mother bought herself new dresses; my father finally got out of his dark suits. He worked for private industry now, that did not want their personnel to look like the proverbial *Beamten* (civil servants). During holidays, I used to pick up my father and his colleagues at the office to accompany them home for lunch. I always enjoyed the walk through the park. There were stories to tell and nature to observe. I would take my soccer ball along and the grown-ups enjoyed kicking it as much as I did. It was a carefree time, and an innocent time as well. One day, when I searched for my soccer ball just off the path, I found a small balloon filled with water, a type of balloon I had never seen. I brought it to my father, and he and his colleagues burst into loud laughter, gently kicked it like a ball, until it burst. It was a condom, of course, but nobody explained its purpose to me. I do not think it was adult shyness, the men seemed to realize that I was totally innocent at that time and not yet ready to be enlightened in sexual matters. Neither did my father do this later on, when my time had come to need such enlightenment very badly.

Times were different, of course, and society had not progressed much beyond Victorian attitudes when it came to the interpretation of sexual matters to growing children. My mother discharged her responsibility to me while I was still at an early age. Before I started elementary school, she had explained to me one quiet afternoon how babies are born. I was fascinated, understood her simple, but clear explanations very well and promptly lost interest in them. I also never wondered about how babies got started in the first place.

I think my mother gave me her explanations because she wanted to protect me from ridicule once I entered school. She knew that children with relatives in the country or workers' kids were far ahead of boys of my class when it came to sexual matters. This did not change for many years. I remember when we worked with plasticine in elementary school, creating little animals, plants and other things, how several boys had great fun forming male genitalia and their female counterparts, which they then united while other kids watched in fascination. I do not think I was the only one who did not understand what the boys were giggling about, but those like me, the innocents, were definitely in the minority.

When I started grade four after Easter 1934, our *Rektor,* or principal, was gone. We surmised that he had simply become too old, but although his replacement was perhaps a little less Victorian, he was definitely not much younger. We understood what was at play when he came to school dressed in his brown uniform as often as circumstances or events would allow. Two more teachers did not return for the new school year. Fortunately, our own teacher Alfons Geisler was not taken away from us. With growing frequency the entire student body was called to special assemblies for the purpose, later very obvious to me, of political indoctrination, explanation of political events, and interpretations of the actions of the government and the *Führer.* These explanations were either given by the principal, who was always in uniform on such occasions, or by delegates from the party, the *SA,* the *Hitlerjugend,* or others.

Before Hitler's ascent to power, the *SA* was seen as the equivalent of the social democratic *Reichsbanner* or the Communist *Rotfrontkämpferbund.* After Hitler had taken over Germany, the *SA* seemed to be at loose ends, especially once the power over Germany and all its institutions was firmly in Hitler's hands. Now, the *SA* was looking for an influential role within the new system. Its members became less popular. Citizens, although more intimidated, had become highly sensitive to any actions that seemed even slightly illegal, which applied to much of what the *SA* was involved in now.

The reputation of the *SA* also suffered by the behaviour of its leaders, which especially in Silesia was a rather unusual group. Although the Silesian *SA* carried a proletarian mantle, quite a few of its leaders belonged to the province's aristocracy. One group of *SA* leaders loved to frequent Waldenburg's elegant Café Enderlein, where their bad behaviour raised much talk of which I picked up a fair amount. From the afternoon visits to the café with my mother, I remembered a huge Chinese vase that stood in a little alcove. I always admired it, but one day in 1934, it was gone. When I wondered about it, mother told me later that the *SA* leader Edmund Heines, during a heavy drinking party with his friends had pulled his revolver and shot the precious vase to pieces.

On July 1, 1934 the papers and the radio reported a coup that Hitler supposedly stopped at the last moment. This coup was planned by his friend Ernst Roehm, the leader of the *SA* who, as it was said later, had his own plans of expanding the role of the *SA* from that of a paramilitary militia to much more powerful functions, eventually to supersede those of the Army. Hitler's response was to order almost the entire upper echelon of the *SA* leadership, many lesser important *SA* men as well, and also a number of other political figures not related to the *SA* to be shot without trial. Among the people, this mass murder was quickly called "the night of the long knives." I remember how distressed our relatives were, and how deeply upset my father was. I think, in his heart and mind, he made his break with the party at this time, when Hitler's wrath for the first time turned against his own supporters and comrades-in-arms. Behind closed doors, he and other people spoke of Hitler's action as plain murder, and worried about the ascendancy of the *SS*, now that the *SA* had lost all its political power. In school, we again had long assemblies where the supposed cause of the revolt, the bad character of Roehm and his friends, was explained to us while Hitler was praised again and again.

Several streets and buildings that had been given the names of members of the new party elite after January 30 — much too fast, as it turned out — had to be renamed again, now receiving the names of Hitler, Goering, and others. Ironically, one name belonging to one of Hitler's victims, Peter von Heydebreck, remained. His name had been chosen as a replacement of the Polish name of Kandrzin (since 1945 Kędrzierzyn), a railroad centre in Upper Silesia. It was obviously politically inopportune to change this once Polish name of the town yet again.

The next event that shook Germany was the death of President Hindenburg on August 2, 1934. I had holidays from school, which we spent with my mother's brother in the picturesque little town of Sprottau (since 1945 Szprotawa), actually the wealthiest small town in Germany. The media had already prepared the people for Hindenburg's imminent death. For one week the entire country was in a state of official mourning. My uncle's house and business was located on the town square of Sprottau, which was dominated by the city hall with its two spires, one from medieval times, the other dating back to the eighteenth century.

From both spires, long banners floated in the wind carrying the colors of Imperial Germany, the national socialist swastika, and the old black and white colours of Prussia. Every day at noon and in the evening, the church bells of the town would ring for one hour. It was a mournful time, I felt at my young age. Whether people were good Prussians or monarchists or not, the demise of President Paul von Hindenburg seemed to weigh heavily on their mind. He was one of the last of the old guard.

How justified this feeling was, became clear when immediately after Hindenburg's death, the law pertaining to "the Head of the German Reich" was proclaimed. It amalgamated the two positions of president and chancellor of the Reich in one person, Hitler. There would be no more *Reichspräsident*. It was also announced that the German armed forces would now give their oath of allegiance to Hitler only. Hitler had gathered the last strands of power into his hands. What did people feel? A referendum was held on August 19, 1934. 96 percent of all eligible citizens went to vote. Of these, ninety-six percent voted for the recent changes. But I remember the first whispered jokes about the authenticity of the elections held in the Third Reich.

New distractions from the recent events were needed. Again, the Jews of Germany became victims of the authorities. We had speakers coming to our school who gave talks or little one-man plays with a strong anti-Semitic slant.

An extraordinary event took place one day prior to the end of the school term before Christmas. To this day, I cannot admire our teacher Alfons Geisler and his courage enough. No doubt, to establish a balance to the constant barrage of anti-Semitism that we were fed lately, he took us to the Synagogue of Waldenburg in December during the Jewish holiday of Hanukkah, perhaps because for Catholic children, no Jewish holiday is as accessible as Hanukkah. The rabbi awaited us in his spacious home next to the synagogue. He and his wife served us little cakes and also let us sample pieces of *mazzen* which, with its flat taste, actually disappointed us. He explained the other Jewish holidays, especially Succoth, which already meant something to us, as on this holiday, he and his wife always built a little arbour on their balcony that we would admire on our way to school. I am sure Alfons Geisler had to face the authorities, but at least outwardly, he remained unscathed. And he helped to remind us that Jewish people were not what they were made out to be in newspapers, posters, the radio, and in the assembly hall of the school.

I was only nine years old in 1934, but I felt the pervasive political terror in Germany. On the surface, 1935 was a peaceful year. Everyday life had settled down somewhat, and a lot of people seemed to be reconciled to seeing everywhere the pictures of Hitler and his minions in their brown uniforms, or being overwhelmed by the ubiquitous Nazi propaganda in the newspapers, the radio, and in films. There were others who maintained their distance from the new regime but had no way to demonstrate their attitude except by not actively taking part in the Nazi way of life, as the vast majority of Germans did.

There were active resisters, but 1935 seemed to be a midpoint. Most resisters, especially Communists and active Christians, had largely been removed from public life; they were now in concentration camps and the general public had by and large forgotten about them. The next wave of Nazi terror, however, had not yet arrived.

Nevertheless, there were constant events which pre-occupied the people's minds. For most, these were happy events calling for much enthusiasm, pride in the re-awakening German spirit, and gratitude to Hitler for making all these things possible without war.

On January 13, 1935, the plebiscite in the *Saarland*, the territory, which had been under French control since the ratification of the Treaty of Versailles, resulted in a vote of 90.8 percent in favour of a return to Germany. Within three days, the League of Nations voted to return the Saar to Germany. There were supposedly spontaneous rallies to thank the Saar population for their vote and to thank the Führer for reclaiming the Saar for the Fatherland. The tiny *Saarland* was the first in a chain of territories and groups of ethnic Germans reclaimed by Hitler with the use of increasingly risky strategies that would eventually, in 1939 in Poland, contribute to the outbreak of war.

The jubilation in Germany about the return of the *Saarland* was beyond anything ever witnessed. We had a special assembly in school and, sadly, on the Sunday following the plebiscite, there were prayers of thanks in Christian churches. In the meantime, most bakers were selling *Saarhörnchen*, cheap pastry in the shape of a capital *S* covered with sugar or chocolate icing. On March 1, the return of the Saar brought about the entry of German troops into the territory and a repeat of the celebrations throughout the country.

Before that day, several thousand boys from miners' families in the Saar appeared in Germany, being placed in a great number of cities, supposedly to have three months of good life after years of hunger and want under French occupation. German families had been signed up to take one of the Saar boys into their homes. On the evening of their arrival in Waldenburg, a woman from our street appeared at our door asking my mother to accept a boy for whom no home could be found. So we ended up with a *Saarjunge*, a boy from the Saar, the middle of three brothers from the mining town of Sankt Wendel. I must say that his presence turned into a fortunate experience. The youngest of the boys was a sweet, chubby kid of eight, the middle one, ours, was a year older than I was, while the oldest was already past 14 and a mature boy of remarkable qualities. The three brothers often spent their free times with us, and I learned an enormous amount about the Saar, its geography, its people and, last not least, its initially-for-us almost incomprehensible dialect. We never saw the boys again after their return home, and a few years later, the occasional correspondence also petered out. But I remember them to this day as kids who must have come from a strong, proud miner's family. They also were good Catholics and I had the impression that they were not too impressed by the various facets of Nazi life in our town. As a matter of fact, while they were warm-hearted and spontaneous and liked us very much, they rarely expressed any wonderment or admiration of what they saw in this, for them, temporary environment. Whether after their return to the Saar little Peter, Werner, and Gustav would be enthusiastic ambassadors for the Third Reich, fulfilling a role that was no doubt the major objective of this highly political project, seems doubtful to me.

For another reason, March was a crucial month in the history of the Third Reich. On March 16, 1935, Hitler renounced the Treaty of Versailles, which opened the doors to rearmament, fortification of Germany's borders, and abdication from all obligations that were part of the treaty. Hitler also reinstated military conscription and one day after his announcement, he staged a carefully prepared military parade in front of the Imperial Palace in Berlin. The parade was watched by more than 500,000 people.

If Hitler had as yet to win over parts of the conservative middle and upper classes, he succeeded during these days with many of them, who now saw in him the saviour of Germany's strength, honour, and power. There were others, however, who expected war at any moment, convinced that the Western allies would not tolerate Hitler's actions, but they were disappointed and would be so on many future occasions when the Western powers gave in to Hitler again and again. I remember discussions in the Koch family that would invariably bring to the fore the worry about war as an eventual result of Hitler's provocations. At the same time, the propaganda machine continued to operate at top strength. At the end of each week, all school children were taken to movie houses during school hours to watch the newsreels. This would soon become quite a routine with full-length movies added, usually of patriotic or Nazi content that was always preceded by the just-released newsreels of the week.

On September 10, Hitler proclaimed a new set of laws aimed at Jewish citizens. All Jews were stripped of their citizenship; they no longer enjoyed the civil rights of a German citizen; and to preserve the purity of the German race intermarriage and relations between Jews and non-Jews were forbidden and severely punished. To be sure that no person of Jewish blood worked for the German state and its numerous offices and departments, every civil servant had to provide proof of "Aryan" ancestry. In October, Italy invaded Ethiopia, the African Empire of Haile Selassie, which hitherto had been quite obscure for most Germans. Italy more than ever was presented as Germany's primary ally and maps went up in school charting the advance of the Italian forces which, by the way, was painfully slow considering the poorly armed state of the Ethiopian armed forces.

In April 1935, I completed my four years of elementary school and left the unforgettable learning environment of my teacher Alfons Geisler's classroom. From a classroom of over 60 pupils, I moved to a classroom of less than 20 in high school. Incidentally, I was the only one to transfer to high school. The other 59 kids in my elementary school classroom came from families that were too poor to afford the monthly high school fee of 20 Marks. True, this fee could be waived, as in my case, when the father's income was limited. But for all these kids, it was vitally important to finish school and learn a trade to become self-supporting as early as possible in their lives.

Regardless of what the Nazi propaganda claimed, poverty was still rampant in our city. I saw that for years in elementary school by the clothes boys were wearing in my class, their coming to school barefoot as long as weather would permit, their heads shaved by their fathers in order not to spend money for a barber's haircut, and many other indicators that all or most of them shared. Quite in contradiction to the propaganda that there was bread and work for every German — which did not actually come true until the re-creation of the German armed forces and the large scale rearmament — there were constant drives for raising money for the poor, used clothing collections, monthly *Eintopfsonntage*, i.e., Sundays where people pledged to only have a simple one-course meal on the table, usually a good soup, and donate the saved money to the state for the support of the poor. After 1935, it was rumoured, however, that these monies actually were directed to rearmament instead of to the poor. Whatever, monies were continually collected on the streets, at work sites, and in the schools. It seemed obvious that this enormous drive to help your less fortunate fellow citizen was also designed to create a sense of community, not on the local level, but on the national level — to create the masses who, as if possessed, chanted at rallies everywhere "*Ein Volk, Ein Reich, Ein Führer*" (One People, One Nation, One Leader).

The big event of the year, for me, was entering into high school in April 1935, which would take me to senior matriculation over a period of eight years. My new school was just around the corner from our house. It was an incredibly beautiful, well appointed school that had been completed just seven years ago. At a time when many communities strove to offer new buildings for their school children, this school seemed the epitome of taste with its works of art — sculptures and frescoes — and its great diversity of facilities. The building faced a large square with lawns and flower beds. Its façade was decorated by two large sandstone sculptures representing industrial and academic learning. In the entrance hall, the ceiling was painted with allegorical scenes relating to education by Martin Sternagel, the artist who had done the ceiling in my father's music room. Sternagel also created the frescoes of abstract flowers and plants on the ceiling of the large assembly hall. There were special facilities for the sciences and the arts and for music, the latter also equipped with movie projectors. There was a large gym and outside, adjoining the school yard, an experimental school garden with a pavilion and an ornamental basin partially filled with water lilies.

There was no way one could feel anything but proud and happy in such an environment. The kids in my grade came from all parts of the city and surrounding district and all of them felt it was a privilege to attend such a school. The general behaviour, therefore, was quite exemplary without any force or pressure required.

Looking back, I consider, with some terrible exceptions, my teachers of that time to be of high calibre. The school being quite new as a full-fledged high school, the average age of the faculty was much younger than that of the adjoining classical high school that had been in existence since the 1850s. I particularly remember our art teacher, Rudolf Kraft, a person whom today, I would call a Renaissance man — a man of broad education and wide interests, a man who could create interest in the arts in every student, and instil in each of us a sense that we were all of us talented in art to a greater or lesser degree. He was a remarkable painter; his woodcuts and engravings were famous. If I can compare him with a well-known German artist, I think of Lovis Corinth, the East Prussian painter who was also a full-blooded, exuberant man of great vitality, even of physical resemblance to our art teacher Rudolf Kraft. It seems incredible to me now, but thanks to teachers like Rudolf Kraft and a few others, at the end of the weekend and of holidays, I always looked forward to going back to class.

Another teacher who had a profound influence on me was our music teacher, Leonhard Rösner, a man of fine features and prematurely grey hair — it looked like finely-spun silver — who had a devotion to music that he instilled in us as Rudolf Kraft did in his field. He was also a man of incredible political courage. He made us familiar with the breadth of music and composers. He played Mendelssohn on the grand piano for us, sang excerpts from Mendelssohn's songs and oratorios, and told us about modern composers who had been outlawed by Hitler because their art was declared decadent and non-German, or they were Jewish like

Mendelssohn, and any performance of their music was therefore outlawed. We had a Jewish boy in our class, Heinz Meyer, the son of a popular merchant, who was at best treated with indifference by some teachers, or at worst with daily, incredibly inhuman insults by other teachers. Leonhard Rösner, though, regularly declared during our music lessons that a person's different religion would not make him into a different human being and that for him, Heinz Meyer was one of us.[3]

Sixty years later I learned from the other Jewish boy in school — his name is Fred — who used to live in our street, how far Leonhard Rösner's courage extended. As I already mentioned in an earlier chapter, by the kids on our street, Fred was not treated any differently for being Jewish — he simply was one of us. This, however, changed when Fred and I both entered high school. All of a sudden, he was treated like a different human being, which caused quite a shock for me, as I did not know how to help or protect him from the wrath of a couple of our teachers. Unfortunately, a good number of kids in school kept their distance from him, no doubt intimidated by anti-Semitic teachers.

Somehow, I remember being glad that Fred was in the parallel stream and not in my classroom. This I must confess in shame, and I am sure this two-facedness bothered me, as after school on the street, nothing had changed between him and myself and the other kids. In 1936, shortly before we moved away from Waldenburg, the boy was evicted from school from one day to another for being Jewish. A few days later, he left town.

I never heard anything about him until 1996 when, to my great joy, I learned that he had survived and now lived in Australia. In 1998, Fred came to visit us in Edmonton, and only then did I learn how our music teacher Leonhard Rösner protected him from the humiliation of being demonstratively excluded from any functions that involved the entire school, such as flag parades and other events when the flag of the Third Reich was flown. On such occasions, Rösner would always keep him after class, or specifically call him to the music room, stating that he needed his help, which might involve dusting the piano, sorting music sheets, or other work that would keep our classmate in a protected, safe environment and save him from public humiliation.

Other teachers were not so human. Our German teacher would invariably enter the classroom with a loud shout of indignation, "What

---

3   Only Heinz Meyer's father survived. He emigrated ahead of his family to Chile. Heinz, his mother, and the rest of the family were prevented from leaving Germany in time. They were taken to a concentration camp and murdered.

is that infernal stench in this room? Oh, it is this Jew boy again!" This boy, Fred, was the sweetest-looking blond boy one could imagine, of impeccable manners and a friendly, trusting disposition.

I heard similar remarks from this German teacher in our classroom. He was a sloppily dressed man with dirty fingernails, poor teeth, and a very unpleasant nature. He loved to torture us by "feeling" our biceps — in doing so, he was so rough that he brought us to tears — and then told us that we were hopeless weaklings. This was, of course, harmless compared to what the Jewish students had to endure under him; but the negative power of this man was enormous. I remember being acutely afraid of him, mentally as well as physically. Mine and other boys' arm muscles seemed to hurt perpetually and we all felt weak and humiliated.

Worse was what our French teacher, who was also our home room teacher, did to the Jewish Heinz Meyer. Our very first French lesson on our first day in this school began with our French teacher telling us that we would immediately learn our first French word that turned out to be a rather complex one, *cordon sanitaire*. Our teacher not only translated this word for us, but explained its meaning, which he described as an empty strip around something that needed to be totally isolated from its surrounding environment. We really did not know what to make out of all this, until the teacher told us he would now apply this word and its meaning. He ordered Heinz Meyer to move into the far corner of the classroom and then asked the students sitting on the benches in front and next to him to move elsewhere. This, he then explained to us, was an authentic *cordon sanitaire*, which would isolate this "dirty Jew" from the rest of us pure German boys. From then on, as long as he was allowed to attend our school, Heinz had to endure this teacher's daily abuse. The teacher's favourite saying was that he felt like beating Heinz, but that only would mean that he would dirty his hands. This went on day after day, since French at that time was a major subject and was taught on a daily basis.

I know I was embarrassed. I know that nobody laughed when our French or German teachers went into their anti-Jewish tirades. But this was the one thing that depresses me and shames me to this day when thinking of an otherwise happy school experience. Before I left this school both Fred and Heinz were evicted. Walter, the third Jewish boy who attended a higher grade in our school, did not return to school one day in 1936. 60 years later when we both lived in Canada, he told me that his father, a medical specialist who was very popular among the poor population of the city, had been warned by the police chief to take his family away from Waldenburg the same day.

Still, for us, 1935 was a good summer. My father seemed quite content and cheerful. Obviously, there seemed to be a bit more money in the house. We took many outings and short trips and frequently went to the spa Bad Salzbrunn next to Waldenburg on Sunday afternoons. Salzbrunn still had a noticeable aura of elegance at that time. It had the best golf course in the eastern half of Germany. The course had been built upon the initiative of the Princess Daisy of Pless, the legendary Englishwoman who had brought sophistication to Castle Fürstenstein during the early years of her marriage to Prince Hans Heinrich XV of Pless. The prince had been gripped by a building mania making his castle one of the largest in Germany, while his wife Daisy with her social skills and beauty made Fürstenstein into a favourite rendezvous of European aristocracy and royalty. The German and Austrian emperors and several European kings, statesmen like Winston Churchill, generals, and artists came to Fürstenstein, especially during the Imperial manoeuvres. In order to accommodate some of the illustrious guests at such times while Castle Fürstenstein was one huge construction site, the *Grand Hotel* was built in Bad Salzbrunn, which showed a luxury, elegance, and pomp unique among German hotels. It was located in a park-like setting with vast terraces where the Sunday five o'clock tea took place, unless inclement weather would keep the guests in the huge, oval-shaped two-story high hotel lobby.

During my young years, the aristocratic glamour from the years before World War I was no longer there, but the hotel, now called *Schlesischer Hof*, was still frequented by a noticeably sophisticated, wealthy, elegant crowd. As the license plates of the fancy automobiles parked in front of the hotel indicated, many of the guests came from across the near border, from Czechoslovakia, but there were also some Polish and Austrian cars. I loved being there with my parents, sipping a sweet chocolate and eating a fancy piece of pastry, listening to the jazz band, and watching the ladies in their slinky dresses on the dance floor. No doubt, some people thought it was silly for my parents to take me to a place where there was seemingly nothing for me except some fancy food and refreshments. But I do sense to this day an atmosphere that I could only grasp from a distance, but which fascinated me. It was a whiff of the big world that was already disappearing from Germany, and which, in this form, would never return. How fortunate I feel that I did have a chance to witness it.

I felt the same awe when we went with my parents to Prague for a weekend. By that time, I knew Breslau, the Silesian capital, quite well. Prague seemed not only larger, but much richer with its ornate old buildings. Although only slightly more populous than Breslau, Prague carried the ambience of a much bigger city, full of elegant stores, cafés, cars, and well-dressed crowds. The huge department store buildings, the richly decorated facades of office buildings and apartment houses impressed me. Perhaps here, my interest in architecture came into play — my mother had subscribed for years to an art and architecture magazine which I eagerly read.

That our world was changing fast became clear when we visited Castle Fürstenstein one Sunday. There were no more guests, indeed the owner's family no longer lived there. Under the blow of the world depression, the Prince of Pless had lost much of his wealth. So the castle was turned into a tourist destination with guided tours offered through the endless halls, salons, stairways, and across the vast terraces that surrounded the huge building on two of its sides. The terraces were adorned by statues, fountains, rare plants, and profuse flowers.

We also went to the *Riesengebirge*, Silesia's highest mountains. At one time, we had been invited by a former colleague of my father from his days at the bank. He had come to visit us and I especially liked his wife, a good-looking, very motherly lady. We met them in the little village of Kiesewald near Agnetendorf (since 1945 Jagniatków), and on Sunday we went on a hike across the mountains into Czechoslovakia to the Peter-baude, more a sophisticated mountain lodge than a *Baude* — a *Baude* would be quite a simple shelter. During the entire hike, my father and his friend very much kept to themselves and seemed to be engrossed in a deep discussion. For me, it was a wonderful hike, which, however, ended on a sour note. We had just crossed back into Germany on a little hiking trail, when three *SS* men in their black uniforms stopped us and started to question my father and his friend in the most aggressive and unpleasant manner. They called us bad Germans for going into a country that was our enemy, and for trying to hide from the border guards by using this little known trail rather than the official broad hiking trail, which could even accommodate automobiles. I was thoroughly frightened, so were the ladies, and the two men seemed to fume in anger, but they refrained from expressing their feelings.

Nevertheless, the happy memories of this weekend trip soon prevailed, until, on the following weekend, my father told me that his old friend had offered him a very good job in Breslau, the provincial capital. This job was with the *Deutsche Arbeitsfront*, the successor to the German labour unions, but it did not involve any party work, and his friend, who had quite a powerful position, reassured my father that no pressure for expressions of loyalty to the party would be placed on him. At this time, my father had decided against accepting this job, but he also told me a later move into a job like this was not out of the question, as the salary was so much better.

I soon forgot about this possibility of a move away from the town of my birth. On August 7, I turned 10 and was by law required to enter the youth organization *Jungvolk*, which was the section of the *Hitlerjugend*

(Hitler Youth) for boys between 10 and 14. Only later did I realize how unusual for a Nazi youth organization our particular unit in Waldenburg was. Its character was obviously shaped by the socio-economic conditions in our hometown. Very few of the kids would have had parents who could afford to buy a uniform for their sons. Thus, at least in the years when I belonged to this unit, no uniforms were permitted to be worn during the scheduled weekly activities. My father was glad that he did not have to buy a uniform for me. Not even our leaders, youngsters like us, although a year or two older, wore uniforms, and the nature of activities was not that much different from what ordinary kids would do in their free time. Hitler had proclaimed the *Reichsjugendtag*, which meant that on Saturdays there was no more school and the entire day was devoted to activities within the *Hitlerjugend*. That was also the case on Wednesday afternoons, when school ended early. My parents were appalled at what this would do to our education, but we kids, of course, found this wonderful; at least I did so, as long as I attended *Jungvolk* in Waldenburg. We would go on hikes, take some food along, make fires, and bake potatoes. There was practically nothing that would betray these hours as part of the official service given by youth to the Nazi Party and to National Socialist Germany. When weather was inclement, we would stay indoors, using the empty office building of an old coal mine that had been closed years ago. There we played cards, fooled around, and did very little which would remind us that we were on duty as *Hitlerjungen*.

Next to these innocent youth activities, Germany's conversion into a true Fascist state progressed rapidly. In September, during the *Reichsparteitag*, the annual party rally at Nuremberg, Hitler proclaimed the so-called *Nürnberger Gesetze*, which took the last rights away from Germany's Jewish citizens. The consequences were felt in our town very quickly. Jewish doctors and lawyers had to close their offices, although in Waldenburg, there was one exception. Dr. Pese, a local Jewish paediatrician who was held in the highest regard by the poor working population because of his devotion and the extra care he gave, received a special, although I am sure most reluctant, permission to re-open his office, after a large group of miners had publicly protested in front of the office building at their mine.

I discovered another sign of protest at the display cases of *Der Stürmer*, the despicable, almost pornographic, rabidly anti-Semitic weekly published by the Nuremberg Nazi leader Julius Streicher. Next to it was the display case of *Das Schwarze Korps*, the official weekly publication of the *SS*. I walked by those cases next to the wide steps leading downhill from the city hall quite often. Several times I noticed that the glass had been shattered. It was always replaced immediately, but one day, I saw that it had been replaced with wire-mesh. On the following day, a Sunday, we walked this way to early mass and discovered that both display cases were covered with human excrement. During the night, someone must have thrown big packages of feces against the two anti-Semitic papers behind their wire-mesh protection. These were, at least during those years, the only visible signs of protest I became aware of in my hometown.

Within our own family, we particularly felt the impact of the new rules emanating from the new anti-Jewish laws, as my Aunt Lisa had been working with the Jewish dentist Dr. Lubinski. He took the law that forced him to terminate his professional life so prematurely, very hard. Neither was he well enough to leave the country, but he died a few months later. My aunt faithfully visited his widow, did errands for her, as for Jewish people shopping soon became an unpleasant task, and took her to the family's garden for some peace and fresh air. Soon, Mrs. Lubinski was in dire straits, as she had no income. So my aunt would bring her meals several times a week, all this becoming more and more dangerous for her, as there were enough people who would watch her come and go and probably reported her to the police. Not long after her husband, Mrs. Lubinski also died. Aunt Lisa, together with a very few courageous souls, went to the Jewish cemetery to attend Mrs. Lubinski's burial.

The continuous impact of propaganda on the average citizen and family was enormous. On the one hand, there was the constant hatred directed at Jews and those who were not prepared to swallow the Nazi propaganda that the Jews were the enemies of the German people. The intense propaganda claimed that there was a conspiracy of all the Jews throughout the entire world which, without the *Führer's* watchfulness and protection, would result in the destruction of Germany and the German race. In addition to the official propaganda, there were graffiti on many walls screaming into one's face *Juda verrecke!* (Death to Jewry).

There was no more free press in Germany, nor ideologically unbiased radio broadcasts. Not a single word could be found or heard in public that would counteract this increasing attack on Germany's Jews. Only in the circle of the family did I hear expressions of sympathy and support for the Jews. Nobody, however, had a solution how to help the Jews and protect their integrity and safety.

Only those who did not follow Hitler were conscious of how deep Germany had sunk within only two or three years.

* * * * *

6   1936–1939
Marching towards War

A different tone marked the years of 1936 and after. No longer was the accent on building a world of peace for the deserving German people. On March 7, 1936, Germany took on the characteristics of a war-like society.

* * *

On January 6, 1936, the *Winter Olympics* opened in Garmisch-Partenkirchen accompanied by a powerful stream of Nazi propaganda. Although small by today's standards, they were a supreme occasion to celebrate the superiority of Germany's sportsmen and sportswomen. To an even greater measure, this celebration was repeated during the 1936 *Summer Olympics* in Berlin. The Third Reich seemed to gain the respect of the entire world.

The world forgot that on March 7, German troops had occupied the Rhineland which, under the terms of the Treaty of Versailles, had been a demilitarized zone since 1919. With marching his troops into the Rhineland, preceded by the reintroduction of conscription in March 1935, Hitler tore the last vestiges of that treaty to pieces. For these decisions, he certainly had the consent of the vast majority of Germans, as proven by the election on March 27, which resulted in a yes vote of 99 percent. Whether this vote was falsified or not did not matter; it was exploited to the limit by the propaganda to prove that the German people stood solidly behind their *Führer*. Nobody could guess how many people worried at what stage Hitler would stop, or at what stage the Allied nations would decide that the only way to stop Hitler would be war.

On Hitler's birthday on April 20, there was the first of the regularly scheduled huge military parades intended to show not only the German people, but also the foreign ambassadors and military attachés accredited in Berlin the increasing military might of the Third Reich and the advancement in armaments provided for the German forces. This was the first occasion I remember that we were taken as an entire school to a movie theatre to be shown the current newsreel followed by a movie of patriotic content. This became a regular event as the years went on. On no other topic was there as much praise heaped as on Prussia and its kings, especially Frederick II. The movies shown in a regular movie theatre as part of our school day included at least three films focused on Frederick II including "The Old King and the Young King," "The Choral of Leuthen," and "Fridericus Rex." There was more than one film celebrating Bismarck as the unifier of Germany and the creator of the Second Reich, of German poets such as Friedrich Schiller, but eventually also of such topics as euthanasia in the infamous film "Ich klage an," (I accuse), that presented euthanasia as the answer to incurable diseases in a manner that at least a few people recognized as a precursor of Nazi policies to come. Even Italian propaganda movies were shown to us, such as "Mario," the incredibly simplistic story of a little Fascist boy who was smart enough to fool all adults who were not Fascists and make them look like helpless and useless idiots. After 1939, these films would be complemented by dozens of actual war films celebrating the heroism of German soldiers and their victories on land, sea, and in the air.

As time went on, there were more and more movies we were taken to, not only by our school, but eventually also by the *Hitlerjugend*. To indoctrinate us even more, we toured army barracks and, during the summer of 1936, we were taken to the big manoeuvres that took place on the historic battlefield of Hohenfriedeberg near Waldenburg, the scene of the victory of Frederick II, King of Prussia, over Austria.

Causes for jubilation and adulation continued to arise. On June 6, Emperor Haile Selassie of Ethiopia arrived in London as an exile. Italy integrated his country into its new empire. Despite all the official celebrations, people privately joked about the incompetent Italian army that had taken so long to vanquish the impoverished, backward African country whose soldiers were shown bravely fighting in their bare feet with outdated weapons. On June 19, the German champion Max Schmeling knocked out the American boxer Joe Louis in the 12th round. The programmed rejoicing presented by the German radio stations knew no bounds. Not only had a German sportsman been victorious over an

American; the outcome of the match was also representative of the superiority of the Germanic race over the Black race.

Even though Germany did not come out at the top during the *Olympic Games*, the entire event was a great propaganda success for the Third Reich. Too many of the foreigners flooding into Berlin were deceived by the image of a well-functioning country with a contented population, loyal to its government. They did not see any evidence of anti-Semitic propaganda, because all traces of it had been carefully removed for the duration of the games.

In July, the Spanish Civil War broke out. Within two months the so-called German volunteers of the *Legion Condor* appeared in Spain. Their military accomplishments were shown every week in the newsreels. In private conversations, however, the purpose of the *Legion Condor* was understood as a military testing unit on the welcome battlefield of the Spanish Civil War.

The belief that war was no longer an impossibility was held by a good number of people, but many more expressed the unshakeable conviction that Hitler's plan was firmly committed to peace and that he would never involve Germany in a war. People held to that belief, even after the first *Vierjahresplan*, the Four Years Plan was introduced, ostensibly to lessen Germany's dependence on the world market and to make the country more self-supporting. All of a sudden, certain items, especially precious metals, became scarce. Gold coins from past imperial times owned by individuals had to be turned over to the state; their possession was now illegal (I watched my father hide our gold coins in the depth of his grand piano). Bicycles and cars began to look plainer, and had less trim of chromium, another precious item. It became obvious that everything was geared towards freeing as many resources as possible for rearmament.

Only now did unemployment finally disappear in the Third Reich, although that claim had been made much earlier. Many things changed affecting everyday life. This was the time, when at least in Silesian cities, whipping cream became scarce, especially on weekends, and rationing of butter was introduced, although this regulation was not rigidly ad-hered to by the merchants until the war began. Enough happened that made a number of people think about a future which might include a horrendous war. Even the triumphant announcement of Japan's joining the German-Italian Pact was viewed by some people with alarm. Huge propaganda posters appeared everywhere celebrating the *Axis Berlin-Rome-Tokyo*, which was to assure peace in the world — a claim not universally believed.

Even though I was very young at this time, I remember a changing mood coming over the country: On the one hand, there was more elation and jubilation about the triumphs of Hitler and his Third Reich; on the

other hand, there was increasing anxiety, tension, and a nervous antici-
pation of things to come even among those who stood solidly behind
Hitler. Still, people expected more and greater things to come. At that
time, I was not yet capable of putting impressions into words very well,
but in hindsight, I am sure that is what I vaguely felt. Such feeling was
exacerbated by what happened in our family.

On February 1, 1936, my father finally gave in to the constant urging
of his friend and started to work for the *Deutsche Arbeitsfront* in Breslau.
It was a well-paid job, he had a wonderful office, he liked his work and
the freedom it seemed to give him, and he enjoyed working side-by-side
with his old friend from his banking days in the 1920s. Nevertheless, my
father was cautious and decided to commute for a while. He would move
his family only once he was certain that the job and the working
conditions were to his satisfaction. For almost six months he was only
home on weekends, reporting how hard it was to find pleasant housing
in Breslau.

Much had been built during the years prior to the Third Reich, but
not nearly enough for the rapidly growing city that had a huge backlog
of unfilled housing requirements after Word War I and the inflation
years. Housing was still built under Hitler, but at a diminished rate, and
the quality and size of these new apartments was noticeably lower than
what had been provided by the housing projects built under social
democratic governments before 1933. In the Third Reich, except in the
very limited privately built housing sector, windows were of noticeably
smaller dimensions, there were no more balconies, and doors looked
plain and cheap.

We were still in Waldenburg when my Grandfather Koch died
unexpectedly. He had led an active, but well ordered life as a retired
gentleman. He had turned over all his businesses to several of his sons,
but retained some responsibility for the management of his other properties. Almost 80 years old, he still rose at six o'clock in the morning,
went to Mass across the street with his wife, had breakfast after their
return home, then went for his daily walk. Upon his return, he had a
second much smaller breakfast, always consisting of a bowl of sour milk
liberally sprinkled with sugar, cinnamon, and tiny toasted bread cubes. I
loved to join him — there was always an extra bowl ready for me.
Afterwards, he would retreat to his desk and take care of his business
matters or receive some visitors. Lunch, the main meal of the day, was
still served exactly at 12 noon, unchanged from his years as an active
businessman. When the noon bells would ring from the church steeple
across the street, my grandparents would rise and say their prayers,
before sitting down to a meal that was always excellent. Both retired for
an hour's rest afterwards, then took care of various things and again sat

down for some refreshments at three o'clock. This was "coffee time" and there was always some cake and some fruit. Afterwards, they both read the daily paper which was delivered around three o'clock. They each sat in their comfortable armchair facing each other, and each chair was placed next to one of the two windows through which the afternoon sun would flood on bright days. They had two canaries that would sing incessantly. Most of the time I would sit next to my grandmother. In between reading, there would be much conversation. These afternoons, which I attended as often as possible even after we moved out of my grandparents' house, belong to the most precious memories of my childhood.

I am including even small details in this description in order to help the reader get a sense of the mood of peace, happiness, security, and beauty that permeated the atmosphere in my grandparents' house. Almost every afternoon while we were sitting there, the church bells would ring as accompaniment of a funeral. While the reason for their ringing was sad, we had long gotten used to it and I enjoyed the bells as part of the special mood of the afternoon in my grandparents' living room.

At half-past-five, the church bells rang again for the Ave Maria. My grandparents would get up from their armchairs and pray. If I think of prayer and what, among other things it does to a person, I think of this time of the day when I prayed with my grandparents. There was a short prayer again at supper which was served at six o'clock sharp.

This was the daily routine of my grandparents, adhered to even long after they had given up their business, which had involved so many people and brought about such a busy household. This routine served them well to their last days. They took excursions, of course, occasional stays in mountain resorts, or a cure in a spa, but not too frequently, as both always felt well. Until his 60s, my grandfather spent three weeks in Norderney at the North Sea each summer.

My grandparents were definitely of the older generation that stood by its values and habits. They took the best of their lives into these last years of my grandfather, and in retrospect, these values and habits not only served them well, they made a lot of sense to me too and instilled values and attitudes in me which I am conscious of to this day. Like my parents, my grandfather also frequently involved me in discussions of a political, historical, and cultural nature, always in keeping with my age level. I wonder now, whether he was aware how much he did for me in preparing me for a difficult future.

From what I just wrote about them, it will be obvious that both my grandparents were deeply religious. They followed the rites and customs of the Catholic Church, but they were pious in a non-ostentatious way.

Their religion was one of deep faith in God and of a deep sense of responsibility towards God and their fellow-human beings. What they taught me has helped me remain a person who believes in God and in Christ, even though I have not been a practicing Catholic since the end of World War II.

On some days, our school day would end early, sometimes even at 11 o'clock. There was only one place I wanted to go before I was expected for lunch at home, and that was my grandparents' house. It was on July 8, 1936 that I arrived at their house just after 11. As always, my grandfather was happy to see me and invited me to partake in a huge bowl of fresh cherries. We sat, we talked, and I ate most of them to his delight. Just before 12, he gently admonished me that it was time to leave, in order not to be late for lunch at my own home. I left the house and immediately crossed the street in order to be able to wave goodbye once more to my grandfather who stood behind the window of his study among his beloved cacti. He waved, I waved and then, all of a sudden, he was gone. Just for a moment, I was puzzled. Then I felt sure he had been called away, perhaps to the telephone, I thought. Happily I walked home.

When I arrived at home, my mother opened the door in tears and told me that my grandparents' maid had just phoned. Grandfather Koch had died 10 minutes ago.

That someone could leave this world so suddenly and unexpectedly was hard for me to grasp; not only for me, but for the rest of the Koch family as well, as my grandfather had been such a physically healthy, mentally active, and optimistic man. The next few days were hard on me. This was the first time that I experienced what a sudden death can do to a family. The mourning was profound and made more so by the many callers who came to pay their respects to the memory of Grandfather Koch, who had been laid to temporary rest in an open coffin in the parlour, and to express their condolences to Grandmother Koch.

The evening before the interment, my grandfather was taken in a cortège followed by a huge number of mourners to the cemetery chapel where a burial mass was held. In the early afternoon of the following day, there was another mass in the cemetery chapel followed by the interment rites. It was a grey day with some occasional rain. It felt chilly, even though it was the middle of July.

After we returned from the cemetery, a reception and dinner were held in my grandparents' parlour that became what is called today "a celebration of life." There were no formal speeches, but people talked about my grandfather and what his presence had meant in their lives at one time or another. On this day, several of his one-time apprentices had returned from different parts of Germany to their former master's house.

Now, they were proud, successful businessmen. There was the group of old people who had worked for my grandfather and were now living, in their retirement, rent-free on the top floor of his house. There was the *Behmpauer,* the farmer by the name of Böhm who since the meagre years of World War I had brought fresh eggs and homemade butter to my grandparents' house once every week. This arrangement had been started during wartime and post-war shortages. When everything was plentiful again, my grandfather still expected Mr. Böhm, who had become his friend over the years, to bring his products every week, and he had always time for a chat and a drink with the old farmer. I loved the *Behmpauer* from the time I was little, because he would let me ride on his knee and talked to me very gently. He was a very strong man with white hair, very bright blue eyes, invariably dressed in a black suit and wearing huge black boots. He looked perhaps formidable, but he was such a gentle man that I was never fearful of him.

I am quoting part one of the obituaries published in the local papers, because it expressed how my grandfather, *der Millionenkoch,* who never made much ado about his wealth, was looked upon in his community.

Keinem, der in Not zu ihm kam, hat er seine Hilfe
versagt. Er war ein stiller Wohltäter der Armen, wie er
ueberhaupt im Stillen und in Zurückgezogenheit gewirkt
und geschaffen hat . . . . .[1]

I missed my grandfather very much, in some ways I do to this day. But his absence from our daily lives became less painful for me and I was spared part of the mourning, because my father had decided to move his family to Breslau after renting an apartment for us on a temporary basis with a plan to build a house of our own as quickly as possible.

We went on a holiday in the mountains where I, for the first time, fell in love — she was a young lady from Berlin, probably seven years older than I. Needless to say, it was love from a distance. We shared a table at mealtimes with her family in the hotel. Off and on, I made some timid conversation with her, but otherwise, I probably just stared at her and then thought of her for the rest of the day.

After this carefree holiday, I only spent a weekend at home, before being sent off to my uncle and aunt in Trebnitz (since 1945 Trzebnica) to be out of the way during the move to Breslau. For me, this was another holiday, as I was with my favourite cousin Christel.

Before my departure, though, I was witness to an unexpected altercation between my father and my Grandmother Hackenberg. When

---

1   No one in need who came to him for help, was ever refused. In his quiet way, he was a benefactor of the poor. This was his way to live for others. . . . .

she told my father that she expected a little apartment for herself in the house he was going to build for his family in Breslau, my father said firmly and rather coldly, "that will not happen; why do you think we are moving away from this street and this town!" This was only part of the reason my father had chosen to relocate his family away from the town of his birth. There was more than one reason, but one of them was my grandmother's tendency to marshal people around herself, especially my mother and myself, without any regard of our own family obligations and plans. I do not blame my father for no longer being willing to tolerate this habit of his mother-in-law. But had he known what feelings he aroused in my grandmother and how his wife would be punished by her mother in revenge, he probably would have found better words than those that exploded in his mind as a result of years of anger and frustration.

I was looking forward with great excitement to our life in the provincial capital. Breslau, a city of more than 600,000 inhabitants, was the only truly big city in Silesia. It offered everything a young boy would dream of, although less than Berlin, Prague, or Dresden, as I decided after brief visits to these cities. Still, Breslau did seem to promise a more interesting and exciting life than the much smaller town of my birth. Besides, as a coal mining town, Waldenburg was generally looked upon as the ugliest and dirtiest town in Silesia.

On the last day of the summer holidays, my parents picked me up in Trebnitz. We arrived in our new street in Breslau only a couple of hours before nightfall. It was a dull, cool day. I liked the green spaces surrounding the house, but I was horrified by our apartment. It had none of the amenities which my parents, especially my mother always insisted on as essential for a comfortable, cultivated home!

Compared to our apartment in Waldenburg, both living room and music room were considerably smaller, the latter lacking all glamour of former times. Everything looked cheap in our new home. There were no tiles on the bathroom walls and the floor was of plain cement. There was no wash-basin and one had to wash oneself over the bathtub. The toilet bowl was of cheap cast iron. Of this material were also all door and window handles while the windows themselves were of the many-paned type, in order to avoid the purchase of much more expensive large-sized sheets of glass. There was no hot and cold water and no central heating but tiled stoves in all rooms, and even they looked cheap! As I soon realized, we had taken up residence in a new suburb of 23,000 people that had been built in one fell swoop in the late 1920s. In terms of space and greenery, the suburb, by the name of Zimpel (since 1945 Sępolno), had been planned very generously. There were also a beautiful school building, two churches and a shopping street right in the centre. Our type of apartment was the second best in size and quality in the entire suburb. It was obvious that a conscious attempt had been made by the planners to save even a couple of pennies for each appliance, door handle, lock and so on, resulting in savings that would accumulate to considerable sums through these methods of standardization permitting large scale purchases. Throughout the suburb, one would be hard pressed to find more than 10 different floor plans — they were also standardized. Only the outside appearance of the houses varied to a slight extent from street to street.

My parents were not too upset with these shortcomings, as they were determined to build their own house as quickly as possible, a dream to be prevented by political developments, as they would soon find out. My father was glad that two of the three other parties living in the house were very congenial. All families in the house also had pianos that were played everyday — each of the five kids living in the house took piano lessons! So my father did not have to worry about annoying overly sensitive neighbours with his daily hours of piano playing. This was most important, as the houses in this suburb were of uniformly light construction and most poorly insulated against sound. It may be hard to believe, but in the evening, I would converse through the ceiling with the boy upstairs directly above my room in a loud voice, but without shouting, and we understood each other perfectly well.

As it turned out, our apartment was also extremely cold in winter. My parents simply bought enormous amounts of coal to keep us warm, all the time looking for a site to build. Towards spring 1937, they found a lovely place in the southern part of town, Breslau's preferred residential area. It was a lot that sloped southward, bordered by a little creek on one side, and by a park on the other. My mother was delighted. The negotiations with the owner of the lot took longer than expected. I was intrigued that during that time, the owner changed his Polish sounding name into a pure Germanic name. He was not alone in taking this step.

In this year, a campaign was started by the party to strongly encourage all citizens with Slavic, especially Polish names to adopt authentic German names instead. More than a third of the kids in the classroom of my new school had pure Polish names, although their families had resided in Breslau or Lower Silesia for many generations. Only two students announced that their parents had followed the dictum of the party and had chosen German surnames for their family. In the *Hitlerjugend*, there was a similar campaign going on, although I did not notice a single case of name change. This was also the year of often substituting very artificial sounding German words for words that had originated in another language, although in a good number of cases, nobody was conscious of using a *Fremdwort*, i.e., a foreign word when, for instance speaking of sauce which from now on was to be referred to with the far less appetizing word *Tunke*! We laughed, but soon, the usage of foreign words in our essays and other papers was marked in red ink and resulted in a lower final mark.

The character of the *Jungvolk* here in Breslau shocked me. Compared to Waldenburg, there was an enormous amount of discipline and control. To wear a uniform was mandatory, and every boy did. There were military-type drills, endurance marches, eternal singing, and a great deal of political indoctrination. These were different kids, none of them as poor as most of the boys in the *Jungvolk* in Waldenburg. I was most unhappy and felt much behind compared to the other boys. Still, there were some good times, as the boys in my group mostly came from the same school, but not the school I attended. Some of the activities were just good clean fun of the kind all boys everywhere used to have. However, not too long after I was assigned to this group, it was split up as, supposedly, we were not sufficiently focused on the mission of the *Jungvolk*. From then on, I felt totally alienated and only reluctantly went to the compulsory all-day Saturday and the Wednesday afternoon activities. I did not have any choice, if I wanted to avoid punishment.

This became the most upsetting fall and winter in my life! I fell from one surprise or shock into the next and after the shortcomings of our home and the threatening nature of the *Jungvolk*, the biggest shock was my new school.

It turned out to be very hard to find a suitable school that started with French as the first foreign language. My parents had told me about the quality of the high schools in the provincial capital, but the better schools were not suitable for me because they had already started with either Latin or English. Eventually, a school was found for me, which by its years and by its building, seemed ancient, a terrible shock after the beautiful, modern school I had attended in Waldenburg. The wooden stairs of the school building were creaking, the floors in the classrooms were plain boards that looked black from the oil that was used to maintain them. The kids, I realized within days, were way ahead of me in general sophistication and especially in sexual matters. Quite a few of them, who mostly came from a working class district called Tschepine — the Nazis never managed to extinguish this good old Polish name — were very tough kids, aggressive, rough, and wise beyond their years.

I felt very lost in my new class of 60 kids (in Waldenburg, we were around 20). I desperately searched amongst the teachers for someone I felt I could trust, or who would understand and protect me. Many of the teachers were quite advanced in years and were distant and authoritarian. Another group of teachers were former professional officers from World War I who had been forced to terminate their military careers as a consequence of the disarmament of 1919. Some were truly pathetic, forever telling us stories from their war experiences. We were bored but let this happen, as this meant we did not have to study.

Other teachers from this group were outright mean and cruel — they seemed to hate their profession and the kids they taught. I happened to be physically weak from birth, and more than one of our physical education teachers, rather than teach me how to gain some strength, would literally ridicule and persecute me and the other weak kids in the class. When we had to climb up on thick ropes, I would usually reach the limit of my strength a few feet above the floor. One of the teachers would then grip the end of the heavy rope and forcefully whip my behind. I was not the only one who received such treatment, and more than once, fresh blood would run down our legs.[2] In the next grade, when I was 13 years old, my math teacher, who would not forgive me for being weak in his subject, would beat my upturned, open hand with a cane until blood would flow from my fingers. His only comment was *"Du Schwein blutest auch noch!"*[3] And he would repeat this procedure a few more times. He was also a teacher who loved to wear his old captain's uniform from World War I whenever he could find the slightest reason.

Cruelty and terror as part of physical education classes was not unique to my school in Breslau. Even in my beloved high school in Waldenburg, one physical education teacher would make us jump from the top of the Swedish ladders, something I had no trouble doing, as this involved only some courage, but little physical strength. Over a period of 15 months, the length of my stay in this school, two boys broke their ankles, but the teacher was not disciplined and continued with this practice seeming to enjoy it even more, as more boys became fearful after the earlier accidents of their classmates.

The biggest problem I had in Breslau, was with our homeroom teacher, who was from another part of Germany and spoke a very pronounced Bavarian dialect that I simply could not understand. He never physically disciplined us, but seemed to take immense pleasure to catch our mistakes, make a cynical remark, and with a nasty grin on his face, enter a comment in his little black book. Many of us were almost paralyzed by fear in his presence. I felt that somehow, I managed to get by in his classes. Somehow, I had gradually found a way to survive among the tough kids, primarily by trying to be as tough as they were. I am sure,

---

2   For years, my reports about these cruel teachers were met with a good measure of understandable skepticism on the part of my wife, herself a teacher, until 1998 when my Jewish classmate from Waldenburg visited us in Edmonton and confirmed what I had related about my schooldays.

3   "You are a pig! You are even bleeding!"

my attempts were quite pitiful, but I was much calmer now feeling fairly adequate among my classmates.

Christmas came, the first Christmas away from Waldenburg with its special celebrations in the houses of my Grandparents Koch and Hackenberg. On the last day of school, we received our report cards. A glance at mine assured me that my marks were actually quite good. Very relieved with the way things had turned out, I walked home and placed the report card on the dinner table next to my father. Looking expectantly at him, I suddenly saw his face turn red and, in a state of agitation, he held the report card in front of my eyes demanding my explanation of the meaning and the cause of the remark my feared home room teacher had written, which I had not even noticed, until my father pointed with his finger at the following sentence: "Koch ist ein gewissenhafter und fleissiger Schüler, lässt es aber völlig an Disziplin, Anstand und Moral fehlen." [4] I had no idea what the teacher meant by these terrible comments, which my father no doubt perceived as a severe criticism of the standards of his own family. Neither could I think of any incidents which might have caused these terrible remarks, as my homeroom teacher had never once corrected my behaviour. My father was beside himself, but little could be done, as the school was now closed until after New Year. For me, this did not turn out to be a very merry Christmas.

As was the custom at this time, it was the boy's mother who would visit the school rather than the father. My mother could not come to terms with my homeroom teacher, who failed to give her the satisfactory explanation she felt he owed her and me. She decided to call on the director of the school, who was not a very effective man. I would not have been surprised to learn he was afraid of my homeroom teacher. What he did, at least, was to send my mother to the teacher I had produced the best marks for, my French teacher. He also happened to be a rather generous man with a good sense of humour, who assured my mother that I was a perfectly decent human being and not to worry about me. Things were not quite as simple for me. I was badly shaken and made most insecure. It took me years to find my bearings and become an ordinary boy or, later, teenager and enjoy life.

Gradually, my feelings towards this school and its teachers turned more and more to the positive and for that I have to thank a few teachers, especially our new homeroom teacher. Dr. Randow had been transferred to Breslau from a small town near Berlin. He was a generous man, who was at once intellectual, practical, and filled with a fine sense of humour.

---

4   "Koch is a conscientious and diligent student, but very badly lacks discipline, decency, and morals."

His major subject was Mathematics where I had become a total failure due to the cruel teacher I had had so far. He also taught Chemistry and Biology. I was not great in Chemistry either, indeed in most sciences, but Biology posed no problem to me. At any rate, in the latter two subjects, I could demonstrate to my new homeroom teacher that I was neither lazy nor stupid. So he remained most tolerant of my weaknesses in Mathematics throughout the remaining five years of school and I suspect that he believed that I simply lacked ability to grasp mathematical concepts and would never do much better, no matter how hard I tried and no matter how good a teacher he was — and he was an excellent teacher. With his practical sense, he simply suggested to my mother that each year a tutor be engaged for me to get me through the final exams so that I would pass to the next grade.

The other teacher I had immense respect for was a Catholic priest, Dr. Gnielinski, who taught Religion, as long as this was tolerated as a subject. He had grown up in the farthest reaches of Upper Silesia, in a village near the town of Rosenberg (since 1945 Oleśno). He made no secret out of the fact that his parents, small farmers, still spoke only Polish. He had the most difficult task of teaching the concepts and beliefs of the Catholic Church while under the surveillance of non-believing colleagues. At this time, in 1938, there came massive changes that practically extinguished the traditions and practices upon which the education in Germany's high schools had been based for generations.

All textbooks were banned from school to be replaced with new texts that exclusively reflected the beliefs and goals of the Nazi party. Most books, of course, were not immediately available and for months or, in the case of Latin and English, for almost three years, we had to study without the benefit of textbooks.

For most of us who had looked forward to English as the second foreign language to be taught, the reform of the curriculum was a great disappointment, as instead of English, Latin was now taught in our type of high school. This change brought one reward: Our Religion teacher Dr. Gnielinski, who had been barred from teaching, as soon as Religion had been outlawed as a high school subject, returned as our Latin teacher — minus his clerical collar he was ordered to replace with a white shirt and tie. We were very happy and we were fortunate as well, as he inspired us reluctant students of Latin to learn to like the language and to work hard. Much later, I was grateful to him and even to the "system" for making me learn Latin because it proved itself invaluable for my interests in other languages and for my entire career.

One day, Dr. Gnielinski no longer appeared in our school. We were sad, but no longer surprised considering the frequent sudden changes we were experiencing. Only after the war did I learn that Dr. Gnielinski had been transferred to the prison at *Kletschkaustrasse* to provide spiritual comfort to the political prisoners, many of whom had been sentenced to death.

Something else disappeared from the scene, and that was the German script our forefathers had used for generations, and which we had used in its slightly modified version, the *Sütterlin Schrift*.[5]. Also abolished was the Gothic script in which books published in Germany had been printed. Both were replaced by the Latin alphabet in handwriting and in printing.

We had a new teacher, who most of the time appeared in his SA uniform, obviously planted in this school as a strong party influence. He was, however, a wonderful teacher and a great human being. The political material filled more and more hours of the curriculum, especially in German. We were indoctrinated to hate all Slavs and, of course, all Jews, and be suspicious and mistrustful of the French and the British and, finally, to consider the Americans as hopelessly uncultured and racially degenerate because of the many "negroes" in the United States. Despite his *SA* uniform, our teacher — in some ways, he was an enigma to us — taught us such loaded subject matters in a not very convincing manner. We were getting enough young teachers, though, who obviously believed in what they were to teach us, and these classes were very unpleasant, because we still had a Jewish boy in our class who was protected by most of us.

The presence of the party also began to intrude into our family life. Within a year of his start with the *Deutsche Arbeitsfront*, my father experienced a terrible blow. His friend who had encouraged him to accept the position was summarily fired, and my father felt utterly alone and abandoned. It became clear now that his friend's position had been precarious for quite some time, and this was the reason he had encouraged my father to join him, in other words to be his ally in this politically highly-charged environment. To this day, I wish this man had never done this to my father who, once more, ended in a terribly difficult position in his job. Again, bitterness, stress, and unhappiness were a daily presence at the supper table when my father could not help but talk about what was happening to him now that he had lost his friend and was surrounded by committed Nazis. 1937, with some exceptions, was not a good year.

One happy memory was *Das Deutsche Sängerfest*, the huge rally that brought over 100,000 members of German choirs to Breslau to fill our

---

5   In 1915 the Sütterlin Schrift, designed by the German graphic artist Ludwig Sütterlin, replaced the old German script in all schools of Prussia — all other German states soon followed this practice.

city with music, fun, and a cheerful mood. Interestingly enough, there were few political aspects to this huge festival — it was perhaps the last of the traditional German rallies that had not been usurped by the party.

During the summer holidays while I was with Grandmother Koch and my Grandparents Hackenberg in Waldenburg, I entered puberty totally unprepared and not knowing what was happening to me. This was the beginning of a most difficult time with my father who had failed so completely to introduce me to the facts of life — which perhaps not too many fathers did at that time — but then interfered with my development to an extent which made me a guilt-laden person who felt sinful, dirty, and weak in the absence of knowing what was part of normal, healthy development.

My mother also entered a difficult time that started with the death of her father on April 13, 1937. He had suffered from what is today called *Alzheimer's Disease*. He was a very proud individual with the bearing of an upright, strong man, but for some time, he had been failing. Every so often, someone would bring Grandfather home, when he had again become lost in the town where he had lived for the greater part of his life. He also would break into tears quite often, which I found most difficult to deal with. It broke my heart to see him cry seemingly without reason.

Grandfather Hackenberg had spent a very happy few weeks with us under the loving care of my mother. It was natural that he would not go out on his own in a city he did not know very well. So in Breslau, we were always with him without him feeling watched or not trusted. Shortly after his return to Waldenburg, he died of a brain hemorrhage. It was tragic, but in hindsight, for him and for the rest of the family, it was the best.

Grandfather Hackenberg's death was the beginning of a severe conflict between Grandmother Hackenberg and my mother who now felt more responsible for her own mother than before her father's death. Unfortunately, in a rather devious way, my Grandmother Hackenberg revived the old conflict between her and my father by impressing on my mother that she must convince my father that we should have a small apartment for her as soon as we would move into our new house, the construction of which had not yet even started. Grandmother Hackenberg was insistent and aggressive and I remember that at the end of each visit in Waldenburg, my mother would leave her mother's home in tears. My father was very much aware of his mother-in-law's campaign, but did nothing to bring it to an end as he had done a couple of years earlier.

In November 1937, my mother had to enter a private hospital for a couple of weeks for surgery and a rather lengthy period of recuperation. Only now do I realize that this was a happy time for my mother. Indeed, whenever I came to see her, she was laughing, enjoying my presence, and that of other visitors. It was obviously a time when she could legitimately disengage herself from a conflict which festered between her mother and her husband.

There were other bad news from Waldenburg. Near where we had lived were the quarters of a Christian fundamentalist group that called themselves *die Bibelforscher* (Jehova's Witnesses). Most of them were ordinary working people. Throughout the year, there was a well publicized court case in which the adults among the *Bibelforscher* were accused of failing as true German parents because they had raised their children in a belief and an ideology that contradicted the goals of the Third Reich. In the media, this group of true believers was portrayed as devious, anti-German, and dangerous. We kids had only a vague idea of the meaning of this campaign, which bordered on persecution of an insignificant, harmless minority. In November, the court delivered its verdict resulting in the removal of the children from their parents and this was justified by the statement of the presiding judge, which went through the world press as far as the United States:

The law as a racial and national instrument entrusts
German parents with the education of their children only
under certain conditions, namely, that they educate them
in the fashion that the nation and the state expect.[6]

I remember that even with our limited comprehension of what this case involved, my friends and I were shocked to hear that children were taken away from perfectly decent parents. These poor people were ridiculed and portrayed as monsters in the press. Pictures of their homes appeared next to the defamatory articles. Only a couple of years earlier, I had passed these houses every day on my way to school — actually, they had been built as very modest post-World War I emergency housing. Soon we heard that among those accused was a woman who had done the washing and ironing for my mother for a couple of years. Her children, one of them my age and whom I knew quite well, were taken away by the state and placed in institutions. A chill went through our family when we realized what ruthless power of the state over its citizens had been proclaimed by this judgment of the court.

By the middle of December, my mother had returned home from the hospital. We had a happy Christmas and on Boxing Day my father took me to the opera for the first time in my life. My father, my mother, my cousin Christel, and I made up a happy group. Richard Wagner's *Lohengrin* was a bit of a heady start for me, but I enjoyed the rather

---

6   Garbe, Detlef, *Zwischen Widerstand und Martyrium. Die Zeugen Jehovas im "Dritten Reich"* *(Studien zur Zeitgeschichte Band 42)*, R. Oldenbourg Verlag, München, 3.Auflage, 1997

attractive staging, the large opera chorus, and the music. I was over-whelmed by the large number of well-dressed people who convened in the foyer during the intermissions, drank champagne, and presented to me a society I had never seen before. I was deeply engaged in following the last act and never noticed until the curtain fell that the two seats my parents had occupied next to me were vacant. Then someone came from behind the stage and took my cousin and me to the back where I found my mother in a rather pitiful state, trembling and gasping for air. The theatre physician, a distinguished looking, but very old gentleman, stood by helplessly repeating again and again, "but Madam, *Lohengrin* has five acts, how could you have attended such a long opera so soon after your surgery!"

It was an extremely cold, snowy night. My cousin was put into a taxi and sent home to Trebnitz. An ambulance took us home and I was instructed to run to our doctor's house as his telephone was constantly engaged. I did find him at home and together, we ran back to our house. He gave my mother an injection and I was sent to get medication from the pharmacy. As it was around two in the morning by that time I had to get the pharmacist out of bed. This upsetting night was the beginning of several years of my mother's dependency on my father and on me.

For almost a year, my mother was bedridden or, at best, would move about only within the confines of our apartment. She was frequently stricken with panic attacks that sapped all her energy and all her courage. Other than during school hours, I ended up being almost as housebound as my mother, as I felt it my duty to look after her, to comfort her, and especially to distract her. She was most grateful. I loved her more than ever, but this was not a productive relationship. My father, who had terrible difficulties in his job as he was being put under pressure to become an open Nazi, was totally overburdened, but gave all he could to his wife. He had little left for me, hardly any attention or love, and was getting stricter and stricter. He seemed to also become mistrustful of my actions and my thoughts. When he arrived home, he expected me at the door prepared to give him a report on my conduct on this day. Only then would he go and say hello to my mother. He was never positive at these moments. As a result, I felt and looked apprehensive, which he inter-preted as guilt. So he would press me more and more to tell him the truth, which to him I only seemed to have reached after confessing to some bad behaviour or thoughts. The reason was, as he once explained to me, that he could not expect my mother to supervise me. Rather, she must be shielded from anything upsetting, especially my bad behaviour.

I truly dreaded these daily minutes of interrogation at the front door in the hallway. I dreamt about them, thought about them while in class, and slowly became a jittery, nervous wreck. Not surprisingly, I also began to act out behind his back. I asked to take Spanish evening classes, a type of wish that was immediately granted. However, other than attending the first lecture and getting my textbook, I rarely went to evening classes but went to the movies instead. I also began to hang around with boys outside the movie house, who taught me how to smoke. As a result, I became a smoker at the age of 12, which I successfully hid from my father for at least three years. I also went for long walks all by myself, something I was allowed to do as long as I described exactly the route of my planned walk. I was always alone, not just physically, but also felt utterly alone in my heart and soul. I was bothered with dark thoughts about running away, even about ending my life. I also wanted to leave school and enter an apprenticeship, as soon as I reached the age of 14. This was one of the few times when my father was utterly reasonable, understanding, and kind. As a result, I gave up this thought after a while and completed my high school. I am grateful that my father took the time to help me in this regard. The thought of running away, however, remained in my mind. I am convinced that it was only my Grandmother Koch and my father's youngest brother Hubert and his wife Käthe who prevented me from doing something foolish and harmful to myself. After my mother felt somewhat better and managed to stay by herself without breaking into panic, my father let me spend about one weekend a month in Walden-burg with my grandmother. Uncle Hubert and his wife lived in the same house, and all three provided a warm, carefree, and happy environment for me, where I was not under any suspicion, where I was free to come and go, and roam about. Nobody ever asked any questions. As a consequence, I never did anything except walk around in town, visit chums from my old school, and – the only thing I kept to myself — smoke cigarettes.

It was these weekends that kept me on the straight and narrow. Later on, when I was deeply into my teen years and the conflicts with my father took on new dimensions, I went for weekends to Waldenburg even more often. My classmates were gradually allowed more and more privileges like going out in the evenings, attending ballroom dancing instruction, and going to movies or to cafés. They also dressed like young adults now. Even though clothing was drastically rationed, my mother managed to get extra points and bought me some nice clothes, but I lacked a decent winter coat. I was given a coat which a distant uncle had worn while he was in Northern India in the 1920s. The cloth itself, I still remember, was superb and most elegant, but the cut of the coat absolutely out of style. Yet, my father insisted that this coat was good enough for me, and even when I told him under tears that this piece of out-of-fashion clothing made me the laughing stock of the school, he did not relent.

Fortunately, Uncle Peter, my mother's brother, understood how hard life was for me. He came to my rescue when I tried to help myself. Secretly I had saved some money, which was not too difficult. While my father gave me a very small allowance for which I had to account for every penny spent, my Grandmother Koch and my other uncles and aunts often discreetly slipped a five-mark-coin into my hand. After I had saved a fair sum, I asked and got permission to visit Uncle Peter, who owned a large drugstore in Sprottau and therefore had "connections" to other businesses. I asked him to help me buy a winter coat without clothing ration points, which he gladly did. I proudly arrived at home in my new coat. My father was furious but did not dare to take the new coat away from me, as I told him that my uncle had bought it as a gift for me. I had to live with the lie I told my father as with many other lies at this time. It was not good for me. I felt without hope; I was often depressed and saw the whole world in a sombre light.

Once before I had taken the law into my own hands. We were still living in Waldenburg; I attended the first grade in high school and had just turned 10. I had begged for a bicycle, but in vain. In the papers, however, there were these little ads for *Edelweiss Fahrräder*, which could be bought by mail order. Their cost was less than 35 marks. All it took was to clip out the coupon, enter name and address on it, enclose a postal money order, and send it to the factory in Deutsch-Wartenberg (since 1945 Otyń) in the northern part of Silesia. This I did after a long period of saving. One day, the bicycle was delivered at the door. My father, who happened to be home for lunch, told the deliveryman that this must be a mistake until I owned up to my actions and explained things. At that time, my father was still a more generous man and laughed and let me have my bike. His further reaction was to buy a bike for himself. During the following summer, the two of use took some bicycle trips, which belong to the happiest memories of my childhood.

Things were very different now. My father was easygoing and funny in the presence of my mother or with friends or guests. Alone with me, he was grim, always suspicious, and absolutely non-giving, in material things and in his attitude towards me as well. It must have been the stress of my mother's condition, which fortunately improved more and more, and the stress in his job that almost destroyed our relationship during these years. When I acted without asking him, he became very angry. As he hardly ever said yes, even to the smallest request of a totally legitimate nature, I eventually stopped asking his permission altogether and simply did what I wanted to do, which again burdened my conscience even more. I believe though, that he was aware of my growing resentment. As time went on, I asked to spend weekends with my grandmother more and more frequently. During the last year or two of school, on the majority of Saturdays, I would proceed to the train station immediately after dismissal from school, spend the weekend in Waldenburg, and take the early train on Monday morning to arrive in Breslau just in time for the first class of the day. I believe my father felt hurt, but he never tried to stop me, and perhaps deep down in his heart, he realized that this was the only way for the two of us to manage living under the same roof.

I never dared complaining to my mother, who was still not really well. Her love for her husband was unqualified, as was his for her. So in her eyes, he could do no wrong. Perhaps she would have felt sorry for me, but she would never have tried to intercede on my behalf — and even if she had, I do not think it would have made a difference.

In late fall of 1937, an unexpected event happened: my father was called up by the Army. He briefly was discharged again after a month or so, but while in the army, he had signed up for courses as a purser, a position of officer's rank. So, it happened that after a brief few weeks back at his hated civilian job, my father was called up again in February 1938. Only later did we realize that his renewed call to the Army was part of the preparation for the *Anschluss*, the annexation of Austria one month later. My father was elated to have escaped the *Arbeitsfront* once more. After the *Anschluss*, many German men who had been called up were discharged from the Army, while my father was sent for his first course leading towards a purser's rank. He never returned to his civilian job again.

It was truly ironic that it took the *army* to make my father happy and fulfilled in his work again, which after all brought him closer to his former, since 1930 never practiced career as a banker. The mood at home also changed noticeably. My father became a bit more reasonable with me. By that time, however, I had become very cautious, believing that at any time things could revert to their former terrible state. Perhaps my father was changing again towards me, but by that time, I was very mistrustful and resentful for past hurts suffered. I was too bitter and remained so — I have to confess that I did not feel like giving my father a chance. It was not a good situation, and no doubt, I suffered under it. I had learned during the really tough times how to manage and manipulate and had found ways to do what I wanted without my father's blessing. Whether I really thought this through or not, I maintained this stance and never returned to a trusting, open relationship with my father.

On March 12, 1938 Hitler marched into Austria. What we saw in the newsreels shown the following week were throngs of people welcoming Hitler and his troops. If it had not been for the German news from Radio Prague, we would not have known of the persecution of the Jewish population of Vienna immediately after the arrival of the German troops, nor of the mass arrests of people loyal to the Austrian Republic. Radio

Prague announced that many of the arrested persons were taken to the concentration camp of Dachau near Munich.

The rejoicing in Germany knew no bounds, reaching a peak a few months later during the *Deutsches Turnerfest* in Breslau, the rally of the German athletes, which was one huge competition, but at the same time a powerful political event. Hitler spoke to the masses. The newsreels and papers showed delegations of Austrians whose female members, with tears streaming down their faces, shook Hitler's hand in gratitude for having been taken home into the Reich. More ominous for those who expected the worst from Hitler, were the unofficial, self-appointed delegations of ethnic German National Socialists from Czechoslovakia and Poland who publicly implored Hitler that theirs be the next countries to be brought back into the Reich. A lot of people who remembered the casual, friendly atmosphere of the *Sängerfest* of two years before, were very anxious about the totally different atmosphere. Everywhere, people were marching to the sound of martial music, everywhere, there were political rallies. The entire city seemed like a huge camp overflowing with people getting ready for war.

There were certainly other signs of preparations for war. A large number of buses from transit systems throughout Germany were withdrawn from their regular service and sent to the Western border with France. No secret was made that along this border, *der Westwall,* the Wall to the West, was being built as an insurmountable protection against the allegedly aggressive French neighbour. In order to replace the buses sent to the Westwall, privately owned excursion buses were turned over to the municipal transit systems and the up-to-now flourishing system of bus excursions came to a complete halt. People became very anxious feeling that something unknown had got into motion and was not going to stop. To add to the latent fear of events to come, private automobiles were requisitioned by the state in large numbers. The exhibition grounds that I passed by streetcar every day on my way to and from school were now filled with row after row of cars. Some of them were returned to their owners, especially after the annexation of the *Sudetenland*. But the huge field was never totally empty of cars, and the increasing or decreasing number of vehicles stored there seemed like a barometer of the political situation and the outlook to the near future.

On October 3, 1938, Hitler marched into the *Sudetenland*, the Czech border region, which was predominantly populated by ethnic Germans. During the preceding weeks, France, Great Britain, and Italy became involved in trying to come to a solution when Hitler no longer made any pretence about his plans to annex all or part of Czechoslovakia. The government in Prague was ready to defend its country, but France did not stand by its treaty obligations to protect Czechoslovakia. The final decision fell during the conference in Munich where the three countries and Germany came to an agreement about turning over the German populated area of Czechoslovakia to Hitler. This happened over the head of the Czech government who was not even invited to attend the conference in Munich. The rape of Czechoslovakia had demonstrated that the western nations were, as yet, not willing to stand up to Hitler and stop his aggression.

When Hitler entered the *Sudetenland*, it seemed like Austria all over again. Radio Prague, however, reported that large numbers of Germans who did not belong to the *Sudetendeutsche Partei* (the Sudetengerman Nazi party) had fled to Prague.

Everything moved at an accelerating pace. Only three weeks before, we had been hiking in the *Riesengebirge* with my father's brother Bernhard and his family. As always, we wanted to cross the border into Czechoslovakia, mainly for the good food there, especially the whipping cream that had become so scarce in Germany, and also for the purchase of some fresh butter, which had been rationed for years. On our way to the Wiesenbaude just across the border, we were confronted with the strong-arm actions of the *SS*. Like all other Germans wanting to cross the border, we were rudely stopped by *SS* men and sent back with some unpleasant remarks about our lack of national pride.

The rejoicing about the return of the Sudetengermans had not reached its end, when another terrible event took place all throughout Germany. It was the early morning of November 10 when I took the streetcar across the city to the airport. The car was full and I stood between many passengers. In the *Scheitnigerstrasse*, I saw that the Jewish shoe store of Christmann had its windows smashed. I wondered whether there had been a break-in during the night. I did not notice anything else unusual other than that the people in the streetcar were uncommonly quiet.

I had a happy reason to go to the airport in Klein-Gandau so early in the morning. I had won a student writers competition and the reward was a flight over the city in a passenger plane. This was my first plane ride and I enjoyed it thoroughly. Above downtown, I noticed that there was a huge cloud of black smoke.

This was a wonderful morning for me and in a happy mood I boarded the streetcar back into town and to my school. On the way, I saw many more broken shop windows and large groups of people standing near them on the sidewalk. I soon realized that these were all Jewish stores, and that something terrible was happening.

When I got to my classroom, the boys talked about the hundreds of smashed-up Jewish stores they had seen on their way to school. They had also heard that during the night, the central railway station had been flooded with Jewish families leaving town. Someone also had seen our Jewish classmate Brinnitzer and his parents rushing to the main station. We all were relieved that he and his family got out of town, but we all secretly worried about where they went and whether their situation would be any different elsewhere.

School was out early, so a few of us walked to the *Schweidnitzerstrasse*, the main shopping street, rather than taking the streetcar home immediately. We always crossed the huge *Schlossplatz* when we took this direction. This was the former parade grounds bordered by the castle, the opera house, a museum, and the city moat. It was a huge expanse of gravel, usually deserted, unless there were political rallies or the occasional circus tent. Today, the square was packed with people all staring in the same direction towards the synagogue, an imposing brick building with a huge cupola that dominated this part of town. The synagogue was on fire, the fire that I had seen from the plane! The flames were shooting high into the air out of the top of the dome, which had slightly tilted to one side.

The people standing around there seemed in a state of happy excitement that I found disgusting. They were all shouting and hollering for the dome to come down. We walked on, but before reaching the eastern end of the square, a roar of a thousand voices rose, as the huge dome crashed to the ground. I will never forget this scene, which reminded me of a celebration of barbarians dancing around a huge bonfire.

Gradually, we became aware that what we saw in our hometown was repeated a thousandfold all across Germany. The radio announced that the action was the angry population's response to the assassination of the Third Secretary Ernst vom Rath at the German Embassy in Paris by a Jewish man. My father thought this seemed impossible, as the action must have been planned and organized well ahead of time.

In the evening, Radio Prague announced that in many places Jewish people were mistreated and that close to 100 persons, mostly Jewish businessmen trying to protect their stores, had been murdered. Later on, the official number was given as approximately 90 persons.

On the following weekend, we went to Waldenburg, where Uncle Hubert had just been released from a three-day confinement in the local prison. The actions of the *Kristallnacht*, as it was called within a couple of days, had been most aggressive in his street, the *Friedländerstrasse* where I was born and had spent my childhood. There were more than six Jewish stores left: the large menswear store of David Korn, neighbour of the Kochs and, a few doors towards the Ring, the beloved Frankenstein toy store, while two houses in the other direction, was Holzer's three-story fashion house. Slightly across the street from our family's house, there were four Jewish businesses in a row: Grünberg's menswear, the Rahmer/Zernick fashion store, the Thomas shoe and leather goods store, and the liqueur distillery of Friedrich/Cohn. Perhaps, the preponderance of Jewish businesses in this section of the street was the reason why the *SA* had been so particularly destructive and wild, as Uncle Hubert described to us. All the stores were smashed up and bolts of clothes were thrown out of the Rahmer store and set on fire. The worst happened in the shoe and leather store of Thomas. The "aroused people," in reality *SA* men in civilian clothes but most of them showing their black jackboots under their long pants, had thrown merchandise from the Thomas store onto the street. Mr. Thomas ran after them and begged them not to destroy the precious articles. He was ready to donate everything to the social welfare department. This was seen by the *SA* as an insult, as no decent German would wish to wear anything from a Jewish store. Mr. Thomas became more and more excited as he was teased and ridiculed by some onlookers. Finally, when a couple of men began to beat him, Uncle Hubert crossed the street, grabbed Mr. Thomas by the hand, dragged him away from the mob, and took him into his own store. Within minutes, the police arrived to arrest Mr.Thomas and my Uncle Hubert.

I had the feeling that the majority of the population seemed to approve of the actions, as anti-Semitism had been fired up by the government to a high pitch for years. Now, the absolute end was reached of any participation of Jewish citizens in the life of Germany. Jewish professionals had already been barred from practicing, and Jews had been removed from the civil service many years ago. Left were Jewish retail businesses, all of them under pressure to sell their properties at ridiculously low price, and then having to pay enormous taxes, which wiped out the meagre profit derived from the forced sale.

How well organized and directed the entire action during the *Kristallnacht* had been became evident — if only to those who dared to think — when one realized that despite the large-scale destruction of Jewish businesses, the major department stores remained untouched. Their Jewish owners were forced to sell their businesses to non-Jewish buyers who, under different, non-Jewish, names, quickly reopened these stores as non-Jewish stores.[7]

Immediately after the *Kristallnacht*, Jewish citizens were completely segregated. They were evicted from their homes and moved into overcrowded *Judenhäuser*, Jew-houses, in the area of the old ghetto along the *Wallstrasse* near the *Karlsplatz*. They were forced to wear the yellow Star

---

7   Among the Breslau department stores, Wertheim became AWG; Barasch was renamed Münstermann & Haedecke; Bielschowski was called Georg Widersum, and so on.

of David on their coats. For their shopping they were severely restricted to a few designated stores accessible for them at certain hours only. They were not allowed to have a radio, or attend concerts, theatres, or picture shows. By law, Jews had to carry an additional first name, Isaac for men and Sarah for women. In their ID cards as well as in their passports, the capital letter J for *Jude* was prominently printed across the front page. They were not allowed to enter public swimming pools, sit on park benches, or use public transportation, taxis, or washrooms. All restaurants and cafés prominently displayed signs announcing *Juden unerwünscht*, Jews not wanted.

Those who could, left Germany. Many, though, did not have any connections to someone in another country, were too old or too ill to emigrate, or, if they were still young enough to do so, felt they needed to stay in order to look after their elderly parents.

While in Breslau we did not know anybody personally who was Jewish — in our part of the city there were no Jews — we were very well acquainted or even friends with some Jewish families in Waldenburg, some contacts going back to the generation of my grandfather. So we were intimately aware of how the life of Jewish citizens was full of daily humiliations, deprivations, and increasing fear for safety and life. This awareness grew in reaction to the relentless barrage of propaganda. My parents and I were very tired of Nazi propaganda and resented its lies and pretences. We began to feel more and more isolated, sensing that the vast majority of people in Germany were of a different mindset, many being almost drunk with pride in this new Germany of Hitler. Perhaps there were more who thought like us, but there was no way to find out for fear of talking to the wrong person and then being reported to the authorities.

My father was deeply grateful to fate that he had managed to stay in the Army since 1937 as this put his by now hated party membership in "neutral." As yet, Hitler had not done away with some symbols of the old *Reichswehr*, the army of the Weimar Republic, which, according to the Weimar constitution, was not permitted to be connected to any party, but only obeyed the German president. After 1935, however, the *Wehrmacht*, as the German Army was now called, fulfilled without exception Hitler's orders. Only the Nazi salute, the raised right arm, was not yet introduced to *Wehrmacht* (army), *Luftwaffe* (air force), and *Marine* (navy). Neither were their members permitted to wear Nazi insignia like the party badge indicating membership in the NSDAP, or attend party functions and rallies in uniform.[8] For my father, this meant that he no longer could be identified as a party member; he was also absolved from any duties to be expected from a member of the party.

Actually, my father seemed to feel better than for a long time, although his chronic stomach condition, which he had been afflicted with since his return from World War I, continued unabated. He never looked well and was always underweight, as he had to be extremely careful with his diet. He went to see numerous specialists in other cities, received costly, often very powerful, and possibly harmful medications that had unpleasant side effects. Nothing helped. He had disappointments in many ways throughout his life, which no doubt negatively affected his physical health. On the other hand, the chronic stomach condition also took a heavy toll on his outlook towards his future. How pessimistic his poor health had made him while he was still a young man, I realized after finding a letter he had written to my mother, at that time his wife-to-be. He was praying, he wrote, that God may grant them just a few years of happiness together before his poor health would end his life prematurely.

In the media and in school, the propaganda against the rump of the Czechoslovak Republic — the *Sudetenland* had been annexed by Hitler — continued unabated. We had more and more young teachers, trained in the Nazi ideology, who overwhelmed us with their indoctrination. However, there were indications that they achieved the opposite of what they intended. There was a gradual, imperceptible resistance amongst many in our class, never expressed towards the teacher, but freely discussed after class. As the years went on, especially during the war, this attitude became not only more pronounced, it became the trademark of our class where only one student was an open follower of Hitler. My high school class became a source of support and strength for me, and to this day I cannot fathom why our class was like this, while the students in the parallel class of the same grade were almost without exception Nazi adherents.

Our negative attitude towards the party and the Third Reich received a boost when weeks of tension and aggressive gestures towards Czechoslovakia reached their climax with the occupation of the rest of Czechoslovakia on March 15, 1939. Only eight hours after the first German troops crossed the border, Hitler arrived triumphantly in Prague and took up residence at its castle that until the day before had been the seat of the Czech president. From the castle, Hitler proclaimed the dissolution of Czechoslovakia and its new status of *Reichsprotektorat Böhmen und Mähren.* Again, there was boundless jubilation in Germany. There were reports that in many towns, even in Prague, the German troops had been received with flowers by the Czech population. We could

---

8   Only the *Waffen SS,* the military units of the SS, practiced the Hitler salute, wore Nazi insignia and altogether functioned like a branch of the Nazi party.

neither confirm nor dispute this any longer, as the night before, Radio Prague had for the very last time, broadcast its German news report, the one which had been a lifeline for us since the advent of the Third Reich.

A few days later, my parents and I went to the *Schlosscafé*, our favourite restaurant in the centre of town across from the opera house. At that time, I was already quite proficient in French, as was my father. We both loved to peruse the Paris daily *Le Matin*, which was available at the café. It was in this paper that I discovered a photograph which was to become famous and still can be found in many history books. It showed the Czech people of Prague lining one of the main shopping streets and watching the German troops enter their city. The faces of the people are desperate, angry, hateful, sad, and tears are streaming down the cheeks of men and women. This is how the people of Prague received the German soldiers.

During this summer, we had a delightful little experience in the *Schlosscafé* while sitting at the corner window of the second floor. From where we sat, we had a commanding view of two streets, the heavy automobile and streetcar traffic, the streams of passers-by and, on winter evenings, the profuse neon advertising. On this particular day, we suddenly heard a commotion on the street when people suddenly flooded across the intersection and brought streetcars and automobiles to a complete halt. In the middle of the intersection, someone had climbed on top of an automobile, took on a dramatic pose, and began to sing! My mother immediately recognized the artist who had just crossed the street from his hotel to the opera house, probably for a rehearsal. The artist was the famous and immensely popular Polish tenor Jan Kiepura. He was really no longer welcome in the Third Reich, but still appeared in opera roles. His real popularity, though, was derived from the operettas of Lehár and other composers which he sang with a powerful, but tender voice and much emotion. His elegant Hungarian-born wife Martha Eggert was often his partner and their duets were loved by people across Europe. Regardless of what the Party thought of them, Jan Kiepura and Martha Eggert were still the darlings of Breslau, as the enthusiastic crowd on the street demonstrated.

This was a beautiful summer, although the mood in the country was sombre. Everybody expected war, even though the propaganda and those who spouted it claimed differently. In school, some of the young teachers still celebrated the disappearance of Czechoslovakia from the map of Europe. When someone asked what would happen to the Czechs, one teacher grandly claimed that they would be *aufgesogen*, absorbed (a much less innocuous word in English). He also showed us the current issue of a monthly party bulletin designed to indoctrinate its members (it could not be bought at newsstands). The entire issue was dedicated to the topic of acquiring additional lands for Germany. As if to support future claims, areas which had either once belonged to one or the other of the German states prior to Bismarck, or which had a racially related population like Holland, the Flemish part of Belgium, and many other countries or areas close to the German borders, were seen as lands destined to become part of the future, much enlarged *Grossdeutsche Reich*. I do remember distinctly how one naive teacher tried to rouse our enthusiasm for the glorious future of our country, but how almost the entire class remained coldly silent.

During this summer, the stress on youth activities under the party was de-emphasized. The Saturday, until now exclusively devoted to *Hitlerjugend* activities, became a regular school day again. It seemed that the schools and their teachers were now sufficiently indoctrinated to be entrusted with the task hitherto the responsibility of the *Hitlerjugend*. I was very happy about this development, as I had long hated spending time in uniform for an entire Saturday.

We crossed the former German-Czech border on several Sundays, but things were not the same in the *Sudetenland*, compared to the times when this area was part of Czechoslovakia. Every town and village was full of slogans, flags, and swastikas. This was even more noticeable to us when we drove through Reichenberg, now the capital of the *Sudetenland*. We noticed that the former German high school was now the seat of the party and its leader. Considering that this building formerly dedicated to the education of children of German citizens of Czechoslovakia now served as the headquarters of the Nazi party made us laugh about the past propaganda about the oppression the Sudetengermans had experienced while under the Czech yoke.

On August 7, 1939 I reached my 14th birthday and was being transferred from the *Jungvolk* for the 10 to 14 year olds to the *Hitlerjugend* for those between the ages of 14 and 18. The transfer was to be effective as of September 1, supposedly a day of honour for me. It became an altogether memorable day for very different reasons!

War was coming. Of that, at least in our family and among my parents' friends, everybody was certain. And everybody in that group freely stated that it was not Poland, France, and England that were steering Europe towards war, but Hitler, with his ever increasing demands on Poland for concessions on Danzig and the Polish Corridor.[9]

---

9   The Polish Corridor was the strip of land in Western Poland consisting of the former German provinces of Posen and Westpreussen that had to be ceded to Poland in 1919 in accordance with the Treaty of Versailles. The object of this change was to give Poland access to the Baltic sea.

There had been a brief outburst of surprise and relief by some when the treaty between Germany and the Soviet Union was signed in Moscow on August 23. Once more, Hitler's propaganda machine demonstrated its utter flexibility and effectiveness. Overnight, the Soviet Union, which until the day before had been the epitome of the Jewish-Bolshevist conspiracy to conquer the world, turned from Germany's arch-enemy to Germany's trading partner and peaceful friend. Gone were the posters that had flooded Germany with messages about the subhuman nature of the people of the Soviet Union. These were replaced by artists, especially musicians and ballet and folk dancers who appeared on German stages within weeks of the conclusion of the treaty.

On August 27, the last Sunday of the month, we went on an outing by car with the Körners. They belonged to the fortunate car owners who still needed their vehicle for business purposes. Owners like us had to turn their car, used only for pleasure, over to the state — another sign of the war being imminent.

The weather was glorious, a late summer day, and the countryside with the harvest in full swing looked beautiful. We did not travel to the mountains, but through the plains around Breslau and ended up near the little resort town of Obernigk (since 1945 Oborniki Śląskie). On its outskirts, we had a wonderful meal in the garden of a country inn, while on the highway alongside the garden, military traffic passed by without interruption.

We were the only guests in the inn's pretty garden. We should have been happy, and in a way we were. We sensed, though, and spoke about it, that such a day would not return for a long time. My father said "this will be the last Sunday where we still have peace."

On the last day of August, we had a prolonged propaganda rally in school. Our director appeared in party uniform, our favourite teacher in *SA* uniform, and several of the older teachers in their World War I officers' uniforms. Speeches condemned Poland for her anti-German actions, including the occupation of the broadcast house in Gleiwitz (since 1945 Gliwice), a phoney accusation based, as it turned out later, on a German action using *SS* men in Polish uniforms to seek a *casus belli*, a cause for war.

When we returned to the classroom, our homeroom teacher seemed very upset and deeply moved. He advised us that our former music teacher, Mr. Neumann, who had been replaced with a lady teacher from Vienna a year ago, had, together with his wife, committed suicide a few days ago. Mr. Neumann, a true musician by heart and soul, a man of such good nature that we never dared or found it necessary to tease him, had been married to a Jewish woman and therefore was fired from his job when he refused to dissolve his marriage to a Jew.

I was very upset. At the end of school, I jumped on my bike and pedaled furiously, not towards home, but to the southern edge of town and into the countryside towards the *Zobten* (since 1945 Ślęża), the mythical mountain of Silesia, venerated by Slavs and Germans alike for thousands of years. Ever since we had moved to Breslau, I not only missed Waldenburg and my relatives, especially my Grandmother Koch, but I also longed for the mountains. Whenever I felt homesick for them, I would climb into our attic from where, on clear days, I could see the outline of this mountain, or I would take my bike and cycle as closely to the *Zobten* as time would permit.

So did I cycle southwards and out of town on this day, using the bicycle path running parallel to the highway, getting closer and closer to the mythical mountain. The weather was beautiful, but it was not a peaceful day. I was upset and there was no peace in my heart. On the highway next to me, but in the opposite direction, there was an endless caravan of army vehicles, heavy trucks, tanks, and supply vehicles moving towards the Polish border.

Eventually, I turned around and made my way home. My mother received me in a state of panic, as she was terribly worried about me. In my state of mind, I had totally forgotten to phone and tell her that I would not be home until later in the afternoon.

"How could you be so irresponsible and ride your bike on the highway on a day like this! Don't you realize that we might have war soon," she said with tears in her eyes.

Next day, the radio announced that German troops had crossed the border into Poland in the early hours of the morning.

* * * * *

Part III
The War Years

T hrough his countless criminal actions, the invasions of more than half
of Europe's nations, the killing of millions, the genocide of the Jews of
Europe, and the ruthless war, the Germans, with few exceptions, followed
their "Führer" to the bitter end in 1945.

When he committed suicide on April 30, 1945, twelve years after his ascent
to power, Hitler left a Germany behind that had sunk to the point of physical,
political, economical, and moral destruction.

7

1939
Hitler's First Victims

The destruction of Poland

On September 1, 1939 the German Army crossed the Eastern border into Poland after weeks of hectic diplomatic activities that included the surprise of a treaty of friendship between Germany and the Soviet Union.[1] The Polish forces resisted fiercely, but with their antiquated equipment could not stop the rapid advance of the German armies. In keeping with their treaty obligations to Poland, England and France declared war on Germany on September 3. After a prolonged battle at the River Bzura, German forces encircled the Polish capital on September 16, but Warsaw only surrendered on September 27, after heavy air raids and bombardments by the German air force that showed no regard for protecting civilian lives. In the meantime, Soviet forces had entered Eastern Poland on September 17. Soon after, Soviet and German troops met at the River Bug. The last resistance of Polish soldiers ceased and on October 1, the war in Poland was over.

At the Western Front, heavily fortified by both parties through the French Maginot Line and the German Westwall, there was no activity except for a few insignificant skirmishes along the border. Poor weather conditions forced Hitler to cancel the invasion of France planned for November 10. On November 30,

---

1   The treaty also provided for an agreement on the division of Eastern Europe between Hitler and Stalin.

the Soviet Union attacked Finland, which defended itself heroically during the infamous "winter war." Naval activities in the North Atlantic resulted in the sinking of the liner Athenia by a German U-boat with a loss of 1,400 lives, and of the British aircraft carrier Courageous with the loss of over 500 lives. This was the beginning of naval activity that caused increasingly severe military and civilian losses on the Atlantic.

* * *

Walking down the hall past the bathroom, I had seen my father shaving while he listened to the 7 a.m. news through the open door. An agitated voice reported that, overnight, a group of Polish soldiers had crossed the Polish-German border and attacked the studio building of the broadcasting station in Gleiwitz (since 1945 Gliwice). With razor and towel in his hand, my father appeared in the dining room, exclaiming "Are we supposed to believe that!"[2] I knew the answer he had on his mind: "Hitler needs a final reason for starting a war."

There had been an endless stream of news of how Poland and the western powers were getting ready for war, while Hitler was praised for trying to maintain peace. But in early August, registration of all males between 14 and 70 had been proclaimed. Hitler had demanded the Free State of Danzig (since 1945 Gdańsk) and part of Polish West-Prussia or, at least a corridor through this province for access to East Prussia. We also heard that Poland, Russia, Great Britain, and Holland were mobilizing their armed forces and that the French government had begun evacuating 16,000 children from Paris.

My father was right. Hardly was the report about the attack on the Gleiwitz station finished when the announcement came over the air, that at 4:45 a.m., German troops had smashed the border gates and had entered Poland. This was September 1, an ordinary workday. As always, I took the streetcar to school. There was no excitement on the streetcar, but at school we were called for a short assembly in the schoolyard. The swastika flag was raised, our principal gave a short speech, and we were sent home, as the school had been designated to accommodate units of the Wehrmacht. On the way home, I realized how the city was suddenly changing. Swastika flags appeared everywhere above businesses and on apartment buildings. The public address system, long held at the ready since its inception several years earlier, blared news and directives to the populace all across town. The already proclaimed blackout was rigidly

---

2   "Soll man das glauben!"

enforced because of the expected air raids by the Polish air force. Heads of households were ordered to pick up their ration cards. All travel other than for military or purposes or common welfare was officially discouraged. At noon, Hitler's speech before the *Reichstag* was broadcast through the public address system and his voice boomed all over Breslau.

By Saturday, the majority of the people seemed to have overcome the first shock of realizing that the country was at war. There were no air raids reported from anywhere and the blackout was hardly noticed during the warm evenings of late summer. When I went shopping with my mother on Saturday, the people in the stores, both customers and sales staff, were highly excited. I think there was relief that there had been no air raids, and that the resistance offered by the Poles had been overcome quickly. Looking back, this was the beginning of at least three years of constant jubilation by the majority of the people celebrating the invincible German forces and the unlimited trust in Hitler's genius and leadership.

On Sunday, September 3, when I felt the oppressive heat in the silence of midday, the announcement came over the radio that Great Britain had entered the war, as Germany had not responded to her ultimatum to pull her troops out of Poland. At suppertime, the French announcement of entering the war followed. "The next world war has begun," was my father's comment.

Ration cards were distributed, which caused only a ripple of nervousness, as people realized that the rations actually provided for more food than a family could consume. Whatever was considered a little "special" such as oranges, bananas, frozen foods (just introduced in Germany a few months before) disappeared overnight. Chocolate and coffee were quite severely rationed. It seemed patriotic, though, to do with less, when it came to such luxury items, and if people missed these little pleasures of everyday life, nobody dared to complain about their absence.

The morale of the population seemed extraordinarily high except among those who had lost a father, a son, or a relative in battle. The war was going extremely well and the exalted mood of the masses reflected the relief that Polish bombs had not fallen on German cities, as had been feared by many, and that not one enemy soldier had stepped on German soil. There was definite unease, however, about the cordial rapprochement between Hitler and Stalin after the years of demonizing the Soviet Union and Bolshevism. I remember that I stared at the large photo in the *Berliner Illustrierte*, showing a Soviet officer in a leather coat with a cigarette held between his fingers in a way unknown amongst Germans, and pointing with the other hand to a large map, marked with the redefined border between Germany and the Soviet Union. The propaganda went into high gear: Pictures in the papers and the newsreels showed Russian trains arriving at Przemyśl on the new eastern border loaded with grain for Germany, and long rows of tank cars carrying oil from the Soviet Union alleviating any worry about Germany's well-known shortage of oil. There was a daily ration of photos and film clips of street scenes in Moscow, and of cultural events, symphony concerts, ballet and opera performances in Russia, which made me (and no doubt others) wonder about the German propaganda, which had previously presented such a one-sided image of the Soviet Union that was characterized by pervasive poverty, absence of anything considered *Kultur* (culture), and streets filled with people in rags. As if to confirm the new image of Russia – hardly anybody spoke of "the Soviet Union" – there was a flood of "cultural ambassadors" from the former Bolshevik hell: theatre groups, ballet groups, folk dance ensembles, and more attractions that appeared even in the small cities. I was learning new things all the time and kept wondering about "the other side." Today, I ask myself how much the local German authorities were ordered to give in to the foreigners. On the marquee of the Palast Theater in Waldenburg appeared not only the name of the *Gaidanoff Music and Dance Ensemble* from Moscow, but also an even larger banner announcing an "Evening of German-Soviet friendship" which sounded grammatically correct but, in its meaning, had little credibility. After the war, German-Soviet friendship was celebrated in East Germany (later the German Democratic Republic) with the identical slogan.

On August 7, I had turned 14. A week later, I was transferred from the *Jungvolk* to compulsory attendance in the *Hitlerjugend*. Our leaders, often barely a year or two older than we, had a hard time to fall in line with the official propaganda and were often laughed at when they praised our friend the Soviet Union as they were ordered to do in strict adherence to the party line. This was one of the low points in the history of the propaganda machine of the Third Reich.

There was renewed jubilation in the media and among a lot of people when Warsaw surrendered. Papers and newsreels had shown the relentless attacks of German dive bombers that destroyed large parts of Warsaw. The newsreels usually were accompanied by applause from the audience in the theatre or, I am ashamed to say, by schoolboys. Now that Warsaw was in German hands, people could see the destruction of entire housing districts, but no one raised any questions about what might have happened to the civilian population. Photographs taken from the air showed the incredible density of workers' housing and, in the better-class districts, the less dense but much higher blocks of flats. In contrast to Germany, where the height of buildings was strictly regulated, in Russian Poland, apartment buildings had no height restrictions. I was intrigued when I saw rows of seven- and eight-story-high apartment buildings, many of them destroyed altogether or collapsing, while those still intact betrayed a great deal of elegance. Warsaw was described as a very densely populated city and the losses of life must have been considerable. In Warsaw, Hitler had started the purposeful terrorizing through air raids of civilians, old people, women, and children, for which Germany was to suffer a deadly revenge.

When hostilities in Poland had ended, extra rations of coffee and chocolates were distributed and, for a few weeks, the blackout was called off. I still remember how I cherished the return of the brilliantly lit main shopping streets in Breslau in the evening, with all the neon signs, the fully lit streetcars and buses. The effect on one's mood was astonishing. Lighted windows and streets, and neon signs now meant peace, while the blackout had reinforced the sense of war, fear, and ultimately, hopelessness.

After the end of the Polish campaign, school days also returned to normal. Our school was vacated by the Wehrmacht and we returned to regular morning school hours. There was more indoctrination than ever, very much so, and in every classroom hung a large map of Europe, which showed where German troops had taken position and what parts of the continent were being integrated into the German Reich or into Germany's sphere of influence in the East. As a regular routine, the entire school attended movies at least once a month, always films of patriotic content that were preceded by a double dose of two newsreels. I think some of our teachers had a truly difficult time dealing with their divided feelings about the war without showing this too much. Others spent large parts of instruction time talking about the war, and related political issues. If they were veterans of World War I, they loved to reminisce about their past wartime experiences.

There were a couple of teachers who almost embarrassed us with their childish delight about Germany's successes. At times, while praising our military progress, they were literally jumping up and down like little children. Other teachers began to talk about the Jewish population of Poland in the most degrading terms. At least in the eastern provinces of Germany, Poles had never been popular, nor were they ever respected. Now, Poland was described as consisting of a tiny decadent upper-class of aristocrats, officers, and artists, while the vast majority were uneducated, not very intelligent, not even intelligent-looking. The image of the Poles, indeed soon of all Slavic people as dumb, ugly, racially inferior, and near subhuman, was being spread throughout Germany.

In peacetime, we had traveled a bit into Poland, to cities such as Ostrowo, Kalisz, and others, and while these cities were not as well-built and well-kept as German cities, I had discovered interesting and beautiful buildings and districts while there. Nothing of that was now shown in German papers or newsreels that portrayed only decay, ugliness, and primitivism.

Whatever the official German media reported about the poverty and decay of Poland, one of the new developments was the sight of German soldiers coming home from Poland on leave. I remember seeing them while waiting for my streetcar transfer in front of the main railway station, where army trains discharged large numbers of army personnel every hour. These soldiers happily started their leave loaded with bolts of cloth, radios, plucked geese and chicken, and sometimes even sewing machines. This was not a very dignified sight, but the authorities did nothing to stop it. The general population did not seem to care. All of a sudden, quietly permitted by the government, an underground economy sprang up that offered clothing material, shoes, coffee, chocolates, tinned fruit from America, and all sorts of other delicacies, even Danish sweet cream, something people had not seen since the good old days before World War I.

This flood of looted stuff lasted for maybe two or three weeks. Then, it seemed Poland had been emptied of its treasures.[3]

Towards the end of September, my father had been transferred to Kattowitz (from 1921 to 1939 and since 1945 Katowice), the capital of *Ostoberschlesien* (Górny Śląsk / Polish Upper Silesia). It was ironic that my father had experienced the end of World War I while stationed in Kattowitz; and now, he would find himself after his first transfer during World War II, once more in this not unpleasant city — in Polish times (after World War I) it was called "Little Paris." He did not come home on leave until Christmas. He had written some letters and postcards which, however, did not seem to say very much.

We celebrated Christmas quite happily until Boxing Day when a friend of my father, who had been stationed in Kattowitz at an earlier time, came to visit us with his family. I remember that sometime during the afternoon, he asked his wife to take their two little girls to my room so that they could play. Then he made my father close the door to the hall and began to relate what he had witnessed in Kattowitz, which he had entered with the first German troops. Right from the beginning of the occupation, the SS seemed to be everywhere in an organized way, driving the Jewish population (that belonged to the more prosperous segment of the city) out of their apartments. SS[4] soldiers mistreated the

---

3   There was to be a repeat after the victory over France in 1940.

4   Before the war, *SS* military units, the so-called *Waffen SS*, had been created. They were elite troops, most feared in the Eastern occupied countries for their involvement in genocide.

Jews with fists and gun butts and spread terror among the families when some of the SS men grabbed some small children and killed them in front of their terrified parents. Our friend said he had not slept for weeks after his stay in Kattowitz and could never banish the heart-wrenching screams of the mothers from his mind. My father also was very agitated. When he had arrived in Kattowitz a few weeks later, the SS units had completed their mission. Still, he was told stories of cruelty and murder by Polish people he had known since his stay in the city at the end of World War I.

This was the first time we had heard about the excesses of the SS in Poland, initially directed against the Jewish population, but soon extending to the Polish population in general and, eventually, covering all of Eastern Europe. This Christmas, we sensed that a frightening, unstoppable, immoral power had entered our lives and the lives of all Germans.

* * * * *

8 | 1940
The Great Surrender

Denmark, Norway, Holland, Belgium, Luxembourg, and France surrender. Lithuania, Latvia, Estonia, and Albania disappear from the Map of Europe.

The English still called it "the Phoney War," at least up to the early months of 1940. There was no military activity wherever German soldiers stood face to face with the enemy. Even though more countries had entered the war against Germany, only small Finland fought bitter battles against the Soviet armies.

On April 9, Hitler took his war to Scandinavia with the German occupation of Denmark and the concurrent landing of German troops at Narvik in Norway on the same day. On June 9, Norway capitulated.

On May 10, Hitler began his assault on the Western Front. By June 22, Holland, Belgium, Luxembourg, and the greater part of France were firmly in German hands. Previously, on June 4, Hitler's armies had forced the British expeditionary force of 370,000 men to retreat from northern France to England. Hitler's fame as strategic genius and invincible commander was established. His popularity among the German people reached new heights. This was the beginning of the widespread belief that Hitler, and under his leadership Germany, would soon rule Europe.

In July, within the prior agreement between Hitler and Stalin, the Soviet Union annexed the three Baltic states of Lithuania, Latvia, and Estonia.

After the Soviet Union also annexed parts of eastern Romania and King Carol II fled into exile, German troops rapidly moved down the Danube and occupied the Romanian capital Bucharest on October 12. Soon after, the fascist regime of Marshal Antonescu was installed.

Germany's ally Italy, which had entered the war during the last stages of Hitler's campaign in France, suddenly found itself fighting British units in its North African colonies. It also lost Ethiopia. As if to gather fame under any circumstances, Italy occupied Albania and invaded Greece at the end of October, only to fail miserably, even losing part of the recently annexed Albania.

People in Germany looked back on the year 1940 as a time of not only many splendid victories, but of relative ease and comfort, and relatively little loss of human lives. Besides, for the last six months of the year, military activities had moved to the periphery, to Romania and to the Southern Balkans. Without prolonged, huge, or bloody battles, but rather through Hitler's new rapid mobile warfare strategy, through diplomatic manoeuvres, and fomenting unrest in some neutral countries, the map of Europe changed a great deal during that year.

Before the end of 1940, it became clear that Europe had only one master, Hitler and, at least for the time being restricted to the East, another master in Joseph Stalin. Italy's Benito Mussolini played the role of only a minor master by the grace of Hitler.

* * *

On New Years Day, my father let me go to Waldenburg to spend a week with my Grandmother Koch. Deep winter had descended on Silesia; I took my skis along. The streets of Waldenburg were almost impassable; there was much more snow than in Breslau, and it was very cold. Indeed, it was too cold for going into the hills around town with my skis.

There had never been many cars in the streets of Waldenburg, but always a considerable number of horse-drawn coal wagons that loudly clattered over the cobblestones. Together with the clanking of the iron brake handles, they created an unforgettable sound. Now, in the deep snow, these carts had their wheels placed on iron sled-runners on which the heavy carts would glide silently along the streets. Almost as silently moved the streetcars that normally made quite a racket. The ubiquitous piles of snow muffled the voices of the people shuffling along the crowded sidewalks. It was an altogether cozy, comforting mood which took hold of one's soul, and I was happy simply being on the street and among people. War seemed far away, until I saw groups of snow shovelers on the busiest square of the city.

The city had never employed motorized snow cleaners. At best, there were a few horse-drawn snowploughs, but generally the streets were cleaned by individual men. These men, mostly strong and fairly young, had all been drafted into the army. They were replaced by a small group of the first French prisoners of war who looked absolutely miserable in their thin winter coats made of light cloth without high collars. As unsuitable for the raw Silesian winter was the rest of their uniform, especially the typical French képi which gave no protection to the ears. The men used their scarves for warming their ears instead of as protection of their neck from the swirling snow and the wind that blew under their collars. French soldiers still wore old-fashioned puttees around their legs above laced leather boots. Altogether, their drawn, red faces, hunched shoulders, and restless moving about showed how much the bitter Silesian cold, which likely they had never experienced in their lives, affected them. Their work seemed to produce few results, and with their shovels they tried in vain to move the huge amounts of snow that obviously called for snowploughs rather than human muscle power.

I observed another, much more upsetting scene on the Ring. There, I discovered a group of women shovelling snow, dressed in ordinary winter coats as if they were going shopping, some of them even wearing hats. They seemed to be under guard of an auxiliary policeman in *SA* uniform. This rather incongruous picture was quickly explained, when I discovered in horror that all these women wore the Star of David and were engaged in forced labour under these terribly hard conditions. As I heard from my Uncle Hubert, there were not many Jews left in town. Quite a few had managed to leave Germany, others had been taken to concentration camps. The remaining men were assigned to work in factories, while their wives were forced to clean the streets or, now in winter, remove the snow.[1]

When I told Uncle Hubert what I had observed, he confided to me that a few days ago, he had taken a thermos bottle of hot tea and a pair of gloves to one of the women, Mrs. K., an Orthodox Jew he knew well. But the policeman ordered my uncle not to approach and talk to any of the women. Neither did my uncle succeed in persuading the police guard to give these items to Mrs. K. Instead, my uncle was taken to the police headquarters the same morning, interrogated, and sent home with a stern warning. When, during the following winter of 1941/1942, my uncle attempted again to bring some comfort to the Jewish women, he was taken to the near concentration camp Gross Rosen (since 1945 Rogożnica). Released after a couple of days, he was sternly warned that

---

1   As snow shovellers these poor women were totally ineffectual; they were weak and would stop very often to warm their hands in their pockets. It was obvious that the primary objective was not the removal of snow but the humiliation and torture of these Jewish women.

the next time, he would not get away that easily. My uncle would be interrogated in the police headquarters several times during the remaining war years, but never taken to Gross Rosen again. Mrs. B., however, a woman in the rag-collecting business and well-known for her garrulous nature, was kept in Gross Rosen more than once for a few days. Unfortunately, upon returning to her hometown, she spread the word of how terrible the conditions were in the Gross Rosen camp and was promptly returned there. Mrs. B. became the talk of the town. Some people pitied her, others thought she deserved what she got. Learning about Mrs. B.'s unfortunate fate, however, the entire town had become aware of the existence of the Gross Rosen concentration camp and what went on there.

Unexpectedly, I had an extended holiday. The snowfall continued so heavily that on the day I was to return home and start school again, the trains did not run, something that had never happened before. In the stores, there was no milk, and restaurants ran out of the food supplies required to keep their menu filled. I did not mind this extra holiday at all, but did not escape the rather subdued mood in town. Somehow, people thought, this would not have happened, had such harsh weather attacked the city in peacetime.

When I finally returned home, another surprise awaited me: there was a severe shortage of coal in Breslau. Although the next coal mines — in Waldenburg — were only 70 kilometres away, no coal for civilian purposes reached the provincial capital. Our family was especially hard hit, as we had not made provisions for heating our flat during the winter, as we had normally done in past years. This winter, we had been certain to move to a different flat with central heating. But this move did not materialize. So when I entered our flat after my unexpected prolonged holiday, I found my mother wearing a heavy sweater, washing dishes in a dishpan on a kitchen chair in the living room. The door to the adjoining music room had been closed off with a heavy blanket. Except for the living room, the entire flat was ice cold.

From now on and for the duration of the war, our flat, which had never been particularly cozy in wintertime, even though my parents had always been generous with the use of coal, would never be well heated. We did manage to get through the winter, as my uncles still had their trucks running to bring supplies to their stores in Waldenburg. As well established merchants, they had little trouble to get at least a modest supply of coal and send it by their trucks to us in Breslau. In order to avoid drawing the attention of the people living in the adjoining houses, the coal was unloaded after darkness,.

The cold weather finally broke in early February; the snow began to melt away. Life seemed to return to near normal. People were in a good mood. There was no news about battles or significant engagements with enemy troops, and the papers showed only occasionally the obituary of a soldier.

The blackout had been reintroduced before Christmas, but otherwise, entertainment like in peacetime returned in full force. Public dancing was permitted again, and the dancing establishments were overflowing with soldiers and their girlfriends. Breslau's large variety theatres and music halls even expanded their programs through matinees to accommodate the growing audiences, which consisted mainly of soldiers. I was one of the beneficiaries, as my father had no objection against my attending the afternoon shows. This was a new world for me, as with the *Liebich Theater*, Breslau had one of the five top variety theatres in Germany.

During the next couple of years, I saw the best acts of ballet, dance orchestras, singers, animal acts, clowns, and stand-up comics. Only if one had an opportunity to attend shows in one of these top-flight theatres would one realize that the government had eased up on the condemnation of jazz and other types of entertainment hitherto considered as foreign and decadent. Such entertainment had always been popular and it was never fully forbidden. A band like Bernhard Etté was permitted to play in the nightclub of the *Eden Hotel* in Berlin, but generally had not been permitted to appear elsewhere in Germany. All of a sudden though, big time entertainment was brought into the limelight to build up the morale of the people, especially the soldiers. So, for the first time, the huge show band of Bernhard Ette (patriotically, the "é" had been dropped in favour of the plain "e") appeared at the Liebich Theatre with three jazz singers, a male singing quartet, and a dancing duo. Only years after the war and exposure to American music did I realize that Bernhard Ette's band was, in appearance, size, type of music, and stage entertainment, an exact copy of the big bands popular at that time in the United States.

There was also the Argentinian tango orchestra of Eduardo Bianco and the pseudo-Russian Ballett of Tamara Beck, whose repertoire ranged from light classical to jazz. These were events in my life as a teenager, and if they filled the stages of the big cities, they were still somewhat kept away from the majority of Germans. What instead was offered to them, loudly, heartily, and patriotically, was the Sunday afternoon *Wunschkonzert,* entertainment mixed with a large dose of propaganda and morale building, provided by the best orchestras of Germany, the most popular singers and entertainers, all of whom donated their artist's fees to the *Winterhilfe,* the official collection for the needy. Everyone suspected that the monies collected would now go to financing the war, as there were really no needy people anymore. Literally everybody was working, even those who would have preferred to be idle, but were not given a chance by the state to avoid work. It was well known that shiftless people avoiding work or not trying to hold on to a job would likely end in a concentration camp where they would be forced to do hard labour.

We did not get out of town as much as in peacetime, since use of automobiles for pleasure was prohibited. Not traveling around the Silesian countryside any longer, we never saw but only heard of the numerous armaments plants, chemical plants, and other war-based industries that sprang up everywhere, mostly in up-to-now purely rural areas. Naturally, not much was said about this in the press. Only the huge synthetic oil plant being built in Waldenburg was celebrated in the press as proof that Germany could be independent of its former oil suppliers. Being close to downtown, this huge construction project could not be hidden from the local population. Besides, once completed and in operation, the plant's permanent stench was a constant reminder of its existence. Neither could the local population ignore the swarms of forced labourers who were employed in the new plant and other industries. Nobody could fail to recognize them by their shabby clothing and the blue on yellow letter "P" (for Polish), or the white on blue "OST" for other Eastern European nationalities, sewn to their coats.

In Breslau, at that time at least, the presence of forced labourers was hardly noticeable, as they were kept in camps on the outskirts of the city. The German workforce had increased enormously. Men, who were not drafted, and especially women, were frequently commandeered from their established jobs in offices, stores, and public services to do factory work which, in contrast to their past jobs, was considered *kriegswichtig* — vital for the war effort. Government departments were consolidated. Stores and shops seemed denuded of sales personnel. Streetcars were all of a sudden overcrowded with women from young age to their late 50s, dressed in overalls or bulky pants (up to now described by the Nazi party as "undignified for a German woman"). This new type of citizen seemed now to dominate the streets on a 24 hour a day basis, as armaments plants and other factories operated 24 hours around the clock. So the streetcars were always full and except for old people, wounded soldiers and some older women, passengers hardly ever got a seat. With nearly always two per motorcar, trailer cars were in short supply. Streetcars pulled the oldest trailer cars that were re-commissioned after having almost been forgotten in some streetcar barn.

The seats were removed from the trailer cars so that people could be packed into the cars like sardines. Smoking was forbidden in streetcars and trailers without seats, as smoking passengers, being constantly swayed by the moving cars, ended up burning holes into the coats of persons standing next to them.

This was the period where by government decree, millions of women invaded traditionally male occupations. Up to now, Hitler had declared the major role of the German woman to be mother, wife, and homemaker. Now, with the draft and specialized armament industries requiring millions of males, the acute shortage of male workers could only be alleviated by declaring work outside the home a patriotic duty for all women. Without exception, on trains and streetcars, ticket takers were now women — towards the end of the war, there were also female "motormen." Most of the letter carriers and other post office staff, street cleaners, and other municipal service personnel were now all female. The bulk of wartime employed women, however, did hard work in factories and in heavy industry. The Nazi propaganda celebrated their war effort and made heroines out of women workers who were pictured with big smiles on their faces and the proverbial headscarf knotted above their foreheads. They were only slightly less admired than the male soldiers.

Spring came early, but with it came the end of pseudo-peace, of the "Phoney War," as the British called it. On April 9, the population was surprised by the news that German troops had invaded Denmark to protect it from an invasion by the Western Allies. As if to confirm this myth, pictures were shown in papers and newsreels of Danish civilians, especially of young women, fraternizing with German soldiers. Much was made of the fact that while German units were occupying Copenhagen, the Danish king was seen taking his customary morning outing riding through the streets on his bicycle. But on the same day, German troops also landed in Norway, and war became real all of a sudden. Between the Norwegian troops and the British forces that had landed at several different locations, the German Army needed much more time than expected, before all hostilities ceased with the British troops retreating across the sea to England, and Norway capitulating to Germany.

Several weeks later though, all attention was directed westwards where Germany had invaded neutral Holland and Belgium on May 10 and within days became engaged in battles with the French army. Again, I cannot forget the enthusiasm in the radio, on the street, in shops, and in restaurants. News of the bombing of Rotterdam caused jubilation; nobody seemed to realize that, once more, Germany had committed a large-scale assault on an undefended city full of civilians. Soldiers returning on leave also described the devastation along the French highways where hundreds of thousands of civilians, fleeing the advancing Germans, were attacked from the air. Soldiers brought more than news from the front. Again, as after the Polish campaign, France was an endless source of luxury goods carried home by soldiers on leave. As I remember, people talked about this with delight, as if the soldiers simply took from this country what they as victors were entitled to.

In school, our teachers again treated us to enthusiastic lectures. Among ourselves, we students discussed the pitiful equipment of the French army; their tanks looked small and ineffectual and, indeed proved themselves as hopeless in battle with German tanks. The French soldiers looked demoralized and weak with their puttees (German soldiers wore ugly black boots which, however, represented strength and power). We could not grasp how France could be so unprepared. Hitler had never hidden his modern weapons during his regular military parades, the last one being the parade on occasion of his 50th birthday, where ambassadors and military attachés from all over the world had watched the new weaponry of the Third Reich.

Hitler was celebrated as the victor in the *Blitzkrieg*, which was over within six weeks. Luxembourg was annexed, Holland, Belgium and more than half of France including its capital – the famous *City of Light* – were occupied. The French government had been on retreat moving from Paris to Bordeaux and eventually to Vichy, which became the capital of unoccupied France.

In Paris, there were banners proclaiming, "Germany is victorious on all fronts." In Berlin, on July 6, the huge victory parade showed the streets festooned with flags and garlands as in peacetime. Nearly everybody expected Hitler's next step, the invasion of the British Isles, to be imminent.

To the disappointment of many Germans, no German troops would land on the British coast, but beginning in August, German bombers and fighter planes began to cross the English Channel in enormous numbers. *The Battle of Britain* began. Again, in the movie theatres, many people never got tired of the whine of the *Ju'87* dive bombers, the rumble of exploding bombs dropped by the *He'98s*, the flickering flames of the burning buildings and, during the day, the huge columns of smoke rising from London and other English cities under attack. On September 6, the British began to talk about *The Blitz*, after Hitler declared all-out war by air against England, and Hermann Goering vowed to Hitler on the German radio "Wir werden die englischen Städte ausradieren!"[2] I have not forgotten the excitement, the enthusiasm in our school among the teachers, and during break in the schoolyard, how a lot of students were enthused about Goering's vow.

Again, people seemed to firmly believe that peace would return to Germany by Christmas. It was not only the elation about the German air offence against England that raised the hopes for imminent peace. After

---

2   "We are going to eradicate the English cities!"

the end of the French campaign, Germany experienced a summer that seemed so much like all the previous summers of peace. Against expectations, the annual Breslau Trade Fair was not cancelled. Although very little of what was exhibited there was available in stores, one was satisfied to merely admire everything that was new. I remember the first camper ever offered in Germany — small by today's standards, but certainly complete — and the first television sets with their tiny screens.[3] We saw the first utensils made out of genuine plastic, of a quality that we would not see until years after the war. The exhibition of agricultural machines and products was larger than ever. The number of exhibitors in the hall of foreign states had shrunk, however. Since 1938, Austria, Czechoslovakia, and Poland had ceased to exist, one after the other. The handicraft products from Yugoslavia, hand-woven carpets, soft red leather shoes, and embroidered blouses, were still much admired for the last time. Within a year, there would no longer be a Yugoslavian nation.

With great fanfare, the *Hitlerjugend* leadership announced in May the action of organizing the German youth in a program of contributing to the war effort during the summer vacations. We were not very excited about the thought of losing our annual month of freedom from school and being put to work instead. Initiative, however, was to be rewarded. Whoever found a summer job and had it approved by his *Hitlerjugend* leader did not have to worry about being commandeered to a summer camp. So most of my classmates and I found rather pleasant jobs. For myself, the daily task was to replace the horse-drawn cart that normally brought fresh produce to our neighbourhood store. I did not get to commandeer the small wagon but had to manoeuvre the daily load of produce in a huge metal basket above the front wheel of a heavy bicycle. Usually three or four trips were involved from the central warehouse to the local store, but by early afternoon I had completed my job and was invited to pick the best produce to take home to my mother — it was even all right to take the entire daily delivery of such delicacies as strawberries; their quantity was often so small that placing them in the store would only cause anger, as the amount allowed per customer was so minimal.

We also went on holidays, although for the first time without my father who did not get leave during this summer. Neither could my mother and I spend the holidays in our usual quarters in the *Isergebirge* (*since 1945 Góry Izerskie* / Iser Mountains) as the *Hotel Augusta* had been turned over to the Wehrmacht. Instead, we went to a smaller place in a charming village at the foot of the *Riesengebirge*. This was rather an old

---

3   In Berlin, the first public *Fernsehstuben* (public television viewing rooms) had been opened.

establishment with a correspondingly elderly group of guests. I did not really like it there and was glad when we returned home. In fall, all the theatres reopened after their summer closure. Seats were becoming scarce, as large sections of the opera house or the playhouse were reserved for the military. The opera buffs were rather annoyed, as it was obvious that not all soldiers sent to opera performances really cared for this kind of entertainment and did not hide their boredom or restrain themselves from being noisy. But culture was promoted on all levels as the medium of bringing the German people together in one great classless experience. Even a third theatre was opened 10 years after two of the traditional four theatres in Breslau had been closed. The great opera stars were engaged to sing in factories during lunch break, but they usually picked lighter fare such as music from operettas. Even the big symphony orchestras would perform in factories, with mixed results. I remember a scene in the newsreels of the Berlin Philharmonic Orchestra performing under the famous Wilhelm Furtwängler, considered Germany's greatest conductor at that time. Unfortunately, the camera rested on Furtwängler's face and his somewhat odd conducting manners far too long, showing the intense shaking of his head for almost the entire time, which resulted in uproarious laughter among the audience in the movie theatre. My mother wondered whether the Nazis were really that naive to think that they could turn the entire German population into lovers of classical music. My father, who was deeply devoted to music and to Wilhelm Furtwängler, was visibly angry when we related this episode to him. He saw in all this the dishonesty and artificiality of the Nazi state.

The same negative feelings were aroused when the Soviet minister of external affairs, Molotov, came to Berlin on a state visit on November 12. At the *Anhalter Bahnhof*, he was received with the highest honours by Field Marshal Keitel, one of the top military men of the Third Reich and, also in uniform, the German foreign minister von Ribbentrop, and a huge honour guard. The papers reported a three-hour meeting between Molotow and Hitler followed by a festive dinner in Hitler's new Chancellery, attended by over 100 high-ranking officials, artists, scientists, and other persons from public life. Molotov had arrived in pouring, ice-cold rain, which, despite the pomp surrounding this visit, seemed symbolic of the reception this visit had among the general population. Our family found the entire affair dishonest and forced, and indeed, the visit did not leave a positive impact on the country.

On November 29, the radio reported that the gothic cathedral of Coventry had been destroyed by German bombs. Hardly anyone had ever heard of Coventry before that day, but the name became a symbol of the impact of war. The mood in our family was becoming more subdued when news reached our city that the entire Jewish population of Warsaw, about 350,000, had been forced behind newly erected walls into a small ghetto. The pictures of overcrowded streets shown in the papers and in the newsreels gave a frightening image of human beings being treated like animals. The detestable order proclaiming the isolation of the Jews became also effective in Germany and depressed us very much, as our family had several Jewish friends in Waldenburg. As in Breslau, some had been able to leave Germany, others obviously had been taken away to concentration camps, and a few were still around but were hardly seen on the street. On our way home from school, we often walked through the *Antonienstrasse*, the quarter where the Jews arriving from Eastern Europe used to make their first stop in Germany. This area of the old town had been part of the ghetto in past centuries. Now, the remaining Jews had all been herded into the *Antonienstrasse* and the neighbouring *Wallstrasse*. We would pass small families, old couples, or single men or women, marked by the Star of David on their coats, but also recognizable by their fearful demeanour. They all looked frightened, averted their eyes from us, and actually made a visible bow around us. Whenever we passed a Jew or a Jewish family, my classmates and I would, without realizing it, cease our usually lively conversation. We felt acutely uncomfortable. I believe now that, in our minds and hearts, we were struggling with feelings of embarrassment and shame.

* * * * *

9 | 1941
New Wars on Two Continents

Africa, the Balkan Peninsula, and the Soviet Union

The Soviets were still proclaimed as the friends of the Third Reich, although people found this harder and harder to accept. Fear-inspiring to them was the thought of German soldiers fighting the Bolsheviks – their numbers, their country, their resources just seemed too vast for Germany.

In February, German troops under Feldmarschall Rommel were fighting in Africa. In April, German armies swarmed all over the Balkan Peninsula. Hitler continued with his Blitzkrieg. The Blitzkrieg strategy continued its success after Hitler invaded the Soviet Union on June 22. The Eastern Front moved across the vast Russian land through heat and dust; the fall brought huge battles fought in rain and mud. The German armies reached the suburbs of Leningrad; they – almost – entered the suburbs of Moscow.

On December 7, the Japanese destroyed the US fleet at Pearl Harbor in a surprise attack. On the 11ᵗʰ, the United States declared war on Japan's allies Germany and Italy. The number of pessimists grew in Germany.

On the Eastern Front the cold arrived – the winds from Siberia, the snow. German soldiers were not prepared for that; neither was the equipment that had served them so well through so many campaigns. For the first time, Hitler's armies were forced to retreat. A sense of unease gripped the German people. They could not help thinking of what happened to Napoleon at Moscow in 1812.

* * *

I was going to have my 16th birthday this year! This milestone would bring some privileges such as attendance of movies restricted to persons 16 years and over and sitting in restaurants without being accompanied by an adult. Most of my classmates had already reached this age – I had always been the youngest in class; some even had already been drafted into the Army. My father thought I was far from that event, while I felt that being drafted would come soon enough. I was becoming quite restless and rebellious, as my father did not give any indication whether with my advancing age, he would give me some more freedom, not even as much as my classmates were already enjoying with the consent of their parents.

To attend concerts, recitals, operas, operettas, or even the variety theatres (these, however, only for matinees) did not present a problem; my father even paid for the admission to these events – and, of course, would interview me about them afterwards. But simply going out for the evening with friends, which would include attending a movie and a visit to a coffeehouse, was absolutely not discussable with my father. I wish I would have ever understood his reasons. Going out with friends was far safer than being out on my own, which I was now determined to do without even giving a hint to my parents. Ahead of me lay a life of pretence, lies, even fraud on my part. If nothing ever happened to me on my clandestine evening excursions, I can only say I was fortunate.

This was a stressful year where the constant conflict with my father assumed more complex dimensions, to which were added the constant, eventually successful attempts on my part, to evade the compulsory attendance of the *Hitlerjugend* activities. I hated to wear the *Hitlerjugend* uniform, to spend four hours of marching, singing stupid songs, listening to propaganda, and praising Hitler. Managing to skip out early or avoid the activity altogether, gave me, as a side benefit, one evening a week during which I could, legitimately, be away from home. Instead of attending *Hitlerjugend* services in the evening between 6 and 10 o'clock, I would go to a movie. Naturally, I soon desired more than one evening per week. I asked my parents to let me take Spanish lessons in evening school, for which my father readily gave his permission. I registered for Spanish, attended the first two or three classes, bought the required textbook (which I always left prominently displayed on my desk) and then skipped classes and went on my secret evening outings instead.

In order to feel safe from detection, I had to stay away from areas where I might run into my friends or acquaintances of my parents. Such precautions, however, took me to the less desirable districts of Breslau. It was not far from the movie theatre I frequented on these nights, that the *Hitlerjugend* leader of the province of Silesia had been attacked by a mob of young people helped by adults who lived in that street. It was a street, by the way, which at night was avoided by most people. The incident was never reported in the papers, but the city was full of the news that the *Hitlerjugend* leader's car, a smallish automobile, had been stopped by a crowd of older teenagers and young adults and toppled over onto its roof; a signal that the *Hitlerjugend* with all its omnipresence was not yet in control of every part of town. The perpetrators might have been the boys and men I spent time with in the pub!

Today I can say that I often felt uneasy amongst these tough individuals and was always concerned how I could keep up with their rough ways and their physical aggressiveness. But I persisted in going to this pub, if even only to rebel against my father. I also must admit that I did not have any difficulties pretending or even lying to my parents when we talked about my Spanish lessons. I felt bad to deceive my mother, but was not troubled with similar feelings when it came to my father. As the weeks went on, I always made sure to learn a few words or phrases from the Spanish textbook. After having been taught excellent French in high school for several years, I found Spanish easy to manage. I became proficient enough that I felt more at ease facing my father.

I realize that I did pay a heavy price trying to deal with my guilt about deceiving my parents. My school marks fell, I often did not sleep well, and I frequently went for long walks in the afternoons, always alone and brooding about my life; at times, I entertained thoughts of suicide.

During this winter, I also became a heavy smoker. Some of us had started to smoke at the age of 12. There were no problems at that time to buy cigarettes, and at least initially, our smoking was more for show and really not part of our personal life. But now, when I was under such, in part self-imposed, pressure, I became a heavy smoker. Unfortunately, I had easy access to cigarettes, even though they had been rationed since the early months of the war. The established quality brands quickly disappeared from the market to be replaced by cigarettes of truly inferior quality. Supplied through the businesses of his brothers and the black market of Balkan cigarettes, my father stayed with quality cigarettes, but never failed to buy his entitlement with his ration cards. Soon, these cigarettes were piled up in a closet by the hundreds of packs. This was a ready-made source for me and I never was short of cigarettes. During spring of this year I ran into my father when I was lighting a cigarette after coming out of the public library. My father laughed and asked how long I had been smoking. This time I stayed with the truth, telling him that I had been smoking for more than three years. My father laughed and shook his head saying, "Well it is too late for me to do something about it, isn't it," and offered me a cigarette when we had visitors on the following weekend.

Despite his severe strictness with me, my father was in a much better mood now. He had completed additional training courses and was placed in a more senior position as an administrative officer. He continued living at home and going to work as in peacetime, except that he was wearing an officer's uniform. I remember his fabulous place of work, a huge villa fronted by a row of three-story high columns on Breslau's most elegant street in the southern section of town. Visiting him there for the first time, I congratulated him to his splendid quarters — he had worked in ugly Prussian military barracks dating back to the eighteenth century until that time. With embarrassment and repressed anger, he confided to me that this had been the villa of one of Breslau's most distinguished Jewish families. The owners had been evicted, the cleaning woman who had already worked in this building under its former owners, had told my father in confidence. The entire family, from grandparents to grand-children, had been transported to the East.

In cities and towns with a smaller Jewish community, the disappearance of Jewish citizens seemed to occur almost clandestinely. In my birthplace Waldenburg, for instance, where by 1938 the Jewish community had shrunk to less than 100 members, the Jews had disappeared altogether from the streets and from the awareness of the city's population. If there were any Jews still in town, they seemed invisible. The last Jew I saw in Waldenburg, and he may have been truly the very last Jewish person in town, was Mr. Töplitz, an elderly widower whom my Uncle Hubert secretly looked after, an effort for which I still admire and honour him to this day. I do not remember what profession or trade Mr. Töplitz had pursued in his younger years; he might have been a lawyer. At some point after 1938, my uncle offered Mr. Töplitz a room in the attic of a small house our family owned. This house was used for storage of china for my uncle's store, and Mr. Töplitz was the only inhabitant. The trusted maid of my uncle brought him food every day, took his washing home and brought Mr. Töplitz messages from my uncle or took messages from Mr. Töplitz back to my uncle. My uncle never entered this house, in order not to raise any suspicion among people on this street. Unfortunately, he would run into Mr. Töplitz every so often on the street.

One time, on a spring evening during that year, Uncle Hubert took his dog for a walk and I accompanied him. We were not too far from Mr. Töplitz's abode when we met Mr. Töplitz. Carefully dressed in a dark suit and carrying a walking cane over his arm, Mr. Töplitz doffed his hat and stopped to talk with us. My uncle tried to get away and pretended not to know Mr. Töplitz, but not without imploring him not to go out before it turned dark. But with a friendly smile, Mr. Töplitz just said, "nobody will recognize me, it is dark already." Unfortunately, Mr. Töplitz's eyesight was very poor. He wore very dark glasses and for him, it might have been

Other events I remember or was told about

81. Nazi Party sports event in the Waldenburg Stadion (1932).

82. After their first East-West Atlantic crossing by plane the three aviators Köhl, v. Huenefeld and Fitzmaurice are welcomed in Breslau by my cousin Christel and my aunt Käthe.

83. Köhl, Fitzmaurice, v. Huenefeld, and the D 1167 BREMEN at the start of the Atlantic crossing in Baldonnel (Ireland) on April 12, 1928.

Other events I remember or was told about

84. The Waldenburg Chamber Choir under Director Herzig. It included three members of the Koch Family: my aunt Käthe, her later husband (my uncle Hubert), and Georg, my father.

85. Balloon ascending from the short-lived airfield in Bad Salzbrunn.

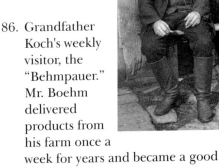

86. Grandfather Koch's weekly visitor, the "Behmpauer." Mr. Boehm delivered products from his farm once a week for years and became a good friend of my Grandfather.

87. The *Comedian Harmonists*, the famous a capella group in the Schauburg Theatre (1932).

Hitler's takeover of Germany

88. Hitler's first broadcast as German chancellor during the night of his election from January 30 to 31, 1933.

89.
The victory parade through the Brandenburg Gate in Berlin.

89a.
The Russian icon my father received from his friend shortly before his friend was murdered by the SS during the night of January 30/31, 1933.

90. One of the first hastily erected Concentration camps.

Indicators of things to come

91. Book burning in front of the Berlin University.

92. First countrywide boycott of Jewish businesses (April 1933).

93. Hitler Youth - the mass organization of German Youth.

Anonymous or hidden art

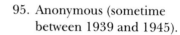

94. Paul Weber (1933).

95. Anonymous (sometime between 1939 and 1945).

96. Theo Matejko (1933).

A few German artists saw Germany's future in works hidden until after WW II.

97. Carl Hofer: Man amongst the Ruins (1937).

My years in Breslau 1936–1943

98. View across the Old Town.

99. Ring (the town square).

𝔐𝔶 𝔶𝔢𝔞𝔯𝔰 𝔦𝔫 𝔅𝔯𝔢𝔰𝔩𝔞𝔲 1936–1943

100. The business section with the LZ 127 Graf Zeppelin, the same airship that I saw cruising above Waldenburg on the same day in 1929.

01. The Cathedral Island in 2001 (Dominsel/Ostrow Tumski).

102. City Hall (Rathaus/Ratusz) in 2001.

103. Petersdorff Department Store (1927) by Erich Mendelsohn.
Our art teacher Georg Nerlich had the courage to take us to this building to explain its significance as an outstanding example of the type of modern architecture that was outlawed by Hitler.

Our family in Breslau

104. 1937

105. 1940

06. 1938

107. 1937

The Eichendorff Oberschule — my high school

108. The teachers (1940).

109. My grade in 1940.

Teachers I will always remember

10. Dr. Gnielinski, Religion and Latin.

111. Dr. Randow, Mathematics & Sciences.

12. Georg Nerlich, Fine Arts.

113. Mr. Hermann, Physical Education.

Concentration camps and deportations

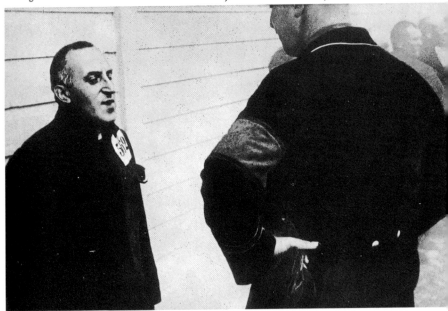

114. Karl von Ossietzky, Author, journalist, and publisher, 1933 imprisoned in concentration camp; 1935 receives Nobel Prize for Peace; 1938 dies in concentration camp.

115. Mortal fear descends on Jewish families.

Reichskristallnacht – November 9, 1938

16. Jewish stores in the Friedrichstrasse, Berlin's main shopping street.

17. Burning synagogue in the Fasanenstrasse in Berlin.

117a. Hitler greets huge crowds at the 1936 Sängerfest in Breslau.

1939 — Last summer of peace

118. Parade in Berlin on Hitler's birthday April 20, 1939.

119. Molotow signs the German-Soviet treaty in the presence of Joseph Stalin and the German foreign secretary von Ribbentrop.

September 1, 1939 — first day of World War II

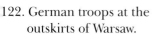

120. German soldiers remove
Polish border crossing.

121. German Ju 87 Stuka
bombers attack
residential quarters in
Warsaw.

122. German troops at the
outskirts of Warsaw.

1940 — Victory in France

123. Victorious German soldiers.

124. Berlin streets are prepared for Hitler's return. Flowers cover the pavement of the Wilhelmstrasse.

1941 — A different kind of war starts in the East

125. Rain and mud in the Russian fall.

126. Snow and cold in the Russian winter.

German film stars keep up morale and ideology

27. Zarah Leander.

128. Marika Rökk.

129. Paul Hartmann and
     Charlotte Thiele in
     "Ich klage an"
     (I accuse) to justify
     euthanasia practiced
     in Hitler's Germany.

The end of the Jewish uprising in the Warsaw Ghetto

Part of the Endlösung — the Extermination of European Jews

130.

131.

132.

133.
The Last Journey –
to the camps and the
gas chambers.

I am prepared for service at the Front

134. Wehrertüchtigungslager Raudten, Silesia, practical and ideological paramilitary training by the SS.

135. Labor Service Camp (RAD Lager) in East Prussia.

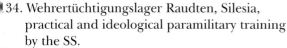

138. My first army barracks in Liegnitz (2002). The 150 year-old Grenadierkaserne has been changed into condominiums in present-day Legnica (Liegnitz). The old Prussian eagle has survived on the building's roof in this now Polish city.

136. Buddies in the Labor Service.

137. My first army photo from my soldier's passbook (1943).

To the Eastern Front

139. I crossed the River Bug into Brest Litowsk on the predecessor of this bridge.

140. The former Brest Litowsk railway station (destroyed in both WWI and WWII).

Брестъ-Литовскъ. Соборъ.

141. I spent my first night in Russia in these barracks that were part of the Brest Citadel.

142. I attended Easter service at the St. Simon Church.

The Pripjet Marshes (Polesie)

A vast land of forests, marshes, lakes and rivers, and of few human beings.

143., 144., 145.

Stachowice

This pretty village in the Pripjet Marshes near the city of Pinsk was my first base as a soldier in Russia.

146. The village street. The two rows of birch trees that once bordered a canal are the last trace of a boulevard that led to a manor house at the outskirts of Stachowice.

147. This platoon of congenial men was m̶ support for the next six months.

148. The family had to make their home in the barn.

149. On a Sunday in front of the farm house we occupied.

Pinsk in old pictures

150.
The Pina River and the town centre.

151.
The Jesuit church.

152.
The main synagogue.

153. Catholic church.

Pinsk as I saw it in 1944

154.
The old railroad station.

155.
The destroyed part of the city.

156.
Only the Apteka (pharmacy) was still there.

157.
Another old picture of the city and the river Pina. In 1944 only the ruins of the church were left.

nightfall already. My uncle worried that Mr. Töplitz's mind might have begun to fail. This was the last time I saw a Jew in Waldenburg, after my childhood years when Jewish families lived all around us in our street. When I returned to Waldenburg a few weeks later, Uncle Hubert advised me that one day, Mr. Töplitz was gone when his maid came with the food to his room. It still seems a miracle that my uncle did not have to suffer the consequences of his courageous actions and end up in a concentration camp.

The pressure, anxiety, and fear suffered by those who harboured or helped Jews in those years must have been horrendous. I have a sense of all that, as for more than half a year, my parents helped shelter a young Jewish woman for a few days every month. Edith was the girlfriend of Lilo, sister of my Aunt Hannchen, the wife of my mother's brother, Peter. The two had met at a boarding school at the *Weisser Hirsch* resort in Dresden shortly before the Hitler years. One day, in 1941, my father advised me with great care and in precise words that from now on we would have a house guest for a few days every month. He and my mother had agreed to the desperate request of my aunt's sister Lilo to please help her Jewish friend who had appeared at Lilo's house late one evening after her parents had been taken away by the SS. We were to be part of a chain of families that were going to take turns in secretly offering shelter to this young woman. Soon after, my father told me not to invite any friends to the house for the following week.

One late evening, our secret house guest Edith appeared and, for the next six or seven days, life at home was incredibly tense and anxious. Whenever the doorbell rang, our guest would quickly retreat to my parent's bedroom and disappear in the large wardrobe behind a thick row of heavy clothing. At night, she slept on the couch in the living room, always fully dressed and with nothing lying around that would betray that someone had been resting there. These visits all happened during the late fall and winter when one would not open windows and due to the blackout, all our windows were curtained off with dark blinds.

I cannot imagine how we would have managed during the hot summer months, when we certainly would have caused suspicion if we had had our windows always shut. It was also fortunate that there were no outsiders in our apartment; by party orders we had to dismiss our maid shortly after the beginning of the war. In addition to the fear of being detected — sheltering or aiding a Jewish person had become a capital offence — daily life was also very stressful, as Edith, as beautiful and elegant as she was, was very subdued but full of suppressed anger. She was not an easy house guest. I do not know how the arrangements had been made, and I only know that other than with our relatives, we had no contact with the other families who were offering shelter. But a day or so before our guest's arrival, a food package would arrive from my relatives who, as businessmen, managed much better in this regard as we did.

One day, my father advised me that Edith had moved to a different part of the country to be with a new set of families. After that, even my relatives never heard of her and we all doubted that she had survived the war. But in 1946, my aunt's sister Lilo met her Jewish friend from boarding school days in Munich. Edith was walking along the street on the arm of an American officer. Surprised and almost in shock, the two women recognized each other, stopped, and looked at each other. But then Edith abruptly dragged her American friend along, all without saying one word. A few weeks later, a postcard from Bremerhaven reached Lilo: "I am on my way to America to get married, and I will never come back," Edith wrote. This one sentence was the last message from Edith to her friend Lilo.

Spring 1941 again appeared to be relatively normal. The sidewalk cafés reopened and the streets were filled with soldiers on leave with their girlfriends on their arms. Good-looking heavy clothing for winter had been hard to obtain or non-existent, which was the case with shoes and boots as well. For the summer, though, there was still enough material available for sewing colourful, light dresses; the girls looked lovely and cheerful. Everybody seemed to be glad to be alive and enjoy life. This summer, it was fashionable to wear open high-heeled sandals (the wedge type) made of colourful cloth and heavy wooden soles. The official propaganda made a fetish out of these sandals, poems were written, and songs were composed and sung about the smart, young women and the wonderful "clip-clop" sounds they made with their wooden sandals. Somehow, I think, the propaganda succeeded, and everybody loved these sandals. During the following summers, people got sick and tired of such footwear, which had lost all its early charm and was now quite common for women and men to wear.

Even ominous events surrounding the war seemed to be taken in stride. General Rommel in Africa became the new hero, and while the battles there remained inconclusive for some time, the German Africa Corps was the subject of great admiration and hero worship. When Hitler started his invasion of the Balkan Peninsula on April 6, the initial shock was also quickly overcome, as the conquest of this largely mountainous area progressed very rapidly. The occupation of the Isle of Crete, however, resulted in great losses among the German paratroopers. Again, the official propaganda exploited the battle for Crete for its own ends, making a spectacle of public mourning that was to unite the German people even more. One did not get the impression, however, that the majority of people was gaining a sense that the war might get a lot bloodier and far less victorious. After all, Crete was securely in German hands now, and so was all of the Balkan Peninsula.

Nothing was secure or predictable. When the war had started on September 1, 1939, it was a fearful day for many people, although the war certainly did not start unexpectedly. More than halfway through June 1941, an event descended on the minds and feelings of the German population that caused the greatest shock of the war so far.

My mother and I were visiting my Grandmother Hackenberg in Waldenburg for the weekend. We had arrived on Saturday, June 21 and spent a pleasant afternoon and evening. On Sunday morning when we were still in bed, my mother's sister Martel who lived with my grandmother, rushed into our room without knocking — most unusual for her — and almost shouted at us "Wir sind in Russland einmarschiert!" (We have invaded Russia!)

German armies had entered the Soviet Union early in the morning of June 22, 1941. The day before, Hitler's Third Reich and Stalin's Soviet Union had still been "friends." The following morning, without any prior warning, break in diplomatic relationships, or declaration of war, Hitler had started another front, this time in the East, facing the huge Soviet Empire with its vast resources and a population far superior in numbers to that of Germany.

I believe that was the first time that the majority of people were not in spontaneous agreement with Hitler's decision. There was a vague sense of unease that from now on, the war might not go so well. Almost everybody expected the Soviet armies to quickly enter at least some parts of Eastern Germany; reminiscences of the rapid Russian occupation of East Prussia in 1914 came alive, and everybody expected air raids and bombings.

My mother and I hastily packed our bags right after breakfast. When we left so prematurely and abruptly, both my grandmother and my aunt were in tears, and so was my mother. We rushed to the railroad station and took the first train to Breslau. The coaches were all overcrowded and we had to stand in the aisle the entire way. People did not talk very much, although they were standing close to each other. Probably, nobody dared express his or her feelings and fears in public. At home, our neighbours were busy, stocking the air raid shelter with fresh water and food, and lugging additional buckets of sand up into the attic. A mood of "we are personally at war" ruled the house, as never before.

Nothing happened during the rest of the day, during the night, or on the following days, weeks, or months. Again, Hitler seemed to win. There were special reports on the radio, often several times a day, about more cities being stormed or occupied, of huge rivers crossed, of battles won, and of huge masses of Soviet soldiers taken prisoners. Within a week, people spoke about more than one million Soviet prisoners of war.

The steadily growing numbers of prisoners were taken as the most reliable measure of Germany's superiority, and people quickly lost their fear of the Soviets. After all, the newsreels proved that compared to German soldiers, the Russians wore shabby uniforms, used cheap, primitive weapons, trucks and tanks,[1] and the country they tried to defend against the victorious Germans looked extremely impoverished. The villages consisted of unpainted log houses with thatched roofs that cowered along unpaved village streets. The number of paved highways was very small. The entire country seemed a vast plain of dust and if there was rain, of thick mud.[2]

Some people suspected that the war reporters had been ordered to show the Soviet Union from its worst side in every respect, but the majority believed what they saw. I think it was the effect of the propaganda as much as the rapid advance of the German armies that cheered up the general population and caused whatever fears and pessimism that had gripped people after June 22, to quickly dissipate.

So again, there was much jubilation in the movie theatres. When scenes of victory were shown, part of the audience jumped out of their seats, stretched out their right arms to the Hitler salute and spontaneously sang the national anthem. What for me and some others was nearly intolerable, however, was the reaction of the audience when the horrendous pictures of the huge, overcrowded prisoner of war camps were shown. The Soviet soldiers looked dirty, their uniforms seemed to fall from their shoulders, none of them were shaved, and often prisoners were shown fighting over a piece of bread. I will not forget the voices in the theatre that loudly uttered derogatory words such as "animals," or

---

1   The seemingly poor quality of Soviet equipment caused amusement and loud derisive laughter in the movie houses. The German soldier, however, would soon learn to appreciate the Russian Sten gun — standard equipment of the Soviet soldier. In contrast to its sophisticated German equivalent, the Russian Sten gun would never become inoperable due to dust, sand, or frost, to all of which German weapons were easily vulnerable. Neither were the Soviet trucks impressive, until the Studebakers were delivered by the USA to turn up near the battlefields in large numbers. The Soviet T34, the standard tank, was shown with a wooden box for a driver's seat. Again, German people laughed about this evidence of the backward Soviet system and again, it did not take long to understand that replacing the T34 was much cheaper, easier, and faster than replacing the sophisticated German tanks.

2   What the newsreels had shown of Poland in September 1939 seemed, in comparison to the Soviet Union, very European and civilized, even though to German audiences the Polish scene had looked incredibly backward at that time.

"pigs." There were reports in the papers about incidents of cannibalism in the camps. Whether they were true or not I cannot say, but typically, for a population steadily bombarded by propaganda, such reports were generally taken as proof that the Soviets were a subhuman race. Indeed, since that time, the term *Untermensch* (subhuman being) was freely applied to Soviet citizens, soldiers as well as civilians.

Of course, when it came to the Soviet prisoners of war, they remained an amorphous mass of human beings for quite some time. The general population never saw a Soviet soldier at close range. Only later were some of them put to work on farms and in factories, and one would be able to look at them as individuals. My first encounter, that involved eye contact with some Russian prisoners turned into a disturbing episode. It was early in July that the fast train I used to visit my relatives in northern Lower Silesia made an unscheduled stop at a small station.[3] Always being curious, I had stepped to the window at the aisle of our express coach to find out why the train had slowed down and eventually crawled to a halt — afterwards, I wished I had not done so. As it happened, parallel to our train, there was a long train of cattle cars filled with Soviet soldiers, obviously on their way to prison camp. Right across from my window, there was a narrow opening of about 2 feet in length in the wall of a cattle car, heavily barred with barbed wire. One Soviet soldier after another crowded to this small slit, the only opening to admit fresh air to the packed cattle car. I remember the first soldier; he had white-blond hair, blue eyes, was wearing a képi and obviously reported to his comrades what he saw. Then others came to the opening. I remember that I was surprised how melodious and gentle the Russian language sounded. I also concluded that these soldiers had been taken prisoner very recently, as they looked neither starved nor dirty. It was the first time that I was confronted with human beings who were caged like animals on a cattle train. It did not take long for a number of passengers to point at the prisoners with their fingers and loudly say "like animals." Here was that terrible word again. I moved away from the window, feeling alienated from the other passengers and their tactless remarks.

Ironically, within a week, I ended up in a camp myself. Very unexpectedly, on one of the last days of school before the summer vacation, we were called out of class and ordered to report to the *Hitlerjugend* district office immediately. After we arrived there, our names

---

3   During the first months of the Eastern campaign, the railway system was especially overburdened with troop and supply trains going back and forth between Germany and the Eastern Front. The scheduled passenger system was still functioning almost as in peacetime, but lengthy delays were not uncommon.

were called. Some of our group were told to go back to school, while about a dozen of us were ordered to go home, pack a small bag with toothbrush and some other items of personal need, and report back within two hours. We had been chosen to attend a camp for preparatory military training. When I arrived at home my mother was away. I left a note about the camp and wrote that I would telephone her, once I had arrived there.

The camp, officially called *Wehrertüchtigungslager*, was a former *Reichsarbeitsdienstlager*[4] located in the tiny town of Raudten (since 1945 Rudna) about 60 miles north of Breslau. For me, the camp was an experience worse than either the Labour Service or the Army in later years. We were all young high school students around 16 years of age. Not everyone in our class was sent to the camp, but we soon concluded that those of us who had shown themselves as not amenable to the goals of the *Hitlerjugend* were sent to this camp to be punished and, perhaps, to be broken of our resistive spirit. As in all Labour Service camps, the standard of housing and hygiene was very basic. So was the food, which consisted of a near starvation diet. It was totally inadequate for the tough daily regime we were forced under. The breakfast, consumed after the *Morgensport*, the morning physical training on an empty stomach, consisted of two slices of rye bread with margarine and beet syrup, and barley coffee. There was nothing else provided till noon. We ate every bite we could get a hold of and in the evenings, succeeded to persuade some of the local citizens to bring us some food and pass it over the fence without being seen. We were allowed to write one postcard a week; food parcels sent by our parents were shown to us and then "donated" to the *NSV*, the national public welfare office.

The camp was under the command of a rather coarse and rough-looking *SS* officer, while each platoon (about 10 boys) was under the leadership of one of the SS non-commissioned officers, all of whom came from the former Czechoslovakia. Needless to say, they were especially fanatical Nazis, who drilled us mercilessly, abused us verbally as weak, lazy, and incompetent, and did their worst work at night. Several of us went through the experience of being called out of bed close to midnight and taken to the main building where our camp officer and the platoon leaders had their rooms. I went through this routine only once. It began

---

4   One of the numerous camps of the *Reichsarbeitsdienst* (the German Labour Service), a Nazi organisation which every German male and female had to attend prior to being drafted for military service. While it was originally started as a means of getting unemployed young men off the streets, later emphasis was placed on physical fitness and political indoctrination.

with being asked quite politely to sign up to join the *SS* voluntarily. As most of us who were taken through this ordeal, I refused. What followed was, in a milder form, not much different from what I had read about interrogation practices of the Soviet secret police. The *SS* leaders began to raise their voices, began to threaten me, and ordered me to do push ups and, finally, to do knee bends while holding a heavy wooden chair by its wooden legs with my arms stretched out. There were moments of rest for further questioning, renewed threats and then the torture continued — and torture it was for me as I was not very strong physically. How I managed to get through this experience without breaking down, giving in and signing the *SS* papers, I do not know. It was like a nightmare, but I was rebellious and proud, that the *SS* had not succeeded in breaking my will. Still, I was too exhausted and demoralized to even speak about it. It was something one was almost ashamed to discuss. As far as I knew, no one in our group had his will broken and signed up for the *SS*.

Without explanation, the duration of the camp was reduced to less then three weeks and we were sent home. I am certain that all the boys I knew were psychologically in a pitiful state. We had been abused and, even though we did not break down, had experienced for the first time in our life the impact of naked, ruthless power, exercised by men who looked like ordinary human beings and who could be quite nice at mealtimes when they sat at our table, or during the brief free time in the evening. I was very angry and bitter. Without really thinking it through, I began to boycott everything that had to do with the *Hitlerjugend*, the party, and with the Nazi indoctrination at school.

I went to the mountains with my mother for a brief holiday and then spent the rest of the vacation with my Grandmother Koch in Waldenburg. There, I was back in a civilized world. I loved to spend the day in the nearby spa of Bad Salzbrunn. Reached by streetcar from Waldenburg, Bad Salzbrunn was an island of peace and beauty. Everything was still in full operation, primarily because most of the hotels and sanatoria were filled with wounded or convalescing soldiers. For them, the concert cafés flourished, as did the small but charming theatre that presented operettas and popular concerts. Some of the best actors and singers had been engaged from Berlin where most of the theatres were closed for the summer season. Yet the memory of the Raudten camp did not fade. When school and *Hitlerjugend* resumed by the end of August, I was a changed person. This did not mean that I was openly resisting. For that I had neither strength nor courage. But I tried to evade whatever smacked of party, *Hitlerjugend*, indoctrination, or whatever conflicted with my beliefs and attitudes.

I stopped wearing the *Hitlerjugend* uniform when this was required on certain school days, and I did not attend the regular *Hitlerjugend* functions anymore. The consequences were not very good, as I was transferred to the *Pflicht HJ*, which was an actual punishment unit used for juvenile delinquents and politically resistant adolescents. I tried my old ways by either attending the first few minutes and then disappearing, or not attending at all. As a result, I was placed under *Jugendarrest*, youth arrest, for entire weekends several times. From all this I was rescued by a fellow a year older than I, an electrician's apprentice who for a few days worked with his master in our house to fix a problem. Helmut came from a tough working class district where he was the local *Hitlerjugend* leader. He was responsible for a unit of the *Marine HJ* (Navy Youth) and ran a rather loose ship, which was no doubt the only way to run such a group in this tough neighbourhood. For some reason, Helmut liked me and I quickly trusted him. He told me he would take me into his unit, register me so that I could get away from the terrible *Pflicht HJ*, as long as I would attend his unit regularly. Nobody in his unit wore a uniform and that would go for me as well.

Helmut became one of the persons I will always remember, because he made my life much easier, practically and psychologically and I knew I could trust him. I also got used to the other guys in Helmut's unit who were pretty tough and rough, but in the end I lost all fear of them and my discomfort in their presence disappeared. I learned to recognize them as decent human beings, even though they were not always free from delinquent behaviour. In a way, they protected me and if after that experience, I have always felt at ease and comfortable among people of the working class, I think this is due to this early experience in one of Breslau's toughest neighbourhoods.

In September, commentaries appeared in the newspapers celebrating the supreme successes of Hitler's strategies on the battlefield. Maps of Europe were prominently displayed everywhere with skilful use of red colour. The observer was confronted with an outline of Europe which, in addition to tiny Switzerland, showed a few unoccupied countries only along the Continent's periphery. The maps also demonstrated that Germany had only one adversary in the West — Great Britain — and another one in the East — the Soviet Union. The other countries, Spain and, to a lesser degree, Portugal, were positively disposed towards Hitler; so were Turkey, Finland, and Sweden. The latter still supplied Germany with high grade ore, essential for its armaments, and had not yet terminated the agreement to permit German troop and supply trains to cross Swedish soil on their way to occupied Norway. At the beginning of the new school term, Germany's might over Europe was appropriately praised during an assembly called for the purpose of the dedication of a new portrait of Hitler, created by a Countess Matuschka, showing Hitler in his party uniform. It was becoming obvious, how the vast majority of the student body was dedicated to the regime; very few of us were not wearing the obligatory *Hitlerjugend* uniform at this special assembly.

How rapidly Europe changed in its character was obvious in the streets of German cities, especially the large industrial centres. Breslau became an international city in several respects, also in our district that was situated close to the *Technische Hochschule*, the technical university. While before the war, I was always intrigued to see the odd dark-skinned student on the streetcar, or even a Chinese or Japanese student, there were hundreds of foreign students now, but all from European countries. Some wore uniforms, especially the very elegant, strongly perfumed Romanian officers who were never seen without a riding crop, and the Hungarians who wore ethnic-looking coats that obviously identified them as members of some organisation. Occasionally, we saw some Spanish officers, members of the Blue Division, sent by General Franco to fight with the German units near Leningrad.

In the northern and western parts of town, however, one saw hundreds of foreign labourers crowding the streets. While none of them had come voluntarily, there were some distinctions. For example, the French labourers obviously enjoyed a bit of status and a degree of freedom. In contrast, the armies of forced labourers from the Balkan countries, especially from Serbia, were treated quite badly, while the Poles, Ukrainians, and Russians were still truly the enemies of Germany in the way they were identified, treated, and exploited. They were kept in the most primitive of barracks, not allowed to enter stores or restaurants, and usually stepped off the sidewalks onto the pavement to make room for German pedestrians. Stories were common about their forced removal from their homes and their subsequent transport on guarded trains to Germany. Rumours about their poor treatment and high death rate due to infectious diseases circulated freely in Breslau and, more so, in Waldenburg where the industries were spread throughout the city and therefore, the foreign labourers were much more prevalent and visible. Only those who were placed on farms had a chance to be treated humanely, although all of them remained at the mercy of their farm bosses.

For ideological reasons, Hitler hesitated as long as possible to employ women in the armament and heavy industry to the extent seen in Great Britain. The alternative was the forced transfer of millions of foreign labourers from the East and Southeast of Europe to Germany. Even before the beginning of the Eastern campaign in June 1941, the Third Reich employed 3.5 million forced labourers. By 1945, their number had increased to 7.5 million. The 2.3 million who came from the Soviet Union were treated most severely. I never saw a German speak with a foreign labourer from the East. Aside from the language problem, this would have been dangerous, leading to prosecution for fraternization. Needless to say, in small towns and villages, the situation was much more casual and humane.

At the Eastern Front, the German forces seemed unstoppable. This, however, was a strange fall season, where an unusual mood gripped the population, even though the victories on the battlefield in the East continued unabated. A certain fatigue seemed to diminish the enthusiasm about the successes of the German armies in the East and the continuing advance towards Moscow. The almost daily fanfares announcing a special news report about yet another battle won had lost their impact. The newsreels, showing the endless columns of beaten Soviet soldiers being marched into prison camp, became boring. When the rains came in October, scenes of German infantrymen losing their boots in the knee-deep mud were shown just a few times too often — this was no longer amusing.

Then came the cold; fires made under trucks to thaw out their engines but also used to heat the morning coffee were soon no longer intriguing. The early Russian winter drove a vague fear into the minds of many Germans. Soon, that fear became very concrete. Soldiers coming back from the front reported temperatures in the range of −40 degrees Fahrenheit, they described how much of the equipment failed, bolts in rifles and machine-guns froze, and how they stripped the ugly padded winter coats off the dead Soviet soldiers and wore them as replacement of the much smarter-looking but totally inadequate winter coats issued to the German soldiers.

At school, at home, and in the streetcars, the mood became very subdued. Leningrad and its surrender seemed within reach and Moscow's suburbs seemed a stone's throw away. By December, vague unease turned into near shock. On December 5, it seemed clear that German troops were retreating from Moscow in the bitter cold. On Sunday, December 7, for us totally unexpected, the news of Pearl Harbour came over the radio at lunchtime. All of a sudden, final victory seemed far away, perhaps uncertain. For the first time in the war, nobody seemed to celebrate a joyous Christmas, and this year, very few people maintained that "next year at Christmas we will have peace."

For me, though, Christmas brought a victory of sorts. One of my chums in school, whose father was well placed in government, invited me to a ski trip to the mountains during the Christmas vacation. My friend's father had connections with a mountain hotel in a remote location on the Bohemian side of the *Riesengebirge*. I was desperate to go, knowing that this would be my only chance to go skiing before being drafted. I mobilized uncles, aunts, and some of my father's friends to speak for me. Finally, my father gave in after much resistance.

On Boxing Day, my friend and I climbed on the early morning train, and after three transfers, we arrived at the little spa of Johannisbad (1918-1938 and since 1945 Janské Láznê) from where a cable car took us to the top of a mountain. I remember my astonishment when I saw a whole settlement of rather luxurious private chalets built in the years of the Czechoslovak Republic – there was nothing comparable on the Silesian side of the mountains. It took three hours of strenuous skiing and carrying a heavy knapsack on the back to reach the remote chalet, but the effort turned out to be worth the struggle. The chalet was so isolated that no produce could be delivered to the authorities. In other words, there was milk and cream, and meat and butter, all from the small farming operation of the chalet manager. It seems superfluous now to mention this, but at that time, nothing of what the chalet offered us was even imaginable for the ordinary citizen. There was wine and, on New Years Eve, champagne. Would I read such a story now, I would quickly conclude that this was a chalet for the party elite. Strangely enough, the opposite was the case. Nowhere had I found such fearless openness in years. The guests shared freely their anger at Hitler and his party and their fear about what was going to happen to us after the lost war – nobody seemed to expect that Germany would win the war. It was no wonder that the New Year's Eve celebration had the ambience of one last great party.

Reality entered our lives when we heard that at the foot of the mountains, at the first railway station of Freiheit-Johannisbad (1918-1938 and since 1945 Svoboda-Janské Láznê), the *SS* were standing ready to confiscate all skiing equipment, including ski boots, to be shipped to the Eastern Front for use by the German infantry. We were told that a large pile of ordinary footwear was lying ready as exchange for the confiscated ski boots. My parents had several pairs of skis at home and I was sure they would be donated. The situation at my friend's family was identical. Understandably, neither of us was in the mood to relinquish our skis to the *SS*. I phoned Aunt Martel in Waldenburg, because she had won many trophies as a ski racer and therefore had received a permit to keep her skis and travel with them unimpeded by the *SS*. She readily agreed to pick up our skis and take them to Waldenburg, as long as we would get them to the Silesian side of the mountains.

This not only saved our skis but also brought us an adventure, the last one of a civilian nature, before we entered the Army. Having to cross the ridge of the *Riesengebirge* into Silesia got us into a ferocious blizzard in which we nearly perished. We had totally lost our bearings when by pure chance we stumbled onto what first looked like a little shed but turned out to be the entrance to a small chalet that had completely disappeared in the snow. This mountain refuge probably rescued us from certain death. I had frozen my ears and my cheeks, and both of us were near total exhaustion. The blizzard ended next morning, but the temperatures dropped to about −40 degrees Fahrenheit. The top of the treeless mountain range was sheer ice.

Close to nightfall, we reached Agnetendorf, the first village at the foot of the mountains, and took our skis to a safe place. We felt like heroes for having evaded the *SS* and survived blizzard, ice, and snow. We had succeeded without the presence or guidance of adults. We had passed our initiation into young adulthood, but it was not the ceremony prescribed by the Nazi party.

* * * * *

10 | 1942
Everyone Knows this is Going to be a Long War, and Who Knows how the War will End...

O f all the six years of World War II, this turned out to be the calmest one, although all the signposts for a bitter end were being set. The general morale was still high, battles were still won, but nothing happened smoothly anymore; or never happened anymore at all.

There were still gigantic battles in the East and hundreds of thousands of prisoners of war were still captured. Yet some of the battles were no longer outright victories for Germany; in some, the Soviet armies seemed to have the upper hand. German planes still flew bombing missions over England, but far fewer than before. And the Allied bombers began to lay waste to the first German cities. Hamburg was firebombed. Air raids seemed to steadily increase in numbers and intensity.

Most special newscasts concerned sunken tonnage of the Allied ships. The German U-boats were the only German weaponry that remained unquestionably successful.

Rommel and the German Africa Corps were still the darlings of the German press and the people, but now Rommel and his soldiers were admired for their fortitude and steadfastness, rather than for their past reckless advances that had chased the British Army from Libya far into Egypt.

So the year 1942 seemed strangely unexciting, but bad news came before its end, many German cities had been heavily bombed. In Stalingrad, the army of General Paulus had been encircled by the Red Army and cut off from all supply

lines except those by air. And after the Allied troops landed in North Africa,
Rommel no longer fought the British on Egyptian soil.
Everything seemed to take a slight turn towards the negative. At Christmas,
everybody was in an anxious mood.

* * *

The era of Hitler's Blitzkrieg, of conquering one country after another seemed to have come to an end, or at least to a standstill, as if all of Europe took one deep breath before the war would return to its former intensity, with objectives, successes, and losses that were unpredictable.

While the war slowed down, life at home assumed a feverish joie de vivre. German cultural life was at a hitherto unknown height and pace. It was fed, promoted, and operated by the party and the state in order to maintain a high morale among civilians and soldiers. Everybody relished life to its utmost.

I must clarify, that the feverish pace of life and culture in the midst of wartime was only visible and palpable in the bigger cities. Nothing of the kind could be noticed in small towns and villages, that often remained peaceful and remote. Everywhere, though, one would find citizens in mourning, because one of their loved ones had died in the war. Neither was the older generation caught up in the hunger for life and pleasure that had gripped the younger men and women, especially the male and female members of the Army and the other semi-military organizations.

Everybody listened to — and hummed — the songs of Zarah Leander, the Swedish actress that had crossed over to Hitler's Germany and became the country's only true star. Her dark voice with its seductive Swedish accent was unique among German entertainers, and her songs became the barometer of the mood of the people. Her songs celebrated love and women — "Only love makes a woman beautiful;" "I give my love for life." True to the mood of 1942, there was a touch of frivolity — "Could love ever be a sin?" And also sentiment and melancholy — "Merci, mon ami, it was wonderful;" "Don't ever cry because of love!" And as the prospects for victory receded, a step further towards pessimism — "I stand in the rain;" "Don't say Adieu to me, say Auf Wiedersehen!" And finally, as defeat became more and more certain, and fear of not surviving rose, Zarah Leander sang in wild defiance, yet in false optimism — "This will not bring the world to an end;" and reflecting the attitude of tens of millions of Germans — "I know, there will be a miracle . . ." No matter how hard Germany's cultural authorities tried, they could not create another popular artist who came even close to Zarah Leander. During the war years, she was Nazi Germany's only superstar!

The hunger of the masses for fun and distraction showed itself in all aspects of the cultural life, mainly in the big cities. Theatres were always sold out. Music halls and nightclubs were full, and books were published in large numbers. More than half of art and literature was merely detestable propaganda in disguise, but what remained, while still controlled by the Nazi propaganda apparatus, was politically untainted and pure enjoyment, and was often of high entertainment value.

I remember the motion pictures of these years. I think I saw them all! The propaganda films to which we were taken during school hours were artistically and technically of superior quality, but all of them had overt and covert messages designed to implant pride in everything German and hatred for everything Jewish, British, French, Bolshevik, and American.

There were the outright anti-Semitic films of gross hatred such as *Jud Süss, Rothschild siegt bei Waterloo*,[1] and *Die Goldene Stadt*,[2] for which Germany's best actors were engaged. They also starred in films that made heroes out of historic figures such as *Ohm Krüger*, the leader of the Boers during the South African War; *Friedrich Schiller*, the German poet; *Andreas Schlüter*, the Prussian architect, *Otto von Bismarck* the German chancellor, and continuing like a series, more films about *Frederick II (The Great) of Prussia*. In every one of these films, the protagonist was portrayed as a superior German character, often ahead of his time, and therefore misunderstood or persecuted, while in the anti-Semitic films, all non-Jewish Germans fell victim to Jewish cunning, perfidy, and dishonesty. These films were fed in a continuous psychological diet to the German population including school children, *Hitlerjugend* members, and soldiers.

There were a handful of films to which people would flock without being ordered or encouraged. These were films of astonishing depth, beauty, sophistication, charm, and wit. They were absolutely apolitical and did not carry a trace of overt or hidden propaganda. Reviewing these films decades later, one comes to the conclusion that the great Hollywood movies and the French films must have been studied intensively as models for these German films. There was the incredibly beautiful and

---

1   ("Rothchild's Victory at Waterloo")

2   Prague during pre-Hitler times is the "Golden City" degenerating under the reign of decadent Czechs and perverse Jews, against whom the German rural minority defends itself. The star of this celebrated film was Kristina Söderbaum, another Swedish actress who had starred in several Nazi propaganda films, frequently in roles where her life ended in suicide by drowning. Amongst the Berliners she earned the mock honorary title of *Reichswasserleiche (the National Drowned Corpse)*.

profound film *Romanze in Moll* by Helmut Käutner, whose main female lead had a character that was absolutely at odds with the ideal of the German woman. There was the charming, sophisticated film *Bel Ami* by Willi Forst who was its director and male lead — in neither role the ideal German male. In the delightful musical *Wir machen Musik*, also by Helmut Käutner, the back and forth between talking and singing by the actors for once did not come across awkwardly as in all other German musical films; Käutner's film was produced along the lines of the successful Hollywood movie musical.

At this time, the movie industry in occupied France operated unimpeded by the German occupation and one of its stars, the charming Danielle Darrieux became popular overnight in Germany with the film *Her First Rendezvous*. Even despite her Slavic features, the Czech actress Hanna Vitova was promoted to stardom with her film *Nachtfalter* (Moths), a rather decadent story. Not too long after her debut in the German film, however, Hanna Vitova Germanized her name to Hanna Witt and appeared in outright propaganda films.

There were more musical films, interestingly most with foreign actors in the main leads. First among these was the incomparable Zarah Leander, probably the only actress in Germany of that time who could be compared to a Hollywood star. She acted in a great number of films, which helped her retain her fame and popularity beyond the war years, even though she did not stay away from Nazi propaganda films. Next to her was the Hungarian Marika Rökk, who was wildly popular because of her talent as a singer and dancer, but she never acquired the true star qualities that Zarah Leander possessed. Marika Rökk starred in the first German color film, in an astonishingly extravagant musical. Also among this group of foreign actors was the Dutchman Johannes Heesters, a smooth, quite charming singer and dancer who became the uncontested top male star in German musical films. He was, however, in no way close to the ideal of the German male promoted by the Nazis.

These foreign actors, while politically harmless, nevertheless contributed enormously to the German war effort. If something supported the morale of the Germans at a time when the news of victories were no longer plentiful, air raids increased in intensity, and daily life became grey and hard, it was the German film industry with its musicals and comedies and the prominence given to its foreign stars.

Next to these was the army of German actors and actresses who were engaged in numerous films, which the German film companies churned out at a frantic pace. From propaganda to neutral films, they were all serving Hitler's objectives of winning this war and shaping Europe according to the Nazi ideology. These actors were reputed to draw exorbitant fees. It would not be wrong to classify them as war profiteers.

My father, who loved good films and movie musicals, had very mixed feelings when he considered how many of these German actors had been colleagues and close friends of the numerous actors of Jewish descent or anti-Nazi convictions who had to flee Germany after January 30, 1933. The same was true of musicians such as the prominent German conductor Wilhelm Furtwängler, and of many writers, sculptors, and painters and, of course, of scientists, philosophers, and other prominent persons belonging to the academic world. They all seemed to readily forget their past artist friends who had been blacklisted after January 30, 1933 and had been forced to emigrate, or were languishing in concentration camps, or had been murdered by the Nazis.

The hand of the propaganda in building up people's morale was also apparent on the concert stage. All of a sudden, the jazz pianist, composer, and bandleader Peter Kreuder returned to the stage of the Konzerthaus in Breslau after years of politically enforced semi-retirement. In the same year, 1942, the *Meister Sextett* was reconstituted, albeit with totally different — non-Jewish — singers. The group recreated the sound of the original sextet, that had been condemned by the Nazis as "decadent."[3]

Also of sudden prominence was *Das Deutsche Tanzorchester von Georg Haentzschel*, later recognized as an unabashed copy of the American big bands. In terms of instrumentation and arrangements, the music of this *German Dance Orchestra of Georg Haentzschel* was true American swing except for its inability to recreate the authentic, easy rhythm of the American bands.

Copies of American jazz records floated around in a kind of black market exchange. One time, even my Aunt Martel who managed a large drugstore in Waldenburg, quickly grabbed a record of jazz music for me, for which she herself had no particular taste. My friends and I cherished the sound of Louis Armstrong's music, the *Tiger Rag*, the *St. Louis Blues*, and of the Andrew Sisters, especially their song that started with the Yiddish words *Baj mir bistu schajn*.

It is hard to imagine how all this charming, easygoing music and entertainment created a carefree, happy atmosphere in movie houses,

---

3   Originally named the *Comedian Harmonists*, after January 1933 for a brief time *Die Komödien Harmonisten*, the group pursued a style that came close to that of the original American *Ink Spots*. As most of the members were either Jewish or foreigners, they were forced to disband during the early stage of the Third Reich. The fact that they were being reconstituted in the later war years says much about the deviousness of German propaganda that now promoted a sound that was certainly decadent by the artistic code of the Third Reich.

musical theatres, cabarets, and dance halls. After all, we were in the third and fourth year of the war. I can only explain this by the fact that in all these places, the majority of the audience consisted of soldiers. These were men on leave from the Front, soldiers housed in local barracks waiting to be commandeered to the Front, or wounded soldiers soon to be sent back to battle, or patients of military hospitals on an evening out, eager to enjoy a few hours of fun and entertainment. All these men were cherishing every minute of freedom from fear, of enjoying pleasant entertainment, often in the company of a girlfriend or a wife. Barely below the surface, however, remained the anxiety about returning sooner or later to war and a hard life of danger and possibly death.[4]

There is another telling memory I have from that time, when we began to feel like adults. I turned 17 during this summer and felt quite comfortable conducting myself, in my appearance and interests as an adult. With one or two exceptions, we were all like that in our class in school. Because we dressed like adults — from hat to scarf to gloves, from dress shirts to ties and bow ties, all items worn every day even in school as "must" items of elegance — we easily gained access to entertainments reserved for adults. We loved to go to the cabaret and dance palace of the *Liebich Theater*, but I preferred the intimacy of the *Kabarett Kaiserkrone* that featured French chanteuses, jazz pianists, and male crooners.

Again, the question will be raised of how we managed to dress in style at a time when everything was rationed and in short supply. Our mothers seemed to be most inventive in either trading something for some material, or having clothing of our fathers taken apart, turned inside out and remade into jackets, coats, skirts, and pants for their sons and daughters, all in the latest style. In addition, on the black market in Breslau, there was still cloth available from the flood of bolts of cloth that had been sent or brought from the large Polish textile centres such as Łódź (between 1939 and 1945 Litzmannstadt).

We often shared a table in a café, cabaret, or a nightclub with soldiers who invariably constituted the majority of the guests. In retrospect, I experience feelings of slight embarrassment when I think of us sitting in the company of soldiers, true adults, while we were trying to look like and be accepted as grownups. Yet I cannot think of a single situation where these soldiers were anything but very friendly to us, treating us as adults, thus adding to the enjoyment of the evening. I am sure that in such situations the soldiers must have thought about us tender, near-adults being drafted very soon and perhaps losing our life

---

4 I vividly remember my own sense of urgency not to miss a moment of freedom and fun while I was awaiting the transfer to the front after the end of boot camp.

in battle a few months later. This sense of a common fate, I believe, created a peculiar empathy between strangers; it brought people closer together than any forced expectation by the state; it was the sense of comradeship that transgressed uniforms and ranks, even nations. To this day, I have a sense of comradeship with the soldiers of other, once hostile nations.

In other ways as well, 1942 was an easier year for me. For once, I evaded party-prescribed summer work or pre-military camp during the school holidays, as our relatives had applied for a permit for me to work on their farm in Deutsch-Kamitz (since 1945 Kępnica) near Neisse, renamed by the Nazis as Hermannstein.[5] I stayed with my great-aunt (sister of Grandmother Hackenberg) and her husband, who, still six feet tall, erect, and with a full head of carefully combed white hair and a large white moustache, looked like a picture of health at the age of 85. He still managed to give some help on the farm. This was a difficult year for my relatives, as my mother's cousin, the owner of the farm, had been drafted into the Army, even though his younger brother had already been killed in the French campaign. Except for my great-uncle, there was only one other man working there, a forced labourer, a Russian, who however, was treated like one of the family; he was strong and always cheerful. I liked him very much, and especially loved to sit with him in the evenings on the front steps, listening to the mournful Russian songs he played on the accordion of my uncle.

My mother's unmarried cousin Martha literally ran the entire farm with the help of two Polish girls, also forced labourers. They were sweet and nice, but also a bit cunning and lazy; they pretended to get easily tired, would sit down and exclaim "Tante Martha stark!" (Aunt Martha is so much stronger than we are.) Aunt Martha was good-natured, but she became quite annoyed with the girls at times, but invariably ended up doing much of their work herself. War was far away. We never heard the sound of foreign aircraft, and transportation was by horse and buggy, which often took us to the other relatives who all had substantial properties. My favourite destination was the mill owned by one of my mother's cousins. Located alongside a little stream in an open valley surrounded by low, but heavily wooded hills, this mill was as romantic as a picture from the nineteenth century.

---

5   To extinguish the slightest indication that at some time, Poles had settled in Silesia, thousands of village and town names were Germanized under Hitler. Similarly, people with Polish last names were strongly encouraged to adopt a German name, which was arranged by the state free of charge.

The relationship with my father was much better that year and he was less restrictive with me than before. I do not think he had modified his standards, but he simply did not feel well enough to uphold expectations he had for my conduct. He often had to stay home from his office, which depressed the mood in the family. I felt guilty but nevertheless, I escaped to spend almost every weekend with my Grandmother Koch in Waldenburg. She was most easygoing and generous with me; she set no restrictions, and fully trusted me. As a result, I behaved better there than at home and was a lot happier. I also was treated like a son by my father's youngest brother Hubert and his wife Käthe, who shared the large second floor in the original Koch house with my grandmother. My uncle was not too well, but my aunt was full of life and to please her, we went to the theatre, to concerts, and on outings into the mountains many times. Between my grandmother and my Uncle Hubert and his wife, I felt happy and relaxed.

I remember a trip with my best friend to the Bohemian part of the *Riesengebirge* where we did a lot of hiking. What stayed with me from that trip, however, was not the idyllic mountain scenery but the last hour of our long hike to the train that was to take us home. In a narrow side valley, just before entering the charming little town of Hohenelbe (1918-1938 and since 1945 Vrchlabí) we came across a smallish concentration camp, obviously full of Jewish inmates of all ages. The barracks and the yard, crowded with inmates behind thick barbed wire, appeared totally incongruous in this picturesque little valley. We recognized the emaciated faces and painful features very well from the road and actually stopped in horror and began to talk about what was confronting us, when a military car came racing up the unpaved road and with angry words, the driver in SS uniform ordered us to move on fast, unless we wanted to be apprehended. The beautiful memories of this trip were extinguished for a long time.

In school, there was no more stress in the classroom. Because of a greatly reduced number of students, the two classrooms of my grade level were amalgamated. Most students had been drafted into the Army and quite a few had already lost their lives in the war. Where there had been two classrooms with more than 100 students a few years before, there were now only about 25 left in one room. Yet there was an invisible wall between the two groups, and our old classroom or what was left of it kept its reserve to the end, as most members of the other classroom were openly Nazi. Overall, however, the general atmosphere was much more relaxed than in past years. The teachers were more easygoing and friendly and far less demanding. I am sure they were affected by the comparatively large number of our former classmates who had died in the war, and the thought that some of us might also be killed within less than a year.

Without really intending to, we took full advantage of this easy atmosphere and played hooky far too often. There was not a day when a few of us were not absent. Instead of appearing in school at eight in the morning, we would gather at the *Oder River* for swimming and boating, while in winter we would go to the luxurious indoor pool downtown, then have a second breakfast in the restaurant, and then go to a movie.[6] At that time, all downtown theatres had begun to show the first feature at 11 in the morning. Our absence from school had to be legitimized in some way or other. I must confess that we forged our parents' signatures, as we always had to bring a note from home explaining our absence on the previous day. I cannot believe that our teachers failed to recognize that these were not the true signatures of our fathers or mothers.

When I think of my youth, especially during the war years, I love to dwell on this year, that for me had more activities and experiences, that one considers part of a happy adolescence than all other years before and after. It pains me, however, that nothing of what I fondly remember involved my father. This was not alone due to our strained relationship and my rebellion against his rigid standards — his failing health removed him from my life. Ever since World War I, when in battle he had lain in ice and snow, he had had an extremely sensitive stomach. After my mother's death, I found letters he wrote to his future wife in the early 1920s, questioning whether they should get married, as he might not live much longer. He was sent to rest cures and special treatments many times, but nothing seemed to help. His stomach condition slowly became more severe and incapacitating, physically as well as emotionally. It is only a few years ago that medical science discovered the *heliobacter pylori* and determined its presence as the cause of chronic stomach ulcers. I am sure this is what gradually killed my father whose condition of what was then called *chronic gastritis* was treated symptomatically only for lack of knowledge of the true cause.

Disregard and inadequate knowledge also existed about the emotional component of my father's illness, which may have been fuelled by the bitterness he harboured about the treatment by his own father. My grandfather was an impressive, loving man with a great sense of humour.

---

6   As with clothing, Silesia was also blessed with a relatively adequate food supply. Our mothers always had some food stamps for bread and cake (Kuchenmarken) left over to give to us. It was no accident that practically to the end of the war, Silesia, had not experienced any air raids. Typically, it was referred to as "Germany's air raid shelter."

I will never understand why he singled out my father from his six surviving sons in treating him shabbily at a time when my father, without his fault, lost his job and lived with his family at the edge of poverty. I remember how my father usually withdrew to another room when this topic was raised, which was not very often, as he did not want to cry in front of my mother and myself.

I admit that at that time I still did not sense any guilt about cheating my father, but I did feel terribly sorry knowing how he went through night after night without sleep because of extreme pain. My father and I did not argue anymore, but we could not share our feelings as I wish now that we could have.

The year 1942 ended with many question marks in people's minds as to the future. Germany had not experienced severe losses, but there were single events, or first instances of what was to reoccur later. These single events and first instances ended up as symbols for a new era in the war, or for something one would never be able to forget.

This began early in 1942 when Hitler assumed the position of supreme commander of the German Army; from then on he only wore military clothing and was never seen again in his brown Nazi uniform.

All year, the Eastern Front moved back and forth, although the German armies did progress to the Caucasus and to the Volga. Too often was territory lost and regained several times.

Everyday, one heard the talk about the *partisans* — guerrillas in today's parlance. This was the new hostile element that had risen in the East like a second army making the entire territory under German control unsafe.

No longer was North Africa a tale of victorious Rommel's heroism. The retreat of the German Africa Corps began with El Alamein in western Egypt and the evacuation of the remaining troops to Italy after the landing of the Allied units in western North Africa. It was the beginning of a new phase in the war and not a few people asked "and how soon will they (the Allied armies) land in Italy?"

Hamburg and Lübeck were the first German cities to suffer the fate of their sister cities Warsaw, Rotterdam, Coventry, Liverpool, and London of being firebombed. Over the remaining years of the war, most large German cities experienced the same fate.

Another first of a phenomenon not to go away for the rest of the war was the genocide of Europe's Jews. Before 1942, most people would only admit that Jews were herded into ghettos in Poland and Russia, or that they had been removed from German soil. But in 1942, stories began to circulate that brought for the first time the concept of *the final solution* to the surface. People could no longer deny that the Jews were not only deported to the East as a source of labour, but that they were deported to be killed there in millions. More and more stories that substantiated these rumours were brought back by soldiers on leave from the Eastern Front. Yet too many people suppressed this knowledge, too many also simply denied it, and too many exclaimed, *"wenn nur der Führer davon wüsste!"* (If only our Leader would know), hanging on to the illusion that Hitler was an honourable man, who would have stopped the killing long ago, if it only would not be hidden from him.

For me, there were three events in the fall of 1942 that gave me certainty about the horror of what was to be called the Holocaust.

When the brother-in-law of my Aunt Käthe came home on leave from Latvia, he was close to a nervous breakdown. Originally, he had been exempted from the draft, since he was managing a large business. Instead, he was made into an auxiliary policeman. Soon after, without being given a choice, he was transferred to one of the infamous *Polizeiregimenter* that worked closely with the *SS* in the killing of Jews and members of Eastern nationalities.[7] Aunt Käthe's brother-in-law came to visit my Grandmother Koch while I was there and told us that he was stationed in the Latvian capital of Riga and was responsible for a volunteer group of Latvians who were delegated to kill the Jews from the large Riga ghetto. He did not do any killing himself, but he had to watch the horrible death scenes day after day. He also recognized that among the Jews who mostly spoke Yiddish, of which he understood enough to sense their extreme fear of death, there were other Jewish families, by the sound of their accent obviously deported from Silesia and from Berlin. He had placed his family in great distress when he considered either deserting or committing suicide. In the end, he followed the urging of his wife and prepared a submission to his commanding officer requesting his transfer to a regular army unit. Within two weeks of his return to Latvia, his wife received a telegram advising her that her husband had died as a result of an accident. She was convinced that he had committed suicide after all.

At that time, one of my classmates, who originally came from *Ostoberschlesien*,[8] told me that in the town of his birth, people secretly talked about "das Vergasen der Juden."[9] This was the first direct reference to the concentration camp of Auschwitz, located in *Ostoberschlesien* near the town that had belonged to Poland between the two world wars.

---

7   The police regiments were close to the SS and given the same tasks, i.e., the rounding up and mass killings of the Jews and the killing of Poles, Ukrainians, Russians, and other peoples.

8   Eastern Upper Silesia, the part of Upper Silesia that had been Polish after the plebiscite of 1921.

9   The gassing of the Jews.

Soon after, one heard off and on nasty remarks or pseudo-jokes ending in "Dich werden sie auch noch vergasen!"[10]

Finally, I was confronted for several months with trains full of Jews on the opposite platform of the railroad junction Königzelt (since 1956 Jaworzyna Śląska), located between Waldenburg and Breslau, where our train had a 10-minute stop. I frequently used this train after visiting my grandmother in Waldenburg. The first time I observed this train, a passenger asked a railway employee who these passengers were and got the answer "Jews from France and Holland." I had quickly noticed that these densely packed trains did not consist of the usual German coaches — the emblems on their sides indicated that they came from France and Holland. I was already familiar with the terrible term *vergasen* – to kill by gassing — and arrived home depressed and full of hate.

One could not believe that Hitler would or could succeed in killing all the Jews in Europe, but the process was well established by 1942 and, at least in Silesia, common knowledge by all those who cared to know.

The final event confirming that during 1942 Germany had arrived at a fateful crossroads signalled the end of the first victorious half of the war. It was the encirclement of Stalingrad, announced on November 19, 1942. Two hundred twenty thousand German soldiers were trapped in the city on the Volga by superior Soviet forces. Hitler refused to permit the retreat of the German troops from their hopeless positions in Stalingrad, although all attempts to break through from the outside and relieve the beleaguered German troops failed. Stalingrad had become the crucible of Germany's invincibility.

Stalingrad became the most terrible of symbols of Hitler's power over people. By the end of 1942, nobody believed that the German soldiers in Stalingrad could hold out much longer. The myth of the invincible German soldier and its invincible leader Hitler had come to an end.

* * * * *

---

10   "Watch out, they are going to gas you too!"

11 | 1943
Reversal of Fortune

S talingrad falls; retreat in the East continues; the battlegrounds of last year's victories return in the news, but now they signal defeat. Air raids are getting heavier. German forces in North Africa capitulate; Allied forces land in Sicily; Mussolini is deposed; Italy declares war on Germany.

* * *

Thinking of the year 1943 and what it would bring, I was anxious and unsettled from its first day on. Soon, I would face my senior matriculation exams to be followed by entry into the Labour Service and later my draft into the Army. I was aware that I would not leave the Army until the end of the war. This meant becoming a prisoner of war before the end of the lost war. The alternatives were even bleaker: I might be discharged after being severely wounded to the extent of remaining a permanent cripple or, more likely, I might be killed in battle. These were constant thoughts I could not ban from my mind.

What affected everyone's mood, however, was the fall of Stalingrad on February 2, 1943. On the afternoon of that day, I happened to be in the *Gloria Palast* to watch a movie when suddenly, the lights came on and the manager appeared on the stage to advise us that the 6th Army had surrendered and the heroic battle of Stalingrad had ended. Across

Germany, the authorities proclaimed a period of deep mourning. All entertainments were discontinued for several weeks; theatres were closed. A pervasive sense that the fall of Stalingrad was the beginning of the end was felt everywhere. The Nazi propaganda, however, did not give up. A new kind of propaganda rolled across the country.

On February 18, the minister of propaganda, Dr. Josef Goebbels, gave his infamous speech in the *Sportpalast* of Berlin to thousands of soldiers, party members, and civilians, to celebrate the unbeatable spirit of Germany that would bring a glorious victory. Goebbels announced a wide range of drastic measures designed to involve every last person in the war effort and ended with his screaming the final sentences: "Do you want total war? Do you want, if necessary, this war more total and radical than we could possibly imagine today?"

We had been called to the assembly hall in school. I do not think that anybody who listened to Goebbels' horrible voice, will ever forget the unending screams of "Yes, Yes, Yes" of the huge enthusiastic crowd that filled the *Sportpalast*. Less than two years later, people could not deny that they got the *Totalen Krieg* (the total war) Goebbels had predicted, but it had turned into a war infinitely worse than imagined, a war ending in total defeat.

I did not look forward to my senior matriculation exams. I had hardly studied during the past couple of years. My competence in mathematics and science was so deplorable that I was seriously worried about not getting a passing grade. If I failed, there would be no mercy such as remaining in school for another year, as the draft would not be postponed (our school had already cooperated by giving us a chance to take the regular senior matriculation exams several months ahead of time). There were close to a dozen written exams to be followed by an indeterminate number of orals, depending on the outcome of the written exams.

I chose to manipulate and sign up for orals in subjects I did well in — German, History, and French — to balance my hopeless standing in math and science. For art history, my chosen option, I worked intensively with my art teacher Georg Nerlich, a well-known painter who had been in deep disfavour with the Nazis and had to become an art teacher in order to support himself and his wife, as he was no longer allowed to sell his paintings. I also ended with an excellent mark in physical education that was solely based on my track and field record. Not very well muscled, I had always done very poorly in gymnastics, especially on single and on parallel bars. However, my phys ed teacher Mr. Hermann, a German golf pro from Brazil, who had been trapped during his holiday by the outbreak of war and was ordered to teach in a German school, told me flatly that I would have to find a way to miss the exam in gymnastics, as otherwise I would spoil my good mark based on my excellent performance in track and field.[1] I did not even consider asking my father to rescue me from this predicament, as I knew only too well that he would refuse. Instead, I found an ally in our family physician whom I visited early in the morning of the phys ed exam pleading for his help. Without saying very much, he wrapped a heavy bandage around my right hand and suspended my arm in a sling; he also certified in writing that I was stricken with severe tendonitis. While this assured me a fine mark in physical education, I had to play the charade of having tendonitis for several days in school, and at home.

There was no jubilation and no glamour when in a simple ceremony the vice mayor[2] of our city handed the senior matriculation certificates to us. We were a sad little group of students who by fate of being younger were still in the classroom, while the majority of our former classmates had long been in the army, quite a few of them already dead in battle. With great difficulty, we managed to arrange for an evening celebration in a third class restaurant[3] to which we invited only one of our teachers. We disbanded after barely three hours, but some of us followed the invitation of the mother of our top student. His parents were in business, which permitted his mother to offer us an incredible spread of good food and drink. I did not dare phone my father to tell him that I would be late. Instead, I did not return home until six in the morning. My father, who was ill in bed, was terribly angry, but he did keep his promise that I could visit relatives in Berlin and in North Germany as a reward for passing my senior matriculation.

My first stop was Berlin, where I stayed with my aunt, a widow who had lost her son in Stalingrad. I arrived on March 2, which brought the city its so far heaviest air raid of the war. The district where my aunt lived suffered terribly, but we all survived. I was glad I was there, because I can say that without my help, my aunt would have lost her apartment, which, when we were allowed to leave the shelter, we found partly in flames. My aunt and I managed to extinguish the fire before it created irreversible damage. Berlin seemed in shambles the next day, but again, I observed

---

1 Physical education was of highest priority during the Third Reich. We had up to five hours of phys ed per week, added to which came another five hours of sports per week in the Hitler Youth. A failure to pass phys ed could result in a failure to pass the senior matriculation exams.

2 Approximately two years later, the Nazis executed this fine man, Dr. Spielhagen, as a "defeatist and traitor" when the city was proclaimed a *fortress* to be defended against the approaching Red Army.

3 A formerly famous inn, named *Das Goldene Zepter,* the Golden Sceptre, where the Prussian King had proclaimed Prussia's War of Liberation against Napoleon in 1813.

the phenomenon that life went on. I could go to theatres and music halls, which still offered top entertainment.

As a matter of record, I must mention that my aunt took me to a friend of hers who suffered through a deteriorating marriage, after her husband, once a high officer in the police of the Weimar Republic and, later in the Third Reich, had chosen to join the *SS*. He quickly rose through the upper ranks, and at the time of my visit in March 1943, this family lived in a luxurious apartment in the heavily guarded compound of Hitler's chancellery, where nothing was missing of amenities and luxury items, which by that time were beyond the reach of the average citizen; neither was there any shortage of rare foods which were purchased in a special store that was not accessible to the general public.

My aunt and I had to pass more than one control point before we reached the elegant house of her friend. It was a strange afternoon. I was in a location where, if it had not been for my aunt, I would not have chosen to be under any circumstances. I was troubled by how my aunt's friend, who made no secret of her hostility against Hitler, nevertheless enjoyed living in such utter luxury on the grounds of Hitler's Chancellery. Actually, as I can gather now, she lived almost on top of the bunker where Hitler ended his life in spring of 1945.

After leaving Berlin, I visited Aunt Käthe in Schwerin, the capital of Mecklenburg, a charming former ducal residence where something approaching peace still reigned. One day, my father called me requesting that I return home immediately. He refused to give me permission to go on to Hamburg, but I did so just the same, with the blessing of my aunt who, like the rest of the family, always felt sorry for my being so restricted by my father. When I did return home a week later, our neighbour told me that my father had received an unexpected leave, which allowed my parents to go to the mountains for a holiday. I followed them to the village of Hain (since 1945 Przesieka), a resort in the *Riesengebirge*, where my father forgave me quite quickly. These were the last holidays we spent together as a family and they were truly harmonious from beginning to end. Looking back, I am very grateful that we had this opportunity to be together.

Soon after, the Labour Service called me up.[4] It was, predictably, a most unpleasant experience, a true waste of time. Personally though,

---

4   The *Reichsarbeitsdienst (RAD)*, was one of the many Nazi organizations. Young men and women were drafted into the *RAD* after completion of high school or of apprenticeship. The *RAD* was run along military lines; its length was shortened from one year to half a year and by *1943* to three months, in order to get the young men into the army as quickly as possible. The RAD never enjoyed any status. Its leaders were generally considered not competent enough to occupy similar or even lesser positions in the armed forces.

there were some compensations for me. First of all, I was assigned to an *RAD* camp in the farthest corner of East Prussia, where I had never been. On the transport by train, I saw much of the countryside between Silesia and East Prussia. I found the latter province a country of great charm. It was a mainly rural province where, for the first time in my life, I realized that non-mountainous country can be attractive, a first impression that would deepen later during my time in Russia and, ultimately, lead me to the Canadian prairies.

The camp was most primitive and even lacked a minimal supply of water. We rapidly became rather dirty and, as we only had one change of underwear in three months, we carried a simply terrible smell on our bodies. Our leaders acted with great pride, although none of them were worth our respect. We were drilled as if we were in an army boot camp and were put to work with primitive tools to dig drainage ditches on private land, while the landowners stood next to us, cursing us for spoiling their rich pastures. We had to endure two or three hours of daily political indoctrination that especially focused on the fate of this borderland which faced Polish settlements only a few miles away. The Nazis had built an entire mythology about the courage of the brave Germans that lived along the eastern border, which for us sounded absolutely ridiculous, as we quickly found out on our first leave (a few hours on Sunday afternoon) that the local people in this remote south-eastern corner of East Prussia all spoke Polish. The village next to our camp had carried the name Zwalinnen (since 1945 Cwaliny) for hundreds of years, but was renamed Schwallen, five years after Hitler took power.[5] One day we were ordered to go *auf Partisanenjagd*, on guerrilla hunt, after groups of Polish and Jewish partisans had been reported on the other side of the border. After we had crossed into formerly Polish country, we found out that the land, the farming practices, the houses, and the people were all identical to the villages we had become familiar with on the German side. We did not locate any partisans, which was a blessing, as our spades were our only weapons, while our leader merely carried a ridiculously small pistol strapped to his belt. Can one imagine anything else but disgust with such pretence? What if we had come across guerrillas who would invariably have carried guns?

A few weeks before the end of our time with the *RAD*, I broke my glasses, which necessitated a trip to the city of Allenstein. The slow train ride there took more than six hours over a distance of perhaps 60 miles,

---

5   In East Prussia, the majority, in Pomerania and Silesia a near majority of all place names were changed by Hitler's edict, as they were of Polish origin and as such conflicted with the history of these provinces as it was taught in the Third Reich.

preceded by a four hour hike from the camp to the railroad station. Again, this was a precious experience, getting to know this remote part of Germany. It was here that heavy fighting took place at the beginning of World War I when the Russian armies flooded into East Prussia. The train trundled slowly through endless pine forests, stopped at every little village and gave me an opportunity to sense how devastating these first months of World War I had been. Everywhere, I saw old fortifications designed to protect this strategic railway line that closely followed the old German-Russian border. I noticed German and Russian soldiers' cemeteries everywhere. The towns where I had to change trains, such as Johannisburg (since 1945 Pisz), looked strangely modern for this backward country, until I realized that their destruction in 1914/1915 had necessitated such extensive rebuilding after World War I.

When we were riding the train back to Silesia, we were all looking forward to being drafted into the Army, because it could only be better than the pathetic Labour Service, which we were grateful to escape from.

For reasons unknown, I had a month's grace before being called up. The weather was wonderful and I escaped from home and spent most of my time with my Grandmother Koch in Waldenburg. More than ever I felt this gritty mining town with its overwhelmingly working class population was my true home. I consciously cherished these last days of my freedom.

For most men, life as a soldier in wartime was rough, tough, cruel, bloody, and dangerous. Hardly anyone survived unscathed, that is without being wounded at least once. Many soldiers were captured long before the end of the war which added years of a prisoner of war life to their existence, and many did not survive. Many were reported missing in action which, in most cases, meant that they were dead. This left a terrible burden on families who, for year after year, long after peace had arrived, hoped against hope that one day, a beloved father, brother, or son might turn up at the door. Too many were killed in action; a likely fate I, as everyone else, was always conscious of, already before being sent to the Front and into battle.

As it turned out, I would be wounded more than once and also carry a life-threatening infection with me when I was brought back from the Eastern Front. Danger to my life did not even end after I became a prisoner of war. There were psychological near-killing experiences that will stay with me to the end of my life. Still, I look back on my years as a soldier and a prisoner as being blessed many times with good fortune.

My military life began with a bit of good fortune, when on the day of being drafted I was sent to Liegnitz in Silesia, a mere 40 miles from my home town Breslau. I had several relatives in Liegnitz. My mother was jubilant about my being stationed there. Grandfather Hackenberg's brother with his large family had lived in Liegnitz from where my mother had only the happiest memories of frequent holidays. She had five cousins there, three girls whose names all started with L, i.e., Leni, Luzie, and Lisa, and two brothers Alfons and Siegfried. I knew them all and they were indeed a kind, cheerful bunch. Luzie had a heart of gold and looked after me whenever I had a pass from the barracks. I adored the tall Lisa who was a rare beauty with long blond hair and finely chiselled features; she sang and played the piano with great talent and skill. And I loved Leni who was short and chubby but a bundle of humour and good will. Alfons was a successful factory owner, so much so that he was exempted from military service. His much younger brother Siegfried was in the Navy.

Quite a few weeks passed before I got my first pass for a Sunday afternoon and was able to see my relatives. By that time, I was through the worst of boot camp training. Although the training continued with unabated intensity, I myself had become toughened to its rigors. I belonged to the Infantry Regiment 51, housed in one of the countless new barracks that had been built as part of Hitler's rearmament program. There were four companies of recruits, each housed in a four-story barracks building of plain character, but with the amenities of showers that, however, were only turned on once a week. Meals were taken in a special building with a mess hall of actually quite pleasant appearance. The food was nourishing based on meeting the physical demands of training; but there was rarely a well-tasting meal. There was a large parade ground in the centre of the complex and numerous garage and storage buildings.

Our company had a rather unpleasant commanding officer, a short man of cruel features who obviously suffered under the shortcomings of his appearance; he was incredibly mean, sadistic, and over-demanding. In his presence, life was hell. But as compensation, our platoon leaders, all battle-hardened soldiers, were very human and decent men; perhaps they tried to balance the horrible personality of the commander. They were tough and their demands and expectations on us were high, but we understood and appreciated their goal of preparing us as thoroughly as possible for survival at the Front and in battle and we followed them willingly. What I respect these four platoon leaders for to this day was their common sense, their ability to deal with young, untrained soldiers by being tough on them without destroying their self-esteem, and for manifesting a character that was deeply admired and respected by us recruits. It is important to understand that the educational background of the platoon leaders was rather modest, while more than half of the recruits were high school graduates. The corporals leading our platoons consisted of one baker (my platoon leader), one candy maker, one butcher, and one farm labourer. They were great guys and, I believe, were representative of the majority of corporals in the Army, while the non-commissioned officers and the full officers were, at least in my personal experience, of far less admirable character, often betraying a complete lack of humane feelings and respect for the soldiers under their command. In Liegnitz, in Russia, and even in prison camp, I met a number of corporals who still are my heroes; they were not outstanding personalities, but they were utterly decent human beings; most of them showed that they cared for us like fathers or big brothers. With dedication, they shared their own experience with us, which became of crucial importance for our physical and psychological survival. Living under their command was positive enough for me to think back of my first nine months in Liegnitz as a tolerable, useful and, perhaps ultimately, life-saving experience.

Another difference to the Labour Service was very evident: the need to prepare us for service at the Front overrode the political indoctrination, which was toned down drastically. Perhaps there was another reason, originating from the fact that more than half of the recruits came from *Ostoberschlesien* (East Upper Silesia) and until the beginning of the war had actually been Polish citizens. How Polish they were in their hearts, nobody could fathom. They were good comrades, but stuck together very much and never talked politics. Some were highly educated, many were young coal miners and others were farm boys. I loved their accent, which was actually based on a Polish dialect of which they fully retained the Polish grammar and syntax while speaking the now compulsory German. It was a charming way of speaking German, and they were all good-natured enough to join us in laughter when we occasionally failed to hide our amusement about their odd-sounding German.

There was a single soldier amongst them who reminded us of the cruelty of the Nazi regime day and night. He was a very good-looking, tall, strong, and intelligent man, the typical blond *Schlonsak,* a member of a Slavic group living in the western Carpathian mountains of Poland. We never found out the reason why he had been imprisoned in a concentration camp for three years; he never spoke one word about it. It was only our platoon leader who asked us to be gentle with this man who had been offered his discharge from the concentration camp provided he volunteered for the Army. This he did, and I can only say with gratitude that he was treated with great respect and affection by all his comrades and the corporals. Unfortunately, I cannot include our master sergeant and our company officer, who somehow had found out that his Polish last name translated into the German word *Hase,*[6] which

---

6   Rabbit in English; Zając in Polish.

easily invited ridicule with its connotation of fearfulness, cowardice, and running away. They nearly destroyed him emotionally, by first calling him *Hase* and as soon as he became visibly anxious and his entire body began to tremble, by shouting at him and threatening him with detention in the barracks lockup. They persisted in this cruel practice, even though everyone knew that as soon as someone stood close to him and looked in his face, he began to shake pitifully and started to stutter. His eyes spoke vividly of his terrible fear. I am grateful to be able to remember that all of us, and all of our corporals understood this man and treated him like a wounded human being that would never lose his fear of others.

Politically and ideologically, I felt much better in the Army. Indoctrination there was, but a lot less than in civilian life. At this time, one still sensed a noticeable adherence to Prussian military traditions – although not all of them were positive and to my liking. They functioned, however, as a balance against the overwhelming Nazi ideology that prevailed everywhere else in Germany. The raised arm as the *Heil Hitler* greeting was only practiced by the military as long as the greeter or greeted were bareheaded, which was rare; otherwise, the traditional placing of the right hand against the soldier's cap remained the rule.

Within this protective shell, the political and military events also seemed to have a reduced impact. When the Allied forces landed in Sicily in July, at the southern tip of Italy on September 3, and a week later at Salerno south of Naples, their presence on the Continent was accepted as a matter of fact rather quickly. I do not know whether at that time, the approaching forces of the Western Allies already raised the welcome thought in many minds of the end of war drawing nearer. Reaction to the news from the Eastern Front was somewhat different because of the widespread fear of the Red Army and of Communism, especially when the reports from the Eastern Front contained a steady flow of bad news signalling a constant retreat, usually disguised by the term of "straightening the front line." German troops had been pulled back from the Caucasus into the Ukraine and on November 6, Kiev fell to the Red Army. These were alarming developments raising the spectre of Soviet soldiers at Germany's eastern borders.

In contrast, developments in Italy, no matter how bad, were seen in a different light. Nobody seemed to be shocked when Mussolini was deposed on July 20. Our commanding officer during his regular morning news report read this particular bit of news with a sneer on his face. Germans had long ago ceased to take Mussolini seriously. The theatrics of "der dicke Makkaroni," (the Fat Macaroni) and the poor performance of the Italian army had been the butt of jokes for years. When the new Italian government, now allied with Great Britain and the USA, declared war on Germany on October 13, this was hardly considered an added threat to Germany.

By September, we were judged as adequately trained for weekend leave in the community. For such an occasion, Liegnitz was the ideal environment. Prior to World War I, the city had been one of the most prosperous in Silesia and the preferred residence of civil servants and the retired middle class. It was also a major garrison of the Imperial Army. When the German forces were drastically reduced to a tiny army of 100,000 men as a consequence of the lost World War I, Liegnitz badly faltered economically. The military no longer provided jobs and filled the places of entertainment and the drinking establishments; even the streetcar system was taken out of service for a number of years. When I spent my first nine months as a soldier in Liegnitz, the city was booming again with entertainment, from opera to concerts to music halls, and bars that ranged from quite elegant and frequented by officers, to pretty raucous places that were always packed to capacity by common soldiers and their girlfriends plus a noticeable number of unaccompanied girls who would be considered prostitutes at other times. I will never forget the noisy, wild nights at a rather large establishment, nicknamed *Die Wanne*[7] where members of the local military bands were playing during their free time. They played a fair number of officially outlawed American tunes, and everyone in town knew the title and the first lines of the lyrics of the *Tiger Rag*. Because this was unofficial Army territory, that was patrolled by the military police, the Nazi party and its observers never interfered. They did not enter places like *Die Wanne*, which explains the obvious tolerance towards jazz there, which, elsewhere, had long been outlawed by the Party as degenerate. I also did not miss a single production at the charming early nineteenth century *Stadttheater* that offered a range of operas, operettas, and plays of astonishing quality. Being garrisoned in Liegnitz where I had the company and support of my relatives who welcomed me to their homes like a son, was one of the fortunate aspects of my army life. I was also fortunate being stationed in a large city like Liegnitz rather than in one of the small Silesian country towns that served as minor garrisons, where soldiers felt like being sentenced to utter boredom when they were on weekend leave.

---

7   *Die Wanne* –The Tub – opened around 1900 as *Luisenbad*. This was initially a high-class place of entertainment and relaxation with an indoor pool, a restaurant, and a concert hall. By the time I frequented this place, it still carried the name of *Luisenbad*, but only the concert hall was left. It was quite notorious, as indicated by its unofficial name *Die Wanne*, which recalled the now defunct swimming pool of the original establishment.

By the middle of September, I was placed under great pressure. We had reached the end of our basic military training, which was to conclude with the transfer of most high school graduates to officers' school. When I had decided to evade the participation in *Hitlerjugend* activities as much as possible, I had also decided never to become an officer of the German Army. I did not, however, expect the degree of force and threat that descended on me when I stated in the interview with the commanding officer that I did not wish to join the officers' corps. He became irate and provoked me into making some unwise remarks, which earned me two weekends of detention. In the end, I did succeed to escape training at the officers' school, but I do not know what entry was made into my military record. The parting remark of the commanding officer that he would make sure that I would be transferred to a unit from which I would not return alive, gave me some indication. Still, no matter how hard he tried to punish me, I was fortunate to survive.[8]

My luck held out for the balance of the year. Instead of being sent to the front immediately as I had expected, I was sent to Berlin with a five-ton truck for the removal of the rubble left after the heavy bombardment of the German capital. The trip from Liegnitz to Berlin was nightmarish. I had completed driving school in September, but had no experience in driving such a huge vehicle on my own for more than 150 miles.

Life in Berlin was quite dreadful by this time, but stationed in barracks south of the city, we were quite safe from bombs. Every morning, I picked up a group of French prisoners of war and their German guards at a camp near our barracks. For the rest of the day, I only had to wait until the truck was loaded, drive it to a dump, and return for the next load of rubble. It was altogether an interesting experience. I got to know Berlin and enjoyed leading a life that was quite free of army drill.

In early November, when I returned with my truck from Berlin, our company, which by now consisted overwhelmingly of *Volksdeutsche* — ethnic Germans from Poland, the Balkans, Bohemia, and Slovakia[9]— was being readied for two weeks of manoeuvre-type training. A leisurely train

---

8   It was a terrible irony that I survived despite my officer's machinations, while most of my comrades who left our unit for officers' school early in September, never returned from the Italian Front, all killed in action during the Battle of Montecassino.

9   This in itself was punishment for me, as this group of reluctant soldiers neither made good soldiers nor were they treated with much respect by the corporals and officers. I felt like an outcast among them, especially since they did not particularly like me. They all stuck to their former nationalities, although they were all classified as *Volksdeutsche* (ethnic Germans), for which their parents had opted. This they had done for the sake of a somewhat better and more secure life; they had not bargained though for their sons being made into German soldiers.

ride of three days took us to Milowitz (between 1918 and 1939 and since 1945 Milovice), a huge military camp close to Prague, that dated back to Austro-Hungarian and Czechoslovakian times. I loved the slow trip on the military train that showed me parts of Bohemia I had never seen before. In the camp, we shared quarters with large numbers of other *Volksdeutsche*, all of them members of *SS* units. They had either naively volunteered or had been pressured to enter the *SS* and were now terribly unhappy and depressed.

Our stay in Milovice ended with an unexpected trip to Prague. On one of the rare occasions where I could speak to our master sergeant from man to man — this happened on the train — I had mentioned to him how beautiful a city Prague was, as I had observed during a couple of visits there with my parents. He then decided that I would be the one to accompany him on a shopping expedition to Prague before our company returned to Liegnitz. I was proud to show him around, although Prague appeared dreary and shabby. I had looked forward to showing my master sergeant the elegant Wenzelsplatz (Václavské náměstí) and the fabulous *Passagen* with their seemingly endless levels and rows of boutiques and cafés.[10] Not entirely unexpected for me, the Wenzelsplatz and the Passagen had lost all glamour. The majority of shops and cafés were boarded up. Yet, there was still a surprising amount of merchandise offered which had long disappeared from stores in Germany.

I experienced another unexpected privilege after our return to Liegnitz. The barracks where I was stationed now, prepared a charitable event, for which we were encouraged to hunt for items to be sold at a large bazaar and raffle. I immediately thought of my Uncle Hubert's china business in Waldenburg and received three days of leave and somewhat unspecified travel documents. They allowed me to arrange a trip that took me through parts of Silesia I had not seen before. It was probably the slowest train I had ever taken in this province, but I got to know an absolutely idyllic part of Silesia. To the delight of the master sergeant, I brought back a lot of china from Waldenburg. For myself I brought back the memory of a nostalgic trip where I was alone and never bothered by military police for my travel papers, because this was such a minor train, travelling through remote parts of the province. Without

---

10 The Václavské náměstí (Wenzelsplatz), the most elegant boulevard of Prague, not only offered fabulous department stores, shops, and restaurants, but also beautiful architecture ranging from eclectic façades from the turn of the century to art nouveau and to 1920s/1930s Czech Moderne buildings. The *Passagen*, connecting one street to another through the middle of buildings and comparable to the arcades in Rome and in London, were unknown in Germany in such size, modern style, and elegance.

being fully aware of it, I now believe that I consciously absorbed everything I saw and experienced, filled with a presentiment that I might never see this country again, or at least not the way it looked at that particular time. I knew the war was lost and that its end would bring incredible changes and upheavals.

And once more, fate smiled on me when Christmas came close. All leaves had been cancelled in order not to burden the overloaded transport system. Only those who could reach their home on foot or by bicycle were given Christmas leave. As I easily could get a bike from my relatives, I got my leave and on December 24, I struggled against an icy easterly wind through rain and snow over the 35 miles of straight highway from Liegnitz to Breslau. It was a miserable ride, as the country looked bleak and the villages, towns, and farms had taken on a shabby appearance after four years of war. I passed the battlefield of Leuthen (since 1945 Lutynia), location of Frederick's II of Prussia victory over Empress Maria Theresia's armies. The tall column commemorating the bloody battle stood forlorn in the midst of bare fields. I arrived at home not just tired, but depressed.

I felt fortunate to be at home for Christmas. My parents and I were in a pensive mood and the singing of the Christmas carols did not sound right, no matter how beautifully my father played his Steinway. I knew that soon I would be at the Front; I had no doubt I would be sent to the Eastern Front.

This was the last Christmas I spent with both my parents.

* * * * *

12 1944
The Beginning of the End

Germany retreats on all fronts – one country after another deserts Germany and joins the Allied powers. D-Day. German troops now fight on all four fronts: France, Italy, Russia and the Ukraine, and Finland. The great Soviet summer offensive begins – in the East and in the West, enemy soldiers stand on German soil. Many Germans still hope for victory – the myth of the miracle weapons returns with the V1 and V2 rockets. Hitler's final levy on October 18: total conscription of all men. Hitler's final offensive fails.

* * *

On January 2, my Christmas leave ended. Through deep snow I struggled back to Liegnitz and returned the bicycle that had taken me home for Christmas. I also returned to the old dreary *Grenadierkaserne*, built in the years of Prussia's glory. Almost 100 years old, it was still a solid building with decorative trims along its façade and, on the roof, huge stone eagles spreading their wings above the central section of the building. I found some postcards from my buddies from boot camp days who had been transferred to officers' school. They were now fighting at the Italian Front. The cards did not say much, but from one of their wounded comrades who had been returned to our unit as a reservist, I knew that they were fighting in Montecassino, engaged in one of the bloodiest battles of the war.

The weeks ahead in the *Grenadierkaserne* meant more boredom. We were simply kept waiting to be put together in units to be shipped to the Front. The interior of the ancient barracks was dreadful and the yard looked deserted.[1] Aside from occasional guard duty, we were quite idle. Could I complain? Certainly not, but every soldier sent to the Front from our barracks had his travel documents made out for the Eastern Front. Perhaps we did not speak about it much, but we were all anxious about being sent into battle in the depth of the Russian winter. The war did not go well anymore in the East, and the worst of our fears was being captured by the Soviet Army.

During the first half of February I was called to the office of the master sergeant who handed me my travel papers with the words: "From that unit you will never return alive!"

Next day, our group of 10 soldiers and one corporal departed for the East on board a scheduled troop train that had its first stop in my hometown Breslau. In Liegnitz, I had checked the timetable on the railway station and was therefore able to phone my parents and ask them to come to the *Hauptbahnhof*, the main station of Breslau — such was the organization of the German railways even at this late stage of the war that I could give my parents the number of the platform where my train would stop for 15 minutes!

On the platform, though, there was bedlam. The train was extraordinarily long and overcrowded. Units of soldiers and individual soldiers were loading and unloading. I was not the only one who had called his family to the station. With my group was Hubert, my buddy since our boot camp days in Liegnitz. He was surprised when he saw his father standing on the platform together with my parents. It turned out that the two fathers were colleagues working in the same building and, by chance, found out each had a son in the same unit on its way east. We were not allowed to leave the train, so both my comrade and I looked out of the window from quite a height down to our parents. It was an awkward position and as there were constant disruptions with people pushing my parents aside or wanting to get at the window, no meaningful conversation was possible. Besides, saying goodbye and knowing that this could likely be the last goodbye in one's life made the entire scene very awkward. The 15 minutes of the train's stopover seemed endless. It was in the middle of the night, but trains were coming and going with great commotion and noise in this bitterly cold February night. When our train finally moved, my parents disappeared in the steam emanating from the

---

1   I visited Liegnitz in 2002 and, to my delight, found the old barracks beautifully restored with decorations and trim cleaned of the decades-old dirt and grime. The entire building now had a noticeable touch of elegance. The old Prussian eagles — today's citizens look at them as Polish eagles — still dominated the entire building, which had been converted into a high-class condominium.

starting locomotive; once more, they appeared between shreds of steam; my father's voice was breaking; he barely managed to call "Auf Wiedersehen;" my comrade's father shed tears; only my mother waved and called with a seemingly cheerful voice after me "Come back, come back!"

I remember every detail of this farewell scene; it had been repeated all over Europe and North America a million times since 1939. Only a few months ago, I had taken my cousin Manfred to this same platform when he returned to his unit in Russia at the end of his leave. Weeks later, he was reported missing. I was the last one of our family who had been with Manfred. He was declared dead sometime after the war.

Had it not been a scene of my own family's life that rolled past me in these few seconds, I would remember this scene with fascination. As it was, of the five people present, two did not survive the next seven months. Six months later, a sharpshooter killed my comrade Hubert, while he was standing at my side. After another month, my father died.

A new phase in my war years was definitely beginning. For the first time in my life, I was away from Germany. Whatever my possessions were during the coming months, I carried them all on my back. From now on I never knew what the following day would bring, and even though my comrades and I never talked much about it, the thought of being killed was always with us.

Compared to that of some of my friends, to my cousin Manfred, or millions of other soldiers, my own experience at the front was relatively short, but it was not an easy one. There were many dangerous or horrifying hours or moments I will never be able to wipe out of my memory. As with the Labour Service or the months in Liegnitz, there were compensations, such as the experience of a hitherto unknown countryside, and of relationships that are equally unforgettable and will remain with me because they have vitally enriched my life.

I was very curious about what impressions Eastern Europe would create for me. So far, I had seen wartime Poland and Russia only in magazines and in the newsreels. The first impression I still have in my mind was the Polish industrial center of Łódź.[2] Our train passed through the city at dawn around eight in the morning. What amazed me was the large number of streetcars, all overflowing with passengers. Łódź was known as one of the ugliest, most poorly planned cities of Europe, but it still impressed with the appearance of a city humming with industrial activity. I was also aware that the city had always had a large Jewish population. How many were left at that time, I did not know, of course.

---

2   Between 1939 and 1945, Łódź was incorporated into the German province of Warthegau and given the German name of Litzmannstadt.

I remember the flat Polish countryside, the large forests, the towns with noticeably many buildings of unfinished character, as their outside walls had not received a layer of stucco. There were churches, often of enormous dimensions, in many cases part of monasteries. Warsaw seemed heavily damaged and what I could see of its streets looked quite deserted. In the centre of the city, the train slowed down and slowly went underground. In the last moment, I saw the huge, modernistic building with the damaged letters *Dworzec Główny* – Central Station. We then crawled through the underground part of the station, a series of white-tiled platforms. I was fascinated, having not expected a modern station like that in Warsaw.

After we emerged from the tunnel, we crossed the frozen Vistula River (Wisła), which looked bleak and deserted. On its opposite bank, we stopped at length at the Praga Station, now named *Warschau-Ost* (Warszawa Wschodnia). Here, I came across one of the many enigmas of the wartime East. It was well known all through the war that the food situation in Poland was desperate; even the Germans, though without pity, admitted that there was hunger in Poland. On the platforms of the Praga railway station, however, there were hundreds of women with large baskets filled with the most delicious baking, from snow-white buns to most tempting pastry; everything, of course was very expensive, but even though the soldier's pay was quite meagre, we always had more money than we knew how to spend. We looked at each other in wonderment. None of us had seen such beautiful baking in Germany for years.

We continued straight east towards Russia and, once more, I discovered evidence of some modern facilities. I noticed that Warsaw was served by a suburban train system with uniformly built stations, all of them modern and attractive, although some imagination was necessary to appreciate their original design, as they all had been heavily damaged in September 1939.

It was night when we crossed the River Bug and rolled into the station of Brest-Litowsk.[3] We were directed to the old citadel, a heavy fortification from Czarist times where, in a maze of deep tunnels and hallways, hundreds of German soldiers spent the night. The air was extremely unpleasant, not only dank but permeated by the stench of the insect powder identified on its package as *"entwickelt von Dr. Theo Morell, Leibarzt des Führers"* (developed by Dr. Theo Morell, the *Führer's* personal physician). There were tables everywhere piled high with the paper bags of this powder. If its stench would only have been an indication of its

---

3   This was the city's Russian name. It was called Brześć nad Bugiem in Polish and now it is Brest in Belarus.

effectiveness! Not a single louse, flea, or bedbug would have plagued a single German soldier on the Eastern Front. Instead, German soldiers were notoriously infested with these insects. Their presence in clothing, hair, and on the skin was most unpleasant and bothersome; worse, they were carriers of infections that took their toll on the effectiveness of the German armies.

We had to stay over for a day — there was no train going east until the next day. Walking around town, we found a badly damaged city. What was left showed the typical Eastern European streets of one- or two-story houses built of brick or wood. The layout of the city centre, however, was impressive with its wide avenues and boulevards. I remember one avenue with a double row of trees in its centre, which guided one's eyes to the tower and the cupolas of a beautiful Greek Orthodox church. Inside, we were captivated by the mosaics, the iconostasis[4] whose gold dimly glowed in the light of the candles and the sunshine of the late winter afternoon. The air was heavy with incense; with its rich bass voices the male choir responded to the liturgy sung by the *pope*, the parish priest. This was a rather incredible and, at this time and location, unexpected experience. Otherwise, there were few people in the streets and the entire city had an atmosphere of being half deserted. We went to a café and bar called *Adria*, reserved for German soldiers only. It was filled with the painful strains of a small string orchestra and was one of the saddest places of its kind I can think of.

Next day, a slow train took us eastwards. By now, I had noticed that all trains had two or three flatcars coupled in front of their engine for the purpose of detonating mines placed on the tracks by partisans. We were now entering the vast area of the Pripiet Marshes[5]. As other soldiers, old hands on the Eastern Front, explained to us, this thinly-populated, densely forested, and swampy land was full of partisans. We left the train in Pińsk[6] and walked from the station, an unexpectedly charming smallish building in yellow stucco, into the centre of town through badly damaged streets that seemed to be absolutely deserted. Combined with the ice-cold temperature of that day and the heavy snow cover, Pińsk gave the impression of a ghost town. There seemed to be no stores anywhere, just some now useless signs such as APTEKA (pharmacy), which I could decipher. There were several large baroque churches with tall spires, and

---

4   The wall of pictures or mosaics of saints behind the altar.

5   Polish Pripiet; Russian Pripiet; Ukrainian Pripjat

6   Polish Pińsk; Russian/Belarus Pinsk

a huge building which, judging by some nasty graffiti, must have served at one time as the main synagogue of Pińsk.

At that time, I was not yet fully aware of the extent of the extermination of the Jewish population by the SS and other German special units in Poland and in Russia; neither did I know then, how many Jews had once lived in Pińsk. During my stay in the Pińsk of 1944, the city was a scene of desolation, and the few humans seen in the streets were almost all German soldiers.

Pińsk has a distinguished history dating back to the tenth century as a trading point on the Pripiet River that in the nineteenth century became part of the Dniepr-Bug Canal system. As I learned after the war, in 1939 the population of Pińsk stood at 50,000 inhabitants of which 80 percent were Jewish citizens who attended 43 synagogues and maintained flourishing trades and a number of factories. Until World War II, there was a steady stream of emigrants leaving Pińsk for North America, South America, and Australia (my Canadian hometown of Edmonton was one of the favourite destinations for the Jews of Pińsk). By October 1942, long before my arrival in Pińsk, not one single Jewish person was left; nearly all of them had been killed by the SS and only a few were able to flee into the marshes and join the partisans.

Our travel papers were changed and we again boarded the train next morning. While we were waiting inside the station building's deserted waiting room, I discovered a large oil painting of a woman walking through the countryside. For me, it was a touch of beauty in this deserted land, permitting a glimpse of the past of this city and its vanished people.

Many years later, I learned that this entire area had been the scene of fierce battles during World War I. Most of the railway station buildings along the railroad had been destroyed. When this area became Polish in 1920, the Polish government rebuilt the stations of which I saw quite a few, in this pleasant, modernistic baroque style. In 1944, the Pińsk Station had become deserted and useless again, as there was no civilian travel any more. The mystery still remains how the painting in the waiting lounge survived and was not destroyed, vandalized, or simply stolen. For me, it became one of the unforgettable small recollections of my wartime experience.

We spent the next night in Łuniniec,[7] a railroad junction with a huge delousing and bathing establishment for the German military. After only a few days in the East, our unit was in dire need of this facility. After feeling clean and no longer plagued by lice, flees, bedbugs, and other

---

7   Polish Łuniniec; Russian Luninyets; Belarus Luninets

vermin at least for a short while, we walked through the small town. In the cold, clear winter night, the reflections in the sky and the deep rolling sounds of exploding grenades indicated that we were very near the front. I felt very lonely and uncomfortable.

After another long train ride, we disembarked in the large city of Minsk with its enormous railway station, built in the ornate Stalinist style, for me the first example of this aberration. We spent the next two weeks in a farmhouse in the little village of Repje and got to know the local *banja*, the Russian bathhouse, which is similar to the Finnish sauna and was a fixture of each village or town. We enjoyed astonishing entertainment facilities for the German soldiers, including movie houses, cafés, and variety shows. In comparison to Pińsk, Minsk was a busy city with many civilians filling the streets that were lined by rows upon rows of dreary four- story workers' flats.

Within two weeks, we were returned to Pińsk and finally stationed with our permanent unit, a squadron of motorized cavalry with a tradition reaching far back into Prussian history. This was also the case of the bigger unit we belonged to, the 4th Cavalry Brigade, both of which had a preponderance of officers with well-known Prussian noble names. I do not mention this for any reasons of pride or importance, but only because the high proportion of officers from the aristocracy was to become a matter of dire consequence only four months later, when an attempt on Hitler's life occurred.

The other contradiction was that, although designated as cavalry, the entire brigade was fully motorized. In the past, the Prussian cavalry with its purebred horses had the image of being highly mobile, capable of surprising the enemy. In modern times, the horses had been replaced by troop carriers or armoured half-track vehicles.

Pińsk still looked like an abandoned city. The country was buried in deep snow, but spring seemed to be in the air. We were taken to our squadron in the village of Stachowice, three villages or approximately 15 miles west of Pińsk. To get there, we traveled on the centuries-old east-west highway, paved sometime in the not too distant past with huge hexagonal paving stones about two feet across. Parallel to the highway ran the equally important east-west railway. As with the neighbouring villages, Stachowice[8] was located about half a mile south of the highway, precisely halfway between the road and the River Pina, which is part of the old Russian Dniepr-Bug and the Oginski Canal systems.

---

8   Polish Stachowice, Russian Stachowiczi; Belarus Stachowice

All around Stachowice the country was flat and there were no church spires or domes rising anywhere above the horizon; the villages seemed to cling to the ground and were hardly visible from any distance. From the first moment on the village of Stachowice intrigued me, although it was exceedingly primitive and poverty-stricken. The houses looked quite alike, without exception built with poles, chinked with mud and straw, and given a coat of mud plaster and whitewash. All had thatched roofs of straw. Their interior consisted of two rooms. The larger one, entered through the single door, was reserved for livestock such as sheep, goats, chicken, and geese, while the only other room was designated as living space for the human inhabitants. Serving for the entire family as kitchen, living- and dining room, and bedroom, this room was dominated by the typical huge stove; its flat top also served as the family's sleeping area during the cold winter months. The windows were small but had decorative wood framing around them. After four years of war, there was no paint left on the framing and neither were there flowers in the boxes outside, nor on the window sills inside.

Facing the village's only street with their gables, the houses lined both sides of the street in its entire length of less than perhaps half a mile. As primitive as they were, the houses somehow gave the village an engaging character. What was unusual and unexpected were the two rows of beautiful birch trees running along the middle of the street between which there was a dry ditch that must have once been a picturesque canal. A very few houses were still inhabited by village people, while most families had been relegated to their primitive, drafty barns when their houses were requisitioned by the German soldiers. We were taken to the village burgomaster who welcomed us with homemade vodka of wartime quality, made of beets and almost undrinkable, not just because of the high alcohol content but because of its terrible flavour.

In the burgomaster's house I saw a small elegant side table with delicate legs and Empire trim with traces of the original gold and white paint still visible. During the next weeks I found a few more pieces of Empire furniture. Asked about the origin of these remnants of an obviously more prosperous time, the burgomaster took me to the western end of the village street where he pointed to a low mound overgrown with weeds and scrub. He spoke enough German for me to understand that this was the location of the former manor house, where the Empire table had come from. The manor house had burned down during World War I and was never rebuilt.

For the first time in my life, I experienced spring in a continental climate. Spring came early in the Pripiet Marshes; temperatures were quite warm, but it seemed to take forever before the country turned green. Sometime in late April or early May, all of a sudden, the appearance of the land changed overnight. Before the trees became green, the meadows broke into bloom, first in red, then in blue, in purple, and finally in yellow. After about one month, the country settled into a rich green with occasional touches of other colors. The sky seemed very high and nearly always cloudless. One day, I climbed on the roof of the barn behind our cottage and, although I only attained a height of 30 feet, I found myself able to look around for miles and miles. I saw the river stretching through rich meadows, partially bordered by trees; I looked across the endless forest, above which I discovered in the west the ruins of the huge churches of Pińsk. I loved the country and this love never left me; it eventually caused me to search, many years later, for a similar countryside in North America as my future home!

If my description of this spring of 1944 spent as a soldier in an impoverished country of a culture quite foreign to me sounds colourful and filled with nostalgia, then this description accurately reflects my feelings at that time and my memory of it. Most of the countryside surrounding Stachowice was not considered safe; actually, the entire Pripiet Marshes were in the hands of partisan units and as a consequence, we were never leaving this little island of a village with its few pastures around it unless we were in a group the strength of at least a platoon, and well-armed and supported by our troop carriers. Even the near highway was off-limits for us, and several times, we found dead German soldiers along its right-of-way; once, we even discovered a man from our squadron, in the water-filled ditch of the dirt road leading from the highway to our village.

In the village, though, we felt protected and comfortable. This sense was only strengthened by the totally different way our squadron was run by our commander, a member of a well-known aristocratic family. There was no senseless drill or barracks routine. Instead, we were trained in ways to help us survive in combat in a hostile country. We quickly developed a natural respect and regard for our commander, his lieutenant, and the non-commissioned officers. Several times we were sent into the forests to hunt for partisans. We hardly ever saw a living soul, but enough dugouts, fire pits, and, almost indistinguishable from the surrounding forest, the narrow trails, used by the partisans.

Only one of our operations turned bloody, near the small but astonishingly picturesque town of Motol,[9] nestling alongside a lake with houses of noticeably better standards than those in most villages. Near

---

9   Later, I learned that this was the birthplace of Chaim Weitzman, the first President of Israel, who attended elementary school in the little town before being sent to high school in Pińsk and, from there for studies in Germany and other countries.

Motol, we became entangled in a couple of skirmishes with partisans who were quickly melding into the near forest. In the shoot-out, we lost two of our men. Both bodies were taken into our vehicle and transported back to Stachowice. It was the first time that I was in the company of a dead person for more than a day. We did not cover their faces that, strangely, never lost their lifelike appearance; but in the extreme heat of the day, it was the smell of their decaying bodies that reminded me of their sad fate.

What we experienced could hardly be called "war." I could not know at that time that I would remain with this platoon until I was wounded. It was at this early stage, still in Stachowice, that we began to grow closer together. It was the occasional time of danger we survived; it was the summer evenings we invariably spent together, because there was nowhere to go; and it was the surfeit of time we had of which we used so much to talk about our lives, our families, and our girlfriends. Later, we would realize how close we had grown to each other and how much we knew about each other's lives when the time came to write to the wives, parents, or girlfriends of those who had been killed in combat.

We were a mixed platoon indeed: two older men in their late forties from Upper Silesia, one a business man, the other a carpenter; another man from the same area, but more Polish than German, who was a coal miner;[10] one fellow with a completed high school education was slated to go to officers' school. There was also my buddy Hubert from the Liegnitz days, and a very young fellow from the outskirts of Heidelberg whom we all looked after, as he seemed so vulnerable. There were two other young miners from near my hometown Waldenburg; the owner of a large farm in Holstein; and our corporal from Westphalia, a decent but inward-turned man in his late twenties. I do not know how much our minds were filled with premonitions during these weeks. We were all, in an unspoken way, quite protective of our corporal, even though, as leader of our platoon, he was our superior — we seemed to feel he would not live very long. He died in the first serious combat our platoon became engaged in.

If someone asked me whether I ever experienced the often misunderstood and, in wartime, overused phenomenon of comradeship, I can truly say that I did as a member of this particular platoon. I felt very safe and comfortable in this group, but only much later did I begin to

---

10 Twenty-three years later, I learned that Karol had survived the war because when I took my aunt from Switzerland who was visiting us in Edmonton in Canada to a travelogue about Poland, Karol was shown in the film as an example of the typical Polish miner with his family in his post-war apartment in Katowice.

comprehend the dynamics of the group and its growth, and why, by extension, I have such positive feelings about a basically inimical environment that in its larger dimensions of the Army, I absolutely detested and hated.

We were a close-knit bunch. As we were not unduly pressured or treated in any demeaning manner by our superiors, we also were tolerant and friendly towards the men of the other platoons, although in a more casual way. The other factor was our isolation. We rarely got newspapers and only halfway through our months in Stachowice did our platoon get a battery-powered radio, which was of surprising strength, capable of receiving stations from all over Europe.

It is a measure of our closeness and trust for each other that we regularly listened to foreign radio stations, a capital offence in Hitler's Germany during the entire war. Almost every night, we hung on the enemy radio stations, not so much because of their news and political broadcasts, but because of the music they played. More than any other songs, we were captured by some American songs Marlene Dietrich had recorded, with the lyrics translated into German by a refugee from Hitler's Third Reich, as I learned after the war. If anything could undermine the morale of the German soldier, it was not so much the foreign news, but songs like those sung by Marlene's seductive voice. Songs like *Fräulein Anni lebt nicht mehr hier* (Miss Otis Regrets), *Sag mir nicht Adé* (I Cried All Night), and others — not to forget *Lilli Marleen*, the song that crossed all enemy lines east and west in many languages and tugged at the heart strings of homesick soldiers lonely for their wives and girlfriends.

There was another station located in England we listened to with always one of us standing on guard outside to warn us about anybody approaching our cottage. This was *Der Soldatensender Gustav Siegfried I*, where we first heard Vera Lynn singing *The White Cliffs of Dover*; and it was not the later so-familiar lyrics, but the voice of Vera Lynn singing this unique melody that brought us close to tears of homesickness.

Once in a while, we would listen to the news broadcast by Gustav Siegfried I. One day, while we were eating our lunch in our cottage the voice from London revealed to us — before we were officially informed by our lieutenant — that the Allied forces had landed at the Normandy Coast. It was the first time I heard the name of General Eisenhower.

This was the 6th of June 1944. Six months ago, the Soviet armies had crossed the old pre-war Polish border; three weeks ago, the German Africa Corps had capitulated in Libya; two days ago, the Allied troops had entered Rome; and now, the Allies had opened a third front in Northern France. Always on guard to watch out for unexpected visitors, we heard the barely audible news of the invasion. We hardly said anything to each other, but our thoughts must have been the same: the war was entering its final phase.

As if to confirm, on June 25 we were loaded with our equipment and troop carriers on the train. For the last time, I took a fond look at the little railroad station building in Pińsk. The train rolled westwards and with some hard to explain feelings of nostalgia, I saw the tall ruined churches of Pińsk disappear at the eastern horizon. On the 23rd, the great Soviet summer offensive of 1944 had begun; it would not stop until it had reached the borders of Germany and the Red Army had occupied parts of East Prussia.

We traveled westwards, more than halfway to Brest Litowsk, before turning back northeast at Kobryn, at another of the yellow post-World War I railroad stations built by the Polish government. At Bereza Kartuska, we unloaded our troop carriers and spent a night in the formerly Polish barracks, that had been built under the czar in the late nineteenth century.

The next day, continuing by road we came close to the Front in the evening, judging by the continued noise of artillery fire. Long past midnight, we drove through the burning town of Słuck (Slutsk in Belarus). I had been in the air raids of Berlin, but Słuck, despite its relative smallness, was like a huge inferno, as flames were consuming literally every building in town. Outside of town, we awaited daylight, but there was no chance to sleep. There were the sounds of exploding grenades, of machine gun fire, of planes above us, and the sight of burning villages around us. We were very apprehensive. We knew that for most of us the morning would bring the first experience of true combat.

There was a dramatic sunrise, in part created by smoke and dust, accompanied by the increasing noise of combat. We were entering wide open, slightly rolling country; it was practically treeless. Everywhere around us, we discovered the wandering columns of dust indicating fast-moving tanks or other armoured vehicles. We felt absolutely helpless and unprotected, as we did not know on what basis we were directed hither and yonder, always in fear of the approaching columns of dust that might or might not be created by enemy vehicles, or our own forces – we never knew. The two older men from Upper Silesia began to weep. They were not cowards, I knew them too well to suspect that, but it occurred to me just very briefly, how lucky I was that I did not have a wife or children waiting at home whom I might never see again after the coming battle.

By the early afternoon, we seemed to have disengaged ourselves from the enemy and took up position on the side of a ridge, crowned by a partially destroyed manor house near the villages of Mokracz and Wiedźma. We found its interior full of wounded German soldiers who were cared for by the lady of the house, a woman perhaps in her forties, of exquisite beauty and elegant manners who spoke German very well, although with a strong Polish accent. To this day, I wonder how she had succeeded in surviving on her estate after the arrival of the Soviets in 1939 because they had made short shrift of the Polish aristocracy, while under the later German occupation, the land was expropriated.

Slightly above the bottom of the hill, we dug our foxholes from where we looked across the picturesque, deceptively peaceful countryside. As night fell, I tried to get some sleep in the small foxhole I shared with Hubert, my buddy from Liegnitz. He rested the first two or three hours, while I took my turn next. I was deadly tired and emotionally exhausted by that time and remained in a vague state between sleep and wakefulness. Unable to distinguish dream from reality, I heard and saw tanks racing across the plain below us, I heard loud Russian voices and thought all that was a bad dream. As I realized later, while it was my turn to sleep, Hubert had also fallen asleep. All of a sudden, terrible noises all around rudely awoke us. Among the sounds of exploding grenades, there was now increasing fire from machine guns and Sten guns. This scary combat continued till noon, when all of a sudden I heard the screams of "*Hooray! Hooray!*" from what sounded like thousands of voices. The scene, which I had observed so many times in newsreels, became real in front of my eyes: hundreds of soldiers in their earth brown uniforms came storming towards us. For the first time, I was shooting at human beings who came closer and closer, until I could distinguish individual faces. At this moment, we heard the sounds of approaching aircraft that turned out to be *JU'87* dive-bombers, the German *Stukas*. As we quickly realized, while we were under heavy fire from an enemy who was now very close to our positions, we also became victims of what is called euphemistically *friendly fire* these days. The German bombs fell not only on the enemy, but also all around us onto our own positions.. The Soviet troops seemed to have experienced severe losses, and those who were not hurt, retreated from the scene of battle.

After everything had been deadly quiet for a time, we dared climbing out of our foxholes and found Rudi, the young fellow from Heidelberg, badly wounded. We took him up to the manor house where the Polish lady immediately took care of him. When an ambulance came to pick him up, he asked us to write to his girlfriend and say goodbye to her on his behalf. He had a smile on his face when he said that. I felt he knew he was dying. I did not know how to cope with such bravery, but I was emotionally frozen. We also learned that we had lost all our leaders under the friendly fire: our commander, our second in command, the lieutenant; and our master sergeant. We found the corporal who was in charge of our platoon dead in his foxhole; our premonition that he would not be with us very long had come true on the first day of combat.

The surviving men seemed to cling to each other after this terrifying experience, but by evening, at sundown, the group fell apart. The replacement for our dead squadron leader and his killed lieutenant arrived, a young lieutenant who immediately ordered us to comb the battlefield for wounded German soldiers. We thought that this was silly, and we told him that all of us had remained on the hillside during the entire length of combat; there would be nothing but dead Russian soldiers in this field. But he ordered us again to follow him, as he marched in the middle of our spread-out platoons and began shooting at the first bodies he came across. I thought he acted out of mercy shooting those who only seemed dead, making sure they would not suffer. To my horror, though, I soon realized that with his Sten gun, he killed all Russians, many of whom were only lightly wounded. Some seemed to expect to be helped, while others begged for mercy. My horror grew, when he asked for volunteers to complete the killing. Not one man of our platoon stepped forward, but there were others who proceeded with the grisly task. I did not feel like saying one word to them for the remainder of the time we served in the same squadron.

A few days later I received my first decoration for this, my first battle, to be followed by more combat and a couple of more decorations that I traded for food in prison camp nine months later. I was also promoted to private first class.

This is all I want to write about my combat experiences. There were quite a few more like that during the next seven weeks. They were basically very similar, but the combat itself got much more vicious. The Russian tanks seemed faster and faster, catching up with our armoured troop carriers that were no match for the Russian T34s. As on the left side of our troop carriers the gasoline tanks were located, while the corresponding right side accommodated our ammunition – everything protected by lightest armour only – we had horrible losses due to explosions and burn injuries.

More and more, we were given the task of holding a section of the front until the other units had completed their retreat. These units also included units of the SS. Being the last ones to retreat from villages, with the Russians entering at the other end, we again and again saw the work of the SS who continued their killing of the villagers wherever they found them – they were Poles or White Russians; there were no more Jews left anywhere.

The rest of my recollections are a mixture of pleasant experiences and horrible incidents. New corporals were assigned to our platoons and, again, we were fortunate to be assigned to a man from East Prussia who had such unique qualities of humanity, humour, practicality and, above all, courage, that I can thankfully say that to a large extent, I owe my survival to him. We could share our innermost thoughts, feelings, and fears with him.

I remember a terrible incident during an operation of clearing a forest of enemy troops and partisans. The latter usually wore civilian clothes; always being well armed they were known to be very dangerous; while retreating they frequently directed their fire at us. We were quite spread out and all of a sudden, I found myself alone in the dense forest when I unexpectedly came across a cowering human figure hiding between the roots of a huge tree. He turned his back towards me, hiding his hands below his chest. I could not see whether he had a weapon in his hands and right away fired several shots at this man and no doubt immediately killed him. After I had turned him over, I discovered that this rather young man was totally unarmed. My platoon leader, who had run to my assistance, went through his pockets and found absolutely nothing, although the local population was obliged to carry identity papers at all times. Whether this was an indication that he belonged to the partisans or not, I was deeply shaken, having killed an unarmed man. To this day, I vividly remember this event. Only someone who has lived and fought in partisan or guerrilla country can understand my reaction and the guilt it produced afterwards.

I like to think of some of the very pretty countryside that was never of a dramatic or grandiose character, but was generally of a pleasant, idyllic nature. There was the odd village that had escaped destruction; it was usually deserted by its inhabitants and reminded me of a romantic painting of better times. Sometimes, there were still geese, chickens, and pigs around, but not one human being.   To us, these rare villages, untouched by war, felt like a picture from a book of fairy tales.

Most of the towns, however, were heaps of rubble. I remember our approach to the larger town of Słonim (Slonim in Belarus), in the middle of one summer night. It was a full moon and we were traveling through the wide valley of the River Szczara. All of a sudden, like a vision, to my right a huge baroque façade of what must have been a monastery church appeared before my eyes. Its view in the pale blue moonlight was dramatic.

I remember the small town of Świsłocz (Svisloch in Belarus)[11] that spread its streets across a gentle hill. There was not a building left in this totally flattened, ghostlike town. As we approached its centre, there, on

---

11   As I later found out, Świsłocz was the birthplace of the Canadian Socialist and leader of the New Democratic Party, David Lewis.

top of the hill among the still smouldering rubble stood a lone bathtub with an old-fashioned shower rising out of it to its full height.

There was the week of unexpected complete idleness after the failed coup against Hitler on July 20, 1944.[12] The 4th Cavalry Brigade to which our squadron belonged, was taken out of service as all its officers — from its commander Colonel von Bischofshausen to our lieutenant — were suspected to be implicated in this courageous political act. They were all arrested and we were without any officers. We were given orders not to leave our temporary camp in a forest, until we received a new compliment of officers. I do not remember any of them except our new lieutenant, a banker from Erfurt, a quiet man of slight stature, not very warlike in his nature, but of enormous courage; he gave us all extra strength at a time when we felt greatly inferior to the Red Army, in strength of numbers and the quality of our equipment.

It became harder and harder not to get depressed. We were almost in the northern half of central Poland now. The continuous, slow retreat of the German armies seemed well planned and, obviously, foreseen. Not only were all strategically important towns destroyed, all railroads were made unusable by special machines that would rip the wooden railroad ties apart so that the pursuing Red Army would be slowed down by supply problems. We were close to Białystok, the big city less than 50 miles from the East Prussian border. In a slightly different direction, I figured I could reach my former Labour Service camp on foot within not more than two days.

The fighting became nastier again and often, we escaped what we considered the worst possible fate — being taken prisoner by the Red Army — by the skin of our teeth. After a couple of especially bad days, we were taken out of combat and placed in the forest near the railroad centre of Łapy. What followed was a week of absolute peace, helped by the fact that temporarily, the front did not move, as the Soviet Army, perhaps also exhausted after weeks of constant advance, did not mount a new attack in this section of the Front.

Fortunately, Łapy was a very pleasant and, for Eastern Europe, rather unique town. It was a small town that had not grown from a village but had been laid out when the railroad from Warsaw to St. Petersburg was built. The town was still fully populated by Poles who ran the railroad and worked in its repair and maintenance shops. All its streets were paved and lined with sidewalks. I was especially surprised to discover one street

---

12 This act took place not too far from where our squadron was in retreat from the advancing Red Army. The distance to Hitler's headquarters *Wolf's Lair* was little more than 100 miles.

of single detached houses, built according to the German concept of *Siedlung* (housing estate). The street was located at the edge of town close to the forest where we camped our vehicles in dugouts as protection against bombs or artillery. These were very pleasant one-family houses with well-kept gardens within their fenced lots. I was so intrigued that I ventured into the first house in this street, where for the next few days I struck up a very short-term friendship, the only instance where I got to know a Polish family during the war. Their home and its atmosphere were in no way different from similar houses in my hometown where I used to go and play with my classmates, sons of skilled workers or miners. I felt very comfortable with this family and in their company emotionally recovered to a degree from the stress of constant combat.

For the first time in weeks, the nights were quiet. Normally, our nights were disturbed by the small Russian observation planes the German soldiers had dubbed *sewing machines* because of the peculiar, low-pitched sound of their single slow engine. These planes would hover over us, dropping flares that turned the night into a peculiar light, sufficient for the pilot to identify our positions. Within minutes we then would be attacked by artillery, only too often by the *Stalin Orgel*, large very mobile trucks that carried batteries of rocket launchers on their flatbeds from which these rockets were launched one after the other in quick succession to cover a specific area with a dense rain of their missiles. Whether for reasons of technical design or for psychological reasons, the *Stalin Orgel* also created a series of horrible, almost panic-inducing sounds. At the sound of the first rocket launched, someone would shout "*Orgel*" and everyone would scoot for his prepared foxhole, hoping to escape a direct hit.

Nothing of that kind plagued us in the peaceful little town of Łapy that, out of a certain nostalgia, I would visit 40 years later during a trip through today's north-eastern Poland. I had no difficulty locating the street and the house where I spent such pleasant hours in the summer of 1944. I found a blond woman in her forties sitting on the steps with a small child on her lap. I venture to think that this woman was the little daughter of former times of the railroad man who had welcomed me to his home in wartime. I did not dare approach her, however, not knowing what might have happened after our platoon had left Łapy after a week during which we had behaved faultlessly.

It was in Łapy, though, that I became seriously ill with constant sensations of nauseousness and liver discomfort. When my body temperature rose to over 101 degrees, I was taken to a field hospital accommodated in the huge, neo-gothic church of the small town of Sokoły. Not much was done for me except giving me rest and lots of fluids. The benches and pews had been removed from the church; its floor was filled by hundreds of soldiers lying around on layers of straw that was host to all sorts of bugs, including thousands of bed bugs that made sleep at night impossible. My condition somehow improved within a few days and I was taken back to my unit. Upon leaving the church, I stood for a while in the shadow of its tall steeple; I looked across the wide empty market square that was surrounded by two story houses that seemed to dream away in the blazing midday sun. Again, there seemed to be no civilians left in the entire town. Sokoły was another town I visited after the war; other than that a number of the old houses were missing, the town had not changed at all.

This experience of passing through towns denuded of their population would confront us day after day. Doing some research 50 years later, I became aware of the formerly high proportion of Jewish citizens in most of these towns, often between 50 to 75 percent. This was true until the German occupation with its genocide of the Jewish population, which reduced the number of Jews in Poland from over three million in 1939 to 45,000 after the end of the war.

In between the burned-out, deserted towns, we passed through a few formerly Polish towns that had been included in the new province of *Südostpreussen* (South East Prussia), created after the defeat of Poland in 1939. There were visible signs of Germanization in these towns, such as new city halls in the centre of the market square, so-called *Feierabend-häuser* designed to meet the recreational, ceremonial, and political needs of the future German population, and some new family homes. I was amazed to see that some of these buildings were still under construction at this time, when Germany experienced a most severe shortage of materials and labour and when the big cities in Germany, under constant bombardment, were in dire need of material for building repairs.

The last town where we noticed this evidence of Germanization distinguished itself in my memory by some German officials strolling across the town square in their notorious brown party uniforms. We slowly crossed the square in our troop carriers, being on our way to our new positions south of town. Amongst many German soldiers, these Nazi officials, called *Goldfasane* (golden pheasants) because of their brown uniform with lots of gold trim, were much ridiculed and detested as leeches and parasites.

This scene was a manifestation of the stubborn belief of especially those close to the Nazi Party, that Hitler would protect them and all of Germany and eventually win the war against all odds. In hindsight, the scene seemed almost unbelievable in view of the nearness of the front. As a matter of fact within 24 hours, Śniadowo was captured by the Red Army. I do so well remember this location and the day — Śniadowo on

August 23, 1944 – as just south of town, I almost got killed in the morning of the following day.

In the late evening of August 23, we had taken positions at the northern edge of a huge golden field where the harvested wheat was still standing in rows of stooks. We knew that somewhere to the south there were Russian soldiers. At that time, when the German forces rarely had sufficient support from artillery and tanks, the Russians often did not bother to start an attack with heavy artillery fire. So we were badly surprised when in the early morning, all of a sudden thousands of Soviet soldiers rose out of the bushes at the other side of the huge field and with frightening *hoorays* began storming towards us. We were quite well armed with machine guns and managed for a while to slow down the advance of the Russian soldiers who jumped from sheaf to sheaf for their protection. It was not long, however, before we observed in great alarm, how masses of Russian soldiers literally raced forward to the left and to the right of our position. Knowing we would be cut off within a minute and then captured, we retreated rapidly to our troop carriers that were hidden in the forest behind us. My Liegnitz buddy Hubert and I quickly loaded our machine gun into our vehicle. We had just finished and I had shut the rear door with my right hand, when I heard some very sharp shots and immediately experienced severe pain in my knee, my right hand, and my thigh. Almost mechanically, I yanked the door open again and pulled myself into the troop carrier with my left hand and before I could look back the driver threw the vehicle in gear and raced away from the scene.

I was almost in shock from the sudden attack and the pain of being wounded, but I do remember that from my lying position on the floor of the carrier, I saw a Russian soldier in a tree nearby aiming his gun at me. He must have been one of the special sharpshooters the Russians had assigned to most of their units. At times, they used ammunition that would explode at first impact and create severe damage. This time, the sharpshooter missed me and we got away. Not too far from the area of combat, several of us – we were all wounded – were loaded into an ambulance and taken across the nearby border of East Prussia to the town of Sensburg (since 1945 Mrągowo) where my hospital time began. Although I was in much pain, my wounds were not life-threatening, but as it turned out, I was going to be a patient in several army hospitals for more than four months!

The first hospital turned out to be a pleasant place, as it was run by a jovial army doctor. I needed a cane and had my arm in a sling but, otherwise, I was fine and mobile. Sensburg was a typical East Prussian small town, neat and clean, though without any buildings of historical or architectural distinction. Its main asset was its picturesque location above a lake where I would take my mother and her sister on a rented rowboat. I had been happily surprised when my mother and my aunt Lisa unexpectedly turned up. We spent several days that were only superficially carefree and relaxed, as the mood in town was very tense and anxious. The lady of the small hotel where my mother and her sister stayed told us that the entire town "*sitzt auf gepackten Koffern*" (was sitting on packed suitcases), as the Russians were not so far away anymore. She herself remembered the devastating Russian occupation of her hometown during World War I, when she was a young girl.

I became very worried when my mother told me that my father was slated to have stomach surgery sometime in September for the purpose of making him fit for front-line duty. I did not like the thought of him undergoing an operation in his weakened state; neither did I want to see him at the Front. He was simply too frail for such demands. My mother, at this time, was visibly more worried about me than my father, as it seemed a question of a week or so before I would be returned to the front. Events took a very different turn, however.

My discomfort with my liver turned suddenly worse and I broke out in jaundice. Our jovial physician examined me and asked me some questions and then sighed and explained to me that I was one of dozens of soldiers coming through his hospital who ended up in the special unit of the other military hospital in Sensburg as victims of an irresponsible medical practice. We all had received vaccinations against typhoid fever, cholera, and other contagious diseases in the most elementary manner. For inoculations, an army medic would arrive, have us line up and take off our shirts and undershirts. He then proceeded "from chest to chest" to inject 1cc of vaccine from a 10cc syringe, without changing or disinfecting the needle. There is no question that the most dangerous viruses were transmitted to thousands of soldiers this way.

It was in the middle of the night a week or more after my admission to hospital that I woke up in sweat after reliving in my dream the scene of being wounded. Only then did I think for the first time of my buddy Hubert and what might have happened to him. The thought caused me to be wide awake and, all of a sudden, in utter clarity I remembered that Hubert had collapsed at my side with a brief shout when the first shot fell. I felt certain that he had died in an instant. The thought of Hubert's likely death came back to my mind repeatedly, but never too long, as I soon became critically ill. I did not learn that Hubert had indeed been killed by the sharpshooter's bullet while he was standing next to me, until my mother happened to meet Hubert's father in Breslau. By that time, my father, his former colleague had also died.

On September 17, my physician called me to his office where he shook my hand and handed me a telegram from my mother. My father had died in the University Hospital in Breslau the night before. The physician vehemently declined my persistent request for compassionate leave, explaining to me that I obviously did not realize how ill I was and how important it was that I would have absolute bed rest for at least a month. Any physical demands on me during this early stage of what he identified as Hepatitis C (Contactiosa) would result in ultimately fatal cirrhosis of the liver within 10 or 20 years. Since he wanted to help me, he would try to receive permission for my transfer to a hospital with better facilities closer to my hometown.

What happened to me during the next few days was an indication of the beginning confusion in the operations of the German Army. My Sensburg physician would have been horrified to learn that the hospital train for which he had me booked turned out to be a string of cattle cars with a layer of straw on the floor. I spent four days lying on the floor of a cattle car with a high fever. I was too weak to eat and this probably saved my life, as the food given to us would have been poison for my inflamed liver. The journey never seemed to end and we circled around this particular part of East Prussia, actually around the town of Rastenburg (since 1945 Kętrzyn) and Hitler's nearby headquarters *Wolfsschanze,* Wolf's Lair, at least three times. Eventually, we left East Prussia. I remember the train thundering over a seemingly endless bridge. Someone told me that we were crossing the Vistula River.

We were unloaded in the city of Hohensalza (between 1918 and 1939 and since 1945 Inowrocław) and placed in an overcrowded temporary hospital, actually a *Sammelstelle,* a collection station, located in an old school building. All the former classrooms were packed with double bunk beds. Someone told me that there were over 500 patients in the building all in the care of a lone, young physician who was still in training as a resident physician. I managed to reach my mother by phone and again, she and my aunt Lisa came to visit me. Those were days of mourning for us. We sat in the visiting room for hours and talked about past times. My mother also managed to scare up some good food on the black market of this strange town, where most people spoke Polish, but were classified as *Volksliste 1* or *2* which meant that a generation or two before, their family included a member of German stock. With such a lineage established, they were permitted to remain in the newly created German province of Warthegau as future German citizens.

All other residents who were not considered eligible for inclusion in the ethnic categories of *Volksliste 1* or *2* were classified as Poles and had to vacate their apartments or houses, and were forced to leave all their possessions behind. They were loaded in trains and transported to the *Generalgouvernement,* the remaining part of Central Poland administered by the Nazi governor Frank who, with the powers of a king invested in his position, resided in Kraków on the *Wawel,* the former castle of the Polish kings. Observance of human rights and political and humanitarian conditions were non-existent in the *Generalgouvernement.* Only elementary schools remained open. This was considered sufficient by the German authorities, as the Poles were seen as potential source of cheap labour only.

My mother left me, greatly worried as my condition had worsened considerably. I received daily injections of liver extract and a special, but totally wrong diet, that, for instance included roast duck, all of which would have eventually destroyed me, if a medical inspection had not visited the hospital and ordered my immediate transfer to a specialist military hospital in the neighbouring city of Gnesen (Gniezno). This time I was transported by ambulance to the train station and placed in a private first-class compartment of a train reserved for high army officers only.

The very competent physician in charge of the Gnesen hospital immediately called my mother from Breslau to my bedside and, in tactful words, let her know that he hoped she would make my last days comfortable; he did not think I would survive much longer. I remember enough of these days to agree with his prognosis, but his highly competent and knowledgeable medical care assured my survival. My mother also helped me enormously, reawakening my desire to get well again rather than die. She was allowed to stay from early morning to late at night and became a source of strength for the entire room, a group of very ill men — all with the same diagnosis of Hepatitis C — of all ages, classes, and originating from all parts of Germany. She also acted as mediator between my two neighbours, a baron from Latvia, member of a famous family on one side, and a streetcar conductor from Strassburg in the Alsace on my other side. In other words, I ended up between a fervent Germanophile and an equally passionate Francophile; their arguments and verbal combat must have helped me keep up my spirits and re-establish my interest in life and in people.

The baron belonged to the Baltic Germans who had lived in Latvia and Estonia for several hundred years. This small ethnic group was constituted entirely of an aristocratic upper class and bourgeois middle class. It was without a lower class; there were no German labourers, or tradesmen; they came exclusively from the native Latvian population.

In former times, many of the Baltic aristocrats had been in the service of the czars, among them many well-known, outstanding diplomats, statesmen, and generals. The Baltic nobles owned large estates with manor houses that often could be classified as palaces. After World War I, though, the newly-created republics of Latvia and Estonia introduced a large-scale land reform that deprived the Baltic Germans not of their palaces and manor houses, but of their land, which was distributed to the Latvian and Estonian rural population.

Although landless and no longer prosperous, after their resettlement from Latvia to Germany according to the agreement between Hitler and Stalin who integrated the Baltic states into the Soviet Union in 1941, the former Baltic landowners were given large estates in the prior-to-1939 Polish province of *Wielkopolska* with its capital of Poznań (in German times Posen). These estates had been owned by Polish noble families for hundreds of years. Once before, in 1908, the Imperial German government narrowly failed to pass a bill that would have expropriated the legitimate Polish owners. 30 years later, after the occupation of the Polish province of Wielkopolska and its integration into the German Reich in 1939, they were evicted from their estates and resettled in the already overpopulated *Generalgouvernement*. In Germany and in the former province of Wielkopolska, now named the *Warthegau*, there were many voices that expressed their reservation with the rich properties that were transferred from Poles to Baltic Germans who had arrived in the *Warthegau* as landless aristocrats.

When my mother felt that she could leave me in this excellent hospital in Gnesen without worry, she returned home and, near the railway station in Breslau met my good friend from high school days with whom I had shared the memorable skiing trip of 1943. He had been wounded and was now working in the hospital transfer office in Breslau. It was easy for him to manipulate the system and, within days, arrange my transfer to Breslau.

So I left Gnesen, again in a special train compartment for my comfort and safety, without having seen anything of this city, one of the most important in the history of Christianity and of Poland.[13]

From the train station of Breslau, I was taken directly by ambulance to the University Hospital where my father had died only 11 weeks

---

13   Since the earliest Middle Ages, Gnesen has always been of supreme importance in the history of the Polish Kingdom and the Polish people. Gnesen had been settled as a centre of pagan cults since the seventh century. In 966 the Polish duke Mieszko I adopted the Christian faith, was baptized, and built a castle. In Gnesen, the Duke Boleslaw Chrobry crowned himself as the first King of Poland; he also called St. Adalbert as a missionary to his kingdom. Adalbert was later martyred and buried in the cathedral of Gnesen.

   In 1000, Emperor Otto III went on a pilgrimage to the grave of St. Adalbert in Gnesen, when Pope Sylvester I elevated Gnesen to an archbishopric and its church to a cathedral. Although accepting Otto III as his sovereign, the Polish king derived much strength and autonomy from this agreement, which became of decisive importance for the development of the Polish Kingdom and the identity of the Polish nation. Very little of this was mentioned during the Hitler years and while I was in Gnesen as a wounded soldier; within the Nazi ideology, the actions of Emperor Otto III were seen as most detrimental for the German nation.

before. This was the most prestigious hospital in Silesia, attended by a number of renowned professors of medicine who, despite their supreme knowledge and experience, had managed to kill my father through reckless medical practices. I was only about two miles from my home, but my mother was plagued with mixed feelings when she came to visit me for the first time. Her thoughts were back at the days she had spent at my father's bedside in the *Bunker*, a deep air raid shelter beneath the main building where all post-surgical patients were placed. It was the location where my father's life had ended, because he was too weak to survive the forced surgery, which should not have been scheduled in the first place, as his weight at that time was less than 100 lbs.

As for me, I received the best possible care and made rapid progress to the point where I was considered fit enough to be the guard of about 25 Russian soldiers who were kept in locked quarters next to the *Bunker* for their use in medical experiments. It was my task to guard them, observe how they spent the day, and record the content of their conversations I had with them — most of them spoke German fairly well and I had been ordered to talk with them as much as possible. The latter I did, but I certainly did not enter everything that had been said in the logbook. I do not know what the nature of the medical experiments was — I had no idea what kinds of injections were given to the prisoners. It was very obvious to me from the beginning that all of them were of remarkable intellectual capacity and were knowledgeable in science, arts, and literature. I led many meaningful conversations with them, but I could not ignore the constantly deteriorating state of their health, the likely result of the injections they were given. I did not tell my mother of my duties, as she was still most uncomfortable when she spent hours in this building every day in order to be at my side.

A week before Christmas I was allowed to visit home for a few hours several times a week. I used this privilege to take the streetcar with my mother to the centre of the city. I was shocked by how much Breslau had deteriorated since I was last there a year ago. There had been no air raids on the city to speak of, but years of war had left their visible traces everywhere. Not a single building had been repaired or freshly stuccoed since the late 1930s and the streets, of which many had always been somewhat grey and darkish, all looked more or less shabby now. The streets were dirty and obviously had not been swept in months. This was understandable as every able person not in the army or in the *Volkssturm*[14] had been sent eastwards to build tank traps, and other rather simple

---

14 The units of 16-year olds and men over 60 that were hastily constituted during the last months of the war.

fortifications designed to delay the expected advance of the Red Army. The centre section of the Russian Front had not moved much for several weeks, but there was undisguised anxiety and premonition among the people of the city.

Little social life was left and there was no entertainment to speak of; except for movie-houses, all theatres were closed. Still, the city seemed to teem with life. Everybody was working and all factories and other enterprises were running on a 24-hour and seven days-a-week schedule. The streetcars were overcrowded day and night, and the main streets in the city centre were black with people.[15] In between, there were units of the military and especially the *Volkssturm* marching through the streets, in part to bring some excitement and enthusiasm among the people. People had become very serious and spoke most guardedly in the streetcars, though in their demeanour, they did not attempt to hide their feelings. Nevertheless, there was still a considerable number of people who were convinced of the inevitable *Endsieg*, the final victory, to be achieved not only by the heroic German soldiers, but primarily by the *Wunderwaffen*, Hitler's secret, but at any moment to be put into action, miracle weapons. The belief in these mysterious weapons, said to be powerful rockets, never faltered in the minds of probably half the population.

Today, one might call this irrational belief in Hitler's power insane or ridiculous, but late in 1944, it maintained an atmosphere of serious- ness and stability and even normalcy in Breslau. Once more, I was home at Christmas, this time only with my mother. We had a Christmas tree, some decent food, and enough coal to be comfortable. We played some records but for the first time did not sing a single Christmas carol. We knew we would break into tears, should we even try to sing one verse.

We did talk at great length about the immediate future, though, and agreed that my mother would have to leave Breslau at the first sign of the Red Army crossing into Silesia. We also talked about where she should eventually turn. We realized that we did not have a single relative left in Central, West, or South Germany. With few exceptions, our families had always lived in Silesia, and those who did not, had returned to Silesia in order to escape the hardships of war that were more pronounced everywhere else. We only had somewhat distant relatives in Aussig an der Elbe (between 1918 and 1938 and since 1945 Ústí nad Labem) in former Czechoslovakia, but we knew that it would be foolish

---

15   This was also a reflection of the sharply increased population of the city. By December 1944, Breslau's population had passed the one million mark.

to be there at the end of the war after what had been done to the Czechs by the Germans since 1938.

We agreed it was essential that my mother would have to move as far west as possible. Through my father, through relatives, rumours, and simply being aware of the developments in Eastern Europe, we knew that horrible crimes had been committed by Germans against not only Jews and communists, but against all the nations in the east and southeast of Europe. The revenge would be terrible.

On Christmas Day we began to sort things out and decide what to take into the cellar for protection, and what we would take along to wherever that would be. For me, that meant next to nothing. I took the small Russian bronze icon my father had been given by his friend who was killed by the Nazis on January 30, 1933, and tied it to my belt with an old watch chain. I also took my father's best watch. I decided to wear my own underwear and put on two extra shirts of mine under my military issue clothing and I took my father's revolver. Both actions — wearing personal clothing and carrying weapons not issued by the military — were against regulations and actually quite risky, as both could be interpreted as preparations for desertion or resistance against the state.

New Year's Eve was very depressing. We had decided to have a good meal and an extra special bottle of wine. Neither did the food taste as good, even though my mother had prepared it with love, nor did we drink much of the wine. I have never again been in a mental state like that. We knew that everything would change and might end in disaster and death and we had no inkling how the coming days and weeks would turn out for us. So we simply ceased to think about what was coming. It was probably the only way to deal with the horrendous fear of the Russians that filled everybody. It was fear for one's naked life; it was fear for being punished for horrible deeds one personally had not committed. It was the fear of being separated, perhaps forever, from one's family and close friends, of being entirely dependent on oneself and having no one to trust and to lean on.

My Christmas leave ended on January 1, 1945 in the morning. I felt relieved that I could get back to the hospital and among soldiers. I did not know where I would end after my imminent discharge from the hospital. I knew that I would see my mother at least once more, but I did not know in what unit and in what section of the front I would end. Again, I refused to think or speculate beyond the end of the day.

* * * * *

13 1945
From Soldier to Prisoner of War

Hitler continues to promise victory. The last German offensive fails; the Red Army rolls into Germany; the enemy stands on German soil in both East and West. With their terror the Nazi establishment turns full force against its own people. Hitler orders the scorched earth policy. The Americans reach Central Germany. I am taken prisoner.

* * *

On January 9, my convalescent leave began; at its completion on January 23, I was to report to my reserve unit in Hirschberg. Being on leave in Breslau was now very different from the early war years. There were over one million people living in Breslau, forty percent more than in peacetime. Rarely beautiful in winter, the city looked now rundown; it was overcrowded with depressed, anxious people. Nobody took care to be well dressed. Everybody had, voluntarily or against his or her will, been integrated into Hitler's war machine. This huge apparatus, however, no longer ran as efficiently as it used to, notwithstanding Hitler's promise in his New Year's message that the war would soon be won. Waldenburg looked much more promising to us. My mother and I were longing to escape from our home that only reminded us of happier years. My mother and I were still in mourning.

Compared to Breslau, Waldenburg seemed an island of normalcy. We felt at home there, among all our relatives who accommodated us gladly and spoiled us with food items hidden in the back of their stores. In Breslau, the Russian Front felt threateningly near. From Waldenburg, however, c.ny 45 miles southwest of Breslau, the Red Army seemed a thousand miles away. The pair of skis that my aunt Martel had rescued for me two years ago came in handy. From the first day of my leave, I wandered through the mountains around town on my skis, always by myself and rarely meeting another skier. These few wonderful days I consciously enjoyed, always realizing that there would be no other time like this for me, at least not here in my home country, in Silesia.

Feeling that the end of the war was rapidly approaching, people were speculating from morning to night about what peace would be like. There were still a lot of people who believed that Hitler would be victorious and Germany would enter a period of never before experienced grandeur. In our families, nobody believed in such an ending. On the contrary, not only did not one of us even remotely hope for a victory, we were all too conscious of how Hitler, the SS, the Nazi party, and even ordinary units of the Wehrmacht had cruelly devastated Eastern Europe and enslaved millions of Poles, Russians, and other nations. For more than two years we had heard of the gas ovens of Auschwitz (between 1918 and 1939 and since 1954 Oświęcim). The concentration camp of Gross Rosen was less than 20 miles from Waldenburg; and throughout this highly industrialized area, there were small out-camps of Gross Rosen. If people had their eyes open, they could not ignore the emaciated concentration camp inmates in their striped clothing.

Even at the once beautiful Castle Fürstenstein, there were thousands of concentration camp inmates put to work in tearing down the terraces and the castle's interior to create, as people speculated, Hitler's new headquarters, or one of his guesthouses.

We actively searched for possible ways for my mother to escape westwards from Silesia. Everybody expected the worst from the Red Army; the British soldiers were expected to be correct but not very sympathetic; the French armies would be driven by thirst for revenge; and in a nebulous way, the Americans had the best press, although nobody had much of a feel of what the American soldiers were really like. All the enemy armies were already deep in German territory. However, not many news reports reached us other than horror reports about all four enemy armies. Many people considered most of the press and radio reports propaganda designed to keep the German population fighting out of fear of the enemy. Only what was reported about the Red Army, the killing, burning, pillaging, and raping received full credence. Everybody in Silesia was very fearful of the impending arrival of the Red Army.

In our family, we had no relatives further west who could have accommodated us. So we continued to talk without coming to a rational conclusion as to where to flee to — I do not remember who first used the word of flight, of fleeing from the Russians; whoever it was in our family, he or she only expressed what we all turned over in our minds all day and during sleepless nights.

On January 12, we realized decisions had to be made. The Russians had stormed out of the two bridgeheads they had maintained on the Vistula north and south of Warsaw since last fall. Within four days, the capital of the last Republic of Poland had fallen. And two days later, Kraków, the old royal capital of Poland, and the industrial centre of Łódź[1] had been abandoned by the German Army. My mother and I decided it was time to return to Breslau immediately and pack our bags.

We arrived in Breslau on January 20 in the late evening and found the city overflowing with refugees. The railway stations were over-crowded, as were the trains bringing refugees from the east. The most emotionally moving scenes were found on the main thoroughfares leading into and out of the city. Endless columns of tired people shuffled silently through the city, filling its main streets with heavily-loaded horse-drawn wagons carrying farmers' or merchants' families, or who-ever might have been fortunate enough to own a wagon and a team of horses. The majority of people, however, were on foot — mothers carrying babies, women pulling little hand wagons loaded with their most precious possessions or an elderly or infirm member of the family. These people told horror stories of struggling along highways in this coldest winter in years, of being strafed by Russian planes, and of leaving dying or dead family members by the roadside. There was neither time nor energy to bury one's loved ones along the way.

It was absolute insanity that the party authorities in Breslau at first forbade the evacuation of Breslau, but on January 20, one day before Breslau was declared a fortified city, ordered via the public address system women and children to leave the city via a road directing the stream of evacuees southwest, away from railroads. This was to force tens of thousands or more onto the icy highways at temperatures of minus 25 to 30 degrees Fahrenheit.

In the afternoon, we went to see our relatives who had already left their home in nearby Trebnitz (since 1945 Trzebnica). They were well known at the *Savoy Hotel* and therefore had managed to get a room for the night. A friend of my aunt Käthe, a factory owner who had been

---

1   Since 1939, it had been called Litzmannstadt, as Hitler had begun to integrate this large Polish city into the Warthegau, the easternmost province of the Third Reich.

allowed to keep his vehicle, had taken them by car to Breslau. They were shattered by the scenes they had witnessed on the highway and were really troubled having traveled in a car while others who had come much further from the east were struggling along, tired, starving, cold, and demoralized, some of them dying by the roadside. We spent the last hour of our visit in the air raid shelter of the *Savoy* and at the all-clear signal, said goodbye to our relatives, promising to follow them soon to Waldenburg. On the way home in the streetcar, we overheard some passengers reporting that our district had been bombed.

We discovered that our house was quite heavily damaged on its upper floor. There was a lot of debris in our apartment and many broken windows, but the walls had remained intact.

As there was no electrical power in the entire neighbourhood, we went to bed. I do not know what went through my mother's mind. My mind was in high gear trying to decide how to leave Breslau without being apprehended by the military police and being shot or, if I would be lucky, not shot but merely sent to the Front. I had my hospital discharge papers that classified me as unfit for active duty, but having all my limbs intact, I did not feel very much protected by this document.

The atmosphere in Breslau had been hectic and politically heated by the party; cases of heroism were constantly announced in the paper and the radio, mostly situations where elderly men, courageous women, and boys still in their teens had committed "deeds of valour," fighting the approaching Bolshevik enemy. This all implied that absolutely every person was now in the service of the fatherland and under command of the Army, the party, or the SS. Hitler had sent his infamous General Schörner to Silesia. His *Feldgendarmerie*, the military police, was greatly feared because of their ubiquitous presence and the quick grabbing of men in or out of uniform. No matter what the papers of their victims said, they were sent to the Front in hastily constituted and poorly equipped units. I was still in Breslau when the practice started, to hang men, and sometimes women, who were accused of evading their duty. These victims were hanged without benefit of the law; they were left hanging for days on town squares and along busy streets in order to frighten the general populace into submission.

This terror was also carried out at the level of higher government. Towards the end of the month, I read that the vice-mayor of Breslau, Dr. Wolfgang Spielhagen, who had attended my senior matriculation, had been hanged for treason and defeatism. For the same reason, the father of my friend Volker Sommer was also hanged on the same day, January 27. Their corpses were left on the gallows in the middle of the *Ring*, the town square of Breslau, for several days.

On January 21 at breakfast, we heard the news that Breslau had been declared a *Festung*.[2] My mother told me that she had cried a lot during the past night, thinking of my father, but she was now grateful that my father was not here in Breslau. In his extremely weak state and with his need for special care and diet, he would not have survived. It was a relief for her to know that he was resting in peace in the military cemetery in Breslau.

In our cellar stood the massive hope chest of my Grandmother Koch that, somehow, had gotten into our possession. It was crafted of beautifully decorated oak, heavy, and sturdy. Into this chest my mother and I placed whatever we thought was of value and importance to the family, although while taking things into the cellar, we could not help thinking of soldiers and civilians soon plundering and stealing what was precious to us. There was still no electrical power and after darkness fell, we got my knapsack and military gear and my mother's two suitcases ready for our departure.

Before that, though, there were two items I felt obliged to take care of that, in hindsight, look absolutely ridiculous. In the shelter of darkness I walked to the next neighbourhood to pay my dentist, finding her just ready to leave the city. When I returned home, my mother was packing two large books, one of them John Knittel's *Via Mala* loaned from one of our relatives in Waldenburg. Both books were very heavy and bulky and took precious space in my mother's suitcase that could have been used for packing items vital for her future. While for the first time in our lives, we were forced to abandon everything and get ready to take our first step into an unknown, frightening future full of death, poverty, insecurity, and multiple losses, with one foot we still remained firmly in our established world where one would always pay one's debts and fulfill all other obligations, often matters of little importance that, nevertheless, were considered a priority in one's orderly life!

---

2   A *Festung* was a fortified city where military law prevailed and civil rights were suspended. The enemy had to presume that any non-military building, even a church, could serve as a defence installation from which the enemy might be attacked. Within a Festung, all civilians, in the case of Breslau men and woman from the age of 10 to 80, were under the orders of the commander of the *Festung*, and could be forced to any type of duty, of a military or civilian nature. A new type of ID card had to be carried by each person; its daily signed and stamped entries were to justify a person's presence anywhere anytime, and would also entitle the bearer to his/her daily ration of food. The latter was one of the most effective measures to enforce people's compliance to military law. To anyone failing to comply, martial law was invariably applied, whether it was a disobedient civilian or a soldier. Refusing an order or suspected desertion were quickly dealt with by shooting or hanging.

Hours before we were ready to leave, our flashlight batteries had given out and we were forced to complete our packing and sorting of papers by candlelight. In silence we carried our heavy luggage to the streetcar. When we arrived at the railway station, I was in shock when I discovered that I did not have my *Soldbuch*, my soldier's passbook, with me. This was a potential death sentence. Would I be stopped by one of the many *Feldgendarmerie* patrols and found to be without my *Soldbuch* I would be brought quickly before an emergency military tribunal, immediately sentenced to death and, without delay, shot or hanged.

I was fortunate not to be stopped on my streetcar ride back to our house where I found the document on my desk. Without electric light and by the dim light of a candle only, in the excitement of leaving home for what likely was to be forever, it had been easy to overlook the *Soldbuch*.

When I got off the streetcar on the square in front of the railway station, my mother was standing there in the ice-cold wind to warn me not to go near the terminal building, because it was swarming with military police. She had, in the meantime, found a railway employee who, for a hefty donation of cigarettes (from my father's supply) agreed to smuggle my mother and myself onto the tracks far beyond the platforms of the terminal building to an empty train destined for Waldenburg; it was to be shunted into the station early in the morning. We thought we would freeze to death in the unheated coach, but eventually, the train was moved into the station and stormed by thousands of desperate people, mainly women and children and some old men, who pushed, fought, and screamed to get onto the train. A young woman got into our compartment; she had five elderly women tied to her waist. There was no other way but to let this group of Polish-speaking Upper Silesians get on the train first. In the ensuing commotion, dozens were left behind, as our and all other compartments had been filled by people who had illegally boarded the train from its other side.

When we arrived in Waldenburg, it was Sunday morning and people were on their way to church. Our relatives had not even had their breakfast when we appeared at their door. I had only three days left of my leave and felt like a hunted deer. I managed to sneak to our old dentist in the late afternoon of the second day, when my aunt phoned to tell me that the *Feldgendarmerie* was active everywhere in the city. Her boss, who still had his delivery van, and my mother, would pick me up at the dentist's office and take me through the dark streets directly to a small suburban railway station where at this time of the day, no military police would be controlling the few passengers. This turned out to be a successful stratagem. I said goodbye to my mother and jumped on the train. After having felt hunted all along, I was relieved when I entered the safety of the barracks of my reserve battalion in Hirschberg.

Huge crowds of people fleeing from the Russians filled the city. Amongst these tens of thousands, I ran into the mother of my former friend from high school who had become a high *Hitlerjugend* official and had stricken me from the list of candidates for the Nazi party, as he had been long aware of my anti-Hitler attitudes. Like others my age who were already in the army, I was to have been drafted into the party on my 18th birthday. Although he detested me by that time, my former friend did me an enormous favour by declaring me as unfit and unworthy to be accepted as a member of the Nazi party. His mother, though, a warm-hearted, spontaneous half-Polish woman from Upper Silesia, still loved me. She gave me a big hug and another kiss mixed with tears when we said goodbye. This was the first of quite a few instances where I ran into old acquaintances in the midst of utter chaos towards the end of the war and after. Except in one instance, I do not know who of those I met in these trying times survived and who died as a result of the events of the war and its consequences. So I have often wondered whether the mother of my former friend "made it," as we said at that time.

Hirschberg was still safe enough to venture out of the barracks and into the streets of the city. As a matter of fact, there were still theatres and bars open, all filled to capacity with soldiers. The entertainment was, of course, not of high calibre anymore, and quite a bit of it was rather coarse. This was no doubt tolerated and perhaps even encouraged, to make the soldiers forget the combat and death that were facing everybody in uniform.

In my teenage years, I had gone to working class pubs in Breslau, but never to the type of bars that I visited now in Hirschberg, all of them at one time high-class establishments for the rich tourists from Dresden and Berlin. In the *Wiener Café* — in spite of its gentle name now a raucous cabaret — I had a rather hilarious experience — although not as much for me as for the audience. The singer of the band, a statuesque woman of slightly advanced years with bleached hair and heavy make-up, picked me out of the crowd as probably one of the youngest, worked her way between the tables in my direction, always singing and swinging her heavy hips, until she landed in my lap and immediately switched to a rather suggestive melody followed by an outright obscene song. It is hard to describe my embarrassment and my fury, especially as I felt I could not get out of my chair, being kept there by the woman's enormous weight. The entire place was noisy with loud applause and roaring laughter. After the singer finally freed me from her weight, I tried to make the best of my embarrassing situation. I stood up and bowed to the crowd as if to acknowledge the applause. But this gesture did not come off as intended. The reaction of the crowd turned to derisive laughter and nobody applauded anymore. My face and my ears were red with embarrassment and I felt I had failed miserably.

Except for guard duties and daily roll call, we were pretty free and quite readily received permission to leave the barracks. I took the suburban streetcar that, in better times, transported tourists right to the foot of the *Riesengebirge*. The primary advantage of this transportation was that although it was as extensive as some rail lines, it was not classified as a railway. Therefore, soldiers could use it without travel papers, and it never seemed to be patrolled by military police, the *Feldgendarmerie*.

Three times I managed to get to the mountains. Each time the trip turned into a different experience. I went to the hotel in Hain where I had stayed with my parents before entering the Labour Service. The proprietor recognized me and since there were no guests present, he and I had one of those rare evenings, when one feels absolutely safe and can share one's political convictions.

Another time, I hiked for three hours to visit my mother's cousin, my other Aunt Lisa who was so beautiful with her classic features and her blond hair. She and her husband and their youngest son stayed in a large hotel in Krummhübel (since 1945 Karpacz), as their hometown Strehlen (since 1945 Strzelin) had already fallen to the Red Army. Aunt Lisa played the grand piano in the empty ballroom; it was as in old times.

During my third visit to the mountains, I took another long hike through the higher mountains and while there felt the atmosphere change from a cold winter day to a day of what the Bavarians call *Föhn*, the Western Canadians *Chinook*, and the dictionaries *a southerly gale*. It turned into an experience where the rapidly changing, wild nature awakens all sorts of emotions in one's soul. I found myself singing, screaming, jumping, and running wildly down the steep narrow path through the forest. All this time, I had a sense of finality that everything I did and experienced, was happening for the last time.

After I returned to the barracks, I wrote a long, emotional letter to a girlfriend I had first met while a young soldier. I told her in kind words I needed to terminate our relationship. Nothing untoward had happened, but I was very agitated that evening and felt that the fewer people I had in my life, the easier I would survive the coming months. I knew that the prisoner of war camp was only weeks, perhaps just days away. I wanted to be as free as possible from worry about people I cared about.

At that time of my life, I passionately loved the mountains. As if to be rewarded for this love, I was blessed with another uninterrupted five weeks of life in the loneliest part of the Silesian mountains. At roll call one morning, our commanding officer, a baron who owned a huge estate in the Silesian Lowlands, asked for volunteers who were experienced skiers to step forward. I am glad I had the courage to do so, as the commander's request sounded like an invitation to join some special unit at the Front. The assignment for myself and four other men, none of them of a higher rank than private first class, turned out to be the guarding of the commander's valuable antique furniture and a number of large steel boxes likely filled with precious items. Within a day, we were on our way by truck into the high mountains, where at a crossing above Oberschreiberhau (since 1945 Szklarska Poręba) a number of local farmers, mostly quite elderly men, were waiting for us with large horse-drawn sleighs. We transferred our load from the truck onto the sleighs. Headed by a snow-clearing sleigh, this column of heavily loaded sleighs made it in one slow five-hour trip to a tiny settlement consisting of one inn and five small farmhouses. From the seventeenth to the nineteenth century, the settlement had been one of the centres of the Silesian glass industry. Although I knew the mountains well, I had never heard of Karlsthal (since 1945 Orle), located alongside the former German-Czech border, the border being the reason for the existence of two fairly large modern houses that had been built as homes for the local customs officers and border patrol members. With the annexation of a part of Czechoslovakia, the *Sudetenland*, in 1938 the houses had lost their original purpose and had been empty since 1938. For the next five weeks, they became our comfortable home. Our work consisted of simply being there to guard the commander's property, to cut wood for the stoves, and to cook our meals. Once a week, two of us would ski to the next village, a trip of close to three hours, to pick up mail, food, and other supplies sent from our barracks in Hirschberg.

I could write a story about these weeks of being in the beautiful mountain country with a few other men of compatible nature. There were never any arguments between us, or strife; our group ruled itself and successfully did so in a democratic manner. Once in a while, we heard the thunder of guns from some far valley and for one week we were showered with burned pieces of paper carried by air currents from the far away burning city of Dresden. Otherwise, we had a wonderful life, a gift of peace that only a very, very few soldiers might have had the chance to experience. We were content, serene, and happy, except when it was our turn to go to the village for mail and supplies. Whoever came back from such an expedition was deeply affected by the uninterrupted stream of civilians fleeing the front line. Some of them had been on the road for several weeks by now and one could see and sense that they would not have the strength and stamina to last much longer. Nearly all of them looked very vulnerable, as they had spent all their reserves on physical and emotional energy. Many were visibly weak by nature, not prepared for an ordeal like that. They were very old, or too young, or had too many others to look after, such as aging parents, or helpless children. Some were obviously true city people, totally unequipped for any physical hardship. I remember one middle-aged couple, obviously Poles, who must have come from a far away small town in the East. The woman, a beautiful person with fine features, was wearing clothes from the late 1920s, a cloche hat, a tight, short winter coat, and impossible shoes. She seemed to have emerged from a fashion magazine of pre-Hitler times. Her husband looked like a small town schoolmaster with his pince-nez, tiny moustache, and his shy smile. We helped them along for awhile, pulling their sleigh, and letting them take their turn to rest on it.

The only other unpleasant location was the old inn in Karlsthal, by itself a very charming place. We liked the people who owned the inn, that is the wife and the children, as the father was at the Front. There were five house guests, however, obviously prosperous women in their fifties or sixties, who seemed to spend the entire day in the dining room of the inn. They were all strident Nazis and kept praising Hitler and bragging about their sons and daughters who had been very successful in the party hierarchy or in the Army. We did not dare enter into any conversations with them, nor speak frankly among ourselves in their presence. I am sure they would have reported us immediately, had they known what our attitude was. These women were dangerous; they were fanatical Nazis. Listening to their loud, boisterous voices, we realized that one was the mother of the most successful pilot in the German air force, famous for having destroyed numerous enemy tanks with his dive-bomber; another woman was the mother of Germany's most famous woman test pilot.

If it had not been for these despicable women, we would have almost forgotten the world beyond the next mountain range and what happened in the other parts of Silesia and of Germany. The Russians had already encircled Breslau on February 15. The city was being destroyed street by street. Budapest had fallen into the hands of the Red Army. The Russians had crossed the Oder River east of Berlin and threatened the German capital. On March 19, Hitler proclaimed that nothing would be left to the advancing enemy; he issued his infamous scorched earth policy. In the west, the Americans had taken Cologne on March 6, and two days later, had crossed the Rhine River via the now famous Remagen Bridge.

On March 22, when much of the snow had melted on the narrow road to Karlsthal, three huge trucks came to load all of the commander's property and take us to Hirschberg. We only had a day there before we were transferred to Glatz (since 1945 Kłodzko), a train ride of eight hours, taking us without stopping through my hometown Waldenburg.

Glatz was a hotbed of military police. I only had wonderful memories of this picturesque city that looked more Bohemian and Austrian than Prussian. In happier times, we had often stopped there to change trains or start long hikes when we spent a weekend or a holiday in the near mountains. The entire county of Glatz – everyone called it the *Grafschaft Glatz* – had this Austrian ambience with its baroque churches and monasteries, religious way stations, modest manor houses, and impressive palaces, everything bedded in the charming hilly countryside with the higher mountains circling the horizon. It was significant that alone among Silesian Catholic towns and villages, the Grafschaft Glatz did not belong to the near archdiocese of Breslau, but to the much more remote archbishopric of Prague. People from the Grafschaft spoke Silesian dialect, but with a different accent. They were generally looked upon as extremely good natured and hard working, steadily plodding along rather than exhausting themselves. The were people who had a gentle sense of humour and were inclined to be a bit naive. Silesians used to call a person from the Grafschaft a *Glatzer Natzel*, an abbreviation of Ignatz or Ignatius, a true Catholic name, if there ever was one, never to be found among Protestants anywhere.

As with other Silesian cities, Glatz had taken on a veneer of grime and dirt, especially noticeable in the washed-out white, yellow, and light blue baroque facades of the many churches and other buildings from the seventeenth and eighteenth centuries. What had become of my beloved Glatz! Not only was it overcrowded with thousands of people fleeing the Russians. Most of them remained in town, swelling the ranks of people needing shelter and food; they hesitated to continue beyond Glatz towards the nearby former Czechoslovakia. They asked themselves whether it would be safe there, after what Germany had done to the Czech people and their state. Still, many thousands did continue into the former Czechoslovakia, oblivious to past history or denying it.

I did not see much of Glatz anyway, as none of us dared to venture out of the barracks, unless being part of a unit dispatched for some specific purpose. We could ask for short leaves, but no one did, as it seemed certain that we would get caught by the *Feldgendarmerie* and immediately shipped to the Front.

The mood in town was depressed. My mother who came to visit told me that people who were not Nazis expected with certainty that the entire Grafschaft would become part of Czechoslovakia. Everybody knew how life had changed for the Czech people after Hitler had annexed their country; nobody expected much good from the future here.

This was the last time my mother and I saw each other until more than a year after the war. It felt, as if I was already in a prisoner of war camp, as I did not dare to leave the barracks and my mother was not permitted to enter the compound. So I stood at the inside of the high wooden fence looking through the slats against the sun, hardly able to make out my mother's face. Whichever way we turned, we could only see a small part of each other's face at any one time. At this last minute, we decided on an address where we could find each other *"wenn alles vorbei ist"* (after everything will be over), a place that was certain to remain part of Germany after the hostilities had ended — we felt quite certain that Silesia would be lost for Germany. We managed to shake hands when the time came to say goodbye; the fence prevented us from giving each other a goodbye kiss. It was a very sad parting.

Three days later, soldiers who were classified as not fit for active duty were put on a train with the destination of Sondershausen in Thuringia. It is hard to describe the relief, the near jubilation in one's heart, when we were advised of this transfer. It meant that the certainty of being captured by the Red Army became a remote, unlikely possibility. With some luck, we would be taken prisoner by the Americans, as long as we managed to get out of Silesia. Our train was to take the last remaining railway that was still in German hands; all other lines in westerly direction were in the hands of the Red Army. We did make it by the skin of our teeth, as southeast of Görlitz, our train was under artillery attack, but we did not stop, nor were we hauled out of the train to defend this last escape route from Silesia to Germany.

We crossed Saxony and entered Thuringia. Spring had arrived and everywhere there were green leaves and blossoms that gave our destination, the small former residence of the Dukes of Schwarzburg-Sondershausen an air of welcome. This was a most picturesque little town with a medieval core of half timbered houses along narrow streets, adjoined by quarters of substantial looking houses from the nineteenth century facing tree-lined avenues, a large park, and like a guardian on the hill above the town, the ducal castle with its stubby clock tower. There was little traffic, and there were, as yet, no refugees coming from the east. It was an idyll that we could enjoy only for a day or two, before we were kept in the barracks, to be ready at a moment's notice in case the Americans would break through the poorly defended German lines.

There were several alerts, but no bombs fell. Our days were dragging and the tension among the men was palpable. No one had a real friend or buddy. We were new to each other, had no common memories or experiences to look back to and, quite frankly, did not readily trust each other. In these last days of the Hitler Reich, unexpressed attitudes were liable to abruptly rise to the surface, and opinions became dramatically polarized. If someone would, after much verbal sparring, declare himself for Hitler, he did so with threatening words and gestures, as if to demonstrate that the power of the Nazis was undiminished. Those who were not for Hitler were severely intimidated. It was extremely risky to utter any criticism, as nobody knew how many were against Hitler and how strongly held their convictions were and whether or not they had the courage to stand by them. I felt most insecure and kept to myself, not wanting to get into political arguments or be reported and possibly be shot days before the end of the war and what was to be freedom after years of Hitler's dictatorship.

I did make one friend, though, a man my age who came from the town of Hadamar near Limburg an der Lahn, east of the Rhine. While we talked about home, he began reminiscing about his sister who was no longer alive. After much hesitation — he must have felt he could trust me — I learned that his sister had been mentally retarded and with many others killed by the Nazis in the large institution at Hadamar. The family had received a telegram one day advising them that their daughter had died of heart failure. I also learned that at Hadamar, this inhuman practice of killing those declared unfit had gone on for several years. Nobody dared to speak about it except within one's family.

My last four days as a soldier were filled with guard duty at a huge depot of food supplies just outside Sondershausen. Break-ins and thefts had been attempted several times, which caused the local military commander to move us to the depot for guard duty. We guarded the perimeter of the otherwise deserted buildings which were filled to capacity with foods and delicacies we had not seen in years. This included the finest chocolates, canned exotic fruits, wine, liqueurs, and champagne. We did live rather in luxury for these few days, until April 10 when a group of American planes bombed the town. I was on guard duty during this afternoon and from this safe distance, I saw every single bomb being released from a plane. I was surprised how slow the bombs seemed to descend towards the ground, and how quickly, after their muffled explosion, huge fires started in the old part of town.

The entire episode did not take more than two minutes. But the centre of town was destroyed.

We were immediately moved back into our barracks. This afternoon became the most tragic, traumatic day of my life. What I had to experience and to endure in the afternoon and the evening of April 10 changed my outlook on life, on my German heritage, and it determined my aims for the future. This experience also made me a person haunted by doubts and guilt for almost 25 years, until I found a man who helped me come to terms with what I was forced to carry out on Tuesday, April 10, 1945, my last full day as a German soldier. The story in the following chapter I called *SEARCHING* tells what happened.

* * * * *

14 SEARCHING

*I*n fall of 1968, I spent a month with the family therapy program of the Montreal Jewish General Hospital, presented by a group of eminent psychiatrists, among them Dr. Isaac Rebner, the most senior member of the group. During those weeks, I not only developed enormous respect and admiration for Dr. Rebner, as a professional and as an individual, I also had the courage to ask for a private meeting with him, where I re-lived the events of April 10, 1945 that haunted my mind and my emotions since that fateful day.

Dr. Rebner not only listened to me – he was the first person with whom I had shared my traumatic memories – he also gently helped me admit to myself that what I had been given as a choice on April 10, 1945 was no choice at all.

Before I left Dr. Rebner's office, he challenged me to put on paper what actually happened, not in the form of a report, but as an expression of my feelings. What I wrote down after my return from Montreal to Edmonton, became a story – no fiction, but a factual story – which I gave the title "Searching." Except for some minor editing, I have left "Searching" as I wrote it 34 years ago.

SEARCHING

As with yesterday and the day before, he had imperceptibly drifted away from the group of tourists he had been traveling with through Germany. Walking through the crowded street he knew so well but had not seen since the spring of 1945, he again caught himself looking for D among the people he passed.

D was the code, his secret code for the man with the crooked left leg stuck in the German officer's black boot, forming with D's straight leg the silhouette of the letter D.

D also stood for Deutschland, and for Death. Above all, D was his code for the man with the D-shaped legs and the Sten gun pointed at him, towering above him against the darkening sky of 25 years ago.

D was Deutschland on the day when Germany had ceased to exist for him. D was Death: D's threat to shoot him, his own urge to kill D, or to kill himself. D meant Death as revenge, retribution, escape from guilt, and redemption of the innocent.

With his eyes cast low, he moved through the busy crowd, oblivious of the faces, young and old, around him. He did not notice the sounds made by tired children dragged along by their impatient mothers, nor the subdued voices of the old couples resting on the benches that lined the sidewalk. The filigree-like church spire pointed out only moments ago by the eager guide and admired by his travel companions, left no imprint on his mind. It was the black silhouette of D's crooked leg that his restless eyes were searching for in the moving crowd; the legs that had marched across this pavement 23 years ago.

For years, he had hesitated and deliberated, finally deciding to return to Germany as a member of a group of tourists studying the country's architecture. Now, as he approached the end of the street, he would soon turn its corner and reach the old army barracks. Like D's silhouette, their red brick buildings had never been banished from his mind. More intensely than ever, he began again to re-live those hours in the spring of 1945, the unextinguished past turning into a vivid painful present in his mind.

It is the 10th day of April 1945. He knows that the end of war is near. He is leaning out of the second floor window of the room of his platoon. He compulsively keeps re-counting the number of the twenty-three concentration camp inmates who are resting in the shadow of the barracks, unguarded and unobserved. All week long, he had watched the heavily guarded grey columns from the concentration camps in the East that were by now in the hands of the Red Army. They were pushed westwards by the *SS* along the highways, that were now crowded with refugees who averted their eyes from the pitiful figures in their striped concentration camp clothes, whose existence they could no longer deny.

The grey ones below his window seem to look alike — exhausted, motionless, faceless. There are no more electrified barbed wired fences or black uniformed guards with their dogs surrounding them. But the grey ones do not look at each other or beyond the low wooden fence, that marks the perimeter of the army barracks. They are quiet as death, as if waiting for liberation, or sacrifice. One of them gets up slowly and urinates against the single tree in the corner of the yard.

Searching for signs of the approaching enemy, his eyes gaze across the silent town towards the gentle hills in the distance, when the bell calls him away from the window. D, their lieutenant, addresses the platoon and reiterates the mission of protecting the fatherland, of preserving the purity of the German race. There will be an execution of the concentra-

Retreat summer 1944

158. Schützenpanzerwagen, the half-track troop carrier that transported our platoon to and from and during battles and skirmishes, attacks and retreats.

159. This is how I remember most of the Russian and Polish towns and villages during our retreat.

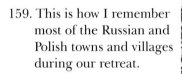

159a. I remember passing this baroque church on the outskirts of Slonim.

160. The war in the East ended for me in Sniadowo in northern Poland when I was wounded in a field like this.

161. The survivors of Stalingrad on their way into captivity. Germany never recovered from the defeat of Stalingrad.

162. "Wollt Ihr den Totalen Krieg?" (Are you ready for Total War?) Rally in the Berlin Sportpalast.

163. Volkssturm. The People's Militia. The last manpower resources are sent to the front.

164. Hitler's terror against his own people: those not cooperating are hanged and publicly displayed.

Surviving victims of Hitler's War

165. The exploited youth of the Third Reich.

166. Hitler among his last conscripts.

168. Millions of Germans fled from the approaching Red Army.

167. Buchenwald concentration camp inmates liberated by U.S. soldiers.

The End

169. May 8, 1945
The destroyed Reichstag
(German Parliament in
Berlin).

170. The destroyed city of Magdeburg.

Prisoners of War

I do not have a single personal photo from my 13 months as a prisoner of war of the American and the French armies. The following pictures, though, are representative of my life as a prisoner of war.

◄70/171. March into captivity

◄72. Early days at Camp Miesenheim near Andernach.

Prisoners of war

173.
Arrival of
prisoners at
camp
Miesenheim.

174.
A close-up of
the Sinzig
camp looking
exactly like the
Andernach
camp.

175. Camp Andernach on
the Rhine in
May/June 1945.

The very difficult postwar years 1945–1948

176. The Neumarkt/Nowy Targ in Breslau/Wroclaw, my hometown I could not return to after the war.

178.
This is how I travelled from Bavaria to Bremen and back in 1946 and 1947.

177. The foto of my first ID card after I had fled the French prisoner of war camp in May 1946.

𝔚𝔞𝔩𝔡𝔟𝔯𝔲𝔫𝔫 1947–1952

179.
My mother and
I lived in the
gable behind
the large tree.

180.
Our only room.

181.
My mother and
her goslings
(1946).

182. With my mother, my aunt
     Hannchen and cousins Klaus
     and Jürgen in 1947.

183. My nephew Hans lived with us
     for a couple of years.

84.
Hans's sister
nes at
Grandmother
Koch's 93rd
birthday in 1952
she died in the
ame year).

1948 The rebirth of Germany

184a.
from left to right:
Dr. Kurt Schumacher, leader of the Socialdemocratic Party; Professor Carlo Schmid, one of the creators of the Grundgesetz, the German constitution; Dr. Konrad Adenauer, the first chancellor of the new republic.

184b. Dr. Theodor Heuss, the first president of the new Federal Republic and Chancellor Dr. Konrad Adenauer.

184c.
A symbol of the "Deutsche Wirtschaftswunder, the German economic miracle. One of the new department stores in Frankfurt.

After the summer of 1948, life is getting better

185. Würzburg 1952.

186. Würzburg 1953.

187. Leaving for Canada - April 1954.

188. Our first Canadian home in Edmonton. My mother and I owned half of the house.

189. Maria Koch née Schuster and myself with Dr. Friedhelm Fabian, best friend from high school days (Karlsruhe 1970).

190. Maria's parents Georg and Charlotte Schuster.

191. Maria's sister Elisabeth Schuster.

Canada 1954 to 2004

192.
Our wedding
on November 9,
1957 in
Edmonton.

194. Visiting in
Germany
(1960).

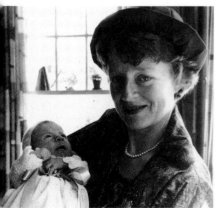

193. Maria with our son George
(1962).

195. Our home in Edmonton before
the trees around it grew tall.

The Kochs

196, 197.
Our Edmonton house and garden.

199. Laurie.

199. George sailing

Europe between the two World Wars, 1918 – 1939

Countries newly created or modified after the end of World War I

Albania (light brown)	Austria (gold)
Czechoslovakia (dark brown)	Estonia (dark brown)
Finland (bright yellow)	Hungary (bright yellow)
Latvia (blue)	Lithuania (light brown)
Poland (dark green)	Soviet Union (light green)
Turkey (light brown)	Yugoslavia (dark blue)

Das Grossdeutsche Reich 1938-1942

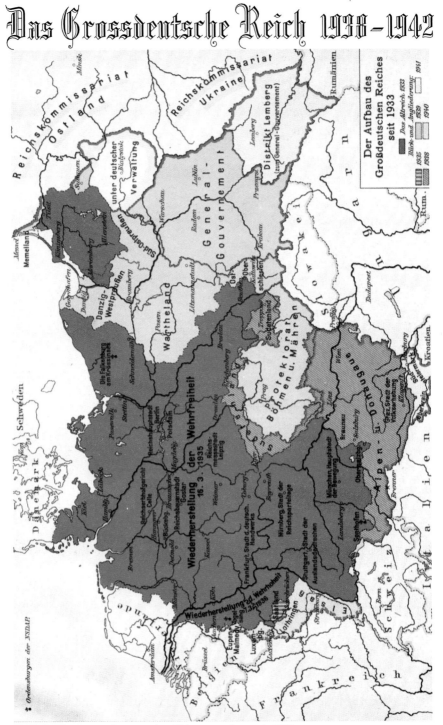

Area in dark-red represents Germany when Hitler assumed power in 1933.
All other shades of red represent further annexations, beginning with Austria in 1938. Not in red are areas unde
German suzerainty (Slovakia since 1939), and those under the control of the National Socialist Party, the
Reichskommissariat Ost (Weissrussland and parts of Russland), and the Reichskommissariat (Ukraine), since 194
Future Plans following a victorious end of the World War II aimed at a Greater Germanic Reich that was to inclu
Norway, Denmark, Holland, the Flemish part of Belgium, and some sections of Eastern and Northern France.

tion camp inmates who had entered the barracks in voluntary surrender. When D asks for volunteers for the execution, only three of 15 soldiers refuse. He is one of three.

Minutes later, behind the high wall of the motor pool, D orders him and the other two who had refused to volunteer for the execution, to dig a pit. With deliberate steps, D measures its dimensions by the length of his boots. For digging, D orders them to use their field spades (the ones soldiers carry attached to their belts).

Frightened and confused, he pushes his spade into the barren soil, remembering the days in combat when he used this little triangle of bluish steel to dig foxholes. More than once, this little spade had saved his life.

One hour later, the sun has disappeared behind the motor pool building, transforming its bright red bricks into a menacing, dark wall. He feels the coldness of the damp earth penetrate his heavy boots. D has been watching with seeming patience. Although the pit is still shallow — a mere foot, he guesses — D orders them to stop digging and wait for his return. Left alone, he suddenly senses a dull pain in the hand that is still gripping the handle of the field spade, as one grips the wrist of a friend in utter fear. What is he to do? Remain and witness the impending murder? Escape and end in the fangs of the roving military police and face certain execution as a deserter?

Still clutching the handle of his field spade, he has not moved from the edge of the pit when D returns with the concentration camp survivors. They are escorted by the volunteers from his platoon, whom only an hour ago he had still called his comrades. Again, he is counting the grey ones. There are still 23 of them. Not one of them has attempted to escape. In total silence and submission, broken only by D's sharp commands, the grey ones are ordered to line up along the edge of the pit.

Dimly, he hears D's command, the single, hard burst of the volley from the soldiers' rifles, followed by the prolonged firing of D's Sten gun. Staring at the grey mass of writhing bodies at his feet, he wants to turn around and scream at the soldiers, "All of you who volunteered shot into the air!" Only D's Sten gun had not been aimed high during the fusillade, he realizes.

He will never know whether D had left the killing of the victims unfinished on purpose. He waits for someone to scream in horror, in pain, in hatred. But all he hears are the muffled groans that rise from the mass of twisting bodies in the pit below.

How much punishment must he accept from D for refusing to volunteer? The ritual of murder and death continues. D orders him and the other two to bury the dying, who are ignored by those who had volunteered for their execution. He remains at the edge of the pit; his boots feel frozen to the ground. He knows that soldiers who refuse orders are quickly executed without court-martial during these last days of the war. Refusing D's order means certain death; and to obey D's order also means death! Perhaps he has only one decision left to make: to refuse and join the dying in the pit. He steps into the pit and raises his eyes. Above him stands D, his Sten gun pointed at him, his straight leg and his crooked leg towering like a huge letter D against the darkening sky.

D's Sten gun motions him and the other two to use their field spades. Field spades are for digging foxholes when under enemy fire, he wants to shout, for digging graves to lay fallen comrades to eternal rest and gently cover their dead bodies with soft earth. Field spades are not meant to be instruments for killing human beings! He sees D's Sten gun pointed at his face and feels a strange pull, as if wanting to throw himself against the black muzzle of the weapon. But with his feet almost buried in the twisting bodies, he does not dare move, afraid of the single, sharp screams of pain breaking from this groaning mass.

Suddenly, he starts swinging his field spade, beginning the task of killing, of murder, of mercy, of liberation. . . . .

The question races through his mind, whether he had been the first to raise his spade. He will never know. Bent low and panting hoarsely, he swings his spade up and down, hears it fall onto the soft mass of human flesh with a dull thud, and wonders whose command his arms and hands are obeying in their rhythmic movements. His eyes closed, he does not see where the sharp blade of his spade is landing. Discerning the cracking sound of skulls being split, he shuts his eyes more forcefully.

His tortured mind remembers the ancient painting in the church of the town of his birth, of the Grim Reaper striding across the field with his horrible grin, swinging his scythe from side to side. Trying to extinguish the image from his mind, he swings his spade harder and harder, not sideways like the Grim Reaper, but up and down. He wants to destroy the Reaper's horrible grin. He wants, instead, to whisper to the dying words of love, of pity, of begging for forgiveness every time he hears the crushing sound made by his spade. Slowly, the writhing and moaning around his feet recedes into utter stillness.

The dying are dead now. They are sacrificed. They are liberated. They have found peace. When D orders him and the other two to step out of the pit and stand against the wall of the motor pool, he briefly experiences a sense of freedom, of peace, until he hears the scraping sound of a dozen field spades. In the pale light of the stars, he sees D and his volunteers throwing earth onto their victims in rapid concerted movements, methodically proceeding in unison alongside the pit like a platoon in action. The pit is shallow. And there is not enough soil to cover the bodies well. Throwing their spades aside, D and his volunteers start trampling down the thin layer of earth in a silent, barbaric, violent dance.

Attaching his spade to his belt and picking up his Sten gun, D commands them to assemble in formation. Silently, he falls in with his platoon and marches through the town's deserted main street. Beyond the last houses, they stop in an open field. There is as yet no sign of the enemy.

Their rifles returned to them, he and the other two are ordered to guard the road, while D and the remainder of the platoon retreat to a barn nearby. Alone now, he senses the utter coldness of the night, which seems devoid of everything human. In body and mind, all senses dulled, he is unable to utter a single word or to speak to his comrades across the road. He wants to cry, but he cannot. He feels as if he has joined the dead.

It is still dark when the soldiers return from the barn, talking and laughing. "He is a good officer, that lieutenant of ours," he hears one of them say and another voice adds, "he is like our buddy."

In the light of the early morning he hears the shooting of the approaching enemy tanks. Wounded, he is taken by the American soldiers to a Jeep with the Red Cross sign on its sides. He would never see anyone from his platoon again.

Twenty- five years later, he finds himself still looking for D, and his restless eyes keep searching the crowded street for the man with the crooked leg.

* * * * *

15 April 1945 – May 1946
A Prisoner of War

The US Army liberates Buchenwald concentration camp. Americans and Russians meet at the Elbe – Germany is cut into two parts. The Red Army enters Berlin. Mussolini is executed near Milan. Hitler commits suicide. Berlin falls to the Red Army. Breslau capitulates. Germany surrenders – Hitler's Third Reich falls apart.

The Big Three meet in Potsdam and divide Germany into four occupation zones.

Atomic bombs are dropped on Japan – Japan surrenders. The Nuremberg war crimes trial begins.

Discord among the Allies creates a divided world. The Iron Curtain descends across Germany.

* * *

After the cold night, the morning seemed even chillier, especially at sunrise. It was then that we heard the rumble of the approaching tanks. Hidden behind last year's tall dried-out weeds, I shared a foxhole with another soldier. We were invisible from the road, but we could see the turret of one tank after another, as it rumbled past us. There was no shooting, even after the tanks had entered the town. A long line of trucks followed the tanks, then it became very quiet again. We did not move nor did we raise our heads; we remained quietly in the foxhole. By noon, the sun stood right above our heads and it became unbearably hot, but we had no choice except to remain in our foxhole until after nightfall.

Around 3 P.M. a civilian coming directly from the road towards us, sauntered past our foxhole. It was obvious that he was not out for a walk in these high weeds. I was certain he was looking for soldiers in hiding.

In the local dialect he assured us that he would not tell anyone about us. Then he turned back towards the road.

Within half an hour, we heard English voices from the road where a jeep had just stopped. Moments later, we saw an American soldier standing at a safe distance from our foxhole. I remember how my foxhole mate whom I did not know began to shout "fair play, boys, fair play, boys." I never found out where he got this inane sentence from and how he thought his words would help. Instead, the American soldier pointed his gun at the two of us and ordered us to raise our hands and get out of our hole. Upon his command, however, he suddenly found himself surrounded by a dozen German soldiers — the entire platoon was rising from their foxholes. Not one of us held a gun in his hands, but the American soldier, I believe, panicked because of the unexpected number of Germans surrounding him. He released a burst from his Sten gun. One bullet hit the back of my head. The bullet grazed my skull, broke the bone, splinters of which I could feel when I reached with my hand to the back of my head. I realized I was bleeding profusely. I also seemed to have lost my sight. I was convinced I was going blind and shouted to the other men to kill me, to shoot me dead. I clearly remember how I yelled "Schlagt mich tot, schiesst mich tot!" (Kill me, shoot me dead!) I then fell back into the foxhole.

I felt myself lifted by my arms and legs out of the foxhole, carried a distance and then put into the seat of a jeep next to the driver. The jeep took off quickly and I realized that the other men were left behind. I do not know what happened to them.

When the jeep came to a stop, I was lifted out of the vehicle and made to sit on something like a box. Someone began to clean my wound and put a dressing on it. I was given some water. Then I was moved again and placed on the ground; I was leaning against something, apparently a tree.

So many times, we had rehearsed our actions when the moment of being taken prisoner would arrive. We would throw away our weapons, raise our hands above our heads, and would not move until told. At least for myself, the prior rehearsing had not worked. While sitting on the ground, still without eyesight, I remember the nightmares I used to have during the previous months about being shot and killed at the last moment of the war. I felt that what I had experienced in my dreams was coming true.

I was desperate and distressed and saw my life ending very quickly. I no longer feared death and if I would remain blind, I did not want to live anymore. I do not know how long I had been sitting there — perhaps a couple of hours. But all of a sudden, I realized that I had regained my sight. I had no explanation for this sudden change.

Years later, when I applied for a veteran's pension, a neurologist suggested that I had experienced an episode of hysterical blindness, provoked by the sudden shock of being shot in the head at the moment when I thought the war was over for me and I had no longer expected to be killed.

The Americans had set up some kind of a bivouac precisely at the entrance to the town. From where I was sitting I saw dozens of white bed sheets hung out of windows and from the roofs. The town had declared that it would not defend itself. This was the reason why I had not heard a single shot when the Americans had been entering the town.

I got my first American chocolate bar and my first American cigarette. I liked the chocolate bar, but the cigarette, with its unaccustomed strong tobacco, made me dizzy. I was afraid that this dizziness might be connected to my wounded head and threw the cigarette away. The soldier who gave me the chocolate conducted a short conversation with me. He asked me what unit I belonged to and whether I was a Nazi. I responded with a repeated No, No. He then asked me whether my head hurt very much and where I was from. I was glad I could manage a simple conversation with my high school English. We were interrupted when a truck full of German soldiers stopped next to us. The driver came over and motioned me to follow him to the truck and join the other Germans. They were all strangers to me. At the front of the platform stood two American soldiers who watched us with their guns at the ready.

I was now on my way to a prison camp, transported in a truck that was becoming part of a growing chain of trucks carrying prisoners westwards. At the bivouac I had been the only captured German soldier. Soon I would be one of a hundred thousand or more in one large camp. There would be many other camps. Between them, they were housing millions of German soldiers. For all of them, the war had ended. Some were relieved and looked forward to a better future. Others looked embittered and were full of resentment.

It was dark when we turned off the highway onto a narrower road leading to a large industrial building where we spent the night in comparative comfort. One of the prisoners, a local, told us that we were inside the large Bleicherode Works that were former potash mines but in recent years had been transformed into underground armament factories. Later I read about the concentration camp Bleicherode and the "subterranean concentration camp *DORA*". I wondered whether this was the place where we spent that night.

Next day, we were brought to the women's prison in the picturesque town of Heiligenstadt. Its courtyard, surrounded by buildings on all four sides, served as a temporary collection point for newly captured prisoners of war. It had an unreal atmosphere, as hundreds of mostly young women hung on the windows behind the bars, laughing, talking, making obscene jokes and obscene gestures to which a good number of the men in the courtyard responded in kind. I felt very weak having lost a lot of blood and bleeding anew; I also ran a fairly high temperature. The bandage around my head that the American soldier had put on the day before was now blood-soaked and dirty. One of the men took me by the arm and began to search for a military doctor of whom we found several among the hundreds of soldiers, easily recognized by the medical symbol on their uniforms. Not one of them agreed to take a look at me. They all gave the same response: once the Americans would separate them from the common soldiers and employ them as prison camp physicians, they would look after the sick. My companion was furious.

One of the ordinary soldiers overheard our altercation with one of the physicians, and introduced himself as an army medic. He immediately requested some instruments and bandages from one of the army physicians. It took the threats of several men to get this request granted. The medic did a perfect job of cleaning the wound on the back of my head and, with the help of another man, put a fresh pressure bandage around my head.

Perhaps a thousand prisoners were brought to the courtyard, before we were all loaded onto semi-trailers. We were now a sizable group filling a dozen or more of the long vehicles that were driven at high speed along the winding roads through hilly Thuringia and Hesse. We all felt like prisoners now. The disintegration of military discipline began to manifest itself in small ways. The medic who had looked after me so well tried to get some of the other men to share their food supplies with me. I was one of the few who had nothing. The bag I had prepared for myself had been left behind when the Americans took me away after I was wounded. No matter how my medic protector tried, nobody parted with a bite of food. It got me very upset, that all around me the men were eating, even chocolate bars and cookies. They all had something and braggingly enjoyed consuming it without shame. I was beginning to learn with what little food one can make do.

Passing through Kassel left a ghastly impression with me. The city was not totally destroyed, but nothing seemed to be intact in the dusty streets filled with debris, through which we were taken. We did not see a single German civilian in the streets. I also remember the little ducal residential town of Arolsen and its beautiful baroque palace a few miles west of Kassel. Its untouched appearance caused me to wonder who was living in this palace right now. Next came a village with a name of similar character, Volkmarsen, where we had a frightening experience. Our long column of semi-trailers stopped outside the village next to an open field. We were allowed to dismount and relieve ourselves, when all of a sudden hundreds of ragged men came storming out of the near forest. They picked up rocks from the field and began to attack us. Several prisoners were badly hurt by the flying rocks. These strangers came closer and closer cursing us and would have probably killed us, if our American guards had not shot their guns into the air and loaded us in great haste back onto the trucks. There were more injuries when rocks hit some of us while the trucks sped away. I did not realize – and neither did anyone else – that these were forced labourers who had just been liberated from their camps and were full of anger and hatred towards the Germans.

We crossed the Rhine by a temporary military bridge late at night and ended in a dark camp that consisted of an area of plain dirt, separated into large compounds by high barbed wire fences. After being on our feet for more than 12 hours while passing through more than a quarter of Germany from east to west in the tightly packed semi-trailers, we were dead tired and let ourselves drop to the ground and fell into a deep sleep.

The first full day acquainted us with this prisoner of war camp. It was located next to Miesenheim, a small village about two miles west of the town of Andernach on the Rhine. The camp stretched over a wide expanse of farmland slightly rising from the Rhine valley towards the west. The western border of the camp was a rail line from which, at least for the first week or two, trains of freight cars pulled up daily to transport prisoners to one of the French harbours where boats were waiting to take the prisoners to camps in the United States – at least we were told so. I could not help looking forward to such an experience.

Instead, I spent one month in this camp, the entire length of its existence. It turned into the toughest month of my life as a prisoner of war. After the first few days, I got a sense of the American way of running a camp. It was obvious that the American soldiers had no particular liking for us, which was not surprising after the discoveries they made in the concentration camps they were liberating during these days. Besides, the war was still on. Still, we were looked after and never mistreated.

I estimate that there were roughly 500 prisoners in each enclosure. They were only enlisted men and non-commissioned officers. In this and the following camp, no leadership structure evolved; neither did the Americans permit or promote such a development. The American prisoner of war camps completely abolished and destroyed the hierarchical pattern of the German Army, which towards the end of the war was more and more based on Nazi ideology. The enclosure next to us was filled with German officers from lieutenants to colonels, ranging in age from young men to high officers in their 60s. I think we all had a hard time to adjust and to survive in the camp, but the hundreds of officers next to us did not set a good example. They seemed physically and mentally poorly prepared for the role of the conquered soldier. In front of our eyes, they engaged in fist-fights about food, which at times provoked laughter from the ordinary soldiers in our enclosure. We thought that especially the older group of officers did not even know how to use their fists and put on a pathetic show for us. We all looked dirty and neglected. Still, even after the worst weeks, the ordinary soldiers seemed to survive better than their officers — perhaps an officer in a dirty uniform without its insignia of rank looked shabbier than the ordinary soldier in his plain uniform.

During the first days, we learned three English words that were going to dominate our lives for the length of our stay in this camp. They were the commands "let's go," "move," and adopted from German, "snell" (quick). There were also a couple of four letter words, one beginning with "f" and the other with "c," that we heard every morning when we were moved out of our enclosure and made to run to an open area, where drinking water in large rubber bags suspended from tripods was waiting for us. There were four spigots from which we could fill our mess tins. On the way back, we passed a row of soldiers who put two small tin cans into each soldier's hand, which constituted our daily food ration. This was very little, but as we received the regular US Army K-rations, we at least received a balanced diet that, no matter how meagre, was highly nutritious and was tasty. The water, of course, was no pleasure to drink as it was heavily chlorinated. It was safe, though, and there were no diseases in this camp.

The lice, bedbugs, and fleas that had tortured us in Russia and towards the end of the war even in Germany, disappeared for good after we received a thorough dusting of DDT powder inside our pants and jackets on the first morning in camp. At this stage, we felt relatively optimistic. The Americans seemed humane in a distant way. We did not worry that we would be mistreated. The mood in the camp was not bad — the majority of the prisoners were glad that the war was over, and everybody was grateful not to have fallen into the hands of the Red Army. But then something unexpected happened which made life very difficult. The rains came!

Even though one could sense a touch of spring in the country, the weather changed dramatically and remained wet and unseasonably cold until the end of the first week in May. Because of being wounded at the moment of capture, I had neither a tarpaulin nor any warm clothes. However, good fortune and desperation helped me to obtain a heavy winter jacket, a special German Army issue for the Russian winter. One day, a truck drove along the outside of our compound from which some

American soldiers threw extra clothing over the fence. I truly fought for this jacket, as if my life depended on it, as it well might have, considering what happened soon.

It rained almost day and night. The temperature was very low, the rain was ice-cold and once in a while changed to wet snow. Within a few days, our compound turned into a mud hole. We spent endless hours on our feet in tight little groups to conserve our body heat and stop ourselves from keeling over. Some of us had a tarpaulin on which we could lay, but even it would become wet and muddy. By the second week, large tents were brought into the compound that gave shelter from rain and wind. But they were insufficient to offer protection to all prisoners. So we had to take turns spending half the time on our feet outside, and half the time inside a tent. Out of nowhere, certain men took over the control of the tents. They were ordinary soldiers — no non-commissioned officer dared to assume this function. Astonishingly, this system worked, and there were no fights.

If some men with unexpected leadership qualities came to the fore, without ever trying to exert power, there were others who betrayed their weakness of character to an increasing degree, as life became more difficult. The men who were heavy smokers had the hardest time to keep body and soul together. Indeed, the consequences of their dependency on tobacco seemed to be the primary cause of death among the prisoners.

We were repeatedly searched during the first few days. I did successfully hide my watch between my legs. The only other item of value, the Russian icon from my father, was inspected many times but not taken from me. Neither food nor cigarettes were taken from any of the prisoners, but by the end of the first week, nobody had any cigarettes left. This was the beginning of a lively trade through the fence. German watches, rings, and army decorations were popular items sought by the American soldiers. Everything was traded for cigarettes, the currency of the camp. I traded my watch and my two army decorations for cigarettes which, in turn, I exchanged for additional K-rations.

I was aware that I deprived those I traded with of food essential for their survival. One time, I did this with a big handful of cigarettes, that an American soldier had pressed into my hand one morning, while I was running past him with my mess tin full of water. When he grabbed my arm, I was, for a moment, even scared that he was going to take me away and tried to evade him. To this day, I do not know why I was the one he singled out of the large crowd to give this dozen or more of cigarettes to. Trading them for food helped me enormously, but probably pushed some confirmed smokers closer to death by starvation. When all the watches, rings, and decorations had been traded away for cigarettes, those confirmed smokers who were married parted with their wedding bands for the going rate of ten cigarettes, and after that, they traded their daily food ration for cigarettes. Now, one would see men fainting and falling to the ground, falling from their squatting position into latrines, getting physically ill, and then die. I cannot give numbers, but I would estimate that perhaps 10 percent died from starvation caused by trading away their food.[1]

I write these paragraphs with deep regret and sympathy which I felt — and still feel — for the confirmed smokers, many of whom were men of otherwise strong character. Their fate was all the more tragic, as only a few weeks later, immediately after the end of the war when the discharges from camp started, the food situation for the remaining prisoners improved dramatically to the point where we were beginning to gain some weight.

It was a day of hope in a double sense when we vacated our horrible camp and, between two rows of American soldiers standing at distances of perhaps 300 feet from each other, slowly dragged ourselves towards the Rhine and to our new camp. We were grateful that we were not pushed and were allowed to sit again and again to gain some strength as we were incredibly weak. It was also a day of hope, as it was the day of Germany's final capitulation.

It was a beautiful, sunny day. The country was green and the church bells were ringing, not very loud, as most German churches had only one bell left. The other bells had been melted into cannons, but nevertheless, for me, the clanging of the single bell across the Rhine was a jubilant sound. It announced that peace had finally arrived.

Our new camp was also bare of all facilities, but the ground was dry and we could watch the Rhine flowing past the camp. And there was water — several taps in each compound that were accessible day and night! The camp was part of the industrial complex of the *Rasselstein* Iron Works and of a huge cement plant. Called *Camp Andernach*, its large expanse is said to have accommodated 50,000 to 65,000 prisoners.

Two days later, on Ascension Day, I looked across the river to the promenade of the town of Neuwied where, perhaps for the first time in

---

1   Much has been written about the alleged severe losses of life in American camps along the Rhine due to the planned starvation of the German prisoners. I can only speak for the Miesenheim camp, where the daily rations were very small but sufficient to keep the prisoners alive, as long as they did not trade their rations away for cigarettes. Not very convincing is a picture showing "starving prisoners in the camp of Sinzig." It is somewhat contradictory, as two of the prisoners were smoking cigarettes that they could have readily exchanged for food.

weeks, the townspeople went for a walk in the sunshine. The church bell was ringing and I had a strong sense of peace having returned. Most of us had taken off our shirts to feel, for the first time in weeks, the sunshine on our skin. We were almost in shock when we looked at our emaciated bodies, but in the sunshine and after more plentiful food issued since the first day in the new camp, we felt quite optimistic and laughed about our appearance. When I took my shirt off, I was perturbed to find the entire back of it hardened with dried blood and the skin of my back blackened with old blood as well. I realized how much blood I had lost and considered it a blessing, as this might have prevented a wound infection for which I would not have found any treatment. I likely would have died of blood poisoning.

The men, usually in twosomes or foursomes, immediately marked off their little squares of territory, kept it clean, and broke off twigs and branches from the bushes and low trees alongside the fence for decorating their small domains. The Americans dumped piles of old lumber which we used in little fire pits. Food was now distributed in large cardboard boxes and in gallon tins for a certain number of men who were expected to divide it. I still marvel that there was no abuse and everything was shared peacefully and then cooked over our little fires. We also began to sleep much better, because the nights had finally turned mild. In the evenings we strolled up and down the wide path leading from the gate through the compound. Everyone seemed eager to talk, about home as it was, about home as he expected to find it, but always about eating. Talk about food became topic number one, replacing sex. When we woke up in the morning, we were quite cheerful.

I opened my little diary which I had carried with me since my days in Russia. I wrote the first entries since before my capture at Sondershausen. I have kept the little black book with its wax-cloth cover to this day.

May 10

We have moved, again we are outdoors, but under all around better conditions; the sunny countryside with its hills cheers me up. And we are just a few metres from the Rhine!

May 11

A very mild night with millions of stars above us. Someone in the next compound plays a violin — how did he manage to hold on to his violin, I wonder — I hear Bach's *Air* and Handel's *Largo*. I cannot help it. I cry and the tears keep flowing.

May 14

For the first time out from behind bars. Five of us are loaded on the back of a truck. I enjoy the sight of the countryside and its towns and villages, and the refreshing wind created by the speeding truck. Compared to Silesian villages, the houses here look somewhat forbidding with their slate roofs and the dark grey stone. We get to Polch in the Eifel. We are put to work, washing tons of mess trays, pots, pans, cutlery, and then clean the stoves, the floors, the walls. All the time we are encouraged to eat; all leftovers, but how delicious! I get to see and taste what is explained to us as peanut butter, by a German-speaking American, a Jewish man, I think; not everybody cares for the peanut butter. As we are ready to drive out of Polch, Germans come out of the houses nearby and bring us several loaves of bread, sandwiches with sausage and one woman even brings us some cake — left over from yesterday, from Sunday, she explains.

May 18

Everybody from the Cologne and Aachen districts is called to the gate. Several hundred assemble there to be told they are discharged to home. Medics are asked to step forward; they are to accompany the transport and come back tonight.

We are speechless. Who would have expected that the first ones of us would get discharged so soon after the end of the war — Germany capitulated only 10 days ago! One truck after the other, packed with prisoners no longer under guard, drives away. There are some sceptics in the crowd who believe that this is all a ruse. The men are probably shipped to places where they are put to work; maybe to France; perhaps even to Russia. But in the evening, the German medics return and report that the trucks took the prisoners right to the Beethovenplatz in Bonn and next to the Cathedral square in Cologne. And the men simply walked away and were free.

May 22

Today was inspection; an American major in a jeep drove through the compound standing next to the driver and saluting us several times. Embarrassingly, several prisoners responded to his traditional military salute with the raised right arm of the Hitler salute!

May 29

We have had three days of rain and everybody is drenched. But it has been a warm rain and we have all managed much better thinking in horror of the cold rainy weeks at the Miesenheim camp. The food is getting more plentiful; there is even delicious white bread distributed every day; some grumble about the *Wattebrot*.[2] The discharges continue. I wait patiently for my turn, knowing it cannot be much longer until I will climb on a truck that will take me home to Silesia. There are noticeably fewer men in our compound. I found a fellow from my hometown, a young miner. We team up together.

Soon, we are joined by a fellow from the Steiermark in Austria who owns a tent. When he gets discharged he leaves us his tent; we take in a fellow from Thuringia. One day, the young miner from Waldenburg volunteers for work in the Ruhr coal mines and there are only two of us left in the tent.

June 2

Yesterday, trucks with discharged prisoners left for Erfurt and Leipzig. Today, Mühlhausen is called up. It is Walter's, my sole remaining tent mate's home district. He urges me to come with him. But I decide to wait for the discharges to Silesia; it cannot be much longer. Now I am all alone in the tent.

June 12

An announcement is made this morning that, for the time being, no further discharges will take place. I am shattered. I feel like I am trapped now. I am very lonely and cannot understand how I could have been so stupid and not go with Walter to Thuringia.

June 14

I am no longer at the Rhine but in the Westerwald![3] I volunteered for a work detail, which turned out to be the setting up of a huge new p.o.w. camp next to the big factory *Keramchemie Berggarten* in the small industrial town of Siershahn. I treasure the memory of the drive along a short stretch of the Rhine and through the hills and forests. From the Autobahn, we saw the beautiful four-towered castle of Montabaur. Here there is no view to speak of.

---

2   Cotton wool bread; the soft North American bread ridiculed by many Germans..

3   The hill country east of the Rhine halfway between Cologne and Frankfurt.

June 20

Every day, we are on the road through the Westerwald to pick up huge cooking cauldrons for the different sections of the Siershahn camp. They all come from former Labour Service camps, many of them located in beautiful castles. We are beginning to form some relationships with the American soldiers that run our work detail. They get us some food, share their cigarettes with us, and are altogether very accessible. So life in the camp is quite bearable. I share a decent tent with a guy from Upper Silesia. He is one of a large group of Polish Upper Silesians, a cheerful bunch; they all used to have Polish citizenship and will be sent home within the next week or so. We have built a small table with a little bench in front of our tent. There are even some flowers on the table. We are no longer hungry.

July 1

The discharges are starting again. The "Poles" are leaving first. I will miss them. If I think, they will pass through my hometown while I am still behind barbed wire!

July 3

Bad news: No more discharges into the Soviet occupation zone or to Silesia which apparently is now in Polish hands.

July 7

Bad surprise: yesterday morning, trucks carrying French insignia arrived. They are full of French soldiers obviously from North Africa. French officers walk through our camp and talk with us. One of them explains that Siershahn has become part of the French occupation zone. That does not sound good! What do they want here?

The answer comes this morning when we see the American soldiers being relieved by the French. Soon after, the Americans leave in their jeeps and big trucks. Now we know why the Americans had been bringing enormous amounts of K-ration packages that we piled up in one of the factory halls after another.

July 30

Enormous changes: the first thing the French did was to cart away all the food supplies the Americans had left. We are now fed by the local population. On their horse-drawn wagons, the farmers from the surrounding villages bring their produce; potatoes and vegetables, no meat.

Hunger is back. I am forced to surrender my good army boots to the French and receive a horrible worn-out old pair of French boots instead. I assume that after the lost war, the French are very poor, having a hard time to supply their newly constituted army.

August 1

The camp is filling up with thousands of German prisoners. After months of only seeing strangers, a few days ago, I discovered the tall half-Czech I was in Russia with. He is in the next camp, and we talk through the barbed wire fence. On the following day, the entire compound next to us is being emptied and filled with different, newly arrived prisoners. I wonder what happened to the Czech.[4]

August 7

My 20th birthday! I am in miserable shape. We have all lost a lot of weight; we are plagued with boils. I have a huge boil on my right cheek and another one on my lip. A German medic offers to open them; he heats a needle over the fire and pokes around my face for what seems an endless time. But he assures me that he might have saved my life, as otherwise the poison might have reached my brain.

Everybody is making "pancakes" from a white powder found in the factory. It is stored in large paper bags with inscriptions that declare the content as glazing powder, obviously for the tiles manufactured in the plant. Everybody throws a handful of the powder in a frying pan and ends up with a not unattractive looking pancake. But it is without any flavour and, of course, of no nutritional value.

Nevertheless, the horrible stuff seems to stay in the stomach forever and kills the craving for food and the perpetual hunger.

August 15

Japan capitulates! Now there is peace in the entire world. It certainly helps me to read the brief bulletins that are affixed to the compound gate every couple of days. In addition, the French have chosen a German soldier to their interpreter — his name is Poldi. He speaks excellent French and I think he comes from a rich, sophisticated family. I observe him talking with the French soldiers; especially the officers seem to like him very much. For us, he is a source of information from the outside. He lives outside the compound in the office building of the factory, that

---

4   Seven years later, I met him in a line-up for a movie in Würzburg.

is right next to the entrance to our compound. He often comes over and shares whatever he knows with us.

August 18

The white powder is getting scarce and has become a black market item. The men still eat it, although several have died under terrible pains. We assume that under certain conditions, the powder hardens in the stomach or intestines resulting in a painful death. But I eat of it, as much as I can obtain. We are all in terrible shape; I am worse than I was in Miesenheim. The French guards, all from Tunisia also complain that they never have enough to eat. They occasionally share their cigarettes with us of which they have plenty. I exchange cigarettes I get from them for the white powder.

August 20

Poldi told us yesterday that there would be a work detail leaving soon. This gave me time to decide whether I should volunteer. Everybody is full of mistrust, and nobody really wants to leave. But I thought, I cannot be worse off anywhere else, even if we should be shipped to France. As it turned out, we were only moved to the town of Altenkirchen, still in the Westerwald. A totally new life of near freedom began last night!"[5]

* * *

My home for the next 11 weeks was the Altenkirchen *Stadthalle,* the civic sports arena. Of modest proportions by today's standards, it comfortably accommodated our group of 200 men in double bunk beds. There was a sufficient number of tables and chairs, decent washrooms, and even showers, that were turned on once a week.

Altenkirchen was a town of approximately 10,000. Its centre was totally destroyed while the streets surrounding it presented a picture of peacetime. Its rail yards, however, had been hit by bombs and were badly damaged. No train could pass through the yards or reach the station building, because there simply was not one piece of unbroken trackage left.

The people of Altenkirchen and its surrounding villages were of incredible kindness and friendliness to us. The town was already over-populated with refugees and families from the heavily bombed large

---

5   This is the end of the prisoner of war camp excerpts in my diary.

cities in the Ruhr, from Cologne, Düsseldorf, and other places. In addition, there were a few hundred people passing through, at any time of the day or night, waiting to hitch a ride with a rare German vehicle or with one of the more frequent American army trucks.

When we arrived at the *Stadthalle*, we were addressed by the French town commander, Lieutenant Maier, and by the burgomaster, a frail old gentleman, no doubt the replacement of the Nazi burgomaster who had ruled the town until its occupation by the Americans and, now, the French.

Lieutenant Maier presented a deal to us. We were to be free to come and go. We were to be employed by the railroad at a regular hourly wage repairing the trackage in the rail yards. We were to administer our own affairs and immediately elect a spokesman and five representatives from our group. There was only one rule we had to subscribe to unconditionally: Should one single prisoner abscond, all of us would be transported immediately to the next camp and go back behind barbed wire.

It may sound incredible, but not one soldier escaped during the entire length of existence of this "camp." Everything worked exceedingly well. Two men volunteered to cook our meals; they were paid through a contribution from each one of us. I still marvel that there was never a fight, or any arguments or trouble to speak of. No doubt, this way of life as prisoners of war was a gift from heaven and Lieutenant Maier, who dropped in once in a while, was very popular. The general harmony was largely due to the personality of our spokesman, an easy-going, highly intelligent man from Stuttgart.

I enjoyed the work for the German railways. We had a retired railroad employee who was still proudly wearing his uniform minus the Nazi insignia. For us, he was Papa Schub, a gentle giant with a great sense of humour. We voluntarily worked hard for him. He had his proudest day, when two months after we had begun our work, the first train from the town of Betzdorf reached the station. He also helped me personally in my attempts to get a letter through to my mother.[6] His daughter had connections to the Red Cross that helped many people trying to get to the eastern parts of Germany. She and I liked each other. On Sundays, I was often invited to the Schub home, where I felt like a normal person again enjoying a typical German Sunday. We got to know more people in town. We were hired by townspeople on Saturdays or weekday evenings to cut wood for the coming winter in exchange for a meal, some

---

6   While the mail service was gradually restored throughout the four occupation zones of Germany, no mail was accepted for the formerly German provinces (including Silesia), that were now under Polish administration.

fruit, or other local products. After a few weeks of solid nutrition and physical work, I felt strong and enterprising enough to go on Sunday hikes through this very picturesque hill country.

I knew I could not go home to Silesia for the time being. The borders were not open and, besides, I felt fortunate to be far away and safe from the Russians. I appreciated that being barred from home while being a prisoner of war, I had the best possible life under the circumstances. I was relaxed and happy these days, and always conscious of my good luck of having survived the war.

It was fall now, it seemed a fall as beautiful as never before. We kept cutting wood almost every evening. We continued to work hard for Papa Schub. Another train was put back into service reaching Altenkirchen from the south.

One day, we lifted the secret of Lieutenant Maier's origin. During one of his visits to the *Stadthalle*, several of us were talking with him, among us a fellow from Upper Silesia whose German carried a heavy Polish accent. Instead of answering one man's question, Lieutenant Maier directed his own question to the Upper Silesian: "*Von wo bist Du zu Hause?*" (Where do you come from?). Immediately I fell in, challenging the lieutenant: "And you are from Upper Silesia too; you just used Polish syntax! Nobody who was not born there would say '*von wo bist Du zu Hause*'!"

With a smile, Lieutenant Maier explained that his family had to leave Upper Silesia during Hitler times. They found life in France very hard. One day, he followed the advice of another young man from Germany and joined the Foreign Legion, but during the war, he had volunteered to join the regular French Army in North Africa. The lieutenant was more popular than ever. Too soon, though, Lieutenant Maier departed from Altenkirchen. On Sunday, November 11, as my diary tells me, he came to our "camp" to say goodbye. One day later, his successor, a captain, appeared. He never entered our building but introduced himself as the new town commander to some of us, who were standing outside the *Stadthalle*, In a friendly voice, he asked our opinion about all sorts of matters. We could answer him truthfully, that we were happy, satisfied, and grateful to his predecessor.

Next morning, it was still dark when I was awakened by a loud voice ordering us to pack and get ready for departure. A terrible melee sprang up throughout the entire building. Everyone was trying to find a window through which to escape. I remember racing down the stairs into the basement, but I soon realized that French soldiers surrounded the *Stadthalle* with their guns at the ready. There was no escape possible.

The trucks transported us to Bad Kreuznach, a camp of bad repute, at one time under quarantine due to an outbreak of cholera. I was acutely aware, that everything would change. Different surroundings required different relationships — I wanted a strong, courageous buddy again. I found the man I was looking for, a fellow I had gotten to know well, a farmer from East Prussia, who was in good health and of a positive nature. We managed to stay close together while approaching the main gate of the camp. We had just passed the gate and entered the camp, when a farmer steering his horse-drawn wagon out of the camp, passed by us quite closely. My buddy kicked me in the side, whispered "*Mach's gut!*" (Look after yourself!), jumped onto the wagon, pushed its driver aside and yanked whip and reins out of his hands. We all wore civilian clothes, but my buddy wearing his leather jacket and his leather cap looked particularly "authentic." He and the owner of the wagon made it out of the camp. Using his wits, my buddy from East Prussia had gained his freedom.

I was surprised at how comfortable and clean the quarters were. The first evening meal was tasty and nutritious. But I was terribly angry at myself. Once more, I had landed behind barbed wire. Once more, I had lost a good buddy. All of it was my fault. I could have been discharged a few weeks after the war, if I had not been so honest, willing to wait until my turn would come — it never came. And I kept the bargain with Lieutenant Maier, as everyone else did and did not escape from the "camp" in Altenkirchen. Since I was still free — even though for little more than one day — when Lieutenant Maier was no longer in charge of us, our bargain was off. But I had been stupid again and had not acted instantly.

I decided to volunteer for the first work detail that would come our way. It took only three days until I and another 200 prisoners were on our way to another camp, where I nearly lost my life. As I found out from a former campmate much later, had I exercised some patience, as he did, I would have spent the next months in an unguarded camp not far from Kreuznach in an arrangement similar to that in Altenkirchen.

I had thought I knew them all: the survival camp of Miesenheim, the primitive but bearable camp at the Rhine near Andernach, the pleasant camp with its many trips to the outside at Siershahn that unexpectedly turned into another survival camp after the French took over, the unusual experiment of giving freedom and responsibility to a group of prisoners at Altenkirchen, the return to life behind barbed wire at Bad Kreuznach. And now, barbed wire once more, but dangerous work, and an atmosphere of long-term confinement that brought out the worst in many people — it was like a true prison! The camp was located on the outskirts of the village of Freisen near the huge former German Army base of Baumholder in the *Pfalz* — the Palatinate.

Although accommodating 200 prisoners, the camp was very small, actually consisting of four former Labour Service barracks placed around a square. Most of us slept in triple bunks, some on a layer of straw on the floor. The food was neither nourishing nor appetizing and after a few months I rapidly lost weight. The camp received a litre of milk per day. As I was obviously the one who looked most poorly, I received a quarter litre each day. As it was skimmed milk, I don't think it did much for me. We worked from Monday to Friday in a huge ordnance depot located about three miles from camp, which we reached sometimes by truck, but usually on foot. We were guarded by Moroccan soldiers under the command of a Tunisian lieutenant who felt very important, always carried a riding crop under his arm and, with his exaggerated gestures, was a rather funny figure. The ordinary soldiers were sullen angry men, who had only been drafted by the French a few months before. They were homesick, and visibly suffered under the unaccustomed cold temperatures and the high humidity. Their uniforms looked like hand-me-downs, and their poor footwear did not protect them from the frequent wet snow. Only later, on a special detail were we under guard of French soldiers from France.

I have few positive reminiscences of the men I shared the camp with. Throughout, there was a depressed mood amongst the prisoners who all seemed resigned to an extended stay in this camp. There were not too many fights, but a great deal of continuous snarling, grumbling, and threatening. Actually, the entire camp was split into numerous small groups of four to six prisoners each. The men stuck with extreme loyalty and secrecy to their little groups, but were standoffish or hostile against the others whom they seemed to look upon as outsiders. It is still hard for me to understand the group psychology, except that it was highly hierarchical in numerous ways.

This was true of the entire camp. First of all, I had never seen soldiers treated with so much disrespect by their superior as were our Moroccan guards. This attitude of disrespect was also assumed by our "leaders" — all former German non-commissioned officers — whom the Moroccan lieutenant commander had appointed for each *équipe* (work detail) consisting of 10 prisoners. This was the first instance in my prisoner of war life, where the old structure of the German Army was revived. As the leaders were chosen on the basis of their former rank, all of a sudden the old master sergeants were on top again and, in their bearing, seemed to manifest their former pride in their rank. To them, it did not seem to matter that they were treated very disrespectfully by the commander. Each morning during roll call, they behaved like loyal dogs serving their master. The ordinary men among us absolutely despised them but, on the surface, were friendly and respectful towards these leaders, who did have some power in the assignments of work, distribution of food at the worksite, and other matters.

We did not meet any of the local people. We only saw them from a distance, except during Catholic mass. But even there, we were kept at the back of the church by our Moroccan guards and never had a chance to talk to the village people. I believe any attempts by them to bring some food to the camp were rejected by the commander, even though we very much could have used the occasional extra bite. We received a large number of books, though, and also the weekend edition of the first daily paper in the French occupation zone, the *Mittelrhein Kurier*, published in Bad Ems. The news it contained were often disturbing, such as the growing divisions between the four occupation zones, or the separation of the Eastern provinces from the former Reich. Nothing, though, created so much turmoil among the prisoners as the descriptions of the conditions in the forced labour camps and the concentration camps that had been liberated at the end of the war by the Allied troops. The majority of the prisoners became very angry about such reports and called them lies that, as they claimed, were fabricated by Jews, who were quickly resuming their power in Germany. Much was made of the fact that the publisher of the *Mittelrhein Kurier* had a first name that could have been Jewish, although especially in southern Germany, this name was quite common among non-Jewish people.

Much of the extreme cliquishness, as is clear to me now, was caused by the situational homosexuality that sprang up, especially among the older men. They were mostly married, but chose a mate among the young prisoners, some of whom were not even 17 years old.[7] Considering how homosexuals were prosecuted in the German Reich, these relationships in the camp were practiced with a modicum of discretion, but they existed in almost every group. Those not belonging to such a group were clearly treated as outsiders, excluded even from ordinary conversations. The result was a preponderance of angry hostile feelings among the prisoners, between the ordinary prisoners and the leaders of the various équipes, and between the prisoners as a whole and the Moroccan guards.

There was anger against one's fate, because, by the end of the year, we read in the paper that the Americans had discharged nearly all their German prisoners, while we were sitting in this miserable camp without any hope of being freed in the foreseeable future. There was only one attempt of escape when three prisoners ran away from their *équipe* during work time. Two of them were caught and never seen again. A third one

---

7   This was not different from the relationship patterns that exist in today's penitentiaries.

had climbed a tree and later quietly joined his *équipe*. On the following morning, our camp commander announced that the two escapees who had been caught were already on their way to North Africa. Horror stories had been traveling through the camp at Bad Kreuznach about the camps in the French colonies. Nobody tried to escape from Freisen anymore, as long as I was there.

We spent a wet, cold winter working on the ordnance depot, where ammunition was collected and stored for the French Army. This often involved hard labour carrying and stacking heavy grenades weighing up to 100 pounds and more. I continued my habit of volunteering and when after a few weeks of work at the depot, men were sought for unspecified work away from the depot, I volunteered hoping for something better than the daily grind at the depot.

As it turned out, we were assigned to handle heavy ammunition that had been collected from the fortifications along the former French-German border, the Maginot Line and the Westwall. After lying around under unknown circumstances for perhaps as long as six or seven years, the various types of grenades were not considered safe and therefore had to be dismantled and exploded on a lonely field, marked off-limits to all civilians. This is where we spent our days, eight to 10 prisoners guarded by two French *poilus*. We unloaded huge, heavy crates, unpacked the ordnance from them, dug 20 foot deep holes shaped like inverted funnels into the ground, then carefully packed each hole with ordnance, tightly closed off its opening with heavy rocks and a thick layer of dirt to get it ready for the explosions expert, a former German Army *Sprengmeister*.

There was danger we were aware of at all times, especially at the task of separating the projectile — the actual grenade — from its shell, that was usually of pure brass and therefore of great value. The separation was accomplished by banging the shell against the edge of a heavy box; always a very dangerous risky task. We also had to handle old land mines of various sizes and shapes.

This very dangerous work had its compensations, though. We were away from the large group all day. Our guards turned out to be decent fellows. From the piles of emptied ammunition boxes, we built a small hut, that provided us with useful shelter against wind, rain, and snow during the long winter months. There we sat around a little stove at break time, and during lunch, when we had a wonderful meal every day. From the village of Osterbrücken in the valley below our worksite, young women came every day carrying baskets full of food, which always included a hot meal. They never disappointed us by not coming, and I remember the days when we saw the women with their baskets emerge like shadows out of the swirling snow or the heavy fog. The food they never failed to bring to us was extremely important for our physical and emotional well-being.

We would have been a peaceful, harmonious group, had it not been for the political discussions that sprung up quite regularly at lunchtime. None of the guards spoke German, so nobody exercised caution. I had considered the members of this group, especially the leader, all decent, likeable fellows. However, once politics became the daily topic, I found myself quite alone. The other men were all staunch Germans and sympathetic to the Nazis. They were fully convinced that Germany had been betrayed by the Jews of the world, and that we all would rise up and fight for Hitler, once he returned from Argentina.[8]

From that time on, my life was very difficult. I became isolated from the group, even though I tried to keep my mouth shut. Still, I was forced to confess my true attitude almost daily, when one man or another would challenge me to swear that I would "fight for Germany's liberation, as soon as the *Führer* comes back." My refusal resulted in being cursed and often enough being beaten up. I had gotten into this situation in other camps before, but being one of many, I managed to get lost in the crowd. In this tight little group, no escape was possible.

Within the camp, there were a few decent guys whom I gradually got to know. So the paradox developed that I preferred the hours spent in the camp where I had some friends, to the time at work, away from barbed wire, where a good meal was part of the day.

The weeks and months in this camp became very monotonous. I only remember the surprise of receiving a letter from Waldenburg on Christmas Eve 1945. It was written by my mother, and an aunt of mine, who had gone back to Silesia and then returned to the Soviet Zone, had taken the letter along. After many months, it reached me in Freisen. It was a true Christmas gift to know that my mother and most of my other relatives in Waldenburg were all right and got by fairly well under the Polish administration. Our relatives from Sprottau were safe in a little village near Würzburg in Bavaria. Sadly, I learned that my Uncle Hubert, the younger brother of my father and a staunch, courageous anti-Nazi, had committed suicide. I did not get the full story until much later, just as my mother did not tell me in this letter that two days after the armistice, she had gone back home all by herself, pulling a little wagon with a few

---

8   When the Soviet Army announced that the charred body of Hitler had been found in the grounds of his chancellery in Berlin, many people considered such news a propaganda lie. There was widespread belief that Hitler had fled to Argentina from where he would, sooner or later, return to liberate Germany.

essential supplies from Waldenburg to Breslau, where she experienced four months of danger and adventure.

For me, the deadly routine of the camp ended on Thursday, March 28, 1946. It was perhaps the first spring day, warm and sunny. After our lunch break, I was sitting peacefully on a rock next to a large pile of 88 mm tank grenades, detaching the projectiles from the shells by banging them sharply against the edge of another box. As always, I took a careful aim, but all of a sudden, I saw an enormous whitish flash in front of my eyes, heard a loud bang and was thrown backwards. I do not think I lost my consciousness, but I was stunned. Like an emotionally detached observer, I saw the other men running towards me, I watched one of them pick up something from the ground next to me and with the words *"Da ist sein Daumen"* (Here is his thumb) gave it to one of the French guards who had already started to bandage my right hand. He packed my torn-off thumb inside the bandage, and when he was finished the other men carried me into the truck of the German explosives expert. The *Sprengmeister* and his truck were the coincidence that probably saved my life, as I was bleeding heavily. He also helped me enormously by not taking me to the prisoner of war hospital in Homburg, as was the standing order, but to a German Catholic hospital, the *Marienkrankenhaus* in the town of St. Wendel in the *Saarland*.[9] This was my second stroke of luck. I might have bled to death before reaching the more distant Homburg.

The events of the rest of the day remain hazy in my mind. I remember the surgeon, Dr. Simon, a small, serious looking man, and I remember the Superior, Mother Canisia, a formidable woman who ran the hospital like an army barracks, but who had a heart of gold.

Next morning, I searched for my right hand. It was heavily bandaged, but it was still there. I was fully awake when Dr. Simon came to see me and gently explained that while he did his best to save my hand, he was not sure I would keep it in the end. The wrist had been split into over 30 pieces of bone, which he had painstakingly tried to fit together. Several fingers on both hands were also badly injured and the exploding shell had taken out a big piece of my leg muscle leaving a deep, heavily bleeding gash, which almost cost me my life. The following morning I was awakened from a daze by the loud screams of a young student nurse who discovered that both my leg and my hand were again bleeding profusely. Over the next days, I needed several blood transfusions.

This small hospital became a place of absolute safety and comfort. The Mother Superior wrote a letter for me addressed to my Sprottau

---

9   The Saar Territory was separated from Germany between 1919 and 1934, and again in May 1945 and placed under French administration.

relatives. One week later, my Aunt Lisa stood at my bedside. It had taken her five days to travel from Würzburg to St. Wendel, a distance of perhaps 120 miles.

For me, it was a blessing that I was not placed in a private or semi-private room. Typical for an older country hospital, I shared the room with five other patients. I was quite weakened and ran a high temperature for a while. I was also still somewhat in shock and depressed. The other patients and my aunt did much for my well-being and beginning recovery. There were, however, upsetting days ahead.

I had been with the newly formed explosives *équipe* from day one. Four months later, I became its first casualty and our *équipe* was immediately disbanded. It was replaced by prisoners who changed daily. From then on, accidents followed each other at the rate of one a week. First, an older member of the *équipe* was admitted whose leg had to be amputated. Next came three men all at once. They were the victims of a large landmine that had been handled by myself several times. It finally blew up, seemingly without any cause. One of the wounded, a young fellow, was very badly hurt, as his windpipe had been cut and could not be repaired. A permanent tracheotomy in addition to the other serious medical conditions was the consequence. The second man had been sprayed by hundreds of small pieces of metal and, while not dangerously wounded, had his face permanently disfigured. The third man, a happy-go-lucky fellow from Braunschweig, was the least injured. With tears in his eyes, he brought the sad news that the week before, a fellow who had been my best buddy in the camp, a gentle man of strong character from Lake Constance, had been fatally injured by an exploding grenade. He died within a minute of the explosion while being carried to a vehicle. He did not know he was dying and said with a weak smile to the man from Braunschweig, *"Nun komme ich weg von hier und bin sicher vor dem Tode."* (Thank God, I get away from here. Now I will be safe from death.)

After these events, we were all very depressed and spent the days quietly. A visit of a French officer, the town commander of St. Wendel, shocked us back into reality. As with all French officers I met, he was very correct, friendly, and humane. Fortunately, through the partly open door, I overheard the later conversation he had with Dr. Simon in the hallway. He agreed that the badly injured young fellow should be discharged from the hospital, once he was ready. The other men — and that included myself — should be sent back to the camp at Freisen in due course.

If I had been certain of something, it was the expectation of being sent home at the end of my stay in hospital. I thanked God for my knowledge of French. Otherwise, we would not have considered escaping from the hospital. Now, the town commander's words had alarmed us sufficiently to prompt us to make our escape instantly. We took the Mother Superior into our confidence. She agreed to help us and also to advise the women of the village that had supplied our *équipe* with food, to expect us and help us along. Next morning, someone from the village brought us some clothes. The same afternoon, we started on our escape.

* * * * *

Part IV
The Aftermath

T he end of World War II left Germany in a state of total political, economic, and moral collapse. Except on the local level, there were no German civil authorities left. Into the offices vacated by former Nazi officials, the occupation powers and their military governments placed the new German civil authorities.

Economic activity sank to a near zero level. Communication systems had broken down. Trains, postal services, and telephones started timidly on the local level and required months, even years before they covered the country.

There was very little food and widespread hunger. There was a severe shortage of housing. Much of it had been destroyed by air raids; housing that had survived, was enormously overcrowded.

Millions were on the move streaming from East to West in search of relatives and family members. Millions tried to get away from the Russian-occupied Soviet Zone, further millions had been expelled from the formerly German territories in the East. Among the millions on the move were former German soldiers discharged from prisoner of war camps searching for their families who often were far from where they had last seen them.

Survival was the big challenge, a challenge that also served to break down moral norms and customs of honesty and decency hitherto generally observed except by criminals. Intense hunger and lack of clothing and shelter seemed to make theft, dishonesty, cheating, lying, and even physical assault permissible, or at least excusable. The Catholic Church declared that "Mundraub," i.e., theft of comestibles, no longer represented a sin.

Such was Germany, or what was left of it, an amorphous area of a hungry, demoralized, lost people that as a political entity did not even exist anymore. And there was no hope. When would there be enough food? And shelter? Would the worthless German mark ever regain its strength? Nobody dared to make any predictions. Estimates for rebuilding the country ranged to as much as 100 years.

16 | 1946
Towards Freedom

*T*here was more hunger in 1946, but there was a beginning of civil government. What was left of Germany had been divided into four occupation zones: the American, British, French, and Soviet zones, the last one quickly becoming a world of its own disappearing behind the Iron Curtain that would separate Eastern Europe from the West for 45 years. All four zones were controlled by military governments.

* * *

May 16, 1946 was the day of our escape. As I found out later, May 16 was also the day when, at the opposite end of former Germany, my mother climbed into a cattle car to be transported from the now Polish Silesia to West Germany.[1]

The three of us sneaked out of the Marienkrankenhaus in St. Wendel after lunch. We walked as fast as we were able to with our wounds and disabilities until we reached the forest. We presented a pitiful picture, and I certainly had felt the eyes of the people on the street all over myself. We looked like three sad figures out of a Biblical story: I had my right arm heavily bandaged and in a sling. My right leg, which still had a huge open gash, was in a plaster cast, and for walking any distance

---

1   At the Potsdam conference in June 1945, the three occupying powers decided to turn over the Soviet-occupied German provinces of Silesia, Pomerania, and the southern half of East Prussia to Polish administration. As Poland had to cede a territory of approximately equal size in Eastern Poland to the Soviet Union, the Polish population from these areas was resettled, primarily in the aforementioned German provinces vacated by their hitherto German population.

I required a cane. One of my companions had his face pockmarked with numerous small black spots caused by tiny pieces of shrapnel from an exploding land mine; he also walked with a bad limp. The third fellow was the least handicapped, but he still had to use a cane. It was a miracle that nobody stopped us either out of sympathy or out of suspicion, which might have led to us being apprehended by the French military police. This was May 1946, and at least in this area, the *Saarland*,[2] such obvious victims of war or prison camp were no longer a common sight on the streets.

We spent a quiet evening with a family in the village of Osterbrücken in the *Pfälzer Wald* (part of the Palatinate). Only a few people in the village knew about our presence, as we stayed off the streets. The first train going east left at 4:30 in the morning. Nobody took us to the station so as not to raise suspicion. We climbed into one of the converted cattle cars of this train that rumbled at a snail's pace stopping at every village and taking in more people going to work. I felt uncomfortable, as this was the first time in many months that I was in public without being under military guard.

Our aim was to cross the Rhine and leave the French occupation zone as quickly as possible. This was not easy, as the only crossing where an ID card was not required was in Cologne in the British zone. To reach Cologne one had to somehow get through the controls at the boundary of the French zone. Even among this group of German working people on this train, I was deadly afraid of being betrayed to the French guards that stood on the platforms of all larger railroad stations. Being apprehended meant the certain immediate transport to a camp in North Africa, the only, for me not discussable alternative being to join the French Foreign Legion.

We passed Bad Kreuznach where we had been in prison camp eight months before. The French military police walked along the platform, but did not inspect the train. The next station was Bingerbrück where we had to change trains. It was at this station that I was ready to give up my freedom when I discovered a French corporal I had gotten to know while living in the open camp in Altenkirchen. I had worked in the kitchen of the non-commissioned officers' casino several times and after work, he and I liked to play chess and talk. He never sounded particularly friendly towards German people in general. Now he was in charge of the Bingerbrück Station Guard and I expected him to notice me because of

---

2   The Saar territory, which had been placed under temporary French administration following World War I, was again given that status after the end of World War II. In both cases, the population voted for a return to Germany.

my pitiful appearance. Indeed, he immediately recognized me, stopping in front of me with what I thought was a malicious grin. I was ready to surrender to him when, at last, his devilish grin changed to a friendly smile. He said something to the two soldiers under his command, touched his képi in a casual military salute, and all three turned around and walked down the platform. We were saved. His is one of the faces I will never forget in my life.

The overcrowded train consisting of a long string of pre-World War I coaches rumbled along the Rhine. Except for Koblenz, there was relatively little evidence of destruction. Whenever the train ran along the embankment of the river, the picture seemed bucolic. With mixed emotion, I noticed the former territory of my prison camp of a year ago at the Rasselstein Works near Andernach, and the other camps I briefly knew at Sinzig and Remagen. The latter was the border station between the French and the British zone.

Nobody in our compartment was afraid for his life or health, but the three of us were afraid of losing our freedom at the last moment. The passengers in our overcrowded compartment saved us from the French military police who, fortunately, only entered the train compartments from the platform side. When the soldiers of the military police opened the door, the passengers pushed against the entrance preventing the soldiers from quickly entering. We were at the opposite side and when we received a signal from one of the passengers that the soldiers had vacated the adjoining compartment, we quickly sneaked out of the compartment and scrambled into the next one, which had just been checked. Not until the train started rolling and immediately entered the British zone were we truly reassured. There was no fear of the British forces. They still maintained camps, but it was known to us that former soldiers caught without papers were taken to a camp, interrogated, and quickly discharged with appropriate identity papers, unless they seemed suspect. We were prepared to accept such an experience, although, as it turned out, it never happened.

We paid little attention to the destruction of Cologne where the cathedral, only damaged, stood like a beacon amongst the endless destruction of the inner city. There were no bridges restored yet, and a number of small boats served as ferries to take us to the right bank of the Rhine. It was a symbolic crossing for us on our way to freedom. By now, we felt quite safe. In this area and in the Ruhr industrial basin, there were more trains running, one of them taking us to the city of Hagen where we said goodbye to each other. I continued north towards Bremen where I had an aunt in the vicinity of the city. But I did not get very far, as it was Saturday evening and in the British zone no trains were running on Sundays. The train simply stopped at a small station to continue on

Monday morning. I decided to walk into the next village, but although I thought that I looked trustworthy and, at least harmless because of my bandaged hand in a sling and my stiff leg supported by a cane, not one of the farmhouses I called at took me in for the night. This was a great shock, as this seemed to be an especially prosperous farming country with large farmhouses and huge barns surrounded by well-tended gardens. On this evening my lifelong prejudice against North Germany began — my later positive experiences in various parts of Bavaria only confirmed and reinforced this prejudice. Still without shelter for the night, I decided to approach the local Lutheran minister — there was no Catholic church in the village. I was angry and frustrated when I met him at the door of the manse. When he asked me in, I was hopeful, but not for long. His first question was whether I was Lutheran. When I explained that I was Catholic, he answered with a startled "*Oh, Oh*" and stated that I could sleep in the small barn in his yard. He ushered me out the door; there was not a word said about a bite to eat. Did he not realize that I was very hungry? I walked straight through his yard at a quick pace and spent the night in some bushes along the highway.

Next day, after a few attempts, I found a kind farmer's family who gave me a big meal. I was close to tears at that time. On Monday afternoon, I reached the town of Sulingen where I found my aunt with her three children in a small attic room. This was Aunt Luzi from Liegnitz who had been so kind to me during my early army days. She had last heard from her husband in January 1945 and was still waiting for him, hoping that he had survived the war. I realized that I could not stay very long, as my aunt had neither money nor food. But she insisted that I take a couple of days of rest. She somehow managed to find some extra food for me.

My destination was a village near Würzburg, where my Aunt Lisa and my other relatives from Sprottau had found a place as refugees. Conditions were much better there and they had written to St. Wendel that they would expect me after my discharge. I still had a long way ahead of me to Würzburg — now I was going south again and would soon leave the British zone. I had only positive feelings about the Americans and was looking forward to crossing into the American zone. The train ended south of Göttingen at the last village before the American zone. I was one of the hundreds of people waiting in the village for the very early morning hours when, still in darkness, some of the local people would guide us across the demarcation line that was patrolled by British and American soldiers. Every house was full of these travelers. Their presence was a daily occurrence, and I admired the people of this village for their kindness.

This was the easiest crossing of all! In no time had our group, led by a man from the village, reached the American zone without having seen a single soldier. Later, I wondered whether there had been an agreement between the military governments of the American and the British zone to let these pitiful, harmless travellers cross the demarcation line. At the first village south of the line, there was a train waiting. Everyone who had just crossed the demarcation line boarded it, but already in Kassel, this group of strangers who had hung on to one another while trying to get into the American zone, split up, each person following his or her own plans.

It was still dark when the train passed through Hannoversch-Münden, a picturesque town in a narrow valley. There were many lit windows — it was the hour when people have breakfast before going to work. This was the first town I saw that looked like peacetime again. Many of the towns or cities I had seen on this journey had been heavily damaged and few of their houses were still lived in and everything was dark. But looking at Hannoversch-Münden with its street lanterns and lit windows was like a step back into my peaceful childhood. I admit that my tears were flowing at this moment.

There was one unexpected hour of danger when I was only 25 miles from Würzburg, my final destination. This was at Gemünden where I had to change to the train to Würzburg. I arrived hours late, long after the last train of the day had departed. I had just settled down in a corner of the large overcrowded waiting room, when a patrol of the American Military Police entered and began to check identity cards. So close to the end of my adventurous journey, I was not ready to be apprehended. I opened a window and jumped out onto the tracks, stepping up onto the platform at its very end, far from the station building. There was an incredibly neglected, filthy, half-destroyed restroom that stank to high heaven. I thought nobody will enter this horrible place and chose the restroom as my hiding place for the night.

This unpleasant night finally passed and early in the morning on a glorious sunny day, I arrived in Würzburg to find the entire central part of the city almost 100 percent destroyed. As I heard, the party leader of Würzburg, Gauleiter Helmut, had declared the city a *Festung*, a fortress to be defended, and Würzburg was promptly bombed by Allied planes. Not a single house had been fully repaired yet, only here and there were temporary small windows set into what once used to be large store windows with attractive displays. People looked shabbily dressed, emaciated, listless. Especially near the main railroad station, there were thousands on the streets who obviously did not want or need to be here but were simply passing through on their way to what often seemed nowhere

— searching for relatives, trying to get home, finding work, or merely drifting across the country.

I found out that a small truck, called *Autobus* would leave for the small village of Waldbrunn where my Silesian refugee relatives lived. Since I could not locate this bus, I started hiking out of town through another village, along the highway through a stretch of forest, then through another village, across a long stretch of fields, into a forest again and, finally emerging from the forest finding myself only a few hundred yards from the village marked, like every other village in this part of the world, by its church steeple. With some asking and trying to understand the heavy dialect of the local persons, I managed to find the house where my relatives lived. This was not my home, but this moment felt like returning home, to people of my family. Being with them was like the start of fully restoring my sense of identity. I had not realized and, indeed, did not realize until much later, how much one's identity is diminished while living away from family, relatives, friends, and acquaintances.

From the first minute, I could see that Waldbrunn was a very poor village. I also found out soon that the generally very modest, small houses all accommodated an extra family or two, families that had lost their homes in air raids, or had arrived as refugees from the East, from Poland, Silesia, East Prussia, Pomerania; or Czechoslovakia, Hungary, or the other Balkan countries. All these people were one way or the other absorbed by the locals with an astonishing degree of practicality, common sense, and readiness to share whatever little they had themselves. Few words were made. The recent arrivals were expected to adopt or at least recognize and accept the local customs and the villagers' daily way of life. Everyone called everyone else by first name. Even the little four year-old called the 80 year-old man or woman by first name; and so did, with a few exceptions, the refugees and bombed-out families from the cities. There had been a fair degree of intermarriage over the centuries. In Waldbrunn, perhaps half a dozen surnames covered at least half the population. To avoid confusion, many locals were as an alternative to their first names also referred to by their house names which, for the outsider were unfortunately obscure in their original meaning.

Other than running water and electricity, there were no amenities in the village. And even though water was free, most people did not waste any water when it came to daily hygiene, changing into fresh clothing, and so on. About a good number of people there was a smell to which, however, we all got used to quite soon. Because overriding a remarkable coarseness while talking to each other and generally coarse habits, the local population generally possessed an innate goodness and kindness, albeit hidden behind very straightforward words. The villagers, with very few exceptions, also exhibited an acceptance of the *Flichtling*, as the refugees were called in the local dialect. *Flüchtling* is what nine million people were called who had the misfortune of having lost home and country as the consequence of the war. It was a word all the refugees hated, but in the village of Waldbrunn, if one was a refugee, one was soon no longer offended when called such. This was in remarkable difference to the horror stories of how terribly many German refugees were treated by their German countrymen.

Because there was this remarkable acceptance of the outsiders, the outsiders felt safe to do some things their way such as enjoying regular sponge baths (there were hardly any bathtubs around). There was a single modern building in the village erected in the 1930s by the Catholic Church where two nuns ran a kindergarten, a first aid station, and a playschool. The building was the pride of the village. On its unfinished lower floor, it had a public bath — unfortunately minus the plumbing that after 12 years still awaited its completion. At each annual meeting of the village council and before elections, the issue about completing the bath came up regularly, but was just as regularly defeated, because, as it was said by the older men on the council, "we have lived here for so many years, and have never had a bath. So why all this commotion now all of a sudden!"

So the refugees continued to carry pails of water to their rooms and washed and washed — their bodies and their clothes. I had hardly arrived at the house of my relatives when the owner commented *"Du bist wohl auch so ein Wasservogel wie die anderen!"* (Are you another one of those water birds?). I had begun to clean myself, understandable after living on the road for so many days.

These first years after the war were very hard for me psychologically, but in Waldbrunn I felt happy and safe, as if I were living in a warm nest. I will never forget the inborn kindness and generosity of the inhabitants. We were never hungry. On Thanksgiving and the other feast days, the good things were shared with us, and during the year, we gladly helped with cultivating and harvesting our hosts' small fields. There was always much work to be done, as a lot of the men worked in the forest, in the quarry, or in the city; and many of the women went to work in the factories and in the households of Würzburg. Employment outside the village was essential, as most farms were so small that they could not provide a living for the owner and his family. Among the 70 or so small farms of the village, there was only one farm that had horses — two of them. All the others had two cows that served as draft animals, milk cows, and sources of food.

There were two inns in the village, two food stores, one bakery, and one butcher. Everyone was a "good Catholic," piously following the customs and precepts of the church, but no one appeared suppressed or falsely pious in a pretentious way. Until the beginning of 1945, they all had had their swastika flags, but the party had not made any great inroads. The last mayor, a party member who was removed by the Americans never lost the respect and gratitude of the people, as he had the guts to march out of the village onto the highway, a white flag in his hands, meeting the American tanks which then left Waldbrunn unscathed. The new mayor, a gentle, kind man, advised me to stay in the village for a couple of weeks, which would be enough time for him to get me an identity card. He could do so without presenting my discharge papers which, as an escaped prisoner of war, I could not produce. Two weeks after my arrival, I was a bona fide citizen of the American zone and resident of the village of Waldbrunn

One day in June, my mother's youngest sister Martel (whom, from early on, I never addressed as "aunt") stood at our door in Waldbrunn. From her I learned that on exactly the day I escaped from the hospital in St. Wendel, my mother, her sister, and my Grandmother Hackenberg had started their journey into the unknown, leaving their hometown of Waldenburg forever. They ended up in a remote corner of North Germany, but at least they were not taken to the Soviet occupation zone that, together with the Eastern European states, was rapidly being isolated from the western half of Europe. It was March 5, 1946, when Winston Churchill spoke in Fulton, Missouri and made his famous reference to "the Iron Curtain" that had gone down from Stettin to Trieste, closing off half of Germany and the Eastern European nations from the West.[3]

For better or worse, I decided to leave Bavaria and join my mother in the *Bremer Heide*, the Bremen Heath. I wish now I had never left Waldbrunn. I did return, but only after a year of hardships and disappointments. To get to Bremen required a three day trip on overcrowded trains pulled by old steam locomotives that always seemed to be short of breath, with some trains only having space left on top of their old, rickety coaches. Shortly after departing from Würzburg, hanging on to the small outside ladder of the coach, I emerged from one of Germany's longest tunnels black as a coal miner at the end of his shift underground. Halfway towards Bremen, I was forced to spend a night in Göttingen where after much pushing and shoving I found a corner in the packed waiting lounge

---

3   People still managed to cross the boundary between the Soviet and the Western zones. But soon, an insurmountable electrified fence went up along this border and also along the German–Czech border. Until 1961, it was still possible for East Germans to cross from East Berlin into the Western sectors of the former German capital. But in summer of that year the last escape route was closed when the Berlin Wall went up.

of the station. I had just bedded myself to what I hoped would be some restful sleep after spending hours of hanging on to the roof of the train, when I had the distinct sense that somebody was looking at me. I opened my eyes and saw a huge rat sitting on the ledge of the wainscoting of the once elegant waiting lounge, ready to jump on my chest. I decided to spend the night outdoors in the chilly air.

I found my mother in good health. We were happy to have found each other, and grateful that we had survived the war. But within a day of my arrival in Brundorf, I knew I had made a terrible mistake in coming here. My mother had been referred to a well-to-do farmer who lived in a huge house. The family consisted of the parents and two daughters; the only son had not come back from the war. There were several unused, well-furnished rooms, but my mother's quarters were in the adjoining barn with its individual stalls for the horses. The stalls were built with solid walls, had very low ceilings and doors, and just one tiny window per stall. In one of them, an old bed, a chair, and a washstand had been placed on the dirt floor. This, I could hardly believe, was mother's room. And irony of ironies, still fastened to the door was the old board with the name of the previous occupant's name, a horse named *Hedda*, which also happened to be my mother's first name! I soon thought that this was symbolic for our relationship with the hosts. The daughters seemed haughty and removed, although they seemed intellectually and in every other way, rather average, ordinary persons, while the mother was forever puttering about her house and garden. Above everybody was the father, a huge man whom we rarely saw in the house. He only came near our abode when once a day he inspected the barn that was looked after by a hired man. I only remember meeting him outdoors towering above us on his huge horse.

We had very little to eat, received nothing from the farmer or his wife except from a full basket of fruit one single cherry with which my mother promptly broke one of her teeth, and a chicken that we had discovered laying dead in the yard. Writing about these seemingly petty experiences, I might appear small-minded and vindictive. The shock of these first weeks in Brundorf, however, left some indelible scars. I feel somewhat fortunate and proud about the way I got through war, prison camp, and the following difficult post-war years. Between memories of many severe but not insurmountable hardships, memories of numerous good people, there is this black spot not only about our start in Brundorf, but also about the 10 months of our life in Bremen in general.

I found the people of Bremen hanging on to their pre-war attitude of haughtiness and feeling on the top of German culture. I found it disgusting that the haughtiness about one's Bremen origin was the more pronounced and the more openly displayed, the lower a person's background was. Besides, my mother and I belonged to the Roman Catholic religion that, before the war, had been almost non-existent in this purely Protestant part of Germany and therefore held in undisguised contempt. I am saying all that *cum grano salis,* as I met a number of very nice people who were true Bremenites. But the overall sense was one of not belonging in this city and this part of Germany both of which felt utterly foreign to me. It was not just the social structure, it was also the language that was either a pronounced *Hochdeutsch* (High German) or *Plattdeutsch* (Low German).

Linguistically, the German spoken in the northern half of Germany belongs to a different strain of German than the dialects spoken in the southern half of Germany, where in the speech of the individual, the local dialect is usually present, ranging from a near unchanged dialect to a faint accent, which results in infinite, charming variations of the German spoken in these parts of the country. The north German person, on the other hand, either speaks *Hochdeutsch* or *Plattdeutsch* which is not a German dialect, but a language by itself, belonging to the group of languages spoken in Scandinavia, the Netherlands, and England.

My primary need was to find work, as I had no income whatsoever, while my mother subsisted on 40 marks per month of her war widows allowance.[4] A week after my arrival in Brundorf, I was on my way to work, leaving at 4:30 in the morning, walking with the help of a cane for two hours through lonely country to reach the huge US Army hospital in Bremen-Lesum. My arm was out of the sling now. I hid the cane in a bush outside the hospital and, with a good deal of pain and a thick bandage around my right leg – my cast had been taken off before I left Würzburg – I managed to do my job as a cleaner on a nursing station.

It was an irony that this lowly work for a non-German employer helped me keep my self-respect amongst the Bremen people who as a group considered the refugees from the East as far beneath them. From the first day, I was happy working in this hospital. I felt treated by the medical staff, the nurses, the patients, and the other Americans with friendly respect. What helped a lot were my Bavarian leather shorts that my mother had brought along from Silesia. While the Bremenites looked upon my *Baierische Lederhosen as* an outlandish garment, the Americans, who all had been stationed at one time or other in Bavaria, greeted me in my *Lederhosen* like a long lost friend.

---

4   The private insurance my father had arranged for us did not come through for my mother until three years later (I was by that time older than 21 and no longer entitled to the insurance my father had paid for my future attendance at university).

What also helped enormously was the provision of a full meal at lunchtime in a special dining room. For the first time I ate from a US Army tray with separate compartments for the various courses, ranging from soup to dessert. The meal was always plentiful, nourishing, and very tasty; and there were always seconds. There was also some food available on the nursing station, most of which I took home for my mother. All day, the loudspeakers were broadcasting the music and news of AFN (American Forces Network), which assured my first intensive exposure to American culture through its music, from jazz to country to swing, and to classical music. I learned about the great US symphony orchestras and their conductors Stokowski, Ormandy, Klemperer, Bruno Walter and the other immigrant artists. I was given the magazines that had been read, and I admired the photography in *LIFE* and the newsreporting in *TIME*. I was also given some books to take home. After the wall that Hitler had built around German culture that had kept us separate from the rest of the world, it felt like a window was opening. My mother, who did not read English, nevertheless perused the magazines and discovered a good number of artists, singers, musicians, painters, sculptors, writers, and actors and actresses who had been household words until Hitler stopped their careers cold in 1933.

Once in a while, the nurse in charge would give me an admissions ticket to the entertainment in the theatre on the hospital grounds. Here I sat among hundreds of sick soldiers who had been assembled from all over the American occupation zone, to wait for a transport ship to take them from Bremerhaven back home to the States. From my theatre visits I remember the live performances of Peggy Lee, Lena Horne, Hazel Scott, and some others. It was a fantastic and very helpful world for me. The medical staff also took care of my leg wound that was slow in healing and after a couple of months managed to close it with the application of various treatments.

After two exhausting months of the two hour-long daily hikes to work, we managed to get a small upstairs room near my place of work. We were glad to escape the oppressive farmhouse in Brundorf, but our stay in the new place was of short duration, as my mother had to protect herself from the advances of the landlord.

With all the hard things I said about the Bremen people, I will not forget the mayor of our small village, who not only took our landlord to task but also immediately got us a different room in what could be called a modern villa. My mother, who was a very outgoing person, was beginning to make friends, first with a family that had moved from Lake Constance near the Swiss border to Bremen many years ago, and later with a sea captain's widow for whom she did a lot of knitting. This wonderful lady did not pay my mother with worthless German marks, but with pieces of her furniture including a nineteenth century desk and a beautiful *Biedermeier* chair. Living between Bremen and the small city of Vegesack that had two theatres, we also finally were able to enjoy the cultural life of both cities.

I still marvel at the cultural life that had sprung up in Germany under the most difficult conditions of starvation rations, shortage of all materials, and bombed-out theatres. There was an explosion of modern theatre productions of authors and dramatists who had been forbidden under Hitler as foreigners, Jews, emigrants, or anti Nazi artists. As in most other cities, in Bremen all theatres had been destroyed, but theatre space was somehow found. I remember my first opera in years, *La Bohème*, being staged in a suburban high school auditorium. *La Voix Humaine* by Jean Cocteau took place in a small Vegesack theatre, where also the good old *Count of Luxemburg* was performed with top-rate actors and singers. Two of these singers I had heard in Bad Salzbrunn in the early 1940s – in more normal times, they had appeared on the Berlin stages. I saw my first American musical, *No No, Nanette*, on the intimate stage of the former ballroom of the *Parkhaus* in Bremen. Everywhere there were enthusiastic audiences, often very simply dressed, and many no doubt very hungry. But the ambience was one of joy, of a sense of discovery or rediscovery. This continued throughout the harshest winter in years. There was no coal for theatres, so the price of admission included two or three pieces of wood for heating. It was still necessary, however, to dress warmly with all one's clothes, as the theatres were very cold. That the actors and singers managed to present a good performance in such harsh settings seems miraculous.

Coming from the near Continental climate of Silesia, we were astonished about the lightly built houses with their single-pane windows. This was fine in summer, and we were also reassured of the mild, usually snowless winters typical for Bremen. Winter 1946/1947, however, arrived with a roar and became the coldest winter in decades. People froze to death in their unheated rooms. My mother froze two of her fingers while knitting in the single room our "flat" consisted of – its walls sparkled with frost like an ice palace. One day the village announced the distribution of firewood on Sunday noon. There were mostly elderly people waiting for their allotment, which turned out to be a tall tree that was still standing on one side of Main Street. Someone got two long ladders and a couple of rather dull handsaws. There was only one other young fellow of my age, and together we climbed up the ladder and onto the branches and cut limb after limb of frozen, still green wood. This was a horrible Sunday, and frustrating afterwards, as the wood, once thawed out, provided enormous amounts of eye-stinging smoke, but little actual heat. It was barely enough for my mother to cook our Sunday meal, which had consumed our entire meat and sausage ration for the week, a quarter of a pound! Equally scarce was the margarine ration of one eighth of a pound (butter was unobtainable).[5] Had it not been for my work with the US Army, I do not know how we would have survived.

By early December my friend and I began to jump the freight trains that transported coal to Bremerhaven for shipment to unknown destinations. One of us threw lumps of coal from the rolling train, while the other ran along the tracks to collect the precious loot. There were hundreds of people chasing after coal, which frequently brought about fistfights, arising from arguments about whose coal it was that ended up on the ground. The tracks were actually well guarded by American military police, but we were all desperate. We were never charged in court but were taken instead by truck to the large underground *Domshof* air raid shelter in the centre of Bremen and locked up for the night. This seemed harmless were it not for the true criminal element that was also locked up there. These dangerous men exercised a regime of terror by stealing from the older people locked up there and beating them up if they did not comply. I remember some ugly experiences that happened to me in the depth of the former air raid shelter.

Things got better just before Christmas arrived. I had met a young woman who was the granddaughter of a well-known Bremen jeweller. His store had been totally destroyed by bombs, but enough of its inventory had been removed beforehand and hidden elsewhere. Upon her suggestion, I became a black market dealer selling jewellery to American soldiers in the hospital for cartons of cigarettes that had assumed the value of hard currency as a replacement of the worthless German mark (at one of the periodic heights of the black market, one

---

5   The rations announced for the four-week period beginning April 19, 1947 were as follows:

Items	for entire month		for one day	
	ounces	grams	ounces	grams
fat/butter/margarine	5.3	150	.3	7.1
meat/sausage	21.2	600	.76	21.4
bread	141.1	4,000	7.6	214.0
flour/oats/etc.	21.2	600	.76	21.1
cheese	2.3	66	.78	21.2
sugar	18.9	510	.6	17.8
milk	3.5	3	1/3 cup	.10 litre
	quarts	litres		

Source: Süddeutsche Zeitung, München (appr. 1977)

carton of 200 cigarettes was worth 5,000 marks). In my dealings, I kept a healthy commission of approximately 20 percent, which allowed my mother and I to finally live quite decently. We were now able to purchase sacks of coal, various food items, and some clothes, all for the cigarettes I had earned. I also went to a farmer in the village where my Grand-mother Hackenberg and my Aunt Martel lived and bought six geese ordered by some American soldiers I worked with in the military hospital. One of the geese was mine. We could hardly believe our good fortune — having a whole goose for Christmas 1946!

* * * * *

17 | 1947 –1948
A New Horizon

On December 2, 1946, the Western Allies announced the economic and political amalgamation of their occupation zones. This was viewed by the German people as the first step of the unification of the four occupation zones. Hopes were raised further when the United States began large-scale food shipments to West Germany in May 1947. On June 5, the Marshall Plan, the decisive American measure to return Europe, including Germany, to economic strength, was announced.

There was little hope in Eastern Europe. On June 21, a failed coup in Hungary ended in a Communist government. Next followed the enforced abdication of King Michael of Romania. A coup in Czechoslovakia finalized the fate of Eastern Europe that was now in its entirety governed by Communist parties, all states being under the domination of the Soviet Union. To this group belonged the Soviet occupation zone of Germany that had been cut off from the other three zones politically, economically, and especially ideologically. While the British and the Americans fostered a budding democratic system in their zones, followed somewhat reluctantly by the French in their zone, the Soviets with terror and brute force turned the Soviet zone into a Communist state.

After the failure of the Big Four conference in Berlin in November/December 1947, that was to pave the way for a democratic, unified Germany, subsequent events moved the country towards a permanent separation culminating in the division of Germany by an insurmountable border.

The Soviet Union also applied rising pressure on Berlin, which on July 4, 1948 was isolated from the western zones; the only communication remaining was by air. The war so feared by the Germans was avoided by the creation of the "Luftbrücke" by the Americans and the British who supplied Berlin with food, coal, and other vital materials until the Soviets abandoned their Berlin Blockade in May 1949.

During this period of extreme tension, the creation of a democratic Germany, restricted to the three western zones, moved forward. On June 18, 1948, the new, convertible German mark was introduced, which was to become the pride of Germany. Overnight, the worthless Reichsmark was no longer in use. Although people were initially stricken by fear, as everybody started with only 40 new marks, they noticed soon that the stores were suddenly filled with all sorts of goods. This was the beginning of a new economy and of a new country, which the French zone joined six weeks later.

On November 30, 1948, Berlin was officially divided, after the deputies of the Soviet sector left the Berlin Rathaus. Now, the birth of two separate German states became reality very quickly. On May 23, 1949, the Federal Republic of (West) Germany was proclaimed with Konrad Adenauer being elected as its first chancellor on September 15. Germany's division appeared permanent after the proclamation of the Communist German Democratic Republic on October 12, 1949.

Three years and three months after the armistice of May 1945, after the elements of a new federal authority had been created step-by-step and the three Western occupation zones were amalgamated, the new German Federal Republic of Germany was proclaimed, based on a democratic constitution that initially was perhaps not understood or accepted by every citizen in the country, but was not resisted or fought against. The political structure created by the guidance and prescription of the military government was a true miracle that formed the basis for the rapid economic rise of West Germany and "Das Deutsche Wirtschaftswunder" (the German economic miracle). The German phoenix was rising from the ashes!

* * *

At the end of January 1947, the closure of the US Army hospital in Lesum was imminent. By that time, I felt secure enough with my English that I accepted a job as dispatcher of the motor pool in the US barracks near the suburb of Grohne. At the same time, I began to think about my future career. I had already abandoned my dream of becoming an architect. Although I sensed that in artistic creativity I would range quite above average, my lack of competence in mathematics and the sciences made me decide against pursuing this career. These were still pre-modern times where architects simply could not function unless they were secure in mathematics and in draftsmanship — the latter I had largely lost due to my wounded and permanently damaged hand. I also asked myself, when the German economy would be strong again to support large-scale building activity? Such conditions seemed many years away.

When I heard about the opening of a new teacher training academy in Bremen, I immediately applied. Although I was worried, as I had hardly read a book in the past five years, I did pass the entrance exams with flying colors. I was asked to present myself to the superintendent of the academy together with my parents, which I found more than odd, being 22 years of age and having gone through war and prison camp. Rather than refuse, however, I asked my mother to accompany me. Thinking of my excellent exam results, I entered the superintendent's office in a victorious mood. He was indeed most charming and praised my knowledge, but then proceeded to explain in a sweet voice that the citizens of Bremen had created the academy with enormous financial effort. Would I not agree with him that in view of such sacrifice the academy should be first reserved for the sons and daughters of Bremen and that refugees would have to come last?

I could not believe what I heard. I rose from my chair without a word, grabbed my mother by her hand and dragged her out of the superintendent's office. On this day, I decided to leave Bremen as soon as possible. I was now determined to enter university to study for a career in high school teaching, perhaps even obtain a PhD. I realized that to be admitted to university would be hard. So soon after the war, there were few universities in operation, and most of them had been damaged to some degree, some very heavily indeed.

I opted for Marburg, one of Germany's better universities, that was located in a picturesque medieval town. My start in gaining admission was promising. I had just set foot on the platform of the Marburg station when I met Suse, a former girlfriend from my high school days in Breslau. She promptly took me to a friend of her mother, an older lady and a proverbial *Studentenmutter*, a "students' boarding mother." Because of university holidays, she had a free room and next morning, it was her turn to help by taking me to the students' padre, who in turn introduced me to the professor who chaired the admissions committee. The interview went well and I returned to Bremen in high spirits. Within two months I would be enrolled at the Marburg University! In preparation, I intensified my black market activities selling more rings and necklaces to my American soldier colleagues at work than ever. I wanted to be well fortified with money and cigarettes before entering university, starting a period of five years without income.

One day, an article in the Bremen daily paper reported the suspension of the Marburg professor who had assured me of my admission. Together with him, four students had been suspended because of right wing activities. In a brief ceremony in the medieval St. Elisabeth Church, they had placed several wreaths with nationalistic slogans, and military flags with the outlawed black, white, and red colors at the coffins of Frederick II of Prussia and Paul von Hindenburg, commander of the German armies in World War I and German president, the last in Hitler's

Third Reich. A few days later, I received a brief note from the Marburg professor expressing his regret that he could not assure my admission to university for the summer session. I struggled with very divided feelings. On the one hand, I seemed to have lost another chance to start my education during this year; on the other hand I was disgusted that I had unknowingly placed myself in the hands of a man whose political convictions I did not share.

Once more, my Aunt Lisa who was still living near Würzburg, became my saviour. When she heard about my disappointment, she approached, without advising me, the professor in charge of admissions at the University of Würzburg. The two turned out to be fellow sufferers, both having a history of tuberculosis and of being treated in the same sanatorium in Silesia. There was a common bond, and I decisively benefited from it!

A few weeks later I received formal notification of my admission to the University of Würzburg, to which the good professor had added a bright red arrow pointing to his handwritten sentence "*so lange Sie die Aufnahmeprüfung bestehen sollten*" (provided you shall pass the admitting examinations). This remark worried me to no end. The headaches, bouts of depression, and palpitations that had periodically stricken me since my escape from the prisoner of war camp now plagued me every day.

For more than four years, I had been far away from any type of educational opportunity. I did not own a single book! The few remaining bookshops were practically bare. In short, I felt singularly unqualified to enter the admissions examinations. My nightmares about the war and the frightful experience before being taken prisoner by the Americans returned in full force. I felt dispirited, physically weak, and emotional labile when I took the train to Würzburg. Again, I spent an entire night on my feet in the packed train, pressed between other bodies. Standing next to me was an opera singer from Munich, who sang aria after aria, and many songs from operettas. She helped me and a few dozens of other passengers through the night with her upbeat mood.

Nevertheless, my knees felt weak when I found myself as one of about 25 candidates waiting in the hall of the philosophical faculty of the University of Würzburg, that consisted of four lecture rooms, four seminar rooms, and a few small offices. The rest of the impressive building was still in ruins. I think, we were all deeply pre-occupied, and no doubt some of us in acute fear of failing the entrance exams. Nobody spoke to any other person. Some candidates looked very confident and important; they were well-dressed, and carried new briefcases, the trademark of the university student. Others appeared in noticeably worn clothes, some in modified army uniforms.

The relief came when the first student emerged from the exam and reported that his exam turned out to be a friendly interview with the admitting professor. All of a sudden our voices returned, as we crowded around the student, a calm, easygoing man from Stuttgart who explained to us in broadest Swabian dialect, that he had answered the professor's first question about what he had read most recently with *"Die Neue Zeitung,"*[1] as all his books had been burned when his family's house was destroyed in an air raid. This was to be the standard question that opened each of the following interviews. Of course, we were examined in a fashion in terms of our general fund of knowledge, our interests, preferences, attitudes, and life experiences. All of us received a pass mark and found ourselves attending university the following week.

Considering the support today's students receive at their entrance into university, in spring 1947 we felt utterly alone and abandoned. There was not a single instruction sheet given to us. Not a soul was there to explain to us the difference between lectures and seminars, or how to use the library. Neither did we understand the rigid ranking order amongst the academic staff, the ubiquitous Latin expressions and terms on various announcements, and the academic titles that had survived from medieval times. What seems strange to me now is how distant the students were towards each other, and with how much formality we communicated with each other. After years of addressing every soldier (except one of higher rank) with the familiar *Du* (thou), we now rigidly adhered to the formal Sie (You) that by and large remained in use throughout everyone's university years. Even in informal groups that regularly met over years, it was Mr., Mrs., Miss, and You. During the first week I became close friends with a student from Breslau. We are still friends today, but we did not progress to the familiar *Du* until close to the end of our university days five years later!

Above everybody and everything were the professors who seemed to reside on the clouds of wisdom. They, at least in terms of that time, all deserved our respect, although many were incredibly traditional and formal. It was obvious that this was their well-established way, and even if they wished to be less formal, they would not have known how to put their intent into practice.

When I returned from Bremen to Würzburg in May 1947, I also returned to the beloved little village of Waldbrunn where I was welcomed by the locals like a lost son. They had an enormous respect for everything

---

1   The first and foremost daily newspaper in the American zone. It was published in Munich on the premises of the former *Völkischer Beobachter*, the major daily of the Nazi Party.

academic, as so few of them ever went to high school. Those boys who did were usually destined to enter the priesthood. Soon, my mother joined me, and half a year later, my Grandmother Hackenberg and my aunt Martel followed us to Waldbrunn. My mother and her two sisters were close together again. In the meantime, their only brother Peter and his small family, formerly from Sprottau in Silesia, had opened a drugstore in a small town not too far from Würzburg.

These were all small indicators of a gradual return to normality. In the cities, the food situation was still critical, but living in a village, we were fortunate. We helped in the fields and with daily chores and were rewarded with food. My mother and I raised our farmer's goslings, in some ways a delightful duty, but also a messy job, as the goslings grew up in our tiny kitchen. In true gosling fashion, the little birds bonded with my mother and even when fully grown would still meet her on the village street when the bus brought her back from town. They accompanied her to the village store and, on one hot summer Sunday when the doors of the church were kept wide open, the goslings even appeared outside the church and then marched single file down the aisle with excited screeching. All five of them settled down next to my mother, who sat close to the pulpit from where the priest threw obvious glances of displeasure in her direction. The children and women giggled, the men smiled broadly, and my mother's face was red with embarrassment.

These were distractions of special charm typical of a small village, where we lived with warm-hearted, truly generous people, and always had the security of having enough to eat, while food was in extremely short supply in other parts of the country. Only much later did we realize how much trauma we carried with us from the experiences of the war years. This explains why I still look back on these years as very hard and burdened with emotional problems one only began to comprehend at that time. Besides, my mother and I were affected by the attitudes of many of our fellow refugees who were full of bitterness about the loss of their homes and possessions. Many were angry and quite a few openly expressed their longing for a return to the Hitler years. Very few made a connection between the crimes Hitler committed in other European nations and the fate of Germany's refugees. Hardly anybody acknowledged the genocide and the other crimes committed by Germans in Hitler's concentration camps. These were the months of the Nuremberg trials at the end of which the surviving top Nazi ministers and generals were sentenced to death. The majority of refugees in our village considered these men as victims, and the Nuremberg trials as show trials based on lies.

The bitterness of many refugees was aggravated by the general lack of comprehension and imagination on the part of the locals when the refugees would describe what they had lived through during past months. Except for some of the males who had been in the army, the villagers had generally not traveled beyond the borders of Bavaria. In their peaceful daily life where few things ever changed, even the Hitler regime had been far less omnipresent than in the big cities. And indeed, their lives, compared to those of the refugees, still seemed to follow the age-old rhythm of seeding, tending the fields, harvesting, and preparing for Christmas and for the numerous other Catholic holidays and feast days. How could they manage to gain a realistic picture of the places where the refugees came from? It did not help that many of the refugees tended to exaggerate the extent of their losses — in retrospect, even a small apartment or a small farm felt like a kingdom lost.

Slowly, the locals began to spread good-natured jokes that there must have been only wealthy people living in the former Eastern provinces, as almost every refugee family claimed to have owned a large house or farm or business "back home." There continued a small degree of moving in and moving away which brought a couple of new families to the village every month. All of a sudden, such a new family conveyed quietly that a family who had been in Waldbrunn for over a year and claimed ownership of a hotel in Breslau, had actually only owned a small house where rooms were rented by the hour! In the case of another family, who raved about their large estate that had been in the hands of the family for generations, it came to light that theirs had been a modest farm, which had been leased from the government.

Conversely, one day a family from Waldenburg appeared in Waldbrunn. The man, a former miner with the thickest of Waldenburg accents, announced that my Grandfather Koch had been a respected businessman and until his death had been called the *Millionenkoch*. My mother was terribly embarrassed, especially as during these days our modest household goods, all from post-war refugee days, arrived. With burning curiosity, the village people congregated around the large van that could have accommodated the contents of a good-sized house. When the doors were opened, there was this pitiful little pile in the far corner, consisting of a small kitchen stove, a desk, and a couple of chairs. First, the villagers shook their heads about these crazy refugees, then they walked away laughing. My mother had the strength and self-control not to break into tears. Only after some time when my mother began to show pictures from former times and a copy of the obituary of my Grandfather Koch from 1936 did we regain our credibility. Thank God, that my mother was free of bitterness and resentment about her fate, which helped give this whole episode a comic touch.

At the bottom of these differences between refugees and local inhabitants was also the caution, even a noticeable mistrust, of the locals towards everything new, foreign, or different, be it religion, language or dialect, or place of origin. On their part, the refugees were hardly conscious of their own, even more pronounced caution or prejudice against the locals, which was understandable in view of their terrible experiences. It could not be avoided that the locals became aware of the comments made by certain refugees about the poor standard of housing, the lifestyle, and the manners amongst the local population. What in hindsight appears miraculous is the fact that both groups, aside from a few individual cases, got along well with each other. The locals retained a very uncomplicated, spontaneous attitude towards the newcomers.

What all this reflected was the very well-established, secure set of traditions and customs, and the strong sense of identity all of the villagers possessed. This, I believe, was the prerequisite and the secret for the wonderfully successful integration of the foreign element into the village population and its culture. This pertained to religious practices, to sports, and especially to the several annual festivities such as the annual *Kirchweih* (the annual parish fair, comparable to a county fair), the *Fasching* (Mardi Gras), the numerous weddings, and other feast days. I foremost remember my first *Fasching* in Waldbrunn, when the farmer in whose house we lived gave me his best black suit, top hat, gloves, and a cane. Following the age-old custom of this day, with my face hidden by a mask, I ran with the other disguised men through the village "terrorizing" the women and children with my cane. I succeeded in keeping my identity hidden all day and only at night during the dance was I recognized when I pulled the mask off my face. I think, on this evening I was fully accepted by the people of Waldbrunn *"als einer von uns,"* as one of us.

As much as I felt at home in the village, my existence during the day in Würzburg was most difficult and unsettled. Dependent on the bus schedule, I arrived at 6:30 a.m. in town, long before the first university classes started, and I did not get home until about seven in the evening. I soon realized that I did not enjoy most of my classes. I had too much free time in town, sat around in the uncomfortable cafés with endless cups of hardly drinkable coffee (there was nothing else to be ordered without ration stamps), or I sat in the library and perused all sorts of books, but rarely those of relevance to my studies. I also had a horror of the future when I would stand in front of a classroom full of children or teenagers as a teacher. Somehow, I knew that I was on the wrong track, which only aggravated my dislike of university. I also found it difficult to study with the intensity required to retain and integrate the material offered by our professors.

There were two exceptions. I delved into English and acquired a considerable fund of vocabulary, grammar, and knowledge in literature, history, and geography far beyond what was required for my university education. My interest was also captured by modern German history that began with the Age of Napoleon. I have to thank Professor Ulrich Noack for nurturing my intense interest in his specialty, Modern European History. Interestingly, he was not the most popular professor among the history students. It was my theory that in this case, it was the topic rather than the teacher that determined popularity. Among the students, there was a deep fascination with medieval German history. I venture to say that consciously or unconsciously, in these early post-war times students were drawn to the glorious age of the Holy Roman Empire and its powerful emperors. In contrast, German history following the Age of Napoleon seemed dry and bureaucratic, ending as it did in the two disastrous world wars and in the Third Reich that had disgraced and destroyed the Germany that the students respected.

I found modern history with its democratic struggles and ideas fascinating. Professor Noack was a man of eloquence, exquisite diction, and elegant appearance. In that regard he was quite unique among his colleagues, who were rather conservative in attitude and outlook as well as in appearance. I very much respected our professor of medieval history, Professor Seidlmayer, a supreme teacher, but I could not get emotionally connected with German medieval history. I was deeply engaged in the English language program and delved into modern English and American literature. However, these two areas of interest were far from sufficient to give my existence at university purpose and goals. I was continually plagued by questions about my future. I felt depressed about my detachment from life at university and most of my classes. Later, I realized that I was still under the trauma of my war experiences and simply was not capable of concentrating on academic studies. Neither did I have the mental strength sufficient for consistent academic work. I was still trying to overcome the burden that I brought home from the war. I still had nightmares. I still caught myself daydreaming, partially to fight the demons of the past, partially to get away from my current life, which I considered an abject failure.

My physical health was also very poor. The long bout of infectious hepatitis continued to manifest itself by its continuous after-effects. I never managed to gain weight, my liver gave me constant trouble, and I could not get the prophecy of the professor at the army hospital in Breslau out of my mind, that I would be lucky to reach the age of 40 before dying of cirrhosis of the liver, the result of the inadequate and improper medical care in the army hospital of Hohensalza during the early, critical stage of my hepatitis. In addition, I had other health problems including a pronounced case of Bell's Palsy that hit me one morning while I was shaving. I was in terror when the right side of my face seemed to freeze to immobility within a couple of minutes. Only the dedicated care of a psychiatrist who was also a neurologist prevented a likely permanent disfigurement of my face. With my consent, he applied new and unorthodox treatments with remarkable success. I also had recurrent bouts of heart trouble, no doubt the results of emotional stress. I had seemingly authentic symptoms, but no organic causes were ever found.

These physical and emotional problems would carry on for several years, albeit to a diminishing but still somewhat incapacitating degree. Whatever self-esteem I managed to rally during these horrible times was supported by the interest of a couple of professors, particularly Professor Noack. He invited me to his home quite regularly and also to the founding meeting of the pacifist *Nauheimer Kreis* through which he hoped to propagate his idea of a neutralized Germany, designed to function as a zone of peace and disarmament between the feared Soviet Union and the threatened Western Allies.

This meeting took place on the evening before the German currency reform on June 18, 1948, which signalled the true beginning of Germany's rebirth as a democratic, economically successful state. It was also the final stage of breaking Germany into two hostile states. Through extreme measures such as the isolation of Berlin from the West, which lasted 10 months, the rigid closure of the border between the Soviet and the Western zones, the Soviets tried to prevent this development out of self-interest and their strategy of spreading their influence through the Western part of Germany and across Western Europe. But in September 1948, the constituent assembly was formed in Bonn and 10 months later, on May 23, 1949, the German Federal Republic was born. The German currency reform soon proved itself an enormous economic success and became the engine that drove Germany's economic miracle.

Despite my deep worries and troubles, I was intensely proud of this development. To this day I consider the Federal Republic of Germany not a democratic experiment, but perhaps the greatest political achievement of the German people. Much ideological and practical support especially from the Americans helped create the German republic out of total chaos. Whoever lived through the end of the war and the hopeless immediate post-war years can appreciate this enormous achievement. Even though I left Germany in 1954 with the intention to start a new life in the New World, I still feel a sense of identity with the Federal Republic of Germany that I no longer possess in relation to the present day Germany or the Germany of earlier times.

* * * * *

18 | 1954–2003
Epilogue

After 1948, Europe was well on her road to recovery, even though Eastern Europe would be waiting for freedom for nearly another 42 years.

By the early 1950s, life for the average West-German citizen provided amenities, comforts, and little luxuries that exceeded those enjoyed in pre-war times. Even though life — at least by today's standards and expectations — was still quite modest in the 1950s, those who were not afraid of hard work were able to create a life for themselves with many rewards and satisfactions, as evident in better housing, clothing, foods, entertainment, and in an increasing number of cases, a motorcycle or a car. For most people, these were never before known luxuries and the sense that all such things were now within reach of the working person, as long as he knew how to save and live prudently, provided an enormous sense of pride, satisfaction, and self-esteem. Annual statistics gave proof of the rising level of prosperity witnessed by the increasing number of telephones, television sets, cars, and so on. True, the cars were modest and often small, but they gave their owners a sense of freedom, autonomy, and independence, of finally being freed from total dependence on public mass transportation. If these acquisitions were of modest size and sophistication compared to what was offered in later decades, this fact was balanced by the enormous sense of pleasure and gratitude for being able to live in a post-war world that rose at an unexpected pace from the ashes of a devastated country with a decimated, morally and emotionally crushed population.

Last not least and dramatically different from the past Weimar Republic, West Germany's citizens of the 1950s and 1960s demonstrated pride in their achievements and respect for the state they lived in with security and success. Unfortunately, it cannot be denied that this West

German success also contributed to the tendency to forget about Hitler's crimes and ignore the legacy of guilt the German people, sooner or later, would have to come to terms with. This did not occur during the successful years of the German economic miracle – it is still troubling the German mind in our times, not necessarily in a positive way.

This is not to diminish the German economic miracle that, while a by-product of Germany's regeneration, was one of the great democratizing phenomena. Class barriers became less harsh. Even if only the truly rich could afford a Mercedes, almost every working person could see ownership of a at least a small car within his or her reach. Instead of the highly organized trips by the Nazi institution KdF,[1] millions of working class Germans now arranged their holidays as individuals, a privilege once reserved for the middle and upper classes.

Few of these amenities were part of my life, as I lived on the shoestring budget of a student. I worked in the early morning hours and after classes in the afternoon and, of course, full-time between university terms. My first job with the US Army did not last very long, as the Würzburg hospital was closed. A subsequent episode as a salesman turned into an abject financial failure. I worked in body shops and wineries, doing jobs that involved heavy physical labour in unhealthy environments, until my Waldbrunn friend Anton managed to persuade his boss to hire me on a part-time, on-demand basis. Anton's boss Emil Bauer was an extraordinary man, a vivacious, temperamental Bavarian who ran a large newspaper and magazine distributorship. He helped me through the following four years of university by tailoring his expectations to my free hours at the university. He paid me well and treated me like all his other full-time employees. While I was quite a loner at university – although I did have a few good friends there – at Mr. Bauer's business, I felt happy and secure and enjoyed the uncomplicated camaraderie amongst the employees for which Mr. Bauer set the tone. He could explode at the slightest reason, but he was also extremely generous, always recognizing good work habits and extra effort. Shortly after I completed my university education, Mr. Bauer died of a stroke, far too young for a man who enjoyed life and people so much. An enormous crowd came to the funeral, among them a large number of poor people – many looking "down at their heels" – whom he had helped along over the years. We all had known that he was generous to a fault, but had no

---

1   *Kraft durch Freude* or "Strength through Joy" was a program of the Nazi party that offered holiday trips to workers at cut-rate prices. Bookings were done through the KdF agency; individual travel remained the preserve of the well-to-do. KdF was terminated with the beginning of World War II.

idea of the extent of his generosity. Even I was not fully aware of it for many years. Only after I applied in the 1980s for my small pension from Germany arising out of the few working years in that country, did I realize that Mr. Bauer had always registered me as a full-time employee and had paid both his and my share of monthly contributions toward my retirement pension. Actually, without the four years of service he registered and paid for, I would have failed to qualify for any pension at all.

With Mr. Bauer's wages, I purchased a small motorcycle with a 125cc motor which carried me to classes and to work and back home every day – a great relief after having struggled daily on my old bicycle for several years over the eight miles of up and down the hills between Waldbrunn and Würzburg. My motorbike also permitted me to take some trips through most of southern Germany. I began to establish contact with members of the families of both my father and my mother. They all managed quite well by now, either in retirement or still proudly working beyond the customary working years.

One Sunday, a converted jeep stopped in front of our house in Waldbrunn and here was my favourite cousin Christel who had, in typical fashion for her, gone through a career from rags to riches within the past four years. She had almost perished from typhoid fever in 1945/1946, after giving birth to my nephew (once removed) Hans, who calls me "*Mein Lieblingsonkel*" (my favourite uncle). He and his sister Ines have always been special for me. With hard work and ingenuity Hans has fully utilized the advantages that the blossoming post-war Germany offered to those who had the courage and the wit to grab the opportunities.

Much of his mother's personality is reflected in Hans. Like Hans, his mother, my cousin Christel, was always a dynamic, enterprising person, ready to work and ready to have fun at any time. After the war, she started to deliver cream and butter to those Frankfurt restaurants and cafés that were frequented by American soldiers and civilians. She began with a Sunday only business, because this was the day, when the restaurants and cafés were likely to run out of cream and other dairy products.[2] My cousin did the deliveries on an old pre-war bicycle with a heavy basket above the front wheel. The business expanded and a used jeep was purchased, that also functioned as the family car. By 1951, my cousin was a successful business woman. In March 1952, Ines, her daughter from her first marriage whose father died as an officer in

---

2   Only businesses catering exclusively to Americans were well supplied with dairy and other products. In German establishments, coffee was of the barley variety; it was served black, as there was no milk except in smallest quantities on ration cards (cream was non-existent). The monthly butter ration was one quarter pound.

Russia, had her first communion. My cousin used this opportunity to also have Hans baptized in the Catholic faith during Sunday mass. This event brought a large group of pious women to tears, as such a belated baptism of a seven-year old boy was a rather unusual event.

These were still very lean years for my mother and I. I borrowed my friend Anton's dark suit, while my mother wore a beautiful summer coat that belonged to a farmer's wife. Thus, the good people of Waldbrunn also helped us look most presentable among the group of wealthy guests at the celebration in my cousin's house in Frankfurt! Actually, I became the object of speculation when one of the guests, owner of a large factory near Frankfurt, decided to pick me as his future son-in-law assuring me of a house and a Mercedes as wedding presents. This offer was somehow characteristic of a part of German society of these years, mainly business-men who worked very hard and were very successful but often failed to observe the constraints of good taste.

I was close to marriage myself at that time, to a young woman whom I liked very much. Her father had died from the consequences of mistreatment in a Japanese concentration camp, while as a widow her mother had become a very controlling, dependent person. I became frightened and terminated the relationship.

At that time I was under great stress because of my final exams, the only exams in four to five years of university studies. The sense of inadequacy I felt when expected to present the knowledge and wisdom gathered during five years was overwhelming. By the time the 12 written exams started, I was a nervous wreck, although I did pass with decent marks. Of the 12 oral exams, I failed the exam in Old English. To this day, I am asking myself where I would have been able to even minimally utilize Old English as a high school teacher. It seemed insane, but as a consequence I was forced to wait for another year to complete the entire range of exams. There were no supplementals in Bavaria like those offered in North America.

I was very disgusted and grabbed the first opportunity to get away. In July 1952, I found out that farm labourers were in high demand in Great Britain. Special arrangements were made for students in terms of transportation, housing, and so on. For two months I tended 200 pigs for a prosperous farmer in Northamptonshire. I was very well paid and well fed, and could save a good part of my wages as we lived almost rent-free in a former prisoner of war camp. We were a happy bunch of young people, students from all over the world, among them a German girl I immediately fell in love with, and a Vietnamese boy studying in Paris, with whom I unfortunately lost contact after his enforced return to Hanoi.

I was extremely happy in England, where I appreciated the different way of life and the English institutions. When I returned home, I firmly decided not to wait for next year's exams but seek work immediately and prepare my emigration to Canada.

In February 1953, my new girlfriend Rita and I spent a glorious Mardi Gras in Munich where she attended university. We were happy, although it bothered me that she felt it necessary to go to confession every morning on our way home from dancing at all-night balls. On the morning of Ash Wednesday 1953, we left for a long hitchhiking tour through Switzerland and Italy. The two countries were bare of tourists, as it was an unusually cold, early spring. There were also gloomy days after the death of Stalin on March 5, 1953. With great astonishment, we observed the resulting mass hysteria. People were crying in the streets, and the streets were a sea of red with the hammer and sickle flags hanging out of thousands of windows, while we were happy that, after Hitler and Mussolini, the last of the three dictators had finally passed from the scene.

Despite the massive mourning, we had a wonderful time in Italy. We lived like royalty in an elegant villa on the Riviera south of Rapallo in the small youth hostel located in the villa's basement that led out to the beach. The single occupant of this huge building, a very old gentleman, only saw us once, but encouraged us to enjoy the garden and the terraces. South of Naples, during our stay in a youth hostel, that was located on the grounds of *Quisisana*, the former summer palace of the Kings of Naples, we felt like royals again when we took in the sweeping panorama that reached from the Vesuvius to Sorrento. We lived like paupers in the youth hostel of the *Casa San Giorgio*, an old monastery in Venice, freezing through the nights and eating our one meal of the day in the soup kitchen for Venice's poor. But we were happy and thought that Italy was the most wonderful country in the world.

While waiting for my immigration papers, I accepted a position as translator and interpreter with the CIA, a most fascinating job that also took me to Berlin in preparation for the summit of the four foreign ministers of the USA, France, Great Britain, and the Soviet Union. But in the last minute the summit was cancelled and we returned to Würzburg.

I half expected to leave for Canada as a young married man. During these last months in Germany, Rita and I met at my cousin's in Frankfurt on many successive weekends, until I discovered that there was another friend and lover in Cologne. I ended the relationship. Three weeks later I boarded the *Italia* in Hamburg. I was on my way to Canada.

* * *

At this point, it is important to enter two observations in this much condensed summary of my life since my arrival in Canada. My life finally turned onto normal, ordinary tracks, and for all intents and purposes, my book should end right here. Out of courtesy to the reader and gratitude to Canada, however, I must, if only most briefly, report on the nearly 50 years of my life in the New World. This is the purpose of the three stars on this page; they indicate that the course of my life experienced a significant break.

From the day of my arrival in Canada, I sensed I was changing into a different person. I became optimistic, task-orientated, and willing to take some risks. I enjoyed everyday life, although at least for the first three years as an immigrant, my life was very modest. I liked people and, for the first time in my life, I became a truly sociable person. Finally, my chronically depressed mood left me for good. I also felt certain that the decisions I had made, beginning with the resolve to leave Germany, were sound.

I had carefully chosen Canada as my future home, although while working for the CIA, I had several offers from American colleagues to come to the States where they would help me to have a good start. I would have quite happily emigrated to the USA, but I was not sure whether I was definitely beyond the age of being drafted, at that time an absolute prerequisite for obtaining American citizenship. So I chose Canada because of being the neighbour of the USA, and of its British traditions that I had learned to appreciate during my stay in England. Just as carefully I chose the specific area of Canada where I wanted to make my home. I voraciously read about the history and geography of Canada and, as I had hoped, I found the wide-open spaces, the vast flat country, and the big sky that had so fascinated me as a young soldier in Russia, in the Canadian prairies.

The masses of emigrants from European countries that moved to Canada year after year predominantly settled in the big cities of Toronto, Montreal, and Vancouver. And indeed, the endlessly long colonist train that took us from Halifax to Montreal continued in its entire length to Toronto, while a group of a mere 25 immigrants continued further west. Our next five travelling days were spent in an old colonist coach with a cast iron stove in one corner. This coach was attached to different local trains, which resulted in frequent stops of several hours that allowed us to explore the smaller towns in Northern Ontario still buried deep in snow, and many other towns and cities further west along the transcontinental railroad. We took a good look at Winnipeg, Regina, Moose Jaw, Medicine Hat, and, finally, Calgary from where we took the night train to Edmonton.

In the early morning of May 5, 1954, the day Dien Bien Phu, the last French outpost in Indochina fell, I arrived in Edmonton. An immigration officer took the only family in our group under his wings. The rest, all single men, were expected to fend for themselves. Nobody in our group complained or panicked.

I liked Edmonton from the moment I arrived. For several hours I explored the city by bus before choosing a district where to find a room. My streak of luck began when I decided on the Southside, on Old Strathcona. This was the proverbial North American residential district with rows of relatively modest houses along tree-lined avenues that charmed me. I had 50 dollars left when I arrived of which 30 dollars went for the rent, which my landlady mercilessly collected from me. I needed a job, which I found in the provincial mental hospital on the outskirts of Edmonton. There was high unemployment in the city at that time, but my prior experience in the US Army hospital in Bremen where I had also worked on the psychiatric station for several months helped me land this job. I made a half-hearted visit to the provincial education department that had by letter promised me a job as an elementary school teacher in a rural area, provided I would pass certain summer school courses thus demonstrating among other aspects my proficiency in English.

To my surprise, I quickly began to enjoy my work in the mental hospital. Without any qualms, I abandoned my plan of becoming a teacher and instead enrolled in the training program for psychiatric nurses. Throughout this book I have refrained from using last names except in the cases of a few exceptional people that had a decisive influence over my life. It is here that I must mention Miss Nessa Leckie, the initiator and creator of the training program in psychiatric nursing that became well-known and respected across North America. Not only did she develop a tremendous curriculum, she single-handedly took on the establishment of the hospital, especially the long-term employees who occupied the senior and middle level positions and, with a few exceptions, were not ready to change their old-fashioned ways of looking after patients. Without Miss Leckie, the hospital would have been a very different place. It was because of her and the advanced treatment setting she aimed for that I stayed.

The three years at this mental hospital stood me in good stead. My short-term economic future was secure. I quickly learned an enormous amount, formally in Miss Leckie's program, and informally through living and working among people who had a different outlook on life, a different way of relating to each other, and different beliefs and customs than those in Germany. Working always in groups helped me greatly to adjust, adapt, and feel at home in my new surroundings and in Canada as a whole.

Six months after my start in Canada, my mother arrived. Together with acquaintances from Würzburg, we bought an older house. A lot of repairs and remodelling was required and, as with so many men in this country, I became a handyman and layman carpenter. We made friends, Canadians as well as Germans. After a brief bout of homesickness, my mother was utterly happy in her new surroundings. She found employment as an auxiliary nurse in hospital, loved her work immensely, and created her own circle of friends. I was most relieved, as my mother had left Germany against the strong objections of the entire family. The true test came when after my graduation in psychiatric nursing, I got married and moved to Saskatchewan. In October 1957 my future wife whom I had known since early student days, came to Canada. I had had my eye on Maria since 1948, the year she had fled from East Germany where as the "capitalist's daughter" of a factory owner she was refused admission to university and was not even permitted to enter into an apprenticeship as a seamstress. Maria had been spoken for and I had my own plans as well. Fate, however, took over in the very last minute!

About three hours before departing from Würzburg on my long journey to Canada, I ran into Fräulein Maria Schuster in the Bahnhofstrasse. I invited her for a cup of coffee and at this late occasion, I learned that her engagement had been broken off, as her future husband had given in to his mother's insistence that he should not marry outside his Catholic faith. After losing her other son in the war and later her husband due to illness, she was understandably very dependent on her son. So I left for Canada with the knowledge that Maria was free and interested — and so was I!

As young marrieds, we lived in the small city of Yorkton in Saskatchewan, both of us working for the provincial department of social welfare. As with every other social worker in the regional office, we had a rural district for which we were responsible. We spent two or three days on the road each week, regardless of snow, ice, cold, blizzards in winter, and of rain and mud in summer. This was a great learning experience, especially for Maria whose bravery in coming to a new country and learning how to drive on often nearly impassable roads was greatly admired by colleagues and clients.

This was 1957, the end stage of the early Canadian prairie culture, when each settlement founded before World War I was still full of life, when the countryside was dotted with elevators to the far horizon, when most roads were rough gravel only, and people lived with a sense of neighbourliness and responsibility for the safety and well-being of their fellow citizens. We experienced blizzards in winter and dust storms, grasshopper plagues, and heat waves in summer, but we loved the beautiful prairie and its people.

As agreed at the time of signing my employment contract, I was assisted by the Saskatchewan government in attending the University of British Columbia School of Social Work for nearly two years, while Maria worked for the Catholic Children's Aid Society in Vancouver. To the annoyance of our colleagues in Vancouver, we both missed the prairies and hated the coastal rains; for the first six months, we were acutely homesick for Saskatchewan. However, Maria loved her job, while I had the great fortune to attend a university with an atmosphere totally different from that of a German university. The structure was democratic, we were close to our professors and, even though the age of the students ranged from the early 20s to the late 50s, we formed a class of students loyal to each other and to our professors. In my second year, I wrote my thesis with the help of a grant from the Leon and Thea Koerner Foundation. The Koerners were refugee-immigrants from Czechoslovakia and had become well-known industrialists in British Columbia. I thought it symbolic that I was assisted in my early immigrant life by other immigrants who had been successful in Canada.

Two days after the end of classes, we left for Europe and while visiting each other's families and friends in Germany, the mail brought me a copy of my thesis and of my masters degree in social work. It had taken us 10 days to cross the USA from Vancouver to New York in our new Austin, going quite far south, as far as Kansas, Missouri, Kentucky, and Virginia. It was an unforgettable way of experiencing this vast country. We slept in our car, made our own breakfast, once at the altitude of over 13,000 feet on top of the Berthoud Pass in the Colorado Rockies. We managed to survive on a total budget of 110 dollars. This trip was also the beginning of our lifelong passion for camping travel in its basic form (tent or truck, no RV as yet).

We spent four years in Regina to fulfill the contractual obligations for my educational leave. Then we returned to Edmonton as a small family of three — our son George had been born in Regina on August 5, 1962. We had hardly arrived in Edmonton when Maria had an offer from the University of Alberta to teach German language. After four years of employment in social work, she returned to her chosen career of teaching

In my career, I eventually chose the administrative stream of medical social work. It was a field with excellent opportunities that enabled me to shift my place of employment about every five years without having to leave Edmonton, which had become our home town in every sense of the word. Even though I never worked in a position of self-employment, I always retained a sense of freedom and autonomy. I knew I was wanted by several organizations and could change employment any time.

The sense of belonging to a large professional community was widened by my membership in the American Hospital Association. I attended conferences and seminars, gave workshops and made many friends. I deepened my knowledge and competence, and got to know all parts of the United States.

When changing jobs, I often took a brief holiday trip. In 1975, I jumped on a Greyhound bus and without planning it, ended in San Francisco. While traveling, I read a book by the American historical writer Barbara Tuchman in which I discovered passages quoted from the diaries of the Princess Daisy of Pless, about whose beauty and fabulous life I had been in awe as a child. Actually, I spent my childhood only about five miles from Daisy's fabulous Castle Fürstenstein that was located on the outskirts of the town of my birth, Waldenburg.

I discovered the first volume of Daisy's diaries in the public library in San Francisco. It was impossible to read this book of over 500 pages in the two days of my stay in San Francisco. The librarian did not hesitate to give me permission to take this book home with me to Canada, copy it, and return it by mail. Such were the days before copyright enforcements and restricted library privileges!

Daisy's diaries immediately fascinated me, as did the descriptions of her humanitarian work in Silesia. I remembered how the poor and the miners in Waldenburg had adored the Princess of Pless who had done so much for them. But I had no idea of the breadth and depth of her social reform projects and the methods she employed towards their realization. I decided to write an article for a professional journal.

Before I had finished Daisy's diaries, however, I had resolved to write her biography, as there was so much that was remarkable in this woman's life and the times she lived through. I was most eager and immediately began my research that led me to hundreds of people and archives in Europe and in North America. In 1976, I began writing Daisy's biography. But I soon found out that with full-time employment that involved among other duties the writing of reports and research projects, I did not have sufficient physical, mental, and creative energy left for writing a biography unrelated to my work. I decided to put my writing aside until my retirement.

I will always remember to thank Barbara Tuchman for becoming a writer. Without her book bringing the diaries of Daisy of Pless to my awareness, I doubt that I would have entered into a writing career so late in my life. I have to thank Daisy of Pless as well, of course, as her personality and life inspired me to learn and discover as much as possible about her pursuits and her fate, most of which had been forgotten or never brought to the attention of a wider public.

Realizing that Edmonton was as good a city as any for writing books, we did not follow the trend of many retirees to escape to a milder climate. Maria and I decided to stay in Edmonton, that has become hometown for both of us. Having been "pushed about" by political circumstances, it is important for us — perhaps more so than for others — to retain a sense of belonging to one place and stay there. Not only do we love Edmonton and Alberta, we also have roots here in terms of friends some of whom have taken the place of relatives which we do not have in this country (I only have a very few relatives left, all of them in Germany). Some of our Edmonton friends, such as the Conradis and Beringers, are like cousins to us, and like uncles and aunts to our son George. Also in Edmonton lives my best friend, Andrew Carlson, the man from Sakatchewan who for me has become the brother I never had.

Retirement came sooner than expected. When I was 62, I had actually reached the age where, thanks to a certain formula, I was able to retire at full pension! I completed one research project for the Government of Alberta but then decided to turn away from social work and devote my entire time to writing non-fiction and to the intensive research required for it.

This research was an adventure in itself often taking on aspects of sleuthing and detective work, done by letter and in person. Especially in relation to my research for the Daisy of Pless biography, a number of trips to my home country, Silesia, now part of Poland, became necessary. These trips were adventures in themselves, but with great effort and political manipulation, they brought me closer to the records pertaining to Daisy of Pless — these were still Communist times and many archives were not accessible to people from the West. My travels to Poland also brought me back to my home country and its now Polish inhabitants. Over the years, both Maria and I have developed a meaningful relationship with modern-day Silesia and respect for its people, something which many former German Silesians do not necessarily share.

In 1989, I published my first book in German, *Schloss Fürstenstein* followed by the biography *Daisy von Pless - Fürstliche Rebellin*, also in German, in 1992. In the middle 1990s followed another biography, *Martin Nordegg — The Uncommon Immigrant*, the story of the son of a Silesian rabbi who became a pioneer in the New World, and the publication in English of the story *To the Town that Bears Your Name*, translated from German by Maria, that Martin Nordegg had written for his daughter in 1912. In 2002, I finally succeeded in publishing *Daisy Princess of Pless — A Discovery*, the biography of Daisy of Pless in English for which I took over all rights and the publishership in summer of 2002. It was on my 77th birthday that I became a publisher and small businessman! Would I have dared doing that under the regulated environment of Germany? I have my doubts.

Now, I hope to bring the book *NO ESCAPE — My Young Years under Hitler's Shadow* the reader now holds in his/her hands to completion in late 2003 for publication early in 2004. All along, my wife Maria has been my partner in my writing and publishing. After 27 years of teaching German at the university, she translated some of my earlier work and is currently the simultaneous translator of this book that I hope to see published in German next year. She knows many of my research partners and has helped me with my research enormously. Together, we share the success and frustrations of researching, writing, and publishing.

For more than 25 years, to a greater or lesser degree, Daisy of Pless has occupied a good part of my time. For exactly 25 years, her portrait by John Singer Sargent hung in our living room. Sold in 2002, the original was replaced by a copy, and Daisy remains with us. Without the inspiration I received from researching her unusual but admirable life, I might have never entered another career, that of a writer.

I would like to say so much more about Canada, the country that has allowed me to resolve and overcome the trauma of my war experiences, as well as the restrictive attitudes and the reactions to them I consider every German's heritage. When I talk about Canada as my home to which I am loyal and committed, and which I love, I am also including the United States. It was the USA and its way of life and its people, its literature and music and arts, that I first got to know and to appreciate through my contact with American soldiers in prison camp, and later while working for the US Army. It was that exposure that helped me decide on Canada as my future home. I chose the West, namely Alberta, unknowingly but fortunately, as Alberta is "the most American" of all Canadian provinces. So has our son George, now a freelance journalist and writer, chosen to stay in the prairies where with his partner Laurie he built a house in the rolling foothills country northwest of Calgary.

My particularly strong relationship with America and Americans has always influenced my political stance and attitudes. As much as I want to, and as much as I owe the reader a fuller explanation, I cannot do so. Entering into this vast, controversial subject would go far beyond the parameters of this book. May it suffice to say the following.

With all my love and loyalty for Canada, I am a "North American" at heart. I am passionately interested in politics and political and social attitudes and tendencies of the New World. That goes for Germany as well, but I am at great odds with the prevailing trends and attitudes in the country of my birth. I also differ with some of the attitudes prevailing in present-day Canada, and I am no longer the passionate Canadian Liberal I once was in pre-Trudeau years. But I love Canada, especially my home, the Canadian West, and I will never cease to do so.

* * * * *

Appendix

Photo Credits

W. John Koch
1,2,5,7,8,9,11,12,13,14,15,17,18,19,20,21,22,23,24,25,26,27,28,
29,30,31,32,33,34,35,42,43,44,45,46,47,48,48,50,51,52,53,54,55,
56,57,58,59,60,61,62,63,67,73,73a,74,75,76,77,82,84,85,86,87,
88a,134,135,136,137,138,146,147,148,149,177,179,180,181,182,
183,181,185,186.187,188,189,190,192,193,194.195,195b,196,
197,198,199

Widawnictwo Arkady
160

Bertelsmann Verlag
184a,184b,184c

Bild und Buch
98,99

Bison Books
123

Bonanza Books
158,159

Brestonline
139,140,141,142

Deutscher Kommunalverlag
16

GeneAct Ste. Hlne
3,4

International News
161,164,165,167,168,178

Nikolay Khmeliarski
143,144,145,150,151,153,154,155,156,157

Stanisław Klimek
101,102,103

Werner Kosmol
108,109,110,111,112,113

United States National Archives and Records Administration
170, 170,171,173,174,175
Neues Berlin
37, 38
Polonia Publishing
176
Portrait of Daisy Princess of Pless, owner unknown
196a
Simon Wiesenthal Center
115, 130,131
Elisabeth Schuster
191
Słonim online
159
Georg Ullstein
36,39,40,41,83,88,93,94,95,97,100,119,120,122,122,124,125,
126,127,128,129,162
Ullstein Bild
89,90,91,92,117a, 118,163,166, 168
United States Holocaust Memorial Museum
116,117,132,133
Waldenburger Heimatbote
6,10,65,66,68,69,70,71,72,78,79,80,81

* * * * *

German-Polish-Czech-Belarus Place Names

Agnetendorf	Jagniatków
Altwasser	Stary Zdrój
Breslau	Wrocław
Dätzdorf	Dzierzków
Deutsch Wartenberg	Otyń
Dittersbach	Podgórze
Dniepr	Dnepr, Dnyapr (*Belarus*)
Freiheit	Svoboda (*Czech*)
Schloss Fürstenstein	Zamek Książ
Gross Rosen	Rogożnica
Hain	Przesieka
Hirschberg	Jelenia Góra
Hohenelbe	Vrchlabí (*Czech*)
Jauer	Jawor
Johannisbad	Janské Lázně (*Czech*)
Kandrzyn	Kędrzierzyn
Königzelt	Jaworzyna Śląska
Köppernig	Koperniki

Landeshut	Kamienna Góra
Leuthen	Lutynia
Liebau	Lubawka
Liegnitz	Legnica
Litzmannstadt	Łódź, Lodz (*Russian*)
Naasdorf	Nadziejów
Neisse	Nysa
Neurode	Nowa Ruda
Niederschlesien	Dolny Śląsk
Obernigk	Oborniki Śląskie
Oberschlesien/OS	Górny Śląsk
Oder	Odra
Ölse	Olszany
Luninetz	Łuniniec, Luninyets (*Belarus*)
	Luninets (*Russian*),
Pinsk	Pińsk, Pinsk (*Russian/Belarus*)
Pripjet	Pripiet, Prypeć (*Belarus*),
	Pripiet (*Russian*),
	Pripjat (*Ukrainian*)
Prag/Prague	Praha (*Czech*)
Rastenburg	Kętrzyn
Raudten	Rudna
Riesengebirge	Karkonosze
Sandberg	Piaskowa Góra
Schwallen/Zwalinnen	Cwaliny
Schweidnitz	Świdnica
Sensburg	Mrągowo
Słonim	Słonim, Slonim (*Belarus*)
Słutsk	Słuck, Slutsk (*Belarus*)
Sprottau	Szprotawa
Steinau	Ścinawa
Trachenberg	Żmigród

Trebnitz	Trzebnica
Oberschlesien, OS/Upper Silesia	Górny Śląsk
Volpersdorf	Wolibórz
Zimpel	Sępolno
Wenzelsplatz	Václavské náměstí (*Czech*)
Zobten	Ślęża